TO DIE FOR GERMANY

TO DIE FOR GERMANY

Heroes in the Nazi Pantheon

JAY W. BAIRD

Indiana University Press

BLOOMINGTON AND INDIANAPOLIS

4p

Manufactured in the United States of America

Library of Congress Cataloging-in-Publication Data

Baird, Jay W.
    To die for Germany : heroes in the Nazi pantheon / Jay W. Baird.
        p.   cm.
    Bibliography: p.
    Includes index.
    ISBN 0-253-31125-X
    1. Germany—History—1933–1945—Biography.   2. Germany—Biography.
3. Heroes—Germany—Mythology.   4. Germany—Intellectual life—20th
century.   I. Title.
DD243.B35   1990
943.086'0922—dc20
[B]   89-45189
                                                                        CIP

1 2 3 4 5 94 93 92 91 90

To the Memory of My Father, Dr. Warren A. Baird
(1905–1975), Surgeon and Historian,
and for My Mother, Helen Siddall Baird,
Who Put a High Premium on Culture.

CONTENTS

ILLUSTRATIONS

Acknowledgments

Many individuals, organizations, and friends have contributed material and moral support during the many years required to research and write this book. The Alexander von Humboldt Foundation and its extraordinary director, Dr. Heinrich Pfeiffer, made it possible for me to undertake a year's research in German archives. Stephen M. Day, dean of the College of Arts and Sciences at Miami University, and my department heads, Richard M. Jellison and Allan M. Winkler, have established a climate conducive to serious intellectual inquiry, and I want to thank them for approving the leaves of absence necessary to complete this work. Donald E. Oehlerts, director of libraries, purchased rare books necesssary to my study. Grants from the Miami University Research Fund were also of considerable assistance. Finally, Jack F. Southard and Debra H. Allison of the Miami University Computer Center offered indispensable support services.

Martin Broszat of the Institute of Contemporary History in Munich extended the hospitality for which his organization is renowned. Many of the ideas developed here arose from lengthy discussions with Elka Fröhlich, Hellmuth Auerbach, Hermann Weiss, Wolfgang Benz, Hermann Graml, and Christoph Weisz. Dr. Hermann-Joseph Busley, Leitender Abteilungsleiter of the Bayerisches Hauptstaatsarchiv, and Dr. Ludwig Morenz were helpful in leading me to sources. Daniel P. Simon, director of the Berlin Document Center, facilitated my work in the important documentary collections housed there. I would also like to thank Dr. Jürgen Wetzel, Archiv Direktor of the Landesarchiv Berlin, Dr. Hans-Joachim Seel of the General Staatsanwaltschaft bei dem Landgericht Berlin, Dr. Werner Volke and Dr. Jochen Meyer of the Deutsches Literaturarchiv/Schiller Nationalmuseum (Marbach), and Dr. Richard Bauer, director of the Stadtarchiv München. I wish also to express my appreciation to Agnes Peterson of the Hoover Institution, who has been of immeasurable help to me over the last twenty-five years. Robert Wolfe of the National Archives and the late Dr. John Mendelssohn also alerted me to several important sources.

I am grateful to the editors of the *Journal of Contemporary History* for permission to quote from my articles on Horst Wessel and Herbert Norkus. Thanks goes also to Frau Minnie Rehkopf of Göttingen for permission to quote from a letter written by her late husband, the Langemarck veteran Willi Rehkopf, to the Deutsches Literaturarchiv.

Several individuals went out of their way to assist my efforts to approach the study of National Socialist film in a professional manner. Among them were Paul Spehr, Patrick Sheehan, David Parker, and Barbara Humphrys of the Library of Congress; Dr. Friedrich Kahlenberg, Leitender Archiv Direktor of the Bundesarchiv (Koblenz); Dr. Gerd Albrecht and Dr. Eberhard Spiess of the Deutsches Institut für Filmkunde (Wiesbaden); and Dr. Gero Gandert and Dr. Werner Sudendorf of the Stiftung Deutsche Kinemathek (Berlin). Manfred Lichtenstein, Stellvertretender Direktor, Staatliches Filmarchiv der DDR, was very helpful in enabling me to view rare prints of the films of Karl Ritter.

I have benefited from discussions with several colleagues, who were very generous with their time. Among them are Michael Kater, Konrad Jarausch, George Mosse, Robert E. Herzstein, John Gillingham, James Diehl, Geoffrey Giles, Otis Mitchell, Gerald Kleinfeld, Larry Wilcox, and Donald Schilling. Michael O'Brien was helpful with his critical reading of the manuscript. Günter Holst aided in the arduous task of the translation of poems, and Hsi-huey Liang kindly shared interview materials on the Horst Wessel case. Lauren Bryant of the Indiana University Press was very skillful in directing the manuscript through the many stages of publication.

This book would not have been written without the loving support of my wife, Sally. Her unselfishness and mature counsel over the years are deeply appreciated. Our children—Lisa Jane, Bryan Eshelman, and Stanford Davis—maintained their sense of humor as they tolerated years of their father's preoccupation with the topic. For the last thirty years, beginning with my student days at the Friedrich Meinecke Institut of the Free University of Berlin, Frau Gisela Rose and Christian and Karin Hauschild have offered their loyalty and generous hospitality in support of my scholarship, and I salute them here. Finally, I would like to thank my colleague Maynard Swanson for giving enduring meaning to an ancient truth, "friendship is the sweetest influence."

Introduction

In the first half of the twentieth century, many in German society embraced the heroic ideology. The German idea of heroism had profound consequences, because ultimately the National Socialists, who were wholly given over to an irrational philosophy of life, succeeded in marrying their mythical ideology to the national state. The German cult of heroism was tied more to death than to life, more to destruction than to victory. Hitler held the memory of the fallen heroes in almost religious awe, and he was much more at home among the dead than he was among the living. His confusion of barbarity with heroism had tragic results. Ultimately in the Third Reich the distinction between myth and reality blurred. It took a tragic war of annihilation to destroy the Third Reich and its pantheon of heroes.

It is the purpose of this book to analyze the world of Nazi mytholgy, to discover its historical origins, and to examine the interplay between myth and reality in German politics from 1914 to 1945. In the Nazi philosophy of death, symbolic figures assume center stage. The death myth of World War I; the martyrdom of Albert Leo Schlageter, killed by the French; the tale of the "Immortals" of the abortive Hitler putsch of 9 November 1923; and the saga of Horst Wessel and Hitler Youth Herbert Norkus all play a role. The careers of major figures from the world of Nazi film (Karl Ritter), music (Hans Baumann), and literature (Gerhard Schumann) are analyzed to mark variations on the theme of heroic nationalism. All three individuals contributed significantly to the formulation of National Socialist aesthetics. Ultimately the Nazis employed all means in their desperate drive for power and glory in World War II. There was no middle ground, no half-way station on the route to national greatness.

This work is written in a style that accurately reflects the historical milieu of the era. National Socialism often took the form of political theater, and the drama of the propaganda battle is conveyed here. Nazi heroic poetry is liberally quoted throughout the book, reflecting the movement's obsession with a mythical realm beyond peopled by heroes of the German nation and the Aryan race.

The work makes no claim to an all-embracing assessment of its central theme. Indeed each chapter could stand alone as representative of one genre of Nazi myth. But, taken together, the chapters form what the purveyors of Nazi propaganda understood to be stations on the road to the national Golgotha. Each of the vignettes presents a discrete facet of what Nazi playwright and poet Richard Euringer defined as the "German Passion." Although the route to national immolation took many peculiar and sometimes macabre turns, the journey remains fascinating and is as strangely unreal as the characters of the Nazi mythmakers themselves. Long dead heroes come to life once more in Nazi ideology and ritual, answering trumpet calls from afar.

The concept of heroism as a form of national identity has many parallels in the past. Throughout history, heroism and antiheroism have gone hand in hand; indeed heroism without antiheroism is inconceivable. The noble Siegfried, the very model of bravery and virtue, was betrayed by the ignoble Hagen. Roland—whom Philippe Aries has called the "model of the secular saint"—was brutally ambushed by the Moorish anti-Christ in the Pyrenees, fighting a rearguard action not only for Charlemagne but also for Christian civilization itself.[1] In turn Horst Wessel, according to the myth, died fighting "Jewish-Bolshevism," so that Germany might live.

Obviously the heroic motif has not been the preserve of Germany, although it assumed its most virulent form there. The concept of the hero was redefined in World War I, when bare-chested men stood against the full force of the weaponry of a technological age. Hero and nation joined, an identification that reached its apogee in Wilfred Owen's poem "Dulce et Decorum Est," which extolled the beauty of sacrifice for England. Although all of the belligerent countries gave their fallen soldiers a prominent place in national ritual, in Germany the subject of the war dead went far beyond national commemoration. There it was to become a philosophy of life, a philosophy born at Langemarck—the battle of Ypres—in 1914.[2]

When the flower of German youth was cut down in the fields of Flanders in a hopeless and strategically bankrupt engagement, the fallen lit a flame— which was considered eternal—in the hearts of their countrymen. The young heroes were heralded as the vanguard of a purified Germanic race of blond warriors, who would return a decadent society to the heroic spirit that once motivated their tribal ancestors. The youth of Langemarck had not died in vain but had won eternal life among the fighting heroes of Walhall.

After the trauma of defeat and the abdication of the kaiser, the blood of the martyrs offered some measure of consolation and hope, as well as the promise of national regeneration. The myth of sacrifice sustained many people through the dark days of the communist revolution, the agony of Versailles, and the indignities of the Weimar Republic. Finally, when the French added insult to injury by occupying the industrial heartland of the Ruhr, a new hero—Albert Leo Schlageter—arose to carry the flag against the enemy.

Schlageter was the very model of a German hero. A pious Catholic youth from the Black Forest, he served as an artillery officer during the war, and he became alienated from the postwar world. Joining a Free Corps, he fought the Bolsheviks in the East and helped to free Riga from the hands of the insurgents. His passion for Germany was so deep that he engaged in hopeless guerilla warfare against the French occupiers. His subsequent arrest, incarceration, and brutal execution led to comparisons with Christ on Calvary. Schlageter was shot by the French on a bleak heath outside Düsseldorf in May 1923. Almost immediately a myth was conceived whereby a tall, slender, blue-eyed German youth, unwavering at the chasm of the abyss, was transfigured into a national saint. The intrepid Schlageter was seen as a star, shining from afar in the dark of the German night. Imitators were not long in coming.

The young National Socialist movement also demonstrated that blood shed for the nation was redemptive. When the sixteen original Nazi martyrs were killed at the Feldherrnhalle in Munich in November 1923, during Hitler's famed Beer Hall Putsch, the blood they shed became the holy water of the Third Reich. The original sixteen heroes inspired the National Socialists to emulate their example and to prepare to die for Führer, Volk, and Fatherland. This heroic mythology became the battle cry of the Nazis in the period of struggle. Upon assuming power, veneration of the "Immortals" became a major component of national ideology and ritual. The ornamental sarcophagi of the sixteen Immortals formed the Eternal Guard at the Temple of Honor on the Königsplatz in Munich, the heart of National Socialism. Ceremonies in their honor became the focal point of party ritual every November thereafter, ceasing only in 1944.

Horst Wessel, the legendary Brown Shirt leader and Joseph Goebbels's most able condottiere in the battle to the death against the Bolsheviks in Berlin, became the subject of myth, legend, poetry, and song. According to the Nazis, Germany in the past had owed its resurgence to eternal youth, and the line of mythical regeneration had passed from Siegfried to Parzifal and, thence, to Horst Wessel in the twentieth century.

Wessel's career as a Nazi leader was meteoric. A son of the upper bourgeoisie—his father was chaplain to Field Marshal von Hindenburg on the eastern front and pastor of the prestigious St. Nikolai Church in Berlin—Horst Wessel was at once a student, a worker, and a National Socialist. He composed the "Horst Wessel Song," and his exploits as commander of Storm Section V in Berlin became legendary. Berlin in the *Kampfzeit* was a political minefield, and Wessel's provocative behavior almost guaranteed his demise. He was gunned down in 1930 in a small apartment in Berlin, where he was living with a former prostitute.

Wessel's long battle for life offered Goebbels the opportunity he needed to give graphic form to the saga of the fighting, dying Brown Shirt hero. A new myth was born, and henceforth the name Horst Wessel became synonymous with heroism. Wessel had won so many converts from the communists in the drab proletarian wards of Berlin, and had made such a name for himself, that the Bolsheviks conceived an elaborate campaign of calumny against him.[3] According to them, Wessel was not a hero at all; instead, he was a pimp, living like a parasite from the earnings of a street tramp. In the world of the radical right and left, there was no room for a rational, measured assessment of Horst Wessel. For the Nazis, Wessel remained what he had always been—a model of bravery and self-sacrifice.

The myth of Wessel found its counterpart in the short life and tragic death of the child martyr Herbert Norkus. The darling of the Hitler Youth and the lodestar of youthful idealism, Norkus epitomized the suffering of the young generation in Weimar Germany. The son of a worker in a drab section of industrial north Berlin, this child of the Volk found a new home with the Hitler Youth. The organization offered him comradeship, order, and fun, the joy of sport, hiking, and boating. It was quite a contrast to his native Moabit, where industrial slime pervaded life in the impoverished district. Early in 1932, while engaged in a dawn propaganda blitz distributing flyers for a coming Nazi rally, Norkus was the victim of a communist stakeout. He was brutally murdered by a gang of communists, who could not have divined that they were slaying a boy who would become a Nazi Immortal. Both Goebbels and Hitler Youth leader Baldur von Schirach molded the legend of Herbert Norkus in the image of Horst Wessel. Young Germany was on the march, and the best had to die so that the nation might live.

Music accompanied Germany on the road to power as well as in the halcyon days of victory. Every great movement has its troubadour, and so it was with the Hitler Youth. Hans Baumann, himself but a youth when he began writing songs of battle and sacrifice in the late 1920s, became the Pied Piper of the Hitler Youth. When the boys and girls sang "today Germany belongs to us, and tomorrow the whole world," they were singing the song of an adolescent aflame with the passion of youth. Baumann longed for change and for a Führer, come from above, who would lead Germany to greatness. He delighted at the sound of pipes and drums and at the sight of columns of German youth marching over hill and dale toward victory. He was thrilled to hear his songs sung by thousands and thousands of German youths on the parade grounds of Nuremberg and in every street and hamlet in the country.

Soon enough Baumann's songs, like the movement itself, beckoned young Germans to conquer and cultivate the beautiful fields of the endless German East. Theirs was to be the consummate joy of creating a universal empire. His songs were well received not only by the Hitler Youth but also by the army and the SS, where they became part of the standard repertoire. To read his story is to recapture the seductive spirit and enthusiasm that moved the youths of Germany to dream of glory on the field of battle as their fathers had before them. Many went to war joyfully, and millions of them found a shallow grave in the steppes of Russia.

Gerhard Schumann offers a marked contrast to Hans Baumann among the circle of poets and writers who created National Socialist aesthetics. His poetry, plays, and radio dramas—like those of other celebrated writers of the period, such as Eberhard Wolfgang Möller and Herybert Menzel—contributed significantly to the heroic philosophy of death in Nazi Germany. Goebbels assigned poets a key role in Nazi propaganda, because they added a deeper dimension to the often mundane world of power politics. In the war that was certain to come, Goebbels expected the leading poets of the Reich to adorn the brow of the German warrior with the laurel crown of victory. Poesy would thus become the handmaiden to Mars, and Schumann assumed a leading role in the elite corps of writers honored by the government.

Schumann attained fame at a tender age. Only twenty-six when he received the National Book Prize in 1936, the young poet shared the vision of Adolf Hitler. He was immersed in heroic thought as an adolescent. At Tübingen University he joined the Brown Shirts, thus bridging the seemingly incompatible worlds of Christian theology and National Socialism. For the young Schumann, the SA was a knightly order in search of the Grail, the German Reich. His early poems are rhapsodies to comradeship, idealism, and the divine illumination of a newborn Reich.

Unlike so many National Socialists, Schumann was a purist and an ascetic. His poems celebrating Hitler and the Third Reich united emotional ecstasy with Swabian reserve, and he did not shy away from attacking, with Voltairean wit, the excesses of the newly arrived *Parteibonzen*. He published several books of poetry, and his works often appeared in leading newspapers. He learned through his experiences fighting at the front that the National Socialist view of heroism exacted a heavy toll. His war poems reflect a deepened sense of seriousness and purpose. Although they praise the joy of comradeship, they nevertheless convey the intense loneliness of all men in the ranks as they faced death so far away from home. The poems also show a tender emotion for the wives and children of the fighting men. Above all Schumann's poetry reflects a sensitivity to the human tragedy involved in the cataclysmic struggle against the enemies of the Reich. Schumann ended the war where he had begun it, faithful to Friedrich Hölderlin's poetic affirmation: "Live on high, O Fatherland, and do not count the dead! Not one too many has died for you."

Like Lenin and Trotsky before him, Goebbels understood that the medium of film was one of the most important weapons in the arsenal of the Third Reich. He acted on the assumption that there were extraordinary benefits to be gained from properly conceived film dramas. Talented directors were considered valuable property indeed and were offered prestige and perquisites. Along with such men as Carl Fröhlich and Veit Harlan, Karl Ritter ranked among the most influential Nazi film directors.

Karl Ritter looms large in this work, because he enjoyed remarkable success in projecting the image of the German philosophy of death. Ritter's influence rested not only on excellent connections to the ruling circles of the regime but also on his talent for historical film drama. As a World War

I fighter pilot, Ritter brought the realism of the front to the Neubabelsberg film studios of *Ufa,* the leading German film corporation. As a graphic artist and film director, he was skilled in the newly emerging technical aspects of the craft. Finally, as a National Socialist, he had all of the attributes that Hitler looked for in a film director: interpretive abilities, a feel for both bombastic propaganda and ideological nuance in his productions, and, above all, blind faith in the basic tenets of National Socialism. Further, Ritter was steeped in rabid anti-Semitism and anticommunism.

Through film, Karl Ritter schooled an entire generation of youth in the beauty of war. There is ample evidence that audiences of Hitler Youth thrilled at his idealization of battle and the nobility of comradeship among the warriors portrayed in his films. *Unternehmen Michael, Urlaub auf Ehrenwort,* and *Pour le Mérite*—film dramas exalting heroism in the Great War— were all enthusiastically received.[4] Ritter's films reflected the increasing belligerence of Germany in the years just before the outbreak of World War II. The films he directed glorifying the Nazi *Blitzkrieg* captured the flavor of bombast and *sang froid,* which characterized Hitler's days of military glory. Through Karl Ritter and the silver screen, Nazi imagery of heroic death probed the outer limits of ecstatic nationalism. Cascading orchestral scores only reinforced the appeal of these films to impressionable audiences.

As always in history, only warfare can decide the validity of a mythical framework. World War II dealt a fatal blow to the National Socialist pantheon of heroes. But en route to its destruction, the heroic ideology controlled the commanding heights. During the days of *Blitzkrieg* victories, Germany was totally immersed in warrior mythology. The battle of Poland, the lightning victory over France, and the war at sea provided ample opportunity for the propaganda of ecstasy. The Führer was recognized as the "greatest military commander of all times," while the intrepid holders of the *Ritterkreuz* were lionized by the propaganda ministry. Even the common foot soldiers were ennobled as protectors of Western civilization. The deadly seriousness of the battle for Russia against the "Jewish-Bolshevik subhumans" was a confrontation made for mythmakers, and Goebbels lost no opportunity to dramatize both major victories, such as the encirclement at Kiev, and tragic defeats, for example, the debacle at Stalingrad.

During World War II, all sectors of German life were employed to buttress Nazi mythology. Although traditional mass rallies, journalism, and radio formed the basis of Goebbels's propaganda orchestration, film, music, art, architecture, poetry, theater, and sculpture all drew variations on the central motifs. Further, the propaganda ministry directed massive theme campaigns at both national and local levels. These involved elaborate preparations for events such as Heroes Memorial Day and Mothers Day and burial ceremonies for the fallen heroes. Further, the ministry directed the writing of individual tracts to be given as gifts to the bereaved. Soon enough, the allied bombing campaign took its toll on German civilians as well, bringing the fighting front to the home front with a vengeance.

As Goebbels attempted to forge effective propaganda in the throes of defeat, he tried to convince the nation that fate had configured only two possible outcomes of the war—either total victory or the "biological destruction" of the German people. His parting cinematic effort to this end was Veit Harlan's *Kolberg*, which called on the German people to hold out when defeat seemed inevitable. The loyal and faithful nation would be rewarded with victory, Goebbels promised, just as the people of Kolberg were in the days of Napoleon.

In 1945 the Nazis ended the fascist era in the twilight of mythology. They had come full circle, because mythology is where National Socialism had begun a quarter of a century earlier in the cafes and beer halls of Munich. The heroes had answered their final reveille. No longer would they be resurrected, only to return to the fighting columns and standards below. The Immortals had joined the endless succession of fallen idols who had preceded them in defeat over the centuries. The light of yet another pantheon of heroes was extinguished forever, giving way to the gods of stronger powers in the endless progression of history.

TO DIE FOR GERMANY

∎ The Myth of Langemarck

No matter how many millennia might
pass, no one can speak of heroism without
remembering the German army in the World
War. Then out of the veil of the past the
iron front of the grey steel helmets will become visible, not faltering and not yielding, a
memorial of immortality. As long as Germans
shall live, they will remember that these were
once sons of their Volk.

Adolf Hitler[1]

In November 1917 the student, soldier, and youthful idealist Walter Flex ended his *The Wanderer between Two Worlds* with the thought that "We died for Germany's glory. Flower, Germany, as a garland of death to us!" His benediction glorified all of the sacrificial dead of the war.[2] During the Great War, propagandists and poets alike joined hands in exalting the blood sacrifice of the youth of Germany, thus transforming carnage into ethereal national revelation. Millions of young men were killed, and their respective nations revered them as true sons of their peoples who had made the supreme sacrifice. But the situation in Germany was unique and had sinister consequences. Only there did heroic death in war become a philosophy of life—indeed, a significant component of the ethos of radical nationalism.[3]

For centuries the beauty of death for the Fatherland had been an important theme in German literature and culture. Heinrich von Kleist celebrated the nobility of a military death in *Prinz Friedrich von Homburg*. The operas of Richard Wagner reveal a peculiar fascination with the redemptive qualities of heroic death. Rainer Maria Rilke, one of the great poets of the twentieth century, inspired the youth of the pre–World War I generation with his *Die Weise vom Leben und Tod des Cornets Chrisoph Rilke*—a narrative in rhythymic prose glorifying loyalty to the death, demonstrated by a youthful standard-bearer of an Austrian cavalry regiment in the war against the "Turkish anti-Christ" in the seventeenth century.

Both high culture and popular culture in Germany were pervaded with the themes of struggle, battle, and death, that is, the redemptive death of the warrior. Nothing was more foreign to this world view than the life of the bourgeois, devoted to pedantic order and the acquisition of wealth, or

1. Hitler pays tribute to the dead of Langemarck, 2 June 1940. (*Mit Hitler im Westen.*)

the values of the worker, mired in materialistic Marxism. Death in battle not only guaranteed eternal life for the martyr but also acted as a resurgent life force for the Fatherland. Death in combat took on the ennobling force of a sacrament. Honor, even more than victory, was the ultimate goal of the hero.[4]

The community of soldiers at the front had a somber beauty of its own, deeply felt by many of the men in the German army. For Otto Paust, the closeness of the soldiers was sweeter than mother's milk:

> Comradeship is stronger than dying.
> Comradeship is greater than death.
> Comradeship is something otherworldly.
> In it glows the spark of the eternal.[5]

For others, the onset of the war offered the promise of redemption for a nation too long sated with corruption, sloth, and self-satisfaction. At last the German Reich could be freed from the shackles of mediocrity and could fulfill the heroic fate willed by destiny.

Seldom in history has an army been inspired more by naive idealism than was the army of woefully unprepared young men who fought in Flanders in the fall of 1914. The final letter of Emil Alefeld from the front reflected these attitudes. Alefeld had been a student at the University of Munich. He was killed a few days before Christmas 1914 in Flanders. His love for Germany lent him courage, and, as he faced the great chasm of the beyond, Alefeld observed:

> We are Germans; we fight for our people and shed our blood and hope that the survivors are worthy of our sacrifice. For me this is a struggle for an idea, the *Fata Morgana* of a pure, loyal, honorable Germany. And if we go to our deaths with this hope in our hearts, perhaps it is better than to have won the victory and to learn that it was only a superficial victory, which did not improve our people spiritually.[6]

The communiqué of the Supreme High Command of the German Army of 11 November 1914 planted the seed that gave birth to the myth of Langemarck: "West of Langemarck young regiments singing 'Deutschland, Deutschland über alles' attacked the first line of enemy positions and over-ran them."[7] This claim, later held in contempt by the German left, became the communion wine of the nationalists, because it revealed the slaughter of the cream of German youth in Flanders.

Several years later Franz Brüchle of the Sixth Bavarian Reserve Division recounted his experiences at Langemarck.[8] According to his account, the young men of the Twenty-second, Twenty-third, Twenty-sixth, and Twenty-seventh Reserve Corps were outrageously overconfident in early October 1914 as they headed west in their troop transport trains toward France. There was no hint of melancholy in their songs, which promised parents and sweethearts their swift return: "In der Heimat, in der Heimat, es gibt ein Wiedersehen." Most of the young men were university and gymnasium students, thrilled with the opportunity thrust upon them at this historic moment in the nation's history. Many had the immature faces of seventeen-year-old boys, and their eyes shone with enthusiasm. They encamped for a few weeks near Lille, behind the front lines, where they received what passed for military training. Many went into battle without even being issued the shovels needed to prepare cover to protect them from enemy fire. And there were too few officers to lead these units. Suddenly, on the night of 26 October 1914, they were ordered into alarm readiness and thrust into the front on the line between Langemarck and Ypers, facing battle-tried English units armed with artillery and machine guns. As a result, the zealous youths, many of them drunk with excitement and bursting into song, were mowed down by the thousands as they attacked the enemy in open fields. Their assault had not been prepared by an artillery bombardment, and the result was senseless carnage.

Hitler, who was attached to the List Regiment in this sector, described his own experiences in *Mein Kampf:*

> We marched silently through a wet, cold night in Flanders, and just as the sun began to disperse the fog, an iron greeting was sent our way and shrapnel and shells exploded all around us; but before the smoke had cleared, the first hurrahs welled up from two hundred voices as the first messengers of death. Then we heard the crack and roar of gunfire, singing and yelling, and with wild eyes we all lunged forward, faster and faster, until suddenly man-to-man fighting broke out in turnip fields and thickets. We heard the sounds of a song from afar which came closer and closer to us, passing from one company to another, and then, just as men were dying all around us it spread into our ranks, and we passed it on: "Deutschland, Deutschland über alles, über alles in der Welt!"[9]

Eleven thousand young men lie buried in the student cemetery at Langemarck, testifying to the depravity of war. Yet through propaganda and poetry, their graves were rendered sacred shrines. They had not died; instead, their souls had passed the earthly boundaries and had been transfigured. Their blood sacrifice had guaranteed the nation's future. The young men of Langemarck became the symbol for all of the German fallen in the Great War. The dead of the Marne, Somme, and Verdun and all of the fighting fronts were subsumed in this symbol of youthful sacrifice. The image of the purity of the youth of Langemarck had an undeniable transcendent force. Theirs was the joyous, endless sleep of the redemptive, for they were vessels of divine grace. Eberhard Wolfgang Möller, who won the National Book Prize (1934–35) for his *The Letters of the Fallen,* concluded his work with an angelic chorus exalting the Langemarck fighters:

> Rest, you youths at Langemarck
> and wait for the coming of spring, . . .
> you will see Germany once more
> and the forests for which you died. . . .
> You will flower in your ranks
> and the summer will sing over you
> of your glory and our gratitude.[10]

The bitter disappointment of defeat in 1918, the unrest and alienation in the wake of the Spartacist revolution, and the political turmoil of the Weimar Republic resulted in a spirit of pessimism and unease in Germany. The stress led to an assault on traditional political, social, and cultural values, which further alienated the nationalists. The memory of the heroic fallen was an issue that united conservatives and the radical right, who fought a running battle with the left over questions related to the war.

Rudolf Binding offered an eloquent statement for the conservatives in his Olympian address in 1924 entitled "German Youth Honor the War Dead".[11] A man of knightly behavior and background—he had been a cadet in the prestigious Fourteenth Hussars—Binding had commanded an independent unit of reconnaissance dragoons in Flanders from 1914 to 1916, attached to the Young Germany Division. His deeply felt love and respect for his fallen comrades and devotion to an idealized German nation based on tradition had inspired several notable war poems, and he was viewed as a spokesman for the traditional Junker ethos.[12] Binding's description of his visit to an encampment of two thousand German youths, gathered to honor the dead in the high Röhn country on the tenth anniversary of Langemarck, was a classic embodiment of neo-Romanticism and secular blood mysticism. Langemarck, he said, had transcended history and had the force of a mythos, eternally testifying to the truth, eternally rejuvenating the nation. The conclave of youth had answered the ennobling call of Langemarck.

Binding joined the company of nationalist youth as if he were entering a Greek temple. The climb itself through the misty moorland into the foggy higher realm of the volcanic Röhn was itself an act of grace, preparing the young knights of the united Bündische Jugend to receive the miraculous healing transmitted by the spirits of the dead. His description of the orderly laying of camp would have delighted Caesar himself. The obedience shown to the youth leaders, the enthusiasm demonstrated in the individually fashioned unit flags that blew proudly in the wind, and the comradeship shown man-to-man all reflected the spirit of Langemarck.

With the coming of nightfall, the boys gathered around a huge, crackling campfire and broke into songs and chants. In the darkness and shadows they formed ranks in a meadow near the forest's edge, where they struck up melodies betokening death and resurrection. A medieval Rhenish mass prepared the youths to receive the solemn words of an honored poet, who reflected on his own experience in the sacred fields of Langemarck. On the next day they engaged in strenuous games, uniting pure spirit with cultivation of the body like their Greek forebears. They planted a monument to their conclave high atop the Heidelstein, where only eagles dared to fly. The scene was made more beautiful by the unity of spirit of those present, where religion, race, and class gave way to the higher good of the Fatherland. As they lowered their flags in honor of the men of Langemarck, theirs was the peace that passeth all understanding. When they sang "Deutschland über alles," like their German brothers had sung it ten years before, the resurrection and return of the heroes was assured.

The dedication of the Tannenberg National Monument in East Prussia in 1927 added significantly to the mythology of the fallen. The Tannenberg Nationaldenkmal Verein e.V. had waged a national campaign to collect funds to build a monument in honor of Field Marshal von Hindenburg and the glorious armies that won the victory of Tannenberg in 1914. The result was the colossal national monument designed by Walter and Johannes Krüger, which lay atop a heroes' burial mound near Allenstein in East

Prussia. The monument was based on the Germanic Stonehenge form, surrounded by walls and high towers. It was to be Hindenburg's final resting place, flanked by monuments mounted by the individual fighting units in the battle. In a classic union of form and function, the monument blended naturally with the East Prussian landscape and resembled the towering castle form of the Teutonic Knights of yore. The graves of the men of the eastern armies were gathered around their leader, who would join them one day when he passed to Walhall.

Near the eightieth birthday of Reich President von Hindenburg in 1927, a gala dedication of the monument took place. Chancellor Stresemann and an illustrious conclave of generals, officers, and men of the Great War joined the throng of eighty thousand people there, gathered to pay tribute to Hindenburg and the war dead. The battle flags and standards of the old military units became icons, celebrating the virtues of an era that did not know the shame of the "war guilt lie" or the dictated peace of Versailles. The field marshal was ultimately laid to rest in his tomb there on his birthday, 2 October 1935.[13]

Increasingly the memory of the war dead became involved in the heated political battles of the day. The socialists and communists attacked the war as a misguided display of the power of the political, social, and economic elite of a corrupt capitalist state. On 11 November 1929 the Social Democratic Party (SPD) organ *Vorwärts* ran an article with the headline "The Lie of Langemarck: A Crime of the High Command—No Deed of Heroism." In a direct assault on the Langemarck memorial ceremony, which had just taken place in the Berlin Sport Palace and where the "Hugenberg press" had celebrated the carnage as sacred revelation, *Vorwärts* claimed that General Erich von Falkenhayn should never have ordered the four reserve regiments of young men into the battle. It was criminal to order boys armed with rifles to launch a hopeless direct assault upon seasoned English units hedgehogged in with machine guns and artillery. Only fools could claim that such a sacrifice, which in a matter of ten days claimed 80 percent losses in some regiments and forty thousand dead, was an exemplary act of heroism.[14]

By the late 1920s, the great wave of war literature had begun, as veterans published volume after volume of reminiscences and literary works dealing with the *Fronterlebnis*. Ernst Jünger celebrated the war experience with Dionysian ecstasy in *The Storm of Steel,* and the posthumous writings of Walter Flex had a wide following. Josef Magnus Wehner wrote *Seven at Verdun* as a "monument to our dead brothers." In *The Belief in Germany,* which became the basis for the film *Stosstrupp* 1917, Hans Zöberlein wrote a testament to the comradeship and love of the Fatherland that he felt during the war, concluding his work with the assertion that "The battle for Germany continues! Volunteers to the front!" Heinz Steguweit's *Youth in the Caldron* was written with the earnest hope that the German warrior would not concede the field to the political cowards of the day but would hold the line in the true spirit of the front. Franz Schauwecker submitted in *Awakening of the Nation* that the political and social order under Kaiser Wilhelm II was so corrupt that Germany had to lose the war "to win the nation."[15]

There were also several feature films dedicated to the theme of national resurgence, most notably *Douaumont* (1931).[16] This Tobis film directed by Heinz Paul focused on the battle of Verdun, the bloodiest campaign of World War I. Its remarkable cast included two officers, Captain Haupt and Lieutenant Radtke, whose names were associated with the heroic storming of Douaumont, as well as units of the German Reichswehr. When it became obvious that the fortress had to be evacuated after a long and bloody struggle, the men of Douaumont dedicated the blood of their fallen to the homeland and announced that "this is the beginning of the end." In that hour of destiny, their faces appeared as if they had been chiseled from marble, as viewers drew parallels with grand scenes from classic Greek tragedy. True heroes know no defeat; instead, they seek annihilation for a greater good. "Ich hatt' einen Kameraden" was struck up, the song of lament for a dead comrade, and, in a moment of high pathos, Beethoven's *Heroic* Symphony accompanied their withdrawal. Footage of long rows of crosses, with the caption "They died for their Fatherland," delivered the message that the heroes of Verdun had sacrificed themselves on their own ravaged hill of Golgotha.

The Langemarck Committee, University and Army was conceived on a dark November day in 1921 in the Garrison Church at Potsdam, where Frederick the Great lay buried. A delegation of students from the University of Berlin and several nationalist organizations joined veterans of the Flanders front in a sad hour in their nation's history. In this period of shame and degradation for the German Reich, they kept the flame burning brightly for their cause. On a pilgrimage to Langemarck in 1928, the German students discovered the herocs' cemetery to be in disgraceful condition, and they determined to build a proper *Heldenfriedhof*. Over the next four years, the Langemarck Committee carried out a national campaign to this end and were successful. In July 1932 the national German student organization solemnly dedicated a fitting monument to the *Langemarck-kämpfer*.[17]

There were countless anniversary celebrations of Langemarck. Alfred Baeumler, professor of philosophy at the Technische Hochschule Dresden, spoke at such a celebration in 1929 before a meeting of the Hochschulring deutscher Art at Castle Boitzenburg. What gave Langemarck meaning, he submitted, was that the heroes had died to change the world. They set the stage for the battle of two world views, where heroism of the blood confronted decadent materialism, the curse of the modern age.[18]

Josef Magnus Wehner, whose *Seven at Verdun* had enjoyed wide readership, gave the speech of dedication. His thoughts revealed his belief in the mystical union of the Reich and the fallen. The address was read simultaneously at memorial ceremonies at all German universities, and it gave new life to the spirit of Langemarck:

> German students, in this hour you now assume the guard of honor before the nameless graves of German youths of the Great War. The transfigured spirits of these grand heroes arise gleaming and unite with yours, person to person and hand to hand and faith to faith and honor to honor and loyalty unto death. They once heroically stormed the hills which spewed forth their murderous fire, bleeding, clearly seen against the background of burning windmills, easy targets for the enemy. They stormed at Wytschaete and Messines, at Dixmuiden, Bixschoote and Paschendaele, at Becelaere, Hollebeke and Langemarck. Storming and dying they became the bearers of the final testament of the Reich.

For Wehner, idea and will had joined in a beautiful union in the fields of Flanders. By singing their song, the dying youths gave expression to the noble idea of freedom. The deeds of the fallen had become immortal:

> The dying sang! The stormers sang. The young students sang as they were being annihilated: "Deutschland, Deutschland über alles, über alles in der Welt." But by singing this song, they were resurrected once more, a thousand times, and they will rise again a thousand times until the end of the Reich. Because the sacred German Reich is not a question of boundaries or countries, it is as infinite as the world itself, created by God, and given to the Germans as an immortal commission. Their song did not perish when they died at Langemarck. The dead heroes became an omen for the German people.

Wehner pointed to the future, to a Third Reich:

> We will have to build the state, not as servants of the state, but as free, farseeing sons of the Reich. We will have the Reich only when power and the inner man flow together in spirit.

Wehner concluded with a vision, as those present were about to meet the heroes:

> They are already beginning to shine, those tender shadows. Happiness wells up on their young faces, the eternal happiness of the immortal. They come and greet us, the survivors, we who are in the twilight, the doubters, the despairing. Now they are more alive than we, and they move about in a joyful mood, singing and saying:
>
> > "Build the columns of the Reich
> > over the corruption of the world!"
>
> The chorus of the men in field gray becomes louder. The Reich is everywhere and its blood witnesses are everywhere. Its heaven glows and its dead shine like the stars.[19]

For Hanns Johst, writing in the *Münchner Neueste Nachrichten*, the words of Wehner were prophetic.[20] Just a few short years before, he submitted, Germany had been lost in Marxist tumult. Materialism, a foreign philosophy of life, stalked the land. Heroes went unrecognized, and their sacrifice was viewed as simply a regrettable loss of life devoid of meaning. Johst claimed that Wehner had sounded the trumpet anew, announcing that the men of Langemarck were the first blood witnesses of the coming Third Reich. A new age of heroism was dawning. The cemeteries of the fallen surrounded the frontiers of Germany with sacrificial altars of the Reich, fortresses of the soul signifying the eternal bond between the dead and the living.

The torch was being passed from Langemarck to the Third Reich. On the anniversary of Langemarck in 1932, the Brown Shirt newspaper *Der SA Mann* took up the theme in a feature article. A delegation of youths, many of them veterans of the war and now members of Hitler's Brown Shirts, made a week-long pilgrimage to Flanders. They were encamped among the crosses of their fallen brothers, and as night fell they gathered around a campfire, where they conjured up images of heroes past and dreamt of future deeds of self-sacrifice. The soil of Flanders, they claimed, had hardly settled over the graves of the young warriors when "the front of the living Langemarck" was born in their hearts. They had proclaimed forthwith that "we ourselves are Germany," recognizing their sacred responsibility. Now a miraculous turn of events was opening the way for the fulfillment of their dream in the Third Reich, led by one of their own, a simple soldier and comrade in the Flanders theater. An SA witness described the euphoria they experienced:

> Night has fallen and our fire blazes on Poelkapelle Hill. At our feet—the graves of Langemarck. Then one of our band stands up and speaks from the heart: "Just as once the rhythm of the gray columns thundered on the roads of Flanders, and just as our young *Wandervögel* brothers in gray coats died here on the field of Langemarck with a song on their lips—so our lives must be like their deed: brave, unselfish, strong and pure. We have two weapons to achieve this: we have our swords and we have our Adolf Hitler."

The Brown Shirts proclaimed themselves the vanguard of historical change in a prophetic affirmation:

> They gazed deep into the black of night and greeted the Germany of tomorrow, born in the breasts of the new young nation. They greet the dead of Langemarck and the German revolution, for which one day they too will die.[21]

With the coming of the Third Reich, the fallen of Langemarck merged with the martyrs of the Feldherrnhalle as inspiration for the new era. The Langemarck veteran Wilhelm Dreysse wrote, "The graves of Langemarck glow with a new heavenly light. *The dead have returned home in us.*"[22] The young Nazi poet, Herbert Böhme, declaimed in "Der 9. November: The Dead of Victory to the Dead of the War":

> We gave force to your words,
> Verdun, Douaumont, Dead Man Hill,
> we took your living form
> and set the hills aflame.[23]

The myth of Langemarck became a basic component of the National Socialist propaganda repertoire. Henceforth the German people were admonished "not to talk about Langemarck, but to live Langemarck."[24] Langemarck ceremonies took place every year, and no less a figure than Martin Heidegger, rector of the University of Freiburg, addressed a rally on this theme in November 1933.[25] Readings on the heroic Langemarck regiments became part of the standard school curriculum as well.[26] A program of scholarships for university study for children of the working class was established and given the title "Langemarck Studium."[27] Countless newspaper articles appeared dealing with this theme.[28]

The front fighter was also a popular subject for radio drama in the classic period of this genre. Perhaps the most outstanding example of radio dramatists was Richard Euringer, a fighter pilot in World War I, who won the first State Prize for Literature offered in the Third Reich for his *Deutsche Passion 1933*. In this radio drama, written in the style of a medieval mystery play, a German front soldier assumes the role of Christ. He suffers the indignity of a crown of barbed wire from the trenches and is crucified by his own people who are led by Jews and Marxists. The front soldier rises again and is redeemed by Adolf Hitler and the National Socialist movement.[29]

Baldur von Schirach, who was always clever at picking themes of propaganda, claimed the Langemarck legacy for the Hitler Youth. With Hitler and the party preoccupied with the mythology of 9 November 1923 and the fallen of the NSDAP, Baldur von Schirach, on Langemarck Day 1934, enthusiastically assumed the mantle of the Langemarck Foundation of German Students. Speaking to the Hitler Youth gathered in Munich, he reflected on the spiritual union of the martyrs of the Great War and the martyrs of the future. Schirach claimed that an entire people stood loyally with the youth of Langemarck and that the dead spoke with a strong voice in every boy and in every girl in the new Germany. They had learned to "live for Langemarck."[30]

A year later the Reich student leader organized a joint ceremony for his Hitler Youth and many of the surviving veterans of Langemarck. The result was a propaganda *tour de force,* as the flag was passed from generation to generation, accompanied by Eberhard Wolfgang Möller's *The Letters of the Fallen,* scored for chorale by Georg Blumensaat. Langemarck Day was not an occasion for mourning, von Schirach claimed. Instead, it was a great day of reunion and an opportunity to rejoice in the resurrection of both the martyrs and the young nation. Turning to the men of Langemarck, the living embodiment of the youthful idealism of 1914, he said:

> In this hall thousands of front fighters are gathered, among them many Flanders and Langemarck fighters. We give you our very special greetings today. You have given us the great gift of the heroic experience. . . . We are spirit of your spirit. You gave birth to the socialism of the front. . . . Look at the millions of our youth! This is the meaning of Langemarck! That we forget ourselves, that we sacrifice ourselves, that we are loyal, that is the message of the fallen to the living, that is the call from the beyond to our times. . . . Because the German dead have risen. With our flags waving we march together with them into eternity.[31]

The "march into eternity" was not long in coming for the second Langemarck generation. Hitler's view of the world had been molded by his own experience at the front, and it was inevitable that he would attempt to succeed where the German Reich had failed. During the course of the German offensive in the west in May 1940, Flanders soon fell into German hands. The OKW communiqué of 29 May 1940 announced that "the Reich war flag is waving over the monument to the German youth at Langemarck, the scene of the heroic struggle in 1914." The meaning of this victory was not lost on Hitler or his propagandists. For them, the German armies were answering the call of the fallen from afar, and they relished the joyous reunion of the living and the dead. It was but a matter of days before Hitler journeyed to Langemarck, which for him was a sacramental experience of the first order.[32]

Dr. Willi Fr. Könitzer, writing in the *Völkischer Beobachter,* noted that the brave youths of the Third Reich had kept the faith with the men of Langemarck, over whose memorial the words of Heinrich Lersch proclaimed: "Germany must live, even if we must die!" Könitzer continued:

> The other, the second Langemarck, has been fulfilled. The day of the greatest German victory has come on the sight of the most tremendous sacrifice of German youth, and its symbol is already flying over the monument. Those who fell for a new Germany now join in a comradely front with those who confirmed this new Germany through their struggle and their death. A Volk which can claim the youth of 1914 as their own can never be destroyed. The young men of the second Langemarck wave are living testimony to that.[33]

Langemarck experienced yet another dramatic event before passing into history. On Langemarck Day, 11 November 1940, Field Marshal von Brauchitsch invited the Hitler Youth leaders serving in the armed forces to Langemarck. There von Schirach spoke on an international radio hookup, heralding the "eternal union of the Hitler Youth and the Wehrmacht." The martyred heroes "had returned home and found eternal peace," he claimed.[34]

Years later Wehner mused on the enduring meaning of Langemarck and the Great War. It had been a religious experience for him and for those who had served at the front. Christ's passion had found its parallel in the deeds of those soldiers, who had sacrificed themselves for the nation. But the tears of Good Friday gave way to the joy of a German Easter and the promise of eternal life. Wehner celebrated this sacrifice in his poem "Vom Blut der Helden Schlägt das Herz der Welt":

> You should neither cry nor grieve,
> for our sacrificial blood was life wine.
>
> God created death as a brother to life:
> The heart of the world beats with the blood of heroes.
> We marched before you through the dark gate
> and shone for your resurrection.
>
> Thus celebrate for us with cheerful, bright resound
> a chant of victory is our funeral music.
>
> Grief's noble gem glows vividly,
> death is short and being is eternal.
> Arise and stand tall proudly proceeding into the light:
> Freedom is already kissing your face.[35]

II

The Martyrdom of
Albert Leo Schlageter

Keep the colors flying, even if you must die.
Motto of Albert Leo Schlageter[1]

Although he was but one of thousands of young men who distinguished themselves in the Great War, Lieutenant Albert Leo Schlageter became a martyr to the German people. Born in Schönau/Baden in the Black Forest in 1894, he was a handsome blue-eyed youth who came to manhood in a tragic period of his nation's history. Germany was bleeding from a thousand wounds. The trauma of defeat, the Bolshevik revolution, and the humiliation of the Versailles Peace Treaty spawned grievous social conflict throughout the country. The Allied blockade of Germany only worsened the conditions of famine and suffering, leaving it vulnerable to foreign attack. Polish insurgents threatened Silesia, and East Prussia lay open to communist penetration. With the nation's proud battle flags in disgrace and its honor sullied, patriots were alert for signs of resurgence. Most of the political parties of the Weimar Republic offered them no hope, and they were offended by bourgeois aggressiveness and tin-plated materialism.

The appalling conditions that followed French occupation of the Ruhr in 1923 set the stage for the birth of a legend of heroism. Schlageter assumed the purple mantle of martyrdom, shedding his blood for the redemption of Germany. Although the facts were more prosaic—he was engaging in acts of sabotage to prevent the delivery of German coal shipments to the French in payment of the war indemnity—Schlageter's death touched a raw nerve in the nation. Almost overnight he was elevated from Free Corps fighter and lawless conspirator to a symbol of the Germanic faith, transcending party and class. Otto Paust's "Song of the 'Lost Troops'" heralded Schlageter as a symbol of deliverance:

Rhine, Ruhr, and Palatinate. And—dungeon's darkness,
Sentence and prison! Troubled, unable to rest—
Golzheimer Heath. Schlageter's death.
Flaming blaze.—Dawn!
Do you remember?

The Third Reich's First soldier!
You kept the faith! You were the living deed.
You are the Reich. You are the nation,
You are Germany's faith, the son of the Volk.[2]

What was the nature of the man behind the myth of Albert Leo Schlageter? Born in a Catholic farming family, he was one of six children. As a boy he loved to roam the hills and valleys of his native Black Forest, to dream under majestic fir trees, and to listen to the tales of war veterans recalling their hour of glory in the German victory over France in 1870. A bright boy at the village school in Schönau, he won a place at the Berthold Gymnasium in Freiburg im Breisgau. There he was consistently a high-ranking student. With the onset of the war in 1914, he volunteered for service in the seventy-sixth Field Artillery Regiment. After a brief training period, he was sent to the western front. Schlageter moved up the ranks quickly, distinguishing himself as much for his bravery as for his mastery of the technical aspects of the artillery arm. He seemed to know no fear. War comrades later reported that Schlageter was often seen charging into enemy shellfire with a lighted pipe in his mouth, and he became something of a legend in his unit. He saw service in sectors ranging from Flanders to the Vosges. Schlageter experienced the living hell of Verdun, and he was wounded there in 1916. He was promoted to lieutenant and received the Iron Cross First and Second Class. Schlageter noted in a letter that, despite the ravages and suffering it brought, war nevertheless "does have its beauty and attraction, especially for us young people."[3]

Schlageter's character was a marriage of youthful bravado and deep-seated religious convictions. During the war he wrote several letters to an esteemed teacher, Rektor Matthäus Lang zu Konstanz, reverently thanking him for his prayers and for those of the pious brothers of the Sankt Konradihaus. In one such letter, Alfred sought advice about entering the priesthood, to which he had felt a calling for several years. "I have prayed to the Holy Spirit and the dear Mother of God for her support in this regard. . . . I have made mistakes and have sinned. . . . But there is nothing that suits my nature more than theology."[4]

As the war progressed, Schlageter became imbued with the traditions of the German army. He was attracted to its ethos of honor and duty, and he had a deep sense of responsibility to the men under his command. He refused the comforts afforded officers when his men fared poorly. Schlageter thought like a fighting man, valuing his comrades-in-arms as the world's elite warriors. He scorned the shirkers and the profiteers on the home front, the pretensions of the reserve, and above all the distant officers of the general staff.[5] He revered the fallen as young knights called home at a tender age. When his brother was killed at Ecurie in 1917, Albert was sorely grieved. In a letter posted to his parents on 17 December 1917, he wrote:

> It is sad that our dear Emil will never again write his blessed Christmas letter. We will miss him terribly, but . . . we can be assured that our dear Emil left this world as a good, brave religious man and appeared before God's judgment seat. God in heaven will not be his judge, but rather his Saviour. . . . Thus we must take the pain we feel at his loss and turn it into a deeply-felt longing for a reunion in Heaven.[6]

It is clear that the war deepened Schlageter's religious convictions. In turn, his faith molded him into a soldier of rare courage.

Like so many of his comrades, Schlageter held firmly to his belief in the final victory. As late as February 1918 he wrote: "I'm really happy that we are finally ready to force a decision; just one more all-out drive and then hopefully the peace we have long hoped for. We will do everything possible to be certain that we get the job done."[7] During the defensive hostilities on the Arras front later that year, Schlageter was proud of the accomplishments of his battery: "The English really took it on the nose in our sector."[8] He had personally crippled six English tanks in the engagement.[9] Loyal to the end, Schlageter was awarded the Iron Cross I in 1918.

When dissolution and revolutionary ferment began to spread in the German armed forces during the last months of the war, there was no question that Schlageter's battery would remain true to the colors. Covering the retreat in their sector, they marched intact across Belgium to their destaging area in Freiburg. There the cannoneers—shattered by the trauma of defeat and fighting back tears signaling their bittersweet memories of shared suffering and danger—raised Schlageter to their shoulders in a display of brotherly affection.[10] Neither the lieutenant nor his men could ever really go home again. The war had radically altered their lives, and they were different human beings. Gradually the men of the unit had become brothers, and they formed a family in the passionate service of the nation. No matter where they wandered, they were driven by the same inner call once expressed by the veteran Major Foertsch: "I've got to get back to my company—I have to get 'back home' to my comrades at the front."[11]

Alienation ate at the soul of Schlageter as he twisted and turned in the lecture halls of Freiburg University, where he had matriculated early in 1919 as a student of national economy. How narrow the vision, how limited the experience of the comical professors and the postpubescent students who had never experienced the storm of steel at the front. This rootless, materialistic world was devoid of meaning for a man who had come to think heroically.[12] When Ernst von Salomon profoundly described the state of

2. Albert Leo Schlageter. (Personal Collection.)

mind of most German veterans in his memoirs, *Die Geächteten,* he could have used Schlageter as a model.[13] Where Schlageter sought truth, he found duplicity. Where he sought love of country, he found communist betrayal and evidence of the Soviet world conspiracy. Where he sought honor, he found nauseating bourgeois avarice and craven clinging to material comforts. Nowhere could Schlageter and his comrades find Germany; nowhere could they find the homeland of their imagination. Edwin Erich Dwinger spoke for many when he explained the reason why:

> The homeland was with them. They were the nation. . . . The front was their homeland, their fatherland. . . . The war was their world, the war dominated them, the war would never let them go. . . . They will always have the front in their blood, the nearness of death, the sense of duty, the grimness, the ecstasy, the shells. . . . The war is over. But the warriors are still marching.[14]

There is little question that Schlageter underwent a personal crisis in the harrowing days after the war. This resulted not only from the revolutionary political, social, and cultural climate of the era but also from the fact that his prospects for suitable employment after university study seemed so hopeless.[15] With the nation in such danger, a future in theology or the priesthood now seemed out of the question. He longed for the reassuring traditions of the old order and was repulsed by the liberal Weimar Republic. Letters to his parents reveal a man who was lost until he came home once more to rejoin his front comrades in the Free Corps von Medem.[16] This offered Schlageter the opportunity to solve his personal problems and to serve a higher ideal—to save Germany from the Bolshevik flood that threatened to drown the country in blood. This remained his calling from the time he joined the old boys from Baden in the Edelweiss Battery at Waldkirch in March 1919 until he was executed by a French firing squad in 1923.

In the spring of 1919, Schlageter was deployed in the campaign against the Bolsheviks in the Baltic region. East Prussia was in danger of being invaded by determined Latvian communists. Estonia had already fallen to the insurgents, and the red flag flew over Reval and Dorpat. Under the command of General Graf von der Goltz, the Free Corps von Medem took part in the successful counteroffensive that liberated Riga in May 1919. According to the regimental history of his unit, "Lieutenant Schlageter personally saved the situation" with a lightning sweep into the city.[17]

Schlageter was very sensitive to the criticism directed against the Free Corps for alleged brutalities in engagements against the communists. He regarded this as unjustified, the actions of the Free Corps paling in comparison to the unspeakable deeds of the murdering, marauding bands of Red Guards. In Riga alone, he noted, the GPU had killed several thousand Latvians and tortured countless others in their subterranean cells of horror.

When Schlageter attended the services in Riga Cathedral to celebrate the liberation, he was all the more convinced that he was serving a righteous cause. He wrote at that time:

> We have a real job to do out here, freeing this country from the most unspeakable crimes and atrocities. . . . It is simply a lie that we are plundering and robbing here. The most insignificant theft is handled much, much more severely than during the war. We have excellent discipline. If this were not so, I would leave immediately and come home.[18]

Schlageter next saw action with the Free Corps von Petersdorff. In August 1919 he took part in the Free Corps mutiny under the notorious commander of the Iron Division, Major Joseph Bischoff, which resulted in the formation of the German Legion. This band, which was outlawed by the government in Berlin, served under the command of the mercurial Russian nobleman Prince Pawel Awaloff-Bermondt. Thereafter Schlageter took part in the disastrous defensive engagement of the forlorn and abandoned Russian Army of the West, which ended in the total collapse of the Baltic front. Following this reversal, he retreated to the relative security of an estate in East Prussia, where he awaited the next call to service.[19] Despite the defeat in the Baltic, Schlageter had been a living testament to Graf von der Goltz's motto for the campaign: "Do what you must—victory or death—and leave the rest to God."[20]

Schlageter's alienation grew with the passing seasons. To him, there was no question of returning home, and he broke contact with his family for the time being. He felt betrayed by a government that he considered cynical and opportunistic. Now that the socialists felt secure with the reins of power, they withdrew their clandestine support for the Free Corps. Worse yet, they unleashed a brutal rhetorical assault on their erstwhile rescuers. Schlageter was of the opinion that the hostility shown by the politicians against those who had saved the country from Bolshevik chaos was totally unwarranted. Mutual hostilities reached a climax in the summer of 1920 when Carl Severing, minister of the interior, remarked: "I most certainly support a strong military force. But what we now have are Praetorian hordes, who have become a plague upon the land."[21]

In the spring of 1920, Schlageter's unit was attached to the Third Marine Brigade Löwenfeld. While engaged in the neutralization of the communist insurgents in the Ruhr, he took part in the bloody class warfare at Bottrop. Later that year, with the victory won, the government dismissed the Brigade Löwenfeld. Once more Schlageter went to the East, leading a Robin Hood existence in support of the Lithuanians in their hostilities with Poland. Submitting to pressure from the Entente powers, Lithuania attempted to intern the German Freebooters, but many of them escaped. According to several popular accounts, most of which have some factual basis, Schlageter subsequently underwent a series of Herculean labors. Dashing westward to escape incarceration, he allegedly swam the Yula River bordering Poland at Tauroggen on a cold and windy night in November 1920. At another juncture, he rejoined the men of his battery encamped for the winter in Lithuania, which had appealed for their help once more. Wilhelm Hügenell, a veteran of those days, recalled:

> Because of a lack of winter clothes and money, that Christmas in Kowno was a miserable one for the men, but a great surprise lay in store for them. Suddenly Schlageter stood before them. He gave all his money and clothes to the surprised men. . . . That was typical of the noble man and comrade Albert Leo Schlageter.[22]

In 1921 renewed trouble broke out with Poland in Upper Silesia, where a plebiscite was to decide the future of the province. In the view of German nationalists, the French had gone far beyond their role mandated by the League of Nations to function as overseers of the plebiscite, even supplying their Polish ally with deliveries of weapons and intelligence information. Schlageter joined the Spezialpolizei, linking up with the Storm Battalion Heinz, a highly secret countersabotage unit under the command of Heinz Oskar Hauenstein.[23] Terror and counterterror were the order of the day. In one notable commando operation, Schlageter took part in a raid that freed twenty-one Germans from a prison in Kosel. Many other undercover operations followed.[24]

After the German victory in the plebiscite in March 1921, the adventurer Wojciech Korfanty unleashed the Third Polish Insurrection and invaded Upper Silesia. Schlageter took part in the legendary victory over the Poles at Annaberg in May 1921, which was won by the Storm Battalion Heinz, Free Corps Oberland, and Heydebreck's Wehrwolves. When the German battle flags were raised high atop the Annaberg on that day, the Free Corps had won a victory that the Nazis celebrated as a chapter in heroism. A dying soldier took pen in hand there, lending poetic vision to the myth of Annaberg:

> Then I saw in the waning afternoon sun
> How they raised our victorious flag,
> It flew so high from the cloister tower
> The flag, the flag which greeted me—
> You proud banner, we raised you up
> From the filth and ruin and mire,
> Now you're back in your honored place,
> And I can die a peaceful death.[25]

Although banned by the German government, the Storm Battalion Heinz continued to operate under the command of Hauenstein. Henceforth it became known as the Organization Heinz. Late in 1921, Schlageter was posted to Danzig—a German city transferred to League of Nations control—where right-wing radicals hoped to establish the infrastructure for a coup. During his stay there, he became the subject of international attention when it was widely reported in the press that he had become a spy in the service of Poland.[26] Hauenstein had in fact assigned Schlageter the dangerous mission of penetrating the Polish underground. Claiming that he stood ready to trade German war ministry secrets for money, Schlageter initially made contact with Lieutenant de Rour at the Hotel Continental in Danzig. De Rour, a member of the intelligence section of the French war ministry, arranged for Schlageter to meet with De Rour's counterpart in the Polish Ministry of War, Rittmeister Dubitsch. Emboldened by the knowledge that it would be compromising for Dubitsch to arrest him in the Free City, Schlageter called on Dubitsch at the Polish consulate. Major Hauenstein personally stood guard across the street as a precaution. Within minutes, Schlageter was revealed to be exactly what he was—a German spy. Dubitsch set him free but, at the same time, published photographs offering a reward for his arrest in the newspapers. He also provided left-wing journalists in Berlin with precisely the sort of slanted materials for which they were hungering. Thoroughly compromised, Schlageter was rendered useless for future service against Poland.[27]

In 1922, Schlageter and Hauenstein formed an export-import business in Berlin. Located on the Linkstrasse, in all probability it served as a cover for the illicit trading and storing of weapons for future use against both foreign and domestic enemies of the nationalist cause. While in Berlin, Schlageter joined the Nazi party, at that point a forlorn, northern bridgehead for the NSDAP in a city dominated by the socialists and communists. He did not take an active part in party activities, although he journeyed to Munich in 1922 to hear Hitler address a meeting of thirty members of the Free Corps Rossbach and Organization Heinz.[28]

Schlageter's unsettled career in Berlin came to an abrupt halt in January 1923, after the French invaded the Ruhr in violation of international law. Both a political gamble and an act of revenge, the invasion fomented a crisis with tragic consequences. Germans from all classes and political parties reacted indignantly. For some, anger threatened to give way to hopelessness. Ernst von Salomon's colorful account of the French advance into Essen reflected the despair.

> At that moment the French moved into the city. I heard their trumpets blowing, and hurried down to the street and watched. . . . I saw the arrogance of the victors, the elegance and the smiles of contempt which bespoke punishment and revenge. The city was delivered to the will of the enemy, its honor sullied, and it was unbearable for those of us who had to suffer through it. . . . Elemental, proletarian rage rushed through me. . . . To think that they

could march in their military splendor while we stood there humiliated, that set my heart afire with rage. The whole morning I walked through the city, totally beside myself.[29]

The passive resistance that greeted the enemy led to great suffering and contributed to the runaway inflation of 1923. Everywhere the French were confronted with the contempt of the Germans. Restaurants refused to serve them; taxi drivers left their cars when French soldiers climbed in; hotels refused them rooms. They were spat upon and terrorized by night. Cries of the "rape of the Ruhr" and "black shame" echoed through the country, and violence was widespread. In a bloody confrontation at the Krupp plant in Essen, thirteen unarmed workers were gunned down, and thirty were wounded. Rumors were rife. There was talk of a "bloodbath at Dortmund" and of a little girl butchered by the enemy outside the Düsseldorf railway station. Matters worsened as the French attempted to establish a separate state in the Rhineland.[30]

Schlageter, like all German patriots, felt the humiliation deeply and answered an inner call to serve his country. The Organization Heinz sprang into action once again, opening the way for what conservatives saw as a page of glory in the history of German heroism. Schlageter set about gathering his old comrades from the Great War and from the Baltic and Upper Silesia. On one occasion he read his flock lyrics by Friedrich Schiller on the theme of freedom:

> So we have to cringe and sneak about on our own soil,
> like murderers, and take what is rightfully ours by
> night, whose dark cloak lends itself only to
> criminality and conspiracy, but which in our case is as
> bright and clear and majestic as the noonday sun.[31]

In January 1923 Hauenstein, operating from his headquarters in unoccupied Elberfeld, assigned Schlageter command of the Essen detachment. For over two months, Schlageter took part in both sabotage and intelligence endeavors directed against the French in the Ruhr. A main function of the group was to dynamite rail lines in an effort to halt the delivery of German coal to France. On several occasions his guerilla raids were successful, and the French were on the alert for further insurgent operations. But the game was up following the dynamiting of a railway bridge at Calcum, which lay on the line between Düsseldorf and Duisberg. On April 5, at the instigation of the French, the Prussian authorities in Kaiserswerth issued a curiously phrased warrant for Schlageter's arrest:

> On the evening of March 15, 1923 at 8:00 P.M., the railway bridge over the Haarbach River near Calcum was blown up. This was probably perpetrated by two young men with the following descriptions. Family name probably Fr. v.

Krampe or von Krause and Albert Leo Schlagstein or Schlageter, who is 20–
25 years old, 1,60 tall, lanky, dark blond, without a beard, good looking with
a confident upright bearing. Speaks with a foreign accent (not a Rhinelander),
wearing black boots, brown sport stockings, gray trench coat and light sport
cap. . . . As a result of the deed, several respected citizens have been arrested
as hostages by the occupation forces, who will not be set free until the perpetrators are put behind bars. Information is urgently requested which will lead
swiftly to the arrest of the guilty parties.[32]

Within a matter of two weeks after the bombing, Schlageter was arrested
by French security forces at the Union Hotel in Essen. Strangely, he had
registered under his own name, although a cache of explosives was in his
possession. The authorities took him first to the building of the Coal Syndicate in Essen, where many German prisoners had been beaten by the
French. Later he was transferred to the prison at Werden, near Düsseldorf.
There Schlageter learned that the police had rounded up many of the
members of the Organization Heinz, including his accomplice Hans Sadowski, as well as Georg Werner, Georg Zimmerman, and the medical
student Alois Becker. On April 14, while the French were preparing their
case against him, Schlageter was able to smuggle a letter out of prison to
Hauenstein:

A hell of a situation. The whole operation is closed down. But be careful. The
whole stinking traitorous mess was traced from me to you. Don't let them get
you. . . . I think we've been betrayed, and the source has to come from inside.
They not only knew what we did, but they had word-for-word evidence of our
future plans. Our men in Essen cannot be used anymore. Be careful around
anyone with the "H" patch. They will pass themselves off as old comrades from
Upper Silesia, but they are really French criminal agents. The fellows will have
to keep their mouths shut and be very careful if they don't want to be chained
three times and led around with a pistol at their breast like me. Greetings to
you and a Heil to all.[33]

During the weeks that passed while Schlageter awaited trial before a
French military court, he wrote several letters to his parents and family.
His case had occasioned considerable attention both in Germany and
abroad, and it was being closely monitored in Berlin as well. Schlageter's
letters reveal a sensitive and tenderly loving son as well as a German patriot
acutely conscious of his emerging role as a national symbol. On 22 April
1923 he wrote to his parents:

A thousand thanks for your letter. Now finally I am relieved to know that you
are well and that with God's help you have endured the shock and pain of the
news. It has been hell here since my arrest on April 7. . . . I do not fear even
the worst sentence, nor does it sadden me. If I were alone on this earth I truly
do not know what could be more beautiful than to die for the Fatherland. My

suffering comes because of you. Day and night. If I could have spared you this, I gladly would face the shells two or three times. Continue to be brave. Keep your hopes up.[34]

After an endless series of interrogations, Schlageter was moved under tight security from Werden to a new prison at Düsseldorf-Derendorf. Unbeknown to the French authorities at the time, the move prevented the escape of their famous prisoner by some twelve hours. Hauenstein had made contact with trusted individuals in the Werden prison, and the plans laid for Schlageter's flight thus came to nought.[35] Instead of freedom, Schlageter faced the trauma of solitary confinement and was forbidden even to exercise in the prison yard. Time hung very heavy on his hands. The German authorities foiled any future attempts at escape when, in a lightning raid on May 12 at Elberfeld, they arrested Heinz Hauenstein and most of the members of his organization.[36]

On May 10, Schlageter and his fellow prisoners were tried by a French military court of five officers, headed by Lieutenant Colonel Blondel. Among the persons attending the trial was "Jürgens," a member of the Organization Heinz who had been in surreptitious contact with Schlageter throughout the crisis. According to the president of the tribunal, in the interest of public safety swift ajudication of the case would follow. The evidence against the defendants was presented in four counts: abetting crimes against the occupation forces, bombing of railway lines, sabotage, and plotting against German agents. The court was able to learn only the barest information from the accused. At the conclusion of the questioning, Schlageter boldly asserted, "I take full responsibility for everything that I have done."[37] The prosecution called for severe punishment to serve as a warning to others contemplating such serious crimes. As the judgment of the court was read, French infantrymen with drawn pistols surrounded the prisoners. Schlageter was sentenced to death, while his accomplices received lesser punishment.[38] A huge crowd stood outside the courthouse building on Düsseldorf's Mühlen Strasse, silently awaiting the verdict. When they caught sight of Schlageter, several men removed their hats in silent tribute to him.

In anticipation of an impassioned response to their actions, the French treated the affair as a military engagement, assigning several units to guard the prison. On the evening after the trial, Schlageter's mind turned toward home, and he wrote his family:

Hear the last but true words of your disobedient and ungrateful son and brother. From 1914 until today I put everything I had to the service of my German homeland out of love and true loyalty. . . . I was not motivated by a wild search for adventure; I was not a leader of a gang. . . . I have never committed a petty crime much less a murder. No matter how people might judge me, don't you think poorly of me. Think of me lovingly in the future, and hold my memory in honor. This is all that I still want from this life. Dear Mother, dear Father! . . . My greatest wish until the last second will be that our dear God will give you strength and comfort, and will make you strong in these difficult hours.[39]

Remarkably, Schlageter had cleared his mind of hatred for his persecutors. In a letter of the same date to "Jürgens," he wrote that, although it was difficult to be executed like a common criminal, nevertheless his mind was at rest and free of anxiety. "Forget life and forgive the prosecution and the jury. I have done both."[40]

With the announcement of the harsh verdict, controversy erupted throughout Germany. Although Chancellor Cuno protested the sentence in the strongest possible terms, parliamentary factions formed that engaged in a campaign of violent rhetoric. While Schlageter was a hero to the nationalists, the left labeled him a mercenary, a right-wing bandit in the service of a corrupt regime.[41]

Public opinion in the areas occupied by the French was forcefully expressed in an editorial in the *Kölnische Zeitung:*

> From the German standpoint, the judgments in Düsseldorf simply cannot be recognized, because the French military court was the result of an illegal entry upon German territory and therefore is devoid of any legal justification. . . . We do not approve of the bombing of railways . . . and if those responsible are indeed guilty, nevertheless their acts are understandable in human terms. The French have shown at many points a ruthlessness, an open hatred, as if they were not facing an equal cultured nation, but instead barbaric tribes of some dark continent. . . . If this brutal treatment causes Germans to well up with a wild hatred against the invaders and forces them to answer illegal violence with illegal violence, then the French have only themselves to thank.[42]

As attention continued to focus on the case, calls for mercy came from several quarters. Schlageter's attorney formally appealed the decision, while the German government exerted pressure through official channels. Despite appeals from Schlageter's parents, the Red Cross, the pope, the archbishop of Cologne, and the queen of Sweden, the French were unrelenting in their decision. On Pentecost, several supporters visited Schlageter in prison and warmed his heart with gifts of cakes, ham, flowers, cigarettes, cigars, and chocolates.

There was no question that Schlageter was preparing emotionally for a martyr's death, and, once his fate had been sealed, he was not distracted from the higher meaning of his life.[43] On May 24, the day before he was shot, Schlageter wrote to his parents: "Take comfort in this, that through it all it was an honor for me to die for the Fatherland."[44] The correspondence that he received during those final weeks touched Schlageter deeply, and he wore some of them over his heart until the hour of his death. One of them read: "Be what you wish; but what you are, have the courage to be completely."[45]

Schlageter's hours were numbered. Poincare, under pressure from Tardieu and the French right to treat the Germans harshly, refused to grant mercy in the case. His order to the military authorities in Düsseldorf to carry out the judgment of the court was received shortly after midnight on May 26. After being informed by a French officer to prepare for his execution, Schlageter sat down at the table in his cramped cell, where he wrote these final lines to his family:

> I am about to go to my death. I will be able to take confession and communion. Farewell until our happy reunion in heaven. Greetings to you all again, Father, Mother and all those in the homeland.[46]

Then he demanded that the French guard leave him alone to take communion from the priest, Father Fassbender. Responding to an officer's request for his last wishes, Schlageter called for a cigarette and rum. Finally, he was driven under maximum security to the place of execution near North Cemetery on the outskirts of Düsseldorf.

At the first light of dawn, Schlageter was executed in a quarry on the barren Golzheimer Heath. The event occasioned bizarre comparisons with the death of Christ, as German nationalists drew parallels between the Golzheimer Heath and Calvary. An infantry company and a squadron of cavalry stood guard at the quarry. Schlageter bid farewell to his attorney Paul Sengstock and Father Fassbender, asking them to greet his parents and "my Fatherland." The manner of his execution was dishonorable according to international standards of military practice. Instead of standing to face his executioners, Schlageter was blindfolded, tied to a stake, and forced to his knees. Father Fassbender, who recovered a wooden cross over the victim's heart, which had been pierced by a bullet, described the scene:

> In the deadly quiet of that place, one heard here and there an expression of impatience. And then, as we waited there, a lark landed directly behind Schlageter and merrily greeted the dawn with a sweet song. This happy spring melody was a devastating contrast to what was about to take place.[47]

At last, the execution squad of twelve men fired their salvo. A sergeant rushed forward and administered the *coup de grace* with a pistol shot to the head. This act wounded German sensibilities more than any other, leading to the charge that Schlageter had been murdered. The French surrendered the body to the German officials at North Cemetery, where the hero was buried in a pauper's grave.[48]

German nationalists responded to the execution with vituperation and rage. Within a day, a cross had been fashioned from birch branches and mounted at the place of execution. Schlageter's old comrades were appalled that he had not been buried in a place of honor. A delegation of them arranged that the body be removed from the alien French coffin, placed in a German zinc and wooden coffin, and moved for a proper burial to the village cemetery at his home in Schönau.

Once Schlageter's body had been exhumed in Düsseldorf, it took an entire week before it was reburied with appropriate honors. The drama that ensued was an extraordinary chapter in postwar German nationalism.[49] The first stage in the martyr's triumphal progress through western Germany took the form of a ceremony in Düsseldorf's North Cemetery. A few hundred people were gathered there, bearing tributes of crosses and flowers. Constanz Heinersdorf, who had been appointed to attend to Schlageter in prison, gave the eulogy, noting that he had been strengthened by the noble character of the man:

> You were inspired solely by a glowing love for our Fatherland. . . . You believed in Germany's future and longed for its rebirth. . . . Through your manliness you knew how to gain even the great respect of your enemies. . . . Yours was a moving, exemplary character. . . . Live on, comrade.[50]

As the coffin was borne out of the cemetery, the band struck up the melancholy old soldier's song "Ich hatt' einen Kameraden."[51]

En route, the body was taken by train to Elberfeld, where it lay in state in the historic Stadthalle. The staging for the ceremony that followed was remarkable. The catafalque had been placed on a podium, banked by lush flowers and ornamental tributes to Schlageter. On all sides the forbidden imperial colors of black, white, and red were in evidence, while candles bathed the scene in a solemn glow. Schlageter's steel helmet and the Reich war flag were draped over the coffin. German army flags, Free Corps colors, and the banners of veterans' associations lent an aura of pageantry and tradition to the ceremony. The crowd was both anxious and despondent, reflecting the sorrow and humiliation that resulted from the French occupation of the Ruhr. According to a witness:

> The Wuppertal has never before seen a memorial assembly of such a magnitude—and so deeply moving—as that witnessed for the murdered hero Schlageter. . . . Sorrowful organ music swelled up through the hall. The *Deutsche Sängerkreis* struck up the soul-piercing motet "Beati mortui." . . . Prelate Neumann now approached the casket to perform the liturgy. After the chants had reverberated throughout the hall, he commenced the ceremony of blessing and spoke the "De profundis" . . . on the theme "O death, how bitter is your reality." . . . May your example of the joy of self-sacrifice live on forever! Down with all parties! One united Volk of brothers! . . . Schlageter's Christianity was exemplary, as was his heroic struggle for our blessed Fatherland. He went to his death like a good soldier of Christ.[52]

Tears streamed down the faces of the onlookers as the casket was carried through the streets of Elberfeld, accompanied by a hundred wreath-bearers as well as uniformed guards of honor. The muffled sounds of a military band were heard as the procession wound its way to the railway station.

As the train proceeded from town to town, it was met with an indescribable outpouring of affection. At many stations, honorary formations of patriotic associations turned out with thousands of mourners. Army reserve units appeared in formation at Hagen, while at Weidenau in the Siegerland hundreds of workers appeared in formation in their blue smocks. All along the route, the outlawed flags and colors of the *Kaiserreich* were in evidence. Artillery units fired honorary salvos over the car bearing Schlageter's casket. At Giessen on the Lahn, students turned out in great numbers, the fraternity men *en couleur*. There the rector of the university praised Schlageter:

> The place where his blood flowed will become a holy shrine for the German people. Some day a free Germany will build a magnificent memorial to keep the name of Schlageter alive for future generations. To be sure those of us here today will not be allowed to erect a stone memorial. But the name of Schlageter will be inscribed in our hearts, where he lives as a glorious example of love of Fatherland, of unwavering belief in the future of the German people and inspiring heroic loyalty to the death.[53]

At Donaueschingen, lying between the Black Forest and the Swabian Jura, Prince Fürstenberg, flanked by local government figures and Reichswehr officers, concluded his patriotic encomium with the ancient German cry for revenge: "Heil, Sieg und Rache!"

Such demonstrations continued through the night as the train snaked its way through the countryside, becoming more heavily laden with flowers and wreaths at every stop. Over thirty thousand people gathered to witness the ceremonies at Schlageter's alma mater, the University of Freiburg. The faculty turned out in their colorful robes and were joined by the uniformed incorporated students and the veterans of Schlageter's old unit in the war, Artillery Regiment Seventy-Six. At last, the train carried him home. On 10 June 1923 his parents, family, and friends, joined by thousands of mourners, laid him to rest in the village cemetery at Schönau.[54]

On the same June morning that Schlageter was buried, a ceremony of considerable importance was staged on Munich's beautiful Königsplatz. A crowd of twenty to thirty thousand people, who had come to hear Adolf Hitler's eulogy for Schlageter, stretched from the podium at the State Gallery across the wide square to the Glyptothek. Uniformed nationalist veterans formed ranks behind their banners, which were furled in black crepe. The political heavyweights who less than five months later staged the abortive Beer Hall Putsch all took part, including Field Marshal Erich Ludendorff in his full dress uniform. Lieutenant Hermann Kriebel, who headed the Fatherland Front, an umbrella organization on the radical right, acted as picador, firing up the crowd with a graphic account of Schlageter's alleged torture at the hands of the French. "Your death will not go unavenged!" he said. "The day will come when your name will be a call to battle! Then we will join in the cry of Heinrich von Kleist: 'Kill them! They will not be asked why at the Last Judgment.' "[55]

Hitler took the podium and drew a parallel between Schlageter's death and that of Johann Palm, delivered by the German police to death at the hands of the French in 1806. Today, he said, the government once again could not do enough to persecute German patriots. Schlageter, a lone German officer, was more feared by the French than ten thousand men in the cowardly Ebert Socialist front. What caused the most pain was not that Schlageter had been martyred but that the weak and divided German people had not earned the honor of his sacrifice. "Schlageter's death should show us that freedom will not be won by protests, but by action alone," he bellowed. Heroic courage only has meaning "when men stand at the helm of Germany who are worthy of such heroism, because they themselves are heroes. And we give this promise today, that we will not rest until the Volk pulsates with the spirit of battle, and until we hear the cry 'The Volk arises! Let the storm break loose!' "[56]

The Schlageter affair became a *cause célèbre* in the ideological battle waged between the right and the left over the coming months and years. The *Rote Fahne* boldly attacked Schlageter as a mercenary in the pay of Krupp monopolists, asserting that "we communists have no reason to spare these bourgeois elitists whose murders of communists and workers are celebrated as deeds of heroism." They charged that Hauenstein was headquartered in Elberfeld, far from the danger zone, where he distributed eighteen thousand marks a day in Krupp blood money to the murderers.[57]

Hauenstein countered that the Prussian minister of the interior, Carl Severing, was directly responsible for the murder of Schlageter. By cooperating with the French and directing the chief of police in Elberfeld to publish the warrant for Schlageter's arrest, Severing allegedly caused Schlageter's incarceration. Severing also ordered the arrest of Hauenstein and the special forces as they were laying plans to free Schlageter from prison.[58] In another assault the right asserted:

> There are forces at work like Severing and Braun, leading Ministers of Prussia who oppose national resistance against the French, even using their offices to suppress it. They stop us from turning the passive resistance in the Ruhr into the active resistance of the entire German people. The enemy are not just on the Rhine and Ruhr, they are—in the name of God—right here at home. And who are they? Socialist Party hacks![59]

Severing vehemently countered the accusations made against him in a speech before the Prussian Landtag on 19 June 1923, denying that the arrest warrant he had authorized had led to the capture of Schlageter. Instead, he charged, internecine strife within the Free Corps had brought it about. Because of their hatred for Hauenstein, Lieutenant Rossbach, Alfred Götze, and Otto Schneider had betrayed Schlageter. The criminal police of Kaiserswerth had arrested Götze and Schneider on suspicion of betrayal of Schlageter, and they had already admitted being in the pay of the French intelligence service. Severing asserted that the worst thing about the affair was that the reactionaries had used the burial to further their schemes to undermine the Weimar Republic. When the wreath from Chancellor Cuno arrived at the funeral of Schlageter, decorated in the black, red, and gold colors of the republic, it was returned with an insulting message: "Delivery not accepted! Keep this for the burial of the Jewish Republic."[60]

Although both Severing and Hauenstein pointed to the slippery figures of Alfred Götze and Otto Schneider as the traitors, subsequent litigation suggested otherwise. Götze had a long criminal record, and during his lifetime he was convicted of theft and fraud as well as falsification and destruction of official records. At the same time that Götze and Schneider were in the service of the Hauenstein special forces, they were spies for the French. This emerged in a sensational Berlin trial in 1928, when Hauenstein produced a star witness who also had been in French employ. Although it was proven that Götze and Schneider attempted to deliver Hauenstein to the French, there was no evidence that they betrayed Schlageter. Instead, evidence emerged that compromised the lily-white reputation of Schlageter. An employee of the Union Hotel in Essen testified that, on the day he was arrested, Schlageter had been intimately involved with a woman at the hotel. He had been drinking heavily, and one way or another the woman learned that Schlageter was hiding explosives in his room. According to the French intelligence officer Allard, she reported this information to the French police in Essen. Since the identity of the woman was not learned, it was never ascertained if she was a French secret agent or merely a woman of loose morals. Hauenstein, assured that Götze and Schneider were the informers, had reported them to the French, which had led to their immediate arrest in April 1923.[61]

The Schlageter affair became all the more serious when Hauenstein contended that he had acted not only in league with Krupp industrialists but also at the behest of several ranking Berlin government officials as well. Although kept a secret at the time, evidence subsequently proved that Hauenstein was indeed engaged in sabotage as an agent of the Reichswehr and the Ministry of Transportation. Far from being an independent band of desperadoes, the Organization Heinz had received money, munitions, and moral support from official sources.[62] Severing was acutely embarrassed, and he protested vigorously to those individuals involved, including the minister of defense, Otto Gessler.[63] The Schlageter case thus took on the added dimension of intragovernmental intrigue. At the same time, it demonstrated the ambiguities of heroism in the postwar world.

The Schlageter affair took a bizarre turn when it was exploited by the communists. Karl Radek, the Soviets' chief liaison man to the German communist party, made a historic speech to a meeting of the Comintern in Moscow in June 1923. Radek praised Schlageter highly, asserting that he "was a brave soldier of the counterrevolution." In arguing for a radical deviation from communist policy vis-à-vis the Free Corps and the reaction, Radek submitted that the working class and the Fascists had, in 1923, the same enemy—the French, who were exploiting German workers in a criminal way. He called for the creation of a united front to fight the enemy:

> The German Communist Party must openly declare to the nationalist petty bourgeois masses: Whoever is working in the service of the profiteers, the speculators, and the iron and coal magnates to enslave the German people will meet the resistance of the German Communist Party which will oppose violence with violence. . . . We believe that the great majority of the nationalist-minded masses belong not to the capitalists but to the workers. We want and we shall find a way to reach these masses. We will do all in our power to make men like Schlageter . . . not wanderers in a void, but wanderers into a better future for all mankind. Schlageter himself cannot hear this declaration now, but we are certain that there are hundreds of Schlageters who will hear it and understand it.[64]

There was little chance that Radek could succeed in his proposal for a fundamental change of course in communist tactics. Despite an effort by the KPD and some components of the German right to cooperate during the summer of 1923, it was a foregone conclusion that this policy would fail. By August 1923, Radek's proposal was already a dead letter.

For German nationalists, the memory of Schlageter was not a question of tactical advantage but one of unwavering devotion. The day after he was shot, the Schlageter-Gedächtnis-Bund was founded in Hanover. Under the leadership of Bundesführer Heinrich Haselhorst and General Secretary Gustav Lauterbach, the Bund central office established an organization that was closely allied with National Socialism and was both progenitor and keeper of the sacred Schlageter cult. Throughout the years of the Weimar Republic, the organization maintained three hundred thirty chapters organized in twelve districts stretching from the Rhineland to East Prussia.[65] The Schlageter-Gedächtnis-Bund was an independent entity, but it was thoroughly National Socialist in its membership, ideology, and use of symbols and rituals.[66]

Lauterbach appealed to the ideal of national unity in a memorial propaganda flyer, which was published on the first anniversary of the martyr's death. "Schlageter," he said, "did not die for the Republic or the monarchy, or for any political system—he died for his Fatherland." A new patriotism must be born, he urged, driven by hatred of the enemy and inspired by a fiery determination to liberate Germany or die in the attempt. For the enemy was strong, and "its goal is the slavery of Germany by forces of international Jewish big business." These foreign and domestic enemies, he contended, must be liquidated to return Germany to itself, and a reawakened people must form a racially united Aryan striking force to inspire the nation—not to talk but to act, not to pose but to die, so that Germany might live. Lauterbach concluded: "Albert Leo Schlageter, we greet you from afar. You are a hero of the nation, the example of what a German officer should be, and the very model of a National Socialist!"[67]

During the years of the *Kampfzeit,* Schlageter became a popular subject of heroic music. Many traditional songs were published with lyrics reworked to convey the emotional intensity of his death. In October 1924, the Turnerschaft 'Schlageter' Berlin—whose motto was "Live loyally, fight fearlessly, die happily!"—modified the verses of "Friedericus Rex wach auf" and "Die Wacht am Rhein" to embrace the Schlageter theme, and the group presented its new songs at a festival evening at that old Berlin battleground, the Saalbau Friedrichshain.[68] The National Socialists belonging to the Treuschaft Hitler celebrated a memorial "in connection with the anniversary of our fallen fighting comrade Albert Leo Schlageter, bestially betrayed by Germans and sadistically murdered by foreigners."[69] Those in attendance heard several songs tailored to the Schlageter theme. To the music of "Kein schönrer Tod," they sang, "He died for us, Schlageter, first hero of liberty."[70] "Deutschland, Deutschland über alles" was reworded to bewail the "black scandal on the Rhine" and scurrilously to attack the Jews:

The traitors must die,
O holy Rhineland, bride of iron
You will be France's death and destruction
When the gray morning of revenge dawns.[71]

To accompany their marches, the SA could lustily render a new version of "Zu Mantua in Banden":

Bound and chained in Düsseldorf,
Beaten like a dog,
Tortured and mocked,
A German officer.
And still his heart so proud and free,
It was in the beautiful month of May,
At Düsseldorf on the Rhine.

O you proud days of battle!
O Riga! Annaberg! . . .
O Mother dear! O you Black Forest!
O red of dawn!—Now a fiery young
Heart goes to its rest.[72]

On the first anniversary of the death of Schlageter, a memorial service was staged at his graveside. Freiherr von Medem, who was Schlageter's Free Corps commander in the Baltic, was the featured speaker, and he reflected on the character of his former comrade-in-arms. Captain von Medem found Schlageter's behavior while a prisoner exemplary, "offering wonderful hope that the German spirit was not entirely lost in the slime of materialism, cowardice and vanity." He would always remember Schlageter standing on the bridge at Riga shortly after its liberation, holding a wounded child in his arms. "There you stood," he said, "a whole man, as strong as the Black Forest from whence you came. When I marched with you through the forests of the Kurland at the head of your battery, there was a happy and noble feeling in us that we haven't experienced since those days: German idealism, pride in knowing that our goals were right for our country, ever ready to do our duty and to die a sacrificial death."[73]

There were countless other memorial ceremonies throughout the country on that first anniversary of Schlageter's death. At Nuremberg there was a torchlight parade through the streets, and thousands of votive candles placed in the windows of homes flickered in the darkness. Addressing an outdoor rally on that warm May evening in the lush surroundings of the Deutschherrnwiese, Rudolf Kötter conjured up the spirit of the dead hero:

> You have redeemed us like that other hero who died on the cross at Golgotha, and you have given us the strength to live and to die just as you did, for your belief in freedom and greatness for our Volk and Fatherland. Albert Leo Schlageter lives![74]

Throughout the 1920s the Nazis were but one of several groups competing for control of the Schlageter legacy. Only a few of his intimate friends were privy to information about Schlageter's critical attitude toward the National Socialists. Had the secret become known, it would have ended the myth cultivated by the party that Schlageter was the "first National Socialist." Oskar Hauenstein had in his possession several letters critical of the Nazis written by Schlageter from the Ruhr in 1923. According to the Free Booter Ernst von Salomon, Schlageter had complained bitterly about the part the National Socialists were playing in the Ruhr. They alone, he said, were prepared to sabotage the solidarity of the resistance for purely selfish political reasons; in 1923 they had not wished to see the party's center of gravity shift from Munich to northern Germany.[75] Consistency, or even truth, had never been a *sine qua non* of Nazi mythology.

There was poetic justice in the difficulty the NSDAP experienced in laying claim to Schlageter. During the bleak days of the party's fortunes in 1925, Goebbels was able to attract only two thousand people to a Schlageter memorial rally.[76] And the the Nazis were not included in the committee established at Düsseldorf in 1927 to plan for the building of the Schlageter National Memorial, under the chairmanship of Max Schlenker of the influential Langnam Verein.[77] The grand edifice was dedicated amid great pomp in 1931, the ceremony attended by the former chancellor Cuno and a host of notables from government, heavy industry, and nationalist circles.[78] For his part, Hitler did not even put in an appearance. Instead, he sent Hermann Göring, who staged a competing rally in the Düsseldorf Planetarium, which was followed by a march to the Golzheimer Heath. Quite predictably, Göring claimed in his address that Schlageter belonged solely to the National Socialists.[79]

The Schlageter National Memorial was an architectural triumph, a felicitous union of landscape, form, and function. Instead of a swastika, a striking Christian cross of iron towered over the heath where he died, suggestive of the promise of resurrection. At the base of the monument, the name Albert Leo Schlageter was inscribed, inviting visitors into an unadorned marble crypt, which lay very low to the ground. There one found the names of all those who had died in the battle for the Ruhr. Friedrich Christian Prinz zu Schaumburg-Lippe described the impression that the monument had on Goebbels, when he first visited it in April 1934.

> Goebbels had never been here since the monument was built. . . . We proceed in a long column. In the middle the "Doctor," ahead two tall SS comrades, carrying a huge wreath. The closer we come to the crypt, lying under a high metal cross, the quieter we become. Not a sound. . . . Before us lies a simple stone tablet. A few words say it all. "Here at the command of France were shot . . . ," so morally incriminating for the aggressor yet so free from petty revenge. Tremendous, really tremendous in its effect. . . . Goebbels stands a long time, staring at the plaque in the crypt. I have never seen his face more serious than at this moment.[80]

The art critic Hubert Schrade had nothing but praise for the monument as well, finding it "a direct architectural expression of the feelings that characterize our thought and beliefs today: the feeling of the Volk becoming." The central rooms and crypt, "sunk into the fateful earth of the Ruhr," delivered, according to Schrade, an unparalleled authenticity to the Germanic Volk community. The memorial, he submitted, was at once organic in form yet monumental in the message it conveyed to the nation—the inspiration to serve the Volk and Fatherland, come what may.[81]

Once they had attained power, the Nazis made every effort to claim Schlageter as their own. The tenth anniversary of his death coincided with the Nazis' assumption of power, and consequently 1933 became a banner

HIER FIEL,
ERSCHOSSEN
AUF FRANKREICHS
BEFEHL,
AM 26. MAI 1923
ALBERT LEO
SCHLAGETER
FÜR FREIHEIT
UND FRIEDEN

...SWILLKÜR, AUSWEISUNGEN, AUSSCHREITUNGE...
DER SOLDATEN, WIRTSCHAFTLICHE MACHTGIER BRACHTEN SCHWERSTES
UNHEIL ÜBER EIN LAND FRIEDLICHER ARBEIT, TROTZ SCHWERSTER WIRT-
SCHAFTLICHER UND SOZIALER NOT STANDEN ALLE SCHICHTEN DER BE-
VÖLKERUNG IN HELDENMÜTIGEM RINGEN FEST ZUM REICH.

3. Schlageter Memorial, Golzheimer Heath, Düsseldorf. The caption reads: "Albert Leo Schlageter was killed here on 26 May 1923 on the orders of the French." (Personal Collection.)

year for Schlageter eulogy. This was the result in no small part of the success of Hanns Johst's play *Schlageter,* which premiered on April 20, Hitler's birthday, at the Staatliches Schauspielhaus on the Gendarmenmarkt in Berlin.[82] Johst dedicated his play to Hitler "in loving honor and eternal loyalty," and the cream of society attended the production. Because the Staatliches Schauspielhaus enjoyed enormous prestige as the official state theater, the cast featured several theatrical luminaries of the era. The legendary Albert Bassermann, Veit Harlan (who later directed *Jud Süss* and *Kolberg*), Lothar Müthel, and Emmy Sonnemann (Göring's future bride) all played a role. The result was a theatrical *Te Deum,* celebrated to honor the National Socialist victory.[83]

Johst used every conceivable device to deliver a play of enormous passion. It mirrored an author afire with *völkisch* ideology and joined nationalistic passion to searing historical retrospection. Schlageter would not have recognized the distorted image of himself in the play, where he emerged as a prophet of National Socialism.

Schlageter—like so much of the expressionist literature that preceded it—was a play based on stereotypes. Such characters as hero, corrupt Weimar parliamentarian, calcified general, redeemable Marxist functionary, and woman as suffering helpmate emerge in graphic delineation. Although radically overdrawn, the characters accurately reflected the dizzying social and political cacophony of the Weimar Republic. The central theme of the work was clear from the outset—an awakened, self-sacrificing youth was to redeem a crucified nation.

In the play, Schlageter's friend, Friedrich Thiemann, voices the alienation of the war veterans.

> God damn it—we were out there serving our country not because someone hired us. . . . Now with the war over . . . our generation is just a bunch of green horns. The old make great speeches . . . they're Party leaders, captains of industry, big shots. . . . Age and titles—that's what the young are supposed to respect today.

Schlageter agreed, complaining that

> the war came . . . and by God the so-called young held the line. . . . I was a lieutenant in the war, and now I'm just Leo Schlageter, a simple farm boy from the Black Forest. . . . now we're an internal cancer, we comrades! . . . But gradually . . . we are sewing on our epaulettes again . . . and one day . . . we will be Germany!

Again and again Johst unleashed attacks against the hated republic. At one point Thiemann argued:

I know all about that crap from 1918 . . . brotherhood, equality, and freedom . . . Beauty and worthiness! Then in the middle of it, hands up! You're
disarmed . . . you're the trash of the Republic!—-No to hell with this whole
ideological smorgasbord. . . . Now we'll cut loose! When I hear the world culture . . . I uncock my Browning!

Schlageter's response was desperate.

Berlin throws you out, plays you for trash!! Adventurers . . . *Feme* murderers . . . This has got to stop! We are blasting away at the wrong enemies! First
action at home . . . the world brothership crowd of 1918 to the wall! Liberate
the Reich from the parliaments. The more the French provoke us, the lower
the bureaucrats kowtow to them.

Johst was skillful at drawing caricatures of political types active in the
Weimar Republic. He painted the socialist Reichstag member Willi Klemm
with caustic irony. Klemm was fat, arrogant, and devoid of patriotism;
heroism and service to the country were foreign concepts to him. Johst
employed the son of a Marxist power broker as an ideological foil. Con-
fronting his father, this patriotic student of the young generation announced that class warfare was dying out. It would be replaced by

the community of blood. . . . You see, papa, the high and low, the poor and the
rich, you're always going to have that. . . . We don't see life in statistics and price
fluctuations, but instead we believe in the human being as a whole. We don't
want to think first about what we earn, but instead about how we can serve our
country. Every individual corpuscle in the bloodstream of the Volk.

Pointing to Schlageter as a symbol of the nation's spiritual and political
reawakening, Johst's student declared:

We young ones who stand at Schlageter's side are not with him because he is
the last soldier of the World War, but because he is the first soldier of the Third
Reich!

Schlageter stood out in the play as a beacon, lighting the way out of the
German darkness. His example heals the political divisions of the past and
reclaims alienated political groups for the *Volksgemeinschaft*. Old Marxists
return to their German roots, and true German women herald the new
dawn. Even the once-faltering Reichswehr general responds to the nobility
of Schlageter: "I hear new columns of marching men ready for action.
Germany awakened!"

The final scene of *Schlageter* is set in the darkness of the Golzheimer
Heath. Trumpets blast a shrill call to the hero's execution. A French military
vehicle provides a dim light, as Schlageter—his back to the audience—is
bound to a stake. Struck from behind, he is forced to kneel before the

unspeakable enemy. Schlageter cries out from the cross: "Germany! A final word! A wish! Command! Germany! Awake! Catch fire! Burn! Burn wildly!" Clearly, Johst intended these final sacred words to become a moral imperative for the entire nation. Schlageter had died so that the nation might live.[84] Hans Stahn, reviewing the play in *Der Angriff,* praised its "prose of reality," calling it a singularly effective production and an appropriate tribute to the Führer on his forty-fourth birthday.[85]

In 1933 fell the tenth anniversary of Schlageter's death, and the Nazis indulged in an orgy of propaganda. Düsseldorf took the lead, staging a Schlageter commemoration that lasted three days. His life, according to the propagandists in Düsseldorf, had educated the nation in German manliness.[86] Three hundred thousand people streamed into the Rhineland for the festivities, and sixteen special trains were employed. Gauleiter Florian sounded a verbal fanfare, noting that Schlageter had demonstrated not only how a German should live but also, and more important, how he should die. The Schlageter-Gedächtnis-Bund staged a grand reunion of the Ruhr veterans in the Tonhalle. Under the motto "Long live the Führer, the Fatherland, and battle to the death," the old boys celebrated their victory lustily, singing their traditional Free Corps and *Landsknecht* songs.[87]

On Friday, 26 May 1933, the Schlageter Memorial Museum was opened with appropriate ceremony, and on the next day Baldur von Schirach addressed a rally of eighty thousand Hitler Youths and students. On Saturday evening, a thousand musicians performed a gala concert on the Oberkassel Rhine banks; a massive fireworks display, which delighted the crowds, concluded their performance. The climax of the commemoration featured a parade of one hundred eighty-five thousand men of the SA, SS, and Stahlhelm to the Schlageter Memorial on the Golzheimer Heath. There Göring addressed the crowd:

> When the shots rang out ten years ago at dawn at this spot, they were heard through the German night and awakened the nation in her weakness and humiliation. In those days the memory of Schlageter inspired us and gave us hope. We refused to believe that his sacrifice had been in vain. Schlageter demonstrated in the way he died that the German spirit could not be destroyed. Schlageter, you can rest in peace. We have seen to it that you were honored here and not betrayed like your two million comrades. As long as there are Schlageters in Germany, the nation will live.[88]

To conclude the festivities, *Schlageter* was performed in the Düsseldorf Schauspielhaus. In remembrance of the event, the townspeople of Düsseldorf presented Hitler with a silver reliquary containing a bullet—the bullet, so it was said, that killed the martyr.[89]

The trumpet call on the Rhine was echoed across the Reich. At Freiburg University, Martin Heidegger extolled the virtues of Schlageter, drawing lessons from his life for the present generation of students.[90] Bernhard

4. Hitler Youth at the Schlageter Memorial, Düsseldorf. (Bayerisches Hauptstaatsarchiv.)

Rust spoke at a night rally at Schlageter's graveside in Schönau, as fires from high points in the Black Forest cast their magic light in the distance. Flanked by the SA Storm Schlageter, Adolf Wagner spoke to a rally at the Feldherrnhalle in Munich, which featured SA, SS, and Stahlhelm units. In Gürzenich Hall at beautiful Maria Laach, the abbot spoke of the essential oneness of the mission of Christ, Hitler, and Schlageter. In Leipzig, the *Feme* murderer Manfred von Killinger addressed a rally of forty thousand people. And at Riga, deep in the Germanic-Hanseatic east, a memorial service was held in the cathedral to pay tribute to the man whom many believed had saved the city further abuse at the hands of the Bolshevik hordes in 1919.[91]

Once they attained power, the Nazis undertook an extensive investigation in an attempt to identify those responsible for the betrayal of Schlageter. As a result, the Gestapo arrested the adventurers Alfred Götze and Otto Schneider in May 1933. During the period of their incarceration in Columbia Haus, the notorious SS prison in Berlin, they were brutally beaten by police commissars Lipek and Kaiser, who sought to extract a confession from them. But the prisoners had allies of their own and were able to play upon the feuds within the higher echelons of the party. Through their SA contacts going back to the Free Corps days, the pair interested an old comrade, the disreputable SA Obergruppenführer Edmund Heines, in the case and quite possibly Gerhard Rossbach as well. Pressure was put on the SS, which concluded its investigation at the end of the year. Dr. Rudolf Diels, who commanded the Gestapo, ordered the release of Götze and Schneider in January 1934.[92]

No sooner had Götze left prison than he set out once more to clear his record. He renewed the vendetta with Hauenstein and raised the stakes. Götze, who had remarkable talents as a dissembler, was not only able to seek and gain a commission in the SS but also, by the force of sheer boldness, emerge as an officer on the staff of Reichsführer SS Heinrich Himmler.[93] From this powerful vantage point, Götze was very effective in furthering his cause.

In the fall of 1934, the SS released to the press the results of the Gestapo's investigation into the Schlageter affair.[94] According to this report, which totally rehabilitated Götze and Schneider, the two were hailed as innocent patriots who had served their country well as members of the Free Corps Rossbach and the NSDAP. These "Old Fighters" had allegedly been the victims of lies spread by Severing and his fellow criminals in the Marxist Berlin government, aided by other political emigrants "now hiding abroad."[95] With the report released to the national press, Götze next turned his attention to Hauenstein, demanding that he retract the false allegations he had spread over the past eleven years.[96]

Hauenstein, who harbored deep bitterness about the matter, counterattacked on three fronts. He paid a personal visit to SS General Kurt Dal-

uege, chief of police for Prussia, to present evidence against his enemies.[97]
Next, he confronted Götze directly to make it clear that despite Götze's
machinations, the men of Organization Heinz would continue to publish
materials accusing him of betraying Schlageter.[98] Finally, Hauenstein contacted the entire membership of the Organization Heinz to seek support
for the steps he was taking. His efforts were not without results. With the
liquidation of Edmund Heines in the Röhm purge of 30 June 1934 and
the loss of influence of the SA, Götze had lost his protector. The SS was
now free to proceed in the case without hindrance. In 1935, after yet
another long investigation by the Gestapo, both Götze and Schneider were
expelled from the SS, and they faded into obscurity.[99]

During the Third Reich, Schlageter was remembered as a hero who
made a blood sacrifice for the rebirth of Germany. Schlageter Memorial
Day—May 26—assumed its place in the annual Nazi calendar, and each
year ceremonial remembrances in his honor took place in Munich, Düsseldorf, and Schönau.[100] In May 1935 the strains of Beethoven's Egmont
Overture filled Munich's Odeonsplatz, where a full dress ceremony was
held at the Feldherrnhalle featuring a host of party and military dignitaries,
the men of SA Storm Schlageter, as well as Sister Bertha, party member
and nurse of the SA, who carried the sacred Schlageter Cross.[101]

It was not public ceremony alone that kept the Schlageter legend alive.
The martyr was given considerable attention in propaganda for German
youth as well. All children were exposed to readings on the subject in their
school primers, and numerous books and pamphlets were dedicated to his
memory.[102] Baldur von Schirach interpreted Schlageter's life as a symphony to love of the nation in his propaganda. At a Hitler Youth rally at
the Düsseldorf National Memorial on Schlageter Day 1934 he said:

> As you look at this grand monument, remember that today the cross of Schla-
> geter towers not only over us, but it casts its shadow over all of Germany and
> this symbol of strength, of spirit, of dedication and sacrifice received its heroic
> incarnation in Schlageter. He went to his death answering only the call to duty.
> Here on this spot the dark earth drank his red blood and he was struck down
> with that cry on his lips which is our call to destiny today: "Oh, you my Ger-
> many!"[103]

Schlageter had joined the Immortals.

III

Sacrifice at the Feldherrnhalle

The Nazi Immortals of 9 November 1923

Nicht in alten Bahnen
ist Gott
Du kannst ihn ahnen,
wo die Fahnen
des Glaubens wehn: am Schafott.

Dort, wo die Teufel rufen:
"Schwör' ab, Hund, oder falle!"
Was sie auch Dome schufen,
uns sind Altar die Stufen
der Feldherrnhalle.

Baldur von Schirach[1]

The march to the Feldherrnhalle on 9 November 1923 in Munich formed the cornerstone of National Socialist martyrology, for on that day the original sixteen Immortals gave their lives for a "reawakened Germany." Every movement of important dimensions must have its fallen, yet with the Nazis this imperative took on a sinister dimension. Blood had returned to blood, spirit to spirit, transfiguring the souls of the fallen. The Immortals had joined the long line of warrior heroes of the epic Germanic past in Walhall, and their legendary deeds inspired future martyrs over the coming years. According to Nazi mythology, their resurrected souls had returned to join the fighting columns of SA, SS, and Hitler Youth, thus guaranteeing the victory of National Socialism.

Hitler centered a secular religion on the blood of the martyrs, lending credence to his affirmation that "one can serve God only in heroic raiment."[2] In his demented ideological world based on racial struggle, heroic death was more beautiful than life itself. The Führer was never more at home than when communing with the souls of the dead. The drama of 9 November became a Station in the Germanic Passion, featuring parallels to Golgotha, the Crucifixion, the Resurrection and return. Hitler thereby wove an epic tapestry from the lives of the martyrs, and the "Blood Flag" became a ritualistic centerpiece in Nazi liturgy. The historic German Passion united the Hitler band around their Führer. It encouraged them in the dark yet glorious days of the *Kampfzeit*, while pointing the way to the future.

Once Hitler came into power, 9 November became a sacred day of remembrance in the National Socialist calendar. Each year, the party members who took part in that historic march gathered in Munich for the pageant of reenactment. The bodies of the Immortals were laid to rest in sarcophagi astride the party headquarters (Führerbau), where they stood "eternal guard" in Professor Paul Ludwig Troost's Temple of Honor. Their blood had become—in Hitler's words—the "holy water of the Third Reich." Reflecting on the meaning of November 1923, Hitler said:

> We who were determined to put an end to a disgusting regime . . . opened the eyes and ears of the entire German Volk and our heroism set an example for the Movement, which it would need later. Above all, the events of 9 November enabled us to fight our way to power legally over ten long years. Be sure of one thing: If we didn't act then, I never would have been able to found a revolutionary movement, to build it and hold it together. . . . The deeds of 8/ 9 November announced not only a new revolution but also a new ideology for Germany. From that day on, the Movement spread out across the whole country.[3]

The Germany of November 1923 was in political, social, and economic chaos. For months Hitler and the men of the nationalist *Kampfbund,* who were gathered in a confusing array of factions, plotted against the Bavarian regime under Minister President Eugen von Knilling and General State Commissar Gustav Ritter von Kahr. The chief of the Bavarian State Police, Colonel Hans Ritter von Seisser, and the commander of the Seventh Reichswehr Division, General Otto von Lossow, offered resolute opposition to the radicals. But Hitler was determined that a decision would be reached in November, come what may.

Five years of humiliation had taken its toll on the insurgents. The terrible disappointment of defeat in the Great War, coupled with abuse on their return from the front, was more than they could bear. Further, they were traumatized by unemployment, Bolshevik insurgency, inflation, governmental instability, and the French occupation of the Ruhr.

Of all the alienated groups in the tattered world of Weimar Germany, the National Socialists presented the ultimate example of hatred and vituperation. For them, Weimar represented a nation of "November criminals," Marxists, cowards, Jews, homosexuals, and assorted political gypsies. Its cultural capital, Berlin, was an asphalt jungle fit only for destruction. Berlin harbored the effete international elite, a covey of parasites gathered at the smoky Romanisches Cafe and at other watering holes around the Kurfürstendamm to plot Germany's total destruction from within. The Nazis queried: "Did two million German heroes perish for this pack of 'Jewish traitors' "? "Did the flower of German youth die in the carnage of Langemarck, Verdun, and the Somme for the Marxist power brokers in the Ebert regime?" "Is true German culture to become utterly ruined by raucous Berlin, which has given way to new-rich Jews in fur coats and shiny new cars, bloated by caviar, cocaine, and lasciviousness?" "Is racial putre-faction to govern Germany's future?" A coup appeared to be the only way out of the chaos.

By November 1923 Hitler had at his disposal about four thousand men, including forces of the SA Regiment München, the Stosstrupp Hitler, Reichs-kriegsflagge and Bund Oberland.[4] Details of the putsch on the night of 8 November at the Bürgerbräukeller on the Rosenheimer Strasse are well known. After a night of confusion, which included Hitler's bungled attempt to proclaim a national revolution and to arrest the leaders of the Bavarian regime, he prepared to lead his forces into the center of the city late on the morning of 9 November. The fact that Field Marshal Erich Ludendorff marched in the first ranks encouraged him to believe that the tide could yet be turned.

It was almost noon when the unarmed columns began to head down the hill from the Bürgerbräukeller toward the Ludwig Bridge over the Isar River. Out front were the flag bearers followed by Hitler, Ludendorff, Göring, Dr. Friedrich Weber, Hermann Kriebel, Ulrich Graf, Dr. Max Erwin von Scheubner-Richter, Wilhelm Brückner, and the SA Sixth Com-pany.[5] Although the bridge was manned by the Bavarian State Police, they were reluctant to hold their ground, and the crossing was taken by force. As the column moved down the Zweibrückenstrasse to Isartor Square, through the narrow Tal past the ancient city walls, it attracted an excited crowd, which shouted support and broke spontaneously into patriotic songs. The streets were teeming as the column turned into the storied Marienplatz, where that morning Julius Streicher had harangued the masses with his nationalist appeals. Johann Aigner, Scheubner-Richter's orderly, described what happened next.

The crowd greeted our march with enthusiastic shouts of "Heil!" and great numbers of them joined the columns. Now as we approached the Feldherrnhalle the same scene greeted us that we had just experienced at the Ludwig Bridge. Except here stronger units were deployed. State Police and Reichswehr troops were in position with mortars and armored cars, and they were ready to shoot. There must have been a thousand men blocking our way. We moved down the Residenzstrasse singing "O Deutschland hoch in Ehren." As a soldier, it was clear to me that only a command was needed to set off a blaze of deadly machine gun and rifle fire. Those of us out front raised our arms once more, yelling to the troops that Adolf Hitler and General Ludendorff were there. Then sud-denly behind us a shot rang out. I turned around to see what had happened as we were fired on from all sides. My comrades and I threw ourselves to the ground and returned the fire. I was shocked to see that my best friend, Kurt Neubauer, orderly to General Ludendorff, lay dying on the street . . . the coun-try's youngest volunteer in the World War. And then I witnessed a heroic deed that will remain with me the rest of my life. The greatest general of the war climbed over my body, and standing tall with his left hand in his pocket, marched right into the line of fire.[6]

Lieutenant von Godin of the state police was intent on holding the line, at whatever cost. Evidence suggests that losses would have been much higher had many of the police not fired into the air to avoid harming their fellow Germans. According to witnesses, desperate officers tore the epaulets off their coats in shame, beside themselves with the tragic dimensions of the event.[7] While Hitler raced off in a car, other survivors were either arrested or went into hiding.

Sixteen men lay dead in the Residenzstrasse astride the Feldherrnhalle. The street was awash with blood, which drenched the swastika flag carried at the head of the column. Thereafter known as the "Blood Flag," it became a relic of great importance in public ceremonies during the Third Reich. Heinrich Trambauer, who carried the banner on that morning, described its transfiguration from flag to holy shroud.

> We gathered in front of the Münchner Kindlkeller on Rosenheim Hill. I was with the II. Battalion, 6th Company Rossbach. . . . Despite my many years at the front it was a tremendous feeling of joy and pride to carry the first flag of our Führer Adolf Hitler to victory. After making the bend through the Theatinerstrasse, we came into the Residenzstrasse, heading for the Feldherrnhalle. A state policeman surged from the Residence Guard, ready to do battle. At that point, we struck up the "Deutschlandlied," but the shooting which claimed our first heroes was the response to our song. Von Stransky, Bauriedl, and Hechenberger were killed in my group. Taking cover, I immediately fell to the ground, the flag under me. Catching my breath, I lay there momentarily, waiting for the right time to escape, because saving the flag meant more to me than my life.

Trambauer, completing his tale of heroism, raced into an apartment building, where he was admitted by a barber. There he removed the flag from the mast and pole, wrapped it around his body, and made his way home where he hid it. Then he continued:

> Despite the repeated attempts of the renegades to trick me into surrendering the flag later, I remained loyal to my Führer and to his flag. Several months later I transferred the flag to the company sergeant-major, and he presented it to the Führer personally after he was released from prison.[8]

Subsequently, Hitler turned the flag over for safekeeping to Reichsführer SS Berchtold at the Reich party rally in Weimar in July 1926.[9] Later it was displayed in the Hall of Standards at the party headquarters in Munich, and it was employed for liturgical use on occasions of great importance as well.

Hitler used the trial of the putschists, which took place in Munich in 1924, to further the radical nationalist cause. During the course of the proceedings, he waged an attack against the "November criminals" as well as the compromised Bavarian ruling triumvirate of Kahr, Lossow, and Seisser. Playing to the courtroom and the media—the trial was widely covered not only in Bavaria but also throughout Germany—Hitler struck the chords of radical nationalism, which thereafter became the leitmotif of Nazi propaganda:

> The deeds of 9 November were not a failure. We would have failed if only one mother had come to me and said: "Herr Hitler, you have my child on your conscience." But I can tell you one thing for certain: no such mother came forward. Quite the contrary, thousands of others did come forward and put themselves at the service of the cause. But the ultimate proof that the 9 November succeeded is in the German youth who rose up like a flood tide and fell in behind our columns. The greatest victory of the 9 November is that it has not led to depression but instead has greatly inspired our people. I believe that the time will come when the masses marching in the street under the swastika flag will be joined by those who opened fire on us. . . . I firmly believe that good German blood will bring us together.[10]

Hitler emphasized that the movement had sacrificed its dead to return honor to the German battle flags, to overturn the Bolshevik world conspiracy, and to avenge the two million young men who died for their Fatherland in the Great War only to be betrayed by a thankless and cowardly republic. By banding together and preparing for self-sacrifice, they represented the true politicized will of the Volk. The 9 November was not the end; instead, it was the first step in the struggle to return Germany to German leadership. In a grand flourish, Hitler transcended the courtroom and returned in spirit to the blood-drenched fields of Flanders:

> The army, which has formed behind us, is growing from day to day, and from hour to hour. I have the proud hope, that the time is coming again when these small battle-ready units will become battalions, then regiments, and will grow to divisions, and that they will raise our old standards out of the filth, and our old flags will wave proudly in the wind once more.[11]

The result, he announced, would be a glorious victory for their just cause. This was the source for what thereafter became the rallying cry at anniversary celebrations once the Nazis took power: "You were victorious after all!"

The dramatic events of November 1923 soon gave rise to many curious myths and legends. Not untypical was the poem by Gauleiter Adolf Wagner, which he claimed was "written in honor of the fallen immediately after the betrayal at the Feldherrnhalle." Such simple poetry and song, which became quite common during the period of struggle, contributed significantly to the cult of the martyrs. It concluded with the lines:

> They marched fearlessly forward,
> Into the deadly fire of the Reaction! . . .
> And there at the Feldherrnhalle
> Sixteen heroes found a martyr's death.
>
> You dead of 9th November,
> You dead, we swear to you:
> Thousands of fighters are still here
> For the Third, the Greater German Reich![12]

The sixteen original martyrs came from diverse social backgrounds, lending credence to Hitler's claim that the movement embraced all classes united by Germanic blood. The group included both professional men and simple workers. Several were members of the aristocracy. Others were salesmen or were associated with banks, whereas the laborers included a tailor, a locksmith, a waiter, and Field Marshal Ludendorff's orderly. All who were of age had served at the front, and several had been officers. Many had been members of various Free Corps units after the war. They were united in a common hatred and contempt for the republic, Marxism, and, in many cases, for the Jews. The eldest was Theodor von der Pfordten, born in 1873. The two youngest were but nineteen—the engineering student Karl Laforce and Claus von Pape, a salesman.[13]

Although some of the fallen had only rudimentary education, others had distinguished university training. For example, Max Erwin von Scheubner-Richter, whom Hitler deemed "irreplaceable," was born in Riga in 1884, studied in Riga, Dresden, and Munich, and took a doctorate in engineering. As early as 1904–05, he saw military action in the liquidation of revolutionary disturbances in Latvia. A volunteer in 1914, he served in the Seventh Bavarian Chevauleger Regiment and won the Iron Cross I for his service in France. Scheubner-Richter was transferred to the foreign ministry in 1915, where his bravery was turned to more adventurous uses. He commanded his own cavalry detachment against the English on an expedition to northern Persia. Following a stint as an intelligence officer assigned to a divisional staff, in 1917 he was posted to the political department of the general staff. He also worked in the section Ober Ost, engaged in preparations for the German occupation of Estonia and Latvia. He was captured during the Russian revolution, sentenced to death, and was saved only by the timely intervention of the German Foreign Office. Later he fought with the White armies attached to General Wrangel in the Ukraine. By 1920 he had returned to Munich, joined the NSDAP, wrote for nationalist causes, and edited the journal *Aufbau*. He was only thirty-nine at his death.[14]

Theodor von der Pfordten was a prominent jurist. The son of a noted chief state prosecutor in Bayreuth, he studied at the Maximiliansgymnasium in Munich and took a law degree at Munich University. Married to Elly Götz, daughter of the Crown Professor, Dr. Wilhelm Götz, von der Pfordten moved up swiftly in the Bavarian Ministry of Justice. A company commander in the Fifteenth Bavarian Landwehr Regiment, he was awarded the Iron Cross II and the Bavarian Cross of Honor. Pfordten was alienated by the policies of the postwar Ministry of Justice, and he argued his views forcibly in a work published in 1919 entitled *Plato's Philosopher King and Its Meaning for the Present*. His contempt for the Jews stemmed from the war years, and he published several anti-Semitic tracts before his death. These included an *Appeal to the Educated Nation of German Blood* (1923). Pfordten edited two law journals and sat as a judge on the Bavarian Supreme Court. Simultaneously, he worked as an editor for the Nazi party in Hitler's suite of offices on the Ottostrasse in Munich. At his death he was writing *The Foundations For the Constitution of the New State* in anticipation of the ultimate victory of National Socialism. When he died, von der Pfordten was fifty years old.[15]

When throughout the 1920s the authorities in Munich forbade ceremonies in honor of those who died in the abortive putsch, they played directly into Hitler's hands. Nazi claims of harrassment commenced when the NSDAP was denied its request to bury the dead in a common grave, a prohibition that Hitler bitterly derided in *Mein Kampf*.[16] As a result, the party was forced to bury them in cemeteries scattered across Munich.[17] In another affront, the police forbade a planned memorial ceremony scheduled for Sunday, 8 November 1925, in the Odeonsaal. In his prohibition, Herr Mantel of the Polizeidirektion München argued that past experience "justified the fear that the planned observance would be used to glorify the November putsch and that it would also lead to marching and demonstrations in the streets."[18]

Despite several earlier bans, Hitler was able to speak at the Bürgerbräukeller in Munich on 8 November 1927. He organized his speech around the charge—to him, unconscionable—that the heroes of 9 November were guilty of "high treason." In a rhetorical flourish, the Führer attacked the pompous "paragraph heroes" of the Weimar legal establishment who, he said, in their stupidity resembled Jewish Talmudic lawyers. Instead, he declared, it was the Jews themselves who were guilty of treason. They had spread unrest in Germany during the war years, had stabbed the front soldiers in the back, and had humiliated those brave heroes on their return home. They had fomented the Bolshevik revolution, had written the despicable Weimar constitution, had misruled the country, and had lived like parasites on the blood of the productive Germanic Volk. Hitler promised that the day was coming when the power constellation would be radically altered. At that time, he said, the basic law would be yanked from the teeth of the Marxists and returned to German hands.

The Nazis would, he promised, continue their struggle to end the chaos in the nation and to mold the congeries of interest groups into the Germanic *Volksgemeinschaft.* The men of the movement would continue to risk their lives for their beloved Germany. Ultimately they would redeem the sacrifice of the two million war dead. This, he declared, was the true meaning of 9 November.

> I know these dead—almost all of them—personally. As they look down from the great beyond, I know that there is only one reward for their deeds and sacrifice, and that is not speeches but work, not memorials but battle. We must continue the mission . . . to strengthen the movement and take the word to the farthest German hamlet. We have to take our great ideas to every factory come what may . . . despite persecution and abuse, always keeping . . . the image of the new Germany, of a new Reich in our hearts—just like our comrades dreamed of it four years ago. . . . This is the only thanks that we can give to our dead. . . . And the day will come when we . . . can build earthly memorials to our comrades who were the first to die. And then we will inscribe the words in stone: "To the true sons of the German Volk, who died when the nation was at its lowest ebb. They died for their belief in a new, sacred German Reich."[19]

More and more, poetry and the arts were used to expound the theme of the heroic dead. Baldur von Schirach, a poet of euphoric romanticism and an enthusiastic organizer of students for the cause, wrote several works that became well known in nationalist circles. The most important of these, "On 9 November at the Feldherrnhalle in Munich," married spiritual and political death motifs.[20] For von Schirach, the reddened steps of the Feldherrnhalle became an "altar," where the blood of the heroes was shed. Running through this poem and the entire corpus of the author's early works was the mystic belief that the blood shed by the party's first martyrs— and all of those to follow in the *Kampfzeit*—was redemptive.

In the poem "Fallen Comrade," von Schirach glorified the bond between the street fighters and the living dead, who had set the example. The souls of the dead were linked with the godhead:

> He lies butchered on the pavement stones
> one who was just like you and me . . .
> For us it seems the sun will never shine again . . .
> as if our last hope was lying here.
> God, your ways are a mystery to us:
> This was a brave comrade.
> Now black ribbon drapes from our waving flags,
> while he has joined his ancestors,
> a brave bearer of great deeds.[21]

The Nazis' annual reenactment of the 9 November death march emerged as the single most important event in the party's liturgical calendar.[22] Once Hitler gained power, he fulfilled the promise to his dead comrades that they would not be forgotten in the Third Reich. Not long after the *Machtergreifung,* an order was sent to Troost—whose architectural and aesthetic design work the Führer so deeply admired—to prepare plans for a monument at the Feldherrnhalle. As a result, the young sculptor and SA man Kurt Schmid-Ehmen was given the assignment. The press made much of the fact that Schmid-Ehmen had grown up on the land, praising the influence that "farm and manual labor had on determining the conception and nature of his work, which reflects a quiet strength."[23]

The Feldherrnhalle monument reflected the influence of Professor Franz Bleeker. Bleeker had designed the memorial to Bavaria's dead in the Great War, which stood before the army museum in Munich. Schmid-Ehmen's work was perched on the west wing of the Feldherrnhalle facing the Residenzstrasse, where the 9 November victims were shot. The monument featured a bronze plaque and a bold swastika encircled in an oak wreath. Crowning it was "that model for all great upward striving and strength, the symbol of Reich authority, the eagle." The names of the sixteen martyrs were inscribed below a dedication that bore the simple message: "On 9 November 1923 at the Feldherrnhalle and at the War Ministry the following men died believing firmly in the resurrection of their Fatherland." Hitler ordered that freshly cut fir wreaths were to adorn the monument at all times.[24]

Hitler also established the *Blutorden* to reward those who had marched with him in 1923. Membership in the Blood Order was highly esteemed within the party. The medal of the order was struck in silver and was attached to a blood-red band bordered in solemn black and white. It showed an eagle in flight clutching a wreath circling the inscription "9. Nov.," with the motto "MÜNCHEN 1923–1933." The other side of the medal featured the Feldherrnhalle crowned by a radiating swastika. It was to be worn uniformly by all members of the Blood Order.[25]

The ceremonies attendant on 8–9 November 1933 climaxed nine months of celebration by the Nazis of their assumption of power. Heroes' Memorial Day, the 1 May pageantry in Berlin, as well as the Harvest Thanksgiving on the Bückeberg in the Franconian countryside all faded in comparison with the splendor of the events in November of that year. Hitler took a personal interest in orchestrating the proceedings, and he established a special office to regulate and control planning for the celebration in 1933 and all subsequent 9 November ceremonies. He placed the Amt für den 8./9. November under the command of SS Brigadeführer Christian Weber. Weber, a horse breeder and a notorious libertine, operated the office from his luxurious apartment in the Munich palace of the former Wittelsbach royal family.[26]

The party took great pains to ensure that those who took part in the sacred reenactment of the Feldherrnhalle march had been legitimate participants in 1923. Opportunists were legion in the frothy days of 1933.

Many of the same politically transfigured individuals who had just joined the party in March (*Märzgefallene*) attempted to insinuate themselves into the ranks of the prestigious 9 November veterans. One measure of control was to limit participation to holders of the Blood Order, all of whom were guaranteed a place in the line of march each year. Accordingly, the party issued strict regulations governing the award. Eligibility was limited to members of the SA, Reichskriegsflagge, and the Bund Oberland who had been deployed on 9 November 1923 and who had belonged to the party before 1 January 1933.[27] Despite unrelenting effort to weed out the ineligible, the problem of membership continued to reoccur.

The central office of Gau Munich–Upper Bavaria coordinated the details of planning for the ceremonies. Early in November 1933, the *Völkischer Beobachter* reported:

> Just as on the Day of German Art when the *Gauleitung* spared no expense to give the Bavarian capital a more festive air, so now it is going about the business of decorating the city for the coming events in a manner commensurate with the seriousness of the day's importance.[28]

Professor Bruno Goldschmitt was named to oversee the visual and decorative propaganda effort, and several architectural firms, artists, and designers were engaged for the preparations. Individual firms were assigned to decorate every main street on the parade route from the Bürgerbräukeller to the Odeonsplatz, as well as each beer hall where groups of Old Fighters were to gather.

The bureaucrats in the Munich Gau Propaganda Office were hard pressed to house adequately the many participants, honored guests, and visitors expected for the event.[29] Accommodations were assigned according to the prestige and influence of the visitors. For many SA men, this meant sleeping on improvised beds of hay in warehouses, barns, and assorted buildings throughout the city. But for prestigious groups, such as the men of Stosstrupp Hitler 1923 and their wives, it meant three days of free accommodations in Munich's leading hotels. Activities of the Stosstrupp included a reception with Hitler at the Brown House and festive *Frühschoppen* breakfasts, luncheons, and dinner banquets.[30] According to Munich wits of the day, the lions at the Feldherrnhalle monument were heard to say to one another, "My, how times change!" And indeed they had.

The Munich police president, Obergruppenführer Schneidhuber, was closely involved in the planning. Several days before 9 November, official announcements were published in the Munich press ordering stores to close between 8:00 A.M. and 2:00 P.M., halting truck deliveries, and stopping the pursuit of business of any kind. The use of automobiles was forbidden throughout much of the city. Orders were issued detailing police control of the scheduled ceremonial transfer of the flags of the Free Corps at the Königsplatz and the reunion celebrations at the brewery restaurants (the Sternecker Gaststätte, Bürgerbräukeller, Löwenbräukeller, Hackerkeller, Hofbräukeller, Wagnersaal, Salvatorkeller, and the Franziskanerkeller). Schedules were distributed for the student torchlight parade, the speech by Goebbels at the Circus Krone, the march itself, the oath of the mayors from all of the cities in Bavaria, and the midnight oath at the Feldherrnhalle of the SS Leibstandarte Adolf Hitler. Planning also included the festival production of Lohengrin at the National Theater and performances of *Alle gegen Einen, Einer für Alle* at the Prinzregententheater and *Magdalena* at the Residenztheater. The Munich police also made arrangements with the appropriate SA and SS offices for a division of responsibilities.[31]

By the time that the first scheduled events commenced, the city of Munich was ablaze with black, white, and red swastika flags and banners. This was in part the result of spontaneous enthusiasm by great numbers of people who supported the Hitler regime, but it was also the result of concerted organizational efforts by the Gau Propaganda Office. With the headline "Munich Goes All Out," the *Münchener Zeitung* reported:

> Special train after special train rolls into our impressive central station these days. The flags of our German Fatherland are waving briskly in the fresh fall wind from the gables of the train station, a festive reception indeed for the many thousands of visitors in Bavaria's capital city. Framed by huge flags in Munich's black and yellow city colors is the welcome: "*Gau Oberbayern* greets the Old Fighters of Adolf Hitler." . . . The streets of the city have really put on their festival attire, and the visitors move about the city looking at the impressive display. . . . Arms dart up in the Hitler salute in all the streets . . . demonstrating that these days, the entire Volk—united as one—has come together as never before in its history. . . . Yes, Munich is turning out in a way that its residents have never seen before![32]

November 1933 brought the last hurrah for the old Free Corps, which were coordinated into the organizations of National Socialism. For the members of the various Free Corps gathered on the Königsplatz at noon on 8 November—including the Bund Oberland, the Free Corps Rossbach, Heinz, Pfeffer, Lautenbacher, and Heydebreck—the surrender of their battle flags to the SA was more a symbolic gesture of unity than a real transfer of power. Yet a certain melancholy overtook the veterans as they listened to their leaders reminiscing about the history of their individual flags and standards. Many of them realized that their day in the sun had passed into history along with their cockades and banners, which were later marched solemnly to the Hall of Honor at the Brown House.[33]

Ernst Röhm, SA chief of staff, spoke to the troops gathered on the square.

In November 1918, as civilians had the audacity to grab the reins of power, our nation was in great danger of falling into bloody Bolshevik chaos as a result of the incompetence of those so-called governing circles. In their helplessness and cowardice they had to call on soldiers once more to help them save Germany. These commanders, who have gathered here today, along with you battle-tried veterans of the Great War, volunteered once again to serve under the old flags in those dark hours and you did your duty. You succeeded in saving Germany from Bolshevism. Your deeds belong to the ages.[34]

Röhm reminded the men of the Free Corps how the government they had saved had betrayed them once order had been restored. The SA had risen to form a united body of political soldiers under Adolf Hitler, guaranteeing a nation free of caste and united in German blood. Together they were comrades one and all, unto death. Playing on the words of the patriotic song "Die Wacht am Rhein," Röhm, who would himself be liquidated in less than eight months, declared: "Germany can be confident [*mag ruhig sein*]! We are standing guard and are fighting the battles."

The evening reunions of the Free Corps were wildly emotional affairs. Meeting with the Bund Oberland and the Deutsche Kampfbund at the Hackerkeller, Dr. Friedrich Weber gave a rousing address on the theme of Germany's salvation under Adolf Hitler. They sang their old songs lustily—many of which would never be heard again—and drank and talked deep into the night. The *Völkischer Beobachter* reported:

> If you wanted to hear good old military music like we used to know it, then you had to be there that night in the Hackerkeller. The band and music of the SS Standarte Hitler really laid it on. The musicians with their drums, trumpets, and flutes really knew how to get through to the hearts and bones of old soldiers.[35]

More than a thousand Free Corps men crowded into the banquet hall of the Hotel Union with their commander, Gerhard Rossbach. The notorious Edmund Heines—now an Obergruppenführer and leader of the SA in Silesia—appeared for his speech wearing the black and white cockade of the unit, to the delight of the old boys. He conjured up many memories of days past when the Freebooters had roamed the Baltic, the Silesian-Polish borderlands, and the Ruhr valley.[36]

At 6:00 P.M. on 8 November, Hitler repaired to the Gaststätte Sternecker in the Tal, where the party had been founded in February 1920. Here he met with the select few who had joined the NSDAP in that year and had remained loyal ever since. At 8:00 P.M., he proceeded across the Isar River to the Bürgerbräukeller. Gathered there were the original Nazi party members who had taken part in the putsch on 8–9 November 1923. To avoid any distraction from the solemnity of the occasion, the Führer excluded the entire press corps from the hall. He proceeded to deliver his message to the "most loyal of the loyal," reflecting on the meaning of the bold decision to act decisively exactly ten years before:

> We were determined to put an end to that regime of shame. . . . On that night and on the next day our young Movement opened the eyes of the entire German people, and set an example of heroism which it needed later. We can say tonight ten years later joyfully and with pride—we were victorious and as a result the year 1923 has become one of the sweetest memories of our whole lives, a memory which moves us to the quick.[37]

As Hitler concluded his message to the faithful, Goebbels was just winding down his "Freedom Rally" across town at the old Circus Krone battleground on the Mars Strasse. Simultaneously, thousands of students carrying torches paraded down the Ludwig Strasse from Munich University toward the Feldherrnhalle for a rendezvous at the Königsplatz with the SA and SS. They added a note of romantic student life as their colorful garb was illuminated in the darkness. Film footage depicts these insouciant students—many of them wearing traditional fraternity regalia—their faces aglow with enthusiasm and innocent idealism on that historic night.[38]

With the arrival of Reichsstatthalter Ritter von Epp, Interior Minister Wagner, Ernst Röhm and the SA staff, as well as officers of the state police and the Reichswehr headed by General Döhla, martial music was heard coming from the Brown House in the distance. At that point Obermusikmeister Windisch launched a spirited *Grosser Zapfenstreich*, mustering all the authority at his command in what must have been the crowning hour of his life. After playing the "Military Prayer" and national anthem, the band withdrew from the Königsplatz through the Propyläen Arch, to the delight of the crowd. Göring gave his blessing to those assembled, announcing that he had just come from the Führer's side. Speaking on the theme of sacrifice, he concluded his homily by asserting that "we have learned that a Volk can only really arise, after it has had to undergo immeasurable suffering."[39]

The events of 9 November were by no means limited to those present in Munich, the "Capital City of the Movement." The radio networks were heavily involved, with programming devoted to the ceremonies, which were coordinated over nearly a day and a half. Besides live coverage of the pageantry, there were elaborate presentations of radio plays, background interviews, music, and poetry recitations.

Listeners on the night of 8 November 1933 were exposed to the kind of refined radio propaganda that Goebbels relished. A program description conveyed the seductive mystical content of that evening's offering:

> The historical night is begun by the Gauleiter of the founding Gau, Pg. Wagner, at 11:10 P.M. The night of the dead. The dead march in. At midnight, a mystical ceremonial play, "The Birth of the Reich." They fight, die and are victorious. Just as the Third Reich was founded.[40]

Religious parallels were drawn throughout the production. Every attempt was made to wed the traditional dogma and liturgy of Easter to the National Socialist epic saga. Just as Christ suffered and died at the hands of the Jews and was later resurrected, so too the noble band of political soldiers— scorned by Marxists and the reaction alike—fought, died, and were miraculously raised from the dead. They also returned to earth in spirit to join the embattled columns, keeping the faith until the final victory. The Nazi *Mysterium* was at once a 9 November mass for the dead and an Easter vigil crowned with hope.[41]

There were several other notable features in radio propaganda. The rooster in the barnyard had hardly greeted the light of dawn when the morning national radio hookup presented a chorale, which began with the song "Wake up, wake up, you German land, you have slept long enough." As accompaniment to breakfast, SA mothers told their personal tales at 8:00 A.M. The cows were milked to a lyrical work by the Brown Shirt poet Heinrich Anacker and a rendition of the "Entrance of the Gods into Walhall." Then it was announced that

> you are listening to the German Radio Network! Today we are commemorating the dead who died for Germany at the Feldherrnhalle on 9 November 1923. At noon we will bring you a live report of the historic march, which will take the Reich Chancellor from the Bürgerbräu to the Feldherrnhalle. . . . They died for us. The Third Reich was born in their blood.[42]

Radio coverage of the march drew parallels with the Stations of the Cross. Victor Dobbert of the Reich Propaganda Command had Christian motifs in mind at every juncture in his conceptual framework for the programming. He accurately conveyed Hitler's desire that the reenactment of the 1923 march offer witnesses the opportunity to take part in a grand ritual of transcendence, at the very place where the original sacrifice took place. In his program notes for reporters, Dobbert likened the ceremony to the mass, "which repeats historical events. The past is brought directly into the present. But the past is not used just as an artifact, but instead the sacrifices of centuries long ago are used to inspire new sacrifices today."[43] Each Station in the Munich Passion was presented as a discrete segment, which was concluded with an affirmation: "Germany, we believe in you."[44]

The parade was indeed a major propaganda spectacle. For some Old Fighters, it was a day filled with memories; for others, it seemed that time had stood still. According to the *Völkischer Beobachter:*

> You know, they are all around us, the reassuring shadows of the dead on this day. They march with their comrades out to the hill over the Ludwig Bridge to the Bürgerbräu. . . . It is a great gathering of the tried and true Old Guard . . . self-assured and ready to do battle, just as they were then. . . . Many

wander out into the November cold and don't even seem to see the decorated streets. . . . But they are sure of one thing: the presence of the dead, that's what brings all Germans together today.[45]

Hitler shared this otherworldly preoccupation. As his Mercedes pulled up to the Bürgerbräu to begin the march at noon, he did not seem to see his loyal followers gathered there to greet him. Instead, he looked right through them, his mind deep in the memories of 1923. He swung into formation behind the Blood Flag, and the parade began to move down the hill toward the Isar River and the Ludwig Bridge. An hour earlier, one hundred ninety-five SA standard bearers had marched with their party insignia to the Feldherrnhalle. They were joined by twenty thousand SA men—six abreast and in two columns—who had marched down the Ludwigstrasse through the Siegestor. By their presence, they signaled the fulfillment of the Nazi battle cry: "You were victorious after all!" Also drawn up on the Odeonsplatz were units from the four corners of Germany, carrying their battle-scarred standards from the *Kampfzeit.* Especially evocative were the black and white colors of the Schlageter-Gedächtnis-Bund, the Oberlanders in their wind jackets and blue hats with the Edelweiss, and the men of the Free Corps Kühne with their black helmets emblazoned in white. The Hamburg delegation turned out with its flag from the underground days of the 1920s.

As the Hitler column crossed the Isar River, a drama was taking place at the Bavarian War Ministry on the Schönfeld Strasse. In 1923, Lieutenant Theodor Casella and Private Martin Faust had been killed there in an attempt to secure the position. Reichsführer SS Himmler and Ernst Röhm of the SA were joined by Minister of Defense Werner von Blomberg. After the playing of the "Bavarian Military Prayer" by Alblinger and the laying of wreaths, Röhm stepped forward to pay tribute to his comrades. "Nothing of any lasting worth," he said, "has ever been created in the world without struggle, sacrifice, and blood. Comrades Casella and Faust! Your blood was not shed in vain."[46]

Led by Julius Streicher and the Blood Flag, the Hitler column, which included a great number of prominent National Socialists, snaked its way through the Isar Gate and the Tal. The line of march included Göring, Kriebel, Graf, Dr. Weber, and Kolb followed by Rosenberg, Christian Weber, Streck, Feder, Sessellmann, Dr. Schulz, and Adolf Wagner. True to the conditions of 1923, there were no bands, and the marchers wore neither hats nor coats. Deadly earnest, Hitler wore a simple Brown Shirt and an Iron Cross. Silent crowds lined the route, and they greeted the Führer with the fascist salute as he passed. The column went by hundreds of oil-burning pylons, each bearing the name of a fallen hero. Belching black smoke, they added an altogether pagan aura to the macabre death ritual. Along the route huge blood-red flags with three slanted Germanic runes—symbolic

5. Feldherrnhalle Memorial March, Munich, 9 November 1935. (Stadtarchiv München.)

of sacrifice (*Opfergedanke*)—waved in the light breeze over the marchers. As the Führer column arrived at the Marienplatz, the ancient central square known for its beauty, the Rathaus *Glockenspiel* struck up the chords of the Horst Wessel Song.[47]

After passing Wein, Theatiner, and Peru Strasse, the column entered the Residenzstrasse. Upon its arrival at the spot where the shots had rung out exactly ten years earlier, a cannon reported in the Hofgarten. It was answered by the fire of artillery pieces stretching across the city. At that point a minute of silence was observed, which brought all pedestrian and motorized traffic across Munich to a halt. Hitler next reviewed the veterans of 1923 who had converged on the Odeonsplatz from their staging positions across the Isar on the Georgenstrasse and the Möhlstrasse. A party journalist reported:

> You can see it in the face of every single man that this march was a profoundly moving experience. They pass in review under their faded and tattered flags— which shine in new glory today—out front the Blood Flag of 9 November 1923.[48]

Hitler then made a very short address prior to the dedication of the new monument for the fallen at the Feldherrnhalle. Musing on the days past, he said:

> We knew that we were carrying out the will of Providence, and that we were being guided by a higher power. Ten years have passed and it is a boundless joy for me today to see yesterday's dreams fulfilled. . . . If our dead of 9 November could see us now, they would shed tears of joy. . . . Now that we have united the whole strength of our nation today, we can give our dead their eternal rest; because this is what they fought for, and this is what they died for![49]

Thereupon Hitler descended the steps of the Feldherrnhalle and proceeded with the ceremony of dedication. To the accompaniment of muffled drums, he approached the memorial, followed by his most intimate paladins. Deeply moved, he listened as the crowd sang the Horst Wessel Song and shouted a round of "Sieg Heils!" Hitler gazed at the monument and saluted the wooden cross that had been placed directly across the street on the wall of the Residenz. In a moment of supreme fulfillment, he shook hands with his faithful Old Guard, which included Göring, Hess, Streicher, Röhm, Rosenberg, Feder, Esser, Wagner, and von Epp. Finally he took leave of the dead, entering his open limousine with Göring, von Epp, and Röhm. The car moved slowly down the Ludwigstrasse, as Hitler accepted the plaudits of the crowd. He returned at midnight to swear in the new members of the SS Leibstandarte Adolf Hitler.[50] With the conclusion of the ceremonies, the pattern had been set that would be followed religiously in subsequent anniversary celebrations.

Because of the tensions associated with the purge of Ernst Röhm and the SA in 1934, Hitler did not stage an anniversary march in November of that year.[51] The climax of 9 November ritual occurred in 1935, with an elaborate reburial of the sixteen martyrs. Troost was commissioned to prepare plans for the building of a heroic burial monument. The Ehrentempel, the Temple of Honor, fulfilled Hitler's dream. Built in neoclassical style at the Königsplatz, the Temple of Honor reflected what Hitler referred to as the German *Tektonik*. Cast in marble, surrounded by columns, and open to the air, the temple incorporated his ideal that true art should express political ideology. The inscription later unveiled at the main entrance to the Haus der Kunst in Munich characterized the Temple of Honor as well: "Art has the mission of ennobling its viewers and schooling them in fanaticism." The temple, conceived in racist ideology, also reflected Hitler's determination to express eternal truths in eternal marble. It was to be but the first step in his grand plan to rebuild Munich in the "Nordic-heroic image." The Temple of Honor was to lie in the center of a complex of party and official buildings, which, had they been completed, would have robbed Munich of the singular appeal of its classic-romantic style.[52]

Frau Gerdy Troost analyzed the heroic form and function of the temple, whose completion her husband did not live to see:

> The Temple of Honor of the first martyrs of the Movement lies between the broad granite Forum, the "community space" of our Volk, and the Führerbau. Faith and readiness for self-sacrifice represent the eternal bonds between a Volk and its leadership. The fallen stand as an "Eternal Guard" for the ideals for which they died. They help guide the decision making in the Führerbau next to them. They inspire those who take their oaths here and the people who make pilgrimages to this sacred place year after year. The greatness and living power of ideology have found their worthy incarnation in this structure.[53]

For Hitler, the temple represented attainment of his desire to bury his honored dead in the heart of the city that he loved so dearly. As he expressed it:

> Early on I resolved that if Providence ever brought me to power, I would bring these comrades out of their cemeteries and honor them and take steps so that the nation could see them, and just as I resolved to do it, so now it has been fulfilled. They have now joined the German Immortals. In those days they had no idea of the Reich of today; they could only dream of it. Because they did not survive to see this Reich, we are going to make certain that this Reich sees them. And for that reason I did not put them in a mausoleum or consign them to some vault. No, just as they laid their chests bare to the blaze of fire in those days, so now they will lie under God's open sky, in the wind and weather, in the storms and snow—always an example for the German nation. Because for

us they are not dead. These temples are no mausoleums, but instead an "Eternal Guard." Here they stand guard for Germany and for our Volk. Here they lie as true martyrs of our Movement.[54]

The planning for the exhuming of the bodies of the martyrs in 1935, as well as the ceremonies attendant on the commemoration of the Temple of Honor, were extraordinary. The Munich *Gauleitung* was commissioned with the orchestration of the events, which were to last three days. No director of a theatrical production ever worked from a script more elaborately detailed.[55] Orders were placed with the Atelier Troost for the creation of sixteen bronze sarcophagi and ceremonial flags for the horse-drawn caissons that bore the bodies. Technical arrangements were made for the placing of four hundred oil-burning pylons along the parade route, each with the name of a hero embossed in gold. Loudspeakers were placed at appropriate points to broadcast the march, and plans were made for the elimination of all artificial lighting during the night ceremonies. SA men with torches lined the entire parade route. Orders detailing their functions were transmitted to the offices of the SS, SA, Wehrmacht, Hitler Youth, and all party organizations involved. The *Gauleitung* commanded that the streets and beer halls be properly decorated and hotels prepared to receive the families of the dead and the many other guests of honor.

Three major events highlighted the anniversary: the midnight transfer of the bodies of the martyrs from several Munich cemeteries to the Feldherrnhalle where they would lie in state, the march on 9 November; and the return of the souls of the martyrs to become the Eternal Guard at the Temple of Honor on the Königsplatz. This three-part framework was intentionally structured on Christian precedents. Battle and struggle were the keynotes of the march from the Bürgerbräukeller; sacrifice characterized the ceremonies at the Feldherrnhalle, while the joy of resurrection followed at the Königsplatz.[56] The flags flying along the parade route corresponded to the conceptual meaning of each segment of the pageant as well. Stages one and two—to the Feldherrnhalle—employed red banners of blood and Germanic runes of sacrifice and mourning. Stage three symbolized victory, highlighted by the use of swastika flags.[57] The musical orchestration was adapted for the progression to each successive Station of the Cross.

By 7 November 1935, the bodies of the fourteen martyrs buried in Munich had been exhumed, and SA Hochland units stood vigil around the clock at the North Cemetery, East Cemetery, and the Forest Cemetery. The remains of Wilhelm Ehrlich and Johann Rickmers arrived by train from Gralow/Warthegau and Vortlage/Westphalia. An honor storm of SA received the caskets at the central station and then transported the bodies to the King's Room of the Wittelsbach Residenz. On the night of 8 November, horse-drawn caissons of the Wehrmacht, accompanied by the roll of muffled drums, transferred the martyrs to their rendezvous at the Siegestor on the Leopold Strasse. There, shortly after 11:00 P.M., they were met by the Old Guard, who had marched from their traditional meeting with Hitler at the Bürgerbräu. At the Siegestor, a host of SS, SA, and party leaders, surrounded by a sea of flags, joined the cortege. The *Völkischer Beobachter* offered a vivid description of what followed:

> Countless torches give off a dim light in the night. The pylons cast their smoky flames heavenward. Thousands and thousands of people on the street greet the dead, as they pass by. Muffled drums can be heard while the metal of the horses' hooves clatter on the pavement and slowly the caissons creak over the Ludwigstrasse toward their goal, the Feldherrnhalle. An heroic symphony . . . An unforgettable experience for those who saw this march.[58]

As the column approached the Feldherrnhalle, the marchers faced a huge blood-red flag draped in the interior. Slowly, the Old Fighters assigned to each sarcophagus moved up the steps of the monument and placed the fallen at the base of a flickering pylon. The first verse of the "Horst Wessel Song" was sung as a funeral dirge, when at a signal ten thousand SA men carrying Swastika flags and banners marched *en masse* into position on the Odeonsplatz. Hitler then mounted the steps alone to mingle with the souls of the dead of 1923. In the darkness of the night, he moved from casket to casket, greeting each comrade individually. This act concluded, he was joined by a select few of his loyal paladins who also greeted the dead.

Throughout the night, sixteen Hitler Youth stood guard at the caskets. Deep into the night, the faithful and the curious filed past the bodies. Hitler's wish, this was to represent an exchange between the living and the dead, linking the martyrs and the *Volksgemeinschaft* in an eternal blood bond.[59] Simultaneously an identical death watch was in place throughout the night at over four hundred points in the Reich, at all those places where National Socialists had been murdered "by Reds or reactionaries."

At noon on the following day, the march formed once more at the Bürgerbräukeller. Ready to greet the participants on their march were representatives from all of the provinces of the Reich, standing guard at the named pylons lining the route. At the precise moment when Hitler reached a pylon, the name of a hero was called out on a sound system that transmitted the proceedings to the city of Munich and to the national radio hookup. Even the tempo of the march was regulated by a telephone communication system placed in buildings along the parade route.[60] Decoration consisted of huge red flags stretching across the street at appropriate intervals. When the Führer's party reached the Feldherrnhalle, sixteen artillery shells were fired, and one by one the caskets were carried from their

6. Feldherrnhalle Memorial March, Munich, 9 November 1933. (Stadtarchiv München.)

places of honor in the hall to the caissons of the Wehrmacht waiting in the street below.

As the parade headed down the Brienner Strasse, the national anthem was played at an authorized "happy tempo" to signify the glory of the risen heroes. The caskets were carried to a platform before the Temple of Honor. The immediate families of the fallen had taken positions there, and the caskets were gently laid at their feet. According to witnesses of the "final call to the colors" that morning:

> Slowly and festively the procession bearing the sixteen coffins approaches the Königsplatz. Through the guard of honor of 3000 Party leaders from the entire Reich, past the leaders and flags of youth . . . The theme of mourning is concluded, giving way to the march of victory of the Movement. The national anthem thunders out across the square victoriously like a magnificent organ in a huge cathedral. . . . Two storms of the SS Standarte Deutschland march into the square. Festive fanfares are blown. . . . In the Temple of Honor the flames from the sacrificial vessels burn at the heads of the sarcophagi. The parade of the dead moves toward its final honors. The caissons wheel into position on both sides of the Temple of Honor. A shell is fired, the national anthem is concluded, and the Führer moves from the Propyläen Temple to a point midway between the Ehrentempel. A second cannon is fired, the flags are lowered to half mast, and the band of the Leibstandarte Adolf Hitler strikes up the "March of Mourning" by Ernst Hanfstaengl. A third shot is heard, and the flags are raised once again.[61]

After a pause, Gauleiter Wagner began the "Final Roll Call" (*Letzter Appell*), a ceremony borrowed from Mussolini's fascist repertoire. As Wagner called off two names from the list of the dead, the Old Fighters and Hitler Youth responded with a "Here!" in unison, a cry that echoed from the Königsplatz out to the city beyond. Two by two—one for each wing of the Temple of Honor—the pallbearers carried the bronze sarcophagi to their final resting places. Ornate tapestries were draped over each body. This was repeated eight times in a solemn and deliberate fashion to the music of the Horst Wessel Song. As each sarcophagus was raised and the Wehrmacht escort honor guard moved off smartly, the sound of the horses' hooves lent medieval imagery to the pageant. As the bodies were laid in the temple, cannons were fired three times. According to the official script:

> The sarcophagi are in place. The fallen of 9 November 1923 have been resurrected and have taken their positions as Eternal Guards, directly between the two buildings of the Führer. The drum roll commences, just as it does with the ordinary changing of the guard.[62]

At that point Hitler entered the temple, and, after a pause for meditation, he laid sixteen wreaths. After he left the temple, the drum rolls were silenced, giving way to the strains of the Badenweiler March. From across the square, the men of the permanent honor guard—the SS Standarte Deutschland—marched through the arches of the Propyläen, strutting across the center of the square to the Temple of Honor. There they assumed a guard that did not surrender its place until the demise of the Third Reich in 1945.

To conclude the ceremonies, Baldur von Schirach administered the oath of membership in the Hitler Youth to twelve hundred boys and six hundred girls.[63] This act symbolized the passing of the torch from the heroes of 1923 to Hitler's young vanguard, the incarnation of the spirit of the Feldherrnhalle.[64] When Gauleiter Wagner called out Horst Wessel's old motto—"Attention: Raise the Flag!"—the *Letzter Appell* had passed into history.[65]

Alfred Rosenberg put the events of 9 November 1935 into an ideological context in a front-page article in the *Völkischer Beobachter*, which was headlined "The Final Roll Call." Rosenberg's tortured analysis was grounded in Germanic blood mysticism:

> For those who visit Munich, seeing these sixteen sarcophagi will admonish them to remember the beautiful race-bound unity of the events at the Feldherrnhalle, which have become symbolic for all of us. The rigorous forms of the buildings and the stark simplicity of the sarcophagi are representative of the basically uncomplicated and rigorous thought of National Socialism. Now the sixteen dead have found their final resting place in the middle of the teeming life of the Capital City of the Movement. . . . Like an ancient grave of our tribal Hun ancestors, yet expressed in the conceptual form of the twentieth century . . . this grave will serve as an eternal declaration of loyalty to that special breed of humanity, which we call the Germanic destiny.[66]

In 1936 the Nazis released the documentary film *Für Uns* (*For Us*), which dealt with the meaning of the 9 November march.[67] A masterpiece of cinematic art, the work compares favorably with Leni Riefenstahl's *Triumph of the Will*. Viewed by a wide audience in feature film theaters, and used extensively as an educational device for youth, it was an important transmitter of fascist ideology. *For Us* created a world far from the throbbing cacophony of twentieth-century industrial and technological alienation. Thoroughly mystical in conception, Führer, Volk, and Fatherland became life's Alpha and Omega in this work. Its singular blend of visual imagery, evocative lyricism, and seductive music created an entirely new reality. Viewers were admonished to become links in an eternal chain bonded in blood and urged to emulate the deeds of the resurrected heroes. The dead offered nothing less than the promise of eternal life in the Volk. This perverted message was at once diabolical and disarmingly effective.

For Us makes excellent use of the architectural splendor of baroque Munich. It begins with a scene of the Isar River, accompanied by the roll

7. Hitler salutes the sixteen Immortals, Temple of Honor, Königsplatz, Munich, 9 November 1936. (Bayerisches Hauptstaatsarchiv.)

of drums and the cadence of marching boots. A solemn reference is made to the revolutionary "stab in the back" of 1918 and the chaos that followed. A closeup of the memorial to the fallen of 1923 offers a counterpoint to the crisp recitation of von Schirach's poem on the Feldherrnhalle. Viewers are immediately swept into a world of German heroes who offered themselves in sacrifice, were resurrected, and returned to live on with their comrades. With the march formed, viewers are presented with footage of the Blood Flag and the Brown Shirts. Hitler, Streicher, Hess, Göring, and Rosenberg merge as one with the other marchers of 1923, several showing the battle scars of the *Kampfzeit*. They pass familiar points in their beloved Munich—the Tal, Marienplatz and the Rathaus, Max Joseph Platz, the Residenz, and the Odeonsplatz. A frame showing Minister of Defense Werner von Blomberg lends added authority to the ceremony, as he lays a wreath for the army at the Feldherrnhalle monument for the fallen. The entrance of the marchers into the Königsplatz is dramatic, as the camera scans the faces of the thronged Hitler Youth. The climax of *For Us* is reached when Hitler climbs the steps of the Temple of Honor to merge with the spirits of the living dead. As the camera focuses on the Führer's face, the urns belch forth their black, oily smoke, which presents a marked contrast to the beauty of the white marble. Muffled drums in shifting cadence reinforce the element of drama. The effect of the whole conveys the sense that one is witnessing an event of world historic importance.

At the conclusion, Siegfried is seen wearing a human face. Hitler becomes a veritable prince of compassion, greeting the survivors individually. In one particularly suggestive scene, he comforts a young girl who is in tears, gently stroking her face, while he touches the shoulder of a grieving widow.

Viewers in the 1930s could not have left the theater without comprehending the message of *For Us*. The flow of German history, and their place in its future development, was clear. The sacrifice of the two million dead in the Great War had been fulfilled by the martyrs of 1923. Hitler showed the way to a glorious future. Nazi film makers had succeeded in creating a powerful synthesis of their heroic mythology.

With the passing of the years, the 9 November pageantry lost its special flavor. Just as the excitement of the Nazi assumption of power gave way to the stale routine of bureaucracy, so too the nature of this celebration changed. It also became routine, the fate of many reunions too often repeated. Heroism had given way to petulant contention, self-sacrifice to bickering and jealousy. More and more the SS was featured at the expense of the Brown Shirts. Gradually, party leaders used the days in Munich to hold meetings. During World War II, they had to be ordered to attend. As the years passed, November came and went with very little fanfare.

Bureaucracy has a life of its own. Christian Weber, director of the Amt für den 8./9. November, busied himself ferreting out persons ineligible to take part in the march. According to a memorandum to all members of the Stosstrupp Adolf Hitler in 1937:

> I am notifying you that we have evidence that certain individuals who did not take part in the march in 1923 in one of our three organizations, or who, if they were members, did not march on 8./9. November, are trying to sneak into the ranks of the Old Fighters of 1923. I urge all Stosstrupp men when they give their testimony under oath to transmit the most exact and carefully considered information. It is not enough that you heard that someone or other was there, but instead you must have personally witnessed the person for whom you are vouching.[68]

Henceforth all members of the Blood Order were required to apply for a new identity card. Detailed instructions were issued clearly delineating those eligible for participation. These included members of the Reichskriegsflagge, Bund Oberland, and SA who participated in 1923 within a five-kilometer radius of the city center. Those outside the limit had to be satisfied with appearing at their Bavarian villages' "White-Blue" maypole ceremonies. All eligible participants had to have two sworn witnesses from 1923, as well as confirmation by their respective company commanders. False declarations resulted in severe punishment.[69]

Gradually stale legalism replaced idealistic commitment to the memory of the martyrs. One of the major events of the 1937 ceremony, for example, was the introduction of a new uniform for the participants in the parade. On 8 October 1937 the *Völkischer Beobachter* went so far as to publish a photograph of a Nazi model in front of the Feldherrnhalle sporting the new outfit. It was difficult to distinguish this picture from an advertisement for the fall offerings in mens' furnishings at the Munich clothing firm Loden Frey. Henceforth a gray windbreaker and an SA cap, "Model 1923," were considered *de rigueur*.[70]

Vanity also raised its ugly head. In 1938, Hermann Kriebel wrote a letter to Rudolf Hess complaining that he, not Hitler's bodyguard, Ulrich Graf, had the right to march next to Hitler:

> In 1933 I marched in the place where I did in 1923—next to the Führer. In 1935 Graf demanded that he march next to the Führer, where he marched in 1923. Since the parade was already formed and the Führer had taken his position, I did not want to make a scene and I quietly relented. Then in 1937 Graf demanded that he march in the place to which he had no right, and I gave in again out of deference to Graf's deed at the Feldherrnhalle (he had thrown himself in front of Hitler when the firing started and was severely wounded). Now I read in the *Völkischer Beobachter* in an article about Graf's sixtieth birthday, that it was he who marched next to the Führer in 1923. This is a falsification of history.[71]

Kriebel complained that it was his right to march next to Hitler because in 1923 he was the military commander of the Deutscher Kampfbund. As a result, he was directly subordinate to Hitler in the chain of command. Kriebel requested that proper documentation be given to the party historians writing the history of 1923, in order that his "name, deeds, and participation would not be overlooked." Further, he asked Hess to clear up the matter with Graf, "since I will not give up my rightful place in the march the next time."[72]

Ernst Schulte-Strathaus of Hess's staff handled the matter for the deputy Führer, and Graf was asked to respond. Graf noted that as Hitler's staff man he routinely appeared with him as they moved into parade formation. Indeed, in 1936 the Führer specifically instructed him to march at his side. Graf answered:

> In 1937, as I arrived with the Führer and also greeted Lieutenant Kriebel, who said to me smirking, "Herr Graf, we should form up like we did in 1923," whereupon I laughed and said "Yes, Herr Oberstleutnant, but then the head of the parade will have to be changed." Then Kriebel said to me, "But I belong to the left of the Führer." Then I said, "No, in 1923 I was next to the Führer." And he said, "Göring doesn't belong over there either." . . . I remained next to the Führer. . . . We started to march and during the whole parade, Kriebel just pouted. . . . I suggest that to clear up the matter, the Führer should be asked where I should march in the future.[73]

Many of the Old Fighters looked forward to 9 November for the camaraderie it offered. For example, in November 1935 Karl Fiehler, the mayor of Munich, invited the veterans of the Landsberg Prison days to a dinner in the Ratstrinkstube of the Rathaus. Hitler himself attended this affair.[74] Seemingly, there was nothing quite like a bittersweet reunion with one's old friends from prison. Friedrich Weber of the Bund Oberland, now a high official in the Reich Ministry of the Interior, wrote to Fiehler:

> I cannot thank you enough— and my wife as well—for the reunion of the old Landsberg comrades in the Ratstrinkstube with the Führer. It really warmed the heart to conclude our wonderful days in Munich by spending those grand hours together.[75]

In 1938 the Stosstrupp Adolf Hitler 1923 cavorted in the countryside at city expense, taking a pilgrimage to the hallowed prison at Landsberg am Lech.[76]

The 9 November also afforded long-forgotten individuals the opportunity for a fleeting place in the sun. Adolf Lenk, billing himself as the "Führer of the former National Socialist *Jungsturm* Adolf Hitler, 1921–1923," mailed a pompous invitation to many highly placed party members to attend a ceremonial banquet on the evening of 9 November 1936.[77] But for many of the thousands and thousands of SA and party men who streamed into the city, the day of remembrance was but an excuse to cavort and carouse in many of the renowned beer halls of Munich.

Matters of real importance were taking place at higher levels. Goebbels used the occasion to launch a triumphal opening of the exhibition "The Eternal Jew." On the evening of 8 November 1937, both Goebbels and Streicher spoke in the Congress Hall at the Deutsches Museum on the theme of the international Jewish conspiracy.[78] On the same day, Göring addressed the entire leadership corps of the NSDAP on the problems of the Four-Year Plan at the invitation of Rudolf Hess.[79] It was Himmler and the SS who used the 9 November pageantry to the best advantage, in time totally overshadowing the SA. The SS proved themselves to be masters of organizational and liturgical detail.

The technical plan for the 9 November 1938 order of formation on the Königsplatz for the Eternal Guard ceremonies gave outward evidence of the altered power relationships.[80] In the square facing the Ehrentempel, which was teeming with Nazi organizations, the SS now outnumbered the SA by at least a four to one margin. Furthermore, the SS assumed a position directly behind the members of the Blood Order. The SA was scattered on the flanks and rear, while lesser party organizations fell in behind. Young women of the Bund deutscher Mädel and the Reich Work Corps took positions on the sides.

The annual midnight ceremonies at the Feldherrnhalle, featuring the swearing in of the SS Verfügungstruppe and SS Totenkopfverbände, provided Himmler the opportunity to highlight his growing power. What had begun in 1933 as a relatively modest event now took on major symbolic importance. Himmler packed the stands on the Odeonsplatz with personal guests that he wished to influence. The scene was very dramatic, and every conceivable symbolic and mystical nuance was employed by the Order. In the black of night, torchlights and flames from burning pylons provided the illumination. SS Obergruppenführer Sepp Dietrich commanded the formation for his old friend, Heinrich Himmler. The *Völkischer Beobachter* described the scene:

> Heavy fog covers the night, which adds to the tone of mystery. Shortly before midnight, Reichsführer SS Himmler appears and takes command. . . . Anxious anticipation wells up among the thousands of people gathered at the Odeonsplatz.[81]

At exactly midnight, Hitler's car arrived at the courtyard of the Wittelsbach Palace. As the Führer approached the Feldherrnhalle, the band of the Leibstandarte struck up the Präsentier March. Hitler, greeting the SS candidates, barked "Heil, SS Männer!" The candidates answered sharply,

"Heil, mein Führer!" The band next played a solemn rendering of the Old Netherlands Hymn of Prayer. At that point, Himmler administered the oath whereby the candidates swore loyalty to Adolf Hitler personally, promising "obedience unto death." Hitler then addressed the men, speaking on the theme of loyalty. He concluded his remarks with an admonition: "I expect you to remain ever true to the motto of the Order to which you have the honor of belonging. Your honor must always and under all conditions be loyalty."[82] At Himmler's command, the band played the SS song of loyalty, "Wenn Alle untreu werden," while Hitler reviewed his new SS men.[83]

The traditional November memorial nearly cost Hitler his life in 1939. A single conspirator, Georg Elser, contrived a plot to kill Hitler by setting a time bomb in the podium where he was to speak in the Bürgerbräukeller.[84] Had Hitler followed his normal schedule on the night of 8 November—he usually spent several hours in the company of the Old Fighters—he might well have been killed. Instead, he left immediately for Berlin by train. En route he received word that a bomb had exploded in the Bürgerbräu, killing seven Old Fighters and wounding sixty others. The fact that Hitler had been spared was interpreted as further evidence that the Führer was a messianic figure protected by Providence. Nazi propagandists claimed that the English, in league with the Jews, were responsible for the bomb plot.[85]

Nazi liturgical specialists exploited the opportunity that freshly spilled blood offered them. Renewed martyrdom on the anniversary of the historic events of 1923 offered the ultimate circumstances for a *Heldentod* scenario. An elaborate ceremony was staged, which commenced with the dead lying in state on the Odeonsplatz before the Feldherrnhalle. Hitler flew to Munich for the ceremonies. At his best on such occasions, the Führer greeted the bereaved before the caskets, offering comfort to the tearful women and children. Newsreel cameramen shot some of the most suggestive footage of the early war years at the event; Hitler so seldom demonstrated sensitivity to the suffering of others.[86] The Munich Philharmonic Orchestra provided moving accompaniment for the solemn funereal theater, which continued with a death march down the Ludwig and Leopold Strasse to a common burial in North Cemetery. Rudolf Hess, seemingly born to the role of a secular priest, addressed the mourners, weaving the death of the 1939 martyrs into Nazi ideology:

> The stream of blood which flows for Germany is eternal—the sacrifice of German men for their Volk is eternal—therefore Germany will also be eternal, the Germany for which you sacrificed your lives. Dead comrades, sleep in the peaceful love of your Volk. . . . The Führer lives! . . . How many tears of joy have been shed for him! . . . The miracle of his rescue has made us believe in him all the more . . . because he has been sent to us on a great mission.[87]

The November remembrance continued on a limited scale during the war, when many Nazis simply chose not to appear. By 1942, interest had waned to such an extent that Bormann was forced to dispatch the following order from the Führer's headquarters:

> On the Führer's orders, I inform you that all Reichsleiter, Gauleiter, and unit leaders are expected to take part in the ceremonies in Munich as usual; Party leaders are also obliged to take part in the ritual at the Temple of Honor. You are expected to arrive in Munich by noon on 8 November.[88]

Mayor Karl Fiehler of Munich, who had once delighted in hosting the festivities, authorized his staff to issue the following ungracious invitation to his comrades in the Stosstrupp Adolf Hitler 1923:

> Unfortunately our reunion on 9 November 1940 will not take place as planned in the Preysing Palace Restaurant, but instead in the home of our comrade Karl Fiehler, im Tannhof, Willroiderstrasse 10. Street car stop Theolindenplatz. In accordance with the war conditions, members should bring along a cold snack.[89]

Considering the magnitude of Hitler's responsibilities during the war, ceremonial diversions to Munich in November of each year might well have seemed a luxury. But such was not the case. Remarkably, Hitler appeared there as late as November 1943. After the Bürgerbräukeller disaster of 1939, the Führer limited his participation to a speech in the Festival Hall of the Löwenbräukeller. Fear that the allies would endeavor to help him celebrate the occasion with a bombing raid forced Hitler to give his annual dinner address in the late afternoon. The traditional march no longer took place; the Königsplatz lay under camouflage and was not considered suitable any longer for the Eternal Guard ceremony. Instead of the usual mass participation by SS, SA, and Hitler Youth, unit representation was limited to symbolic formations of one hundred men. Although schools were dismissed, the sacred day of National Socialism was no longer proclaimed a national holiday.[90]

Goebbels attempted to combine the traditional All Saints Day and Sunday of the Dead with the 9 November anniversary. In that way, memory of those gone before would inspire bravery in the difficult days ahead in the war. Goebbels wrote:

> Especially now in wartime it is of the greatest importance that we give our attention to planning this day. We commemorate those who died for the Movement, the dead of the Great War and of this war, but also our ancestors, who live on in us and our children and thereby have given eternal life to our Volk. At the same time we will be remembering the victims of the bombing of our cities.[91]

The propagandists tried to lend Hitler's Munich appearances something of the magic of bygone days. In 1942, the *Völkischer Beobachter* reported:

> As early as 4:00 P.M. the Festival Hall of the Löwenbräukeller was filled. . . . This year there are great numbers of Wehrmacht and Waffen SS military uniforms in evidence. A number of the younger men in the armed services have added the Knight's Cross to the Blood Order. The symbols of the past and the present are united in them, and they are already leading us to a happier future.[92]

On that occasion, Hitler made only the most casual reference to the martyrs before launching into an address on the military and political themes of the day.

In 1943, the year of the disaster at Stalingrad, the collapse of the African front, the Italian "betrayal" of Germany, as well as the relentless bombing of the Reich's cities, Hitler decided to come to Munich yet again. It was to be his last such appearance, because all 9 November activities were canceled in 1944.[93] There is no evidence to suggest that they were missed by party members.

The Nazi elite schools for youth celebrated the example of the 1923 martyrs until the bitter end. At the elite Nazi school for boys, the Napola Ballenstedt, for example, the cadets engaged in a 9 November pageant as late as 1944. Following the playing of a Händel duo for cello and piano, a cadet addressed the corps:

> We are in the midst of an epochal time that will decide Germany's life or death. A 9 November. Twenty years have already passed since those men, whom you never knew, died in Munich. The Reich was born again at that hour; and now you will fulfill its promise. All those who died for the Greater German Reich stayed with the flag, they never weakened, they were loyal to the Führer. Be worthy of the dead who went before you! Be worthy of our ancestors who protected our blood! And be loyal followers of the Führer.[94]

Official death ceremonials and faith in the apotheosis of martyrs are functions of sovereign state power. Martyrs come and martyrs go. So it was for the heroes of the Feldherrnhalle. Within a few days after the entry of American forces into Munich in 1945, the monument to the fallen of 1923 was removed from the Feldherrnhalle.[95] In July 1945, in one of the stranger ironies of German history, Michael Freiherr von Godin—the same officer who ordered his troops to open fire on those marching with Hitler in 1923— was named chief of the Bavarian State Police.[96] The new regime announced that the Temple of Honor would be transformed into a "monument of peace." According to this plan, the sarcophagi were to be melted down and molded into two gigantic bells, which "would toll for friendship and understanding among nations."[97] But, in fact, the ghosts of the martyrs stood their Eternal Guard for two more anniversaries. Finally, in January 1947, the Temple of Honor was dynamited, and the bodies of the fallen were buried yet again in several Munich cemeteries.[98] On 9 November 1946, the Communist party of Germany held a rally attended by six thousand people at the Feldherrnhalle. German history had come full circle.

IV

Goebbels, Horst Wessel, and the Myth of Resurrection and Return

Die Fahne hoch! Die Reihen dicht geschlossen!
SA marschiert mit mutig-festem Schritt,
Kameraden, die Rotfront und Reaktion erschossen,
Marschier'n im Geist in unseren Reihen mit.

Die Strasse frei den braunen Bataillonen,
Die Strasse frei dem Sturmabteilungsmann!
Es schau'n aufs Hakenkreuz voll Hoffnung schon Millionen
Der Tag für Freiheit und für Brot bricht an!

Horst Wessel[1]

During the years of the "period of struggle" in Weimar Germany, Goebbels gave new meaning to the Nazis' irrational world view with his use of myths, which served to cloak a brutal reality. The most effective of these myths grew out of the conditions of the political civil war waged by the paramilitary forces of Weimar Germany's most radical parties—the Nazis and the communists.[2] The blood myth—which featured the death of a noble warrior, his resurrection, and ultimately his spiritual return to the fighting columns of Brown Shirts—was the most compelling theme of all, and it found its apotheosis in the saga of Horst Wessel. Of this storied martyr it was said: "You will never be forgotten, you were Germany's best son."[3]

The development of the myth of resurrection and return must be viewed against the background of Nazi ideology and practice. The epic of the fighting, dying warrior who through his sacrifice won not only glory but also eternal life struck a responsive chord.[4] Party leaders baptized their following in the blood of the fallen and inspired them with irrational motifs, which, taken together, formed a coherent ideological structure. Based on the primacy of Aryan racial superiority and the theory of "Jewish-Bolshevik subhumanity," the Hitlerian world view proferred a heroic, elitist, warrior ethos and explained the battle for Germany and the soul of the *Volksgemeinschaft* by employing neoromantic, quasi-religious themes.

Goebbels learned through his experiences as a graveside orator that, through the proper use of propaganda, defeat can be transformed into victory. The homilies he delivered in Berlin cemeteries over the bodies of

8. Hitler greets his wounded SA men during the *Kampfzeit*. (Personal Collection.)

slain SA men celebrated the theme of the noble dead fighter and occasioned an emotional response among those present that approached religious transcendence. Using rhapsodic flights from reality, Goebbels merged Nazi myths with pagan warrior motifs and shrouded the whole in the incense of mysticism.[5]

For Goebbels, it was insufficient to intone chants over the bodies of countless SA men. He was convinced that generalities do not move the masses; only easily identifiable symbols serve such a purpose. The agony and death of Horst Wessel, killed by communists in the winter of 1930, was exactly the theme that the Gauleiter needed to offer his propaganda the unifying symbol it lacked.

The Wessel mythology and liturgy was entirely Goebbels's conception, and he approached the theme with great intensity. Indeed, there are curious parallels between the protagonist of his own partly autobiographical novel *Michael* and the life of Horst Wessel.[6] Michael, like Wessel, lived three lives in one—as a soldier, worker, and student. He, too, died for the Volk and was resurrected to eternal life. Whereas the nationalist martyr of *Michael* perished in a mine accident, Goebbels delivered Wessel from a banal death in questionable circumstances and gave him ennoblement as a warrior hero, a prince among the party's Immortals. There is little question that he was fascinated by the model Sturmführer. Goebbels noted in his diary that he came to realize that Wessel was a figure of epic proportions only after the shooting. While visiting the desperate Frau Wessel, Goebbels wrote, she "described Wessel's life for me. It is like a Dostoevski novel: the idiot, the worker, the prostitute, the bourgeois family, continual remorse, agony without end. That is the life of this twenty-two-year-old idealistic visionary."[7]

Horst Wessel became the source of myth and legend, celebrated in poetry and song, biography and film, party ritual and indoctrination. Town squares and streets were named after him, as were units of the German and Italian armed forces. Hitler named an SA section in his honor, and his grave remained a Nazi shrine until 1945. He was revered as the composer of the party anthem, the "Horst Wessel Song," and hailed as an exemplar of bravery, comradeship, love of country, and self-sacrifice for Führer, Volk, and Fatherland. By exalting Horst Wessel as the greatest of the SA stalwarts—a fighting Germanic troubadour who died that the nation might live—Goebbels lent symmetry to his propaganda.

It is difficult to distinguish the legendary from the historic Horst Wessel.[8] The future hero came from solid bourgeois roots. He was born in 1907 in Bielefeld, Westphalia, the son of the Lutheran minister Dr. Ludwig Wessel, who was later called to the pastorate of St. Nikolai, Berlin's oldest church. With the coming of World War I, Horst's father was posted as chaplain to the headquarters of Field Marshal von Hindenburg. His subsequent death taught Horst at an early age the meaning of "sacrifice for the Fatherland," and he was raised in the traditions of ardent nationalism. As a result, Horst was active in both the Bismarck Bund—the paramilitary youth section of the German Nationalist Peoples' Party—and Captain Ehrhardt's Free Corps Viking youth organization. Both groups, however, disappointed him, because they lacked his own radical zeal.[9]

Wessel had a rebellious nature that could find no rest outside of action. Having taken the *Abitur* at a humanistic Gymnasium, he matriculated in 1926 at the University of Berlin in the field of law. But he found much of the university world irrelevant to the needs of the day.[10] His contempt for the system knew no bounds, and the fraternity that he joined, the Kösener SC, although a fertile bearer of nationalistic alienation, was nevertheless a training ground for a future professional elite.[11] He found its aristocratic pretensions and political passivity totally out of place in Germany's hour of need. Wessel would have none of it—his stomach welled up with nausea at the sight of bourgeois hypocrisy and Marxist arrogance alike. He discovered his true home only when he joined the SA in the fall of 1926.[12] According to Wessel, "*Bismarckbund,* that was fun and games. Viking, that

9. Hitler visits the graves of fallen Old Fighters. (Personal Collection.)

was adventure, stirring up putsches, playing soldiers. The NSDAP on the other hand was political awakening. They had an ideology, which was totally foreign to the combat leagues."[13]

For Wessel the Nazi party was the fulfilment of his longings. At home among SA comrades, he found an outlet for his condottiere spirit and radical Germanic ideology. To fight for Adolf Hitler and Dr. Goebbels—called "der Oberbandit" by his enemies—was to taste of life's sweetness. Wessel was struggling for a new world—for a nation united under the Führer, liberated from parliamentary chicanery and greed, a world free from "communist blood terror" and the conditions of squalor, hunger, and unemployment that fathered "Jewish-Bolshevism." For Wessel, the dream of a future Third Reich was worth dying for, and he sacrificed the comforts of university life and career for the hardships of a common laborer and political soldier. By day he wore the proletarian clothing of a construction worker and chauffeur, by night the brown uniform of the SA.

Wessel was sincere in his misguided idealism. His heart went out to the hungry, the unemployed, the poor, and the suffering. Deep down he had much in common with his communist archenemies—they both sought radical solutions to nearly insurmountable problems. Wessel revealed his true feelings in an autobiographical sketch that he wrote for the central archives of the Nazi party:

> The parties on the right soon noticed that they couldn't count on the NSDAP, and they called us National Bolsheviks or National Marxists because of our socialist posture. In fact they were correct. For the National Socialists all in all had more sympathy for the Red Front Fighters League than for the Stahlhelm. . . . I tried to understand all the parties, and it finally dawned on me that in the red camp there were just as many, perhaps even more fanatical, idealists ripe for martyrdom than on the other side. Added to that was the whole shocking realization of the unbelievable delusion and abuse of the entire working class. And that's how I became a socialist.[14]

Clearly, Wessel's successes in the proletarian sections of Berlin were the result of the credibility he enjoyed because of his identification with the oppressed. He carried through on his seemingly naive goal of becoming "one with the Volk."

Wessel was convinced, in his distorted world view, that one could save German culture only by doing battle for it. He gave expression to Nazism's politics of the deed when he remarked:

> Whoever is convinced that Germany of today is not worthy of guarding the gates of true German culture must leave the theater . . . the salons . . . the studies . . . their parents' houses . . . literature . . . the concert halls. He must take to the streets, he must really go to the people . . . in their tenements of desperation and woe, of criminality . . . where the SA is protecting German culture. . . . Every beer hall brawl is a step forward for German culture; the head of every SA man bashed in by the communists is another victory for the people, for the Reich, for the house of German culture.[15]

All party records, diaries, and documents point to one conclusion—Horst Wessel was loved by his comrades. He looked upon himself as a fighter and as such was typical of his generation—individuals who were too young to fight in the Great War but for whom Langemarck, Verdun, and the Somme spelled heroism.[16] He achieved recognition in the Berlin SA as a leader, a speaker, and a composer of party songs. In a short time he had distinguished himself and was named Standartenführer of Storm Section 5 in Friedrichshain, deep in proletarian Berlin. Because of his personal bravery, organizational abilities, and charisma—he was only twenty-one years old and his head swam with youthful enthusiasm—Wessel was able to transform a small pack of intimidated, ragamuffin SA men into a fighting corps of desperadoes. Erwin Reitmann, who served in Wessel's unit, pungently conveyed the atmosphere of their district:

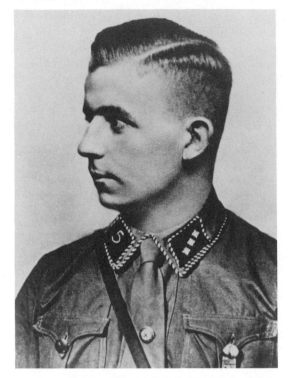

10. Sturmführer Horst Wessel. (Bundesarchiv.)

It seemed as if east Berlin had always been a Marxist domain. They were exceedingly strong in the section of Friedrichshain. With the Silesian Station close by! This was the arrival point of all the Galician Jews, Polacks and the other assorted trash from Eastern Europe. Silesian Station! The area means wild, hateful streets, thieves' dens, subhumans, and pimps. This is Marxism's true milieu, and here they have nested in and taken over. Around this station stretches Friedrichshain, a city in itself with more than 340,000 inhabitants. This gloomy neighborhood was to become the battleground of Horst Wessel.[17]

From the SA bars (*Sturmlokale*), Keglerheim on the Petersburger Strasse and the Möve on the Grosse Frankfurter Strasse, the men of Storm 5 fanned out in all directions agitating for the cause.

Under Wessel's leadership, the Nazis successfully challenged the KPD on its home ground. Terror and counterterror became a way of life for Storm 5. It was a source of great irritation to the communist leadership that the Berlin Nazis—once a laughing stock—were campaigning vigorously in the formerly solidly red districts of the city. They added insult to injury by converting many communists to the Nazi cause. Wessel's unit was composed for the most part of former members and supporters of the

KPD.[18] Further, Goebbels launched an assault on the foe in his newspaper, *Der Angriff,* while continuously bombarding Berlin with a torrent of flyers and pamphlets as well as colorful posters. The communists answered in kind in *Die Rote Fahne,* edited in the party's headquarters on the Bülowplatz. Both sides understood that the real battle was to be won or lost in the streets. The Red Front Fighters League counterattacked with a vengeance, launching brutal assaults on the Nazis both in the streets and in their pub strongholds.

Erwin Reitmann gave a dramatic account of the nature of the violence:

> Our weekly meeting was cut short because of the planned counterstrike. . . . Our goal was to storm a red pub hangout which was the command station for the terror activities. Our Storm was divided into several groups, which were to meet at prearranged places. What we encountered was not exactly reassuring. Wild apppearing shadowy figures were loitering and wandering in the dark. . . . After forming up on a dark side street, we stormed into the notorious pub like lightning. It was very crowded, and the owner and the communists turned pale with fear and didn't say a word. . . . Horst jumped up on a pool table and laid it on the line: "The red murder band in this neighborhood has been terrorizing the decent citizens for years. We give you fair warning, don't lay a hand on any National Socialist workers. Otherwise you're going to taste the sting of the fists of German workers. If there is as much as but one more incident, then God help you! An eye for an eye, and a tooth for a tooth." And so the red terror was broken by Horst Wessel here too, and the suffering in the neighborhood ceased for the time being.[19]

Wessel understood the importance of music as an inspiration for political battle. It was characteristic of the SA to break into song while marching through the embattled streets of Berlin, and their music served at once as effective propaganda and as a boost to Brown Shirt morale. His innovation of organizing a wind instrument band on the communist model (*Schalmeienkapelle*) won considerable attention as a propaganda device in the neighborhoods. Wessel gained an assured place in the Nazi pantheon by setting his poem "Die Fahne hoch" to music. The song became popular in Berlin, and it was enthusiastically received at the Nuremberg party rally in August 1929. It was ultimately adopted as the anthem of the NSDAP.[20]

The meteoric career of Horst Wessel ended as dramatically as it had begun. In mid-1929 he became enamored of a prostitute named Erna Jaenicke, whom he had first encountered at the "Mexico" bar being beaten by pimps. In September he moved out of his mother's house on the Jüdinstrasse, sublet a room at Grosse Frankfurter Strasse 62 in Friedrichshain not far from his *Sturmlokal,* and moved in with Jaenicke. His enthusiasm for the Party and its work declined drastically, a development which was a bitter disappointment to the entire Berlin SA. As a result, Goebbels urged Wessel's bosom friend Richard Fiedler to broach the subject with him. But this only offended Wessel, who maintained that the disrespect shown his beloved Erna—his future bride, a daughter of the proletarian masses and the Germanic Volk community—was nothing but petty bourgeois prejudice.[21] He continued to live on the edge of poverty, supporting Jaenicke from his earnings as a construction worker—despite the fervent pleas of his mother.[22]

Other developments hastened Wessel's demise. His brother Werner, who was also active in the Berlin SA, was killed with several of his comrades in a skiing accident shortly after Christmas 1929. This wounded Horst deeply, worsening his psychological and physical condition. He became seriously ill and was on the edge of a nervous collapse. Finally, he was a hunted man; several flyers—complete with his address—circulated in the neighborhood calling for his murder. A band of communists succeeded in killing him at the very time that his star was fading rapidly.

The circumstances of Wessel's death remain clouded, largely because the facts in the case were distorted by communists and Nazis alike.[23] The criminal trial records reveal that Frau Salm, Wessel's landlady and the young widow of a former member of the Rote Frontkämpferbund, set up the killing. Engaged in a dispute with her tenant over the rent as well as the presence of Jaenicke, and irritated by the constant disturbances caused by Wessel's meetings with his SA men, she turned in desperation for help to the desperadoes of the Storm Section City Center of the Red Front Fighters League. Ali Höhler left his lair—the notorious communist pub Der Bär, which lay on the Dragonerstrasse, a few blocks from KPD headquarters—in the company of several accomplices and planned the attack in the apartment of Salm on the Grosse Frankfurter Strasse. There, with Jaenicke looking on, Höhler shot Horst Wessel several times, yelling at him, "You know what this is for."[24] Wessel fell to the floor in a pool of blood. It was an hour before he received any medical treatment. Although SA comrades were summoned for help, they refused to call a Jewish doctor from a neighboring apartment to the scene. Valuable time was also lost while the SA ferreted out compromising documents among Wessel's possessions before calling the police. Although he was seriously wounded, Wessel did not die immediately. From 14 January to 23 February 1930, he lay dying of his wounds in a pavilion of Friedrichshain Hospital.

The communists made every effort to shield the party from blame for the shooting. Heinz Neumann and others in the KPD leadership conceived a plan to present the affair as nothing more than a squabble among pimps that ended tragically. On the night that the action squad was deployed, however,the communist functionary Max Dombrowski returned to Der Bär, where he warned those attending a communist cell meeting that anyone divulging the secret of the involvement of the KPD would be shot.[25] Salm was summoned to the Karl Liebknecht Haus and told that she was to hold firm to the claim that the shooting resulted from a squabble among

11. Goebbels speaks at the grave of a murdered SA man, Berlin, summer of 1932. (Bundesarchiv.)

pimps.[26] Further, before the Rote Hilfe, the party welfare organization of the KPD, spirited Höhler into hiding in Prague, he was instructed to contend that he had acted out of jealousy and passion. According to this story, Jaenicke had been his girlfriend but had left him for Wessel. Höhler was also ordered to testify that he himself was a pimp.[27] During the trial that followed, Dombroski claimed that Fritz Löwenthal, the communist lawyer who represented the defense, had visited him in prison on behalf of Rote Hilfe. Löwenthal told Dombroski to testify that the communists had no involvement whatsoever with the alleged crime of passion.[28] The communists were so successful in this ruse that, down to the present day, unsuspecting journalists and historians have uncritically accepted misinformation—skillfully conceived in the Karl Liebknecht Haus in the winter of 1930—as the incontrovertible truth in the Wessel murder case.

Höhler, embittered by the way the KPD had exploited and betrayed him, took his revenge in court. *Tempo* reported:

> The Wessel trial reached its high point Tuesday with the questioning of the chief defendant, Ali Höhler. Höhler, a robust dark blond man with rather drawn facial features, pale from eight months behind bars, stands completely composed gesticulating forcefully in the prisoners' dock, and describes in detail how he shot Wessel: "I shot when I saw Wessel reach for his pocket and was sure that he was grabbing a gun."[29]

Höhler attacked the KPD for spreading the rumor that he was a pimp and a police spy. This was not the case at all, he declared, a defense corroborated by the testimony of Jaenicke. The truth, he vehemently asserted, was that "this fairy tale about my being a pimp was spread by the Party—in fact at my meetings with Party officials I was told to say that I was jealous of Wessel because he stole my girlfriend Erna from me."[30] Höhler also castigated his former party comrades for sending him to Prague without adequate means of support. He claimed that those responsible for his safety had stolen the money meant for his provision for a wild drinking spree in Berlin. Höhler was left like a hounded animal to starve in Prague, and he was forced to return home. Worse still, according to Höhler, some in the party intended to have him killed.

While the communists attempted to wash their hands of the affair, Goebbels exploited it. During Wessel's extensive period of mortal agony as he lay in Friedrichshain Hospital, Goebbels issued daily news releases on his condition. These reports, reminiscent of wartime high command communiques, asserted that Wessel had been struck down in the flower of his youth, the victim of a cowardly attack by a "pack of murder-crazed, degenerate communist bandits." In contravention of every moral standard, these "subhumans," having failed to kill the innocent Wessel, undertook to invade the sacred precincts of a hospital ward to dispatch the noble hero there. But they were met by "battle-ready SA men" who gave them a "deserved thrashing." The KPD Central Committee, answering in *Rote Fahne*, claimed that Wessel was nothing but a despicable pimp who had been living as a parasite from the earnings of Jaenicke.

Invective of this nature only enhanced Goebbels's fighting spirit, and his accounts of visits to the bedside of the young hero were reported with religious solemnity. He noted that Wessel's eyes still shone brightly with confidence in the future victory of the movement, peeking out from bandages concealing a face mangled beyond description by communist butchers. A magnificent floral tribute gave eloquent testimony to the love felt for him by all classes, Goebbels continued. Children of workers brought garlands of violets, farmers and miners offered wreaths, and old women on street corners cried for him. Seemingly no group in the nation remained untouched by the martyrdom of Horst Wessel. But neither this outpouring of love and affection nor the sweet balm of comradeship offered by the SA stopped Wessel's steady demise, and he sank into a deep fever. Blood poisoning had sealed his fate, and a team of surgeons, which included the Nazi luminary Dr. Leonardo Conti, could not turn the tide. The end came on the night of 23 February 1930.

Goebbels offered a vivid description of his witness to the death, resurrection, and return of Horst Wessel:

> As I stand at his death bed, I can hardly believe that this was Horst Wessel. His face is waxen yellow, and his wounds are still covered with bandages. . . . His crumpled cold hands are adorned with flowers—white and red tulips, and violets. Horst Wessel has passed away. His earthly remains lie here mute and silent. But I feel it in my bones—I'm absolutely sure of it—his soul was resurrected, to live among us all . . . and he is marching in our columns![31]

The behavior of the communists contributed to Goebbels's plans to make the burial of Wessel a major propaganda event.[32] Authentic film footage offers dramatic evidence of the events that took place. Curiously, Hitler was absent from the proceedings, a situation attributable to security precautions.[33] In an effort to avoid violence, the Berlin police severely limited the numbers in the official party and forbade the SA to march alongside the body. After honor guards of SA and uniformed fraternity representatives had withdrawn from their vigil beside the body, the cortege began its mournful journey through the streets from the Wessel home toward the St. Nikolai Cemetery. A surprise awaited them all. An excited crowd of between twenty and thirty thousand people milled in the streets, awaiting the funeral procession. As the column appeared, a riot erupted, and the communists sang the Internationale at a fever pitch. On the Koblankstrasse, they surged forward in a vain effort to overturn the carriage bearing Wessel's body and to seize the swastika flag draped over the coffin as a trophy.

Shots rang out, but, once the armored cars of the police reached the scene, a measure of order was restored. Only with great difficulty did the column make its way along the Prenzlauerstrasse to the gates, where yet another shock awaited the mourners. Greeting them on the walls of the cemetery was graffiti: "A Final Heil Hitler to the Pimp Horst Wessel!"—boldly emblazoned by red propagandists the night before. "We had to swallow our rage. Keep calm!" Goebbels wrote.

Inside the cemetery grounds units of the SA, the Stahlhelm, and several other organizations presented a colorful spectacle. The pastor of the St. Nikolai Church spoke, as did Captain von Pfeffer, commander of the SA, who also offered a wreath from the Führer. After other brief testimonials, Göring laid Wessel's SA cap on the coffin; students presented the dark blue cap of the Kösener SC (Berlin) and the light blue of its brother house, Alemannia (Vienna).

The chanting mob outside the barricaded cemetery interrupted the proceedings as they hurled a virtual hailstorm of stones over the walls at the mourners, who scattered like rabbits to take cover behind gravestones and monuments. Only the SA held their positions, realizing in the words of Nazi chronicler Wilfred Bade that "this was an hour of supreme test for the Movement."[34]

At last Goebbels began to speak. Gesturing theatrically, he spewed forth the venom and hatred that characterized his rhetoric. According to those present, he seemed to transcend the world of the living, conjuring up in some miraculous way the soul of the martyr. He was, after all, giving birth to a myth that would follow the party through varying fortunes from 1930 until its destruction in 1945:

> When in the future, in a German Germany, workers and students march along together, then they will sing his song, and he will march with them. . . . The brown soldiers are already singing it in every corner of the country. In ten years children in the schools, workers in their factories, and soldiers along the roads will sing it. His song has made him immortal! . . . A soldier of the German revolution! Just as always, hand on his belt, proud and upright, with his youthful smile, striking out ahead leading his comrades, always ready to sacrifice his life, he will remain with us in this way.

At this juncture nature seemed to favor Goebbels. Suddenly, the sun shone through the dark clouds and illuminated the swastika flags, which began to wave in a light breeze. To those present, it was a sign of special grace, testifying that Horst Wessel had indeed passed over to the heavenly realm. Gesturing toward the sky, Goebbels shared his visionary experience:

> I can see columns marching, endless, endless. A humiliated people rises up and begins to stir. . . . It joins in step behind the standards. . . . The flags wave,

12. Funeral cortege for Horst Wessel, Berlin, 1 March 1930. (Bundesarchiv.)

drums resound, the pipes are jubilant; and a million flutes join in the song of the German revolution: "Die Fahne hoch!"[35]

From this point on, the myth of resurrection and return became standard fare in the Nazi propaganda repertoire.

The memory of Horst Wessel acted as a magnet, drawing new members to the Nazi party.[36] Testimony to his manly virtues and lofty sense of purpose became the order of the day.[37] The light sentences meted out to the murderer and his accomplices—Höhler received only a six-year sentence for manslaughter—fueled Nazi indignation. According to the *Völkischer Beobachter*:

> This sentence is so outrageous, that one wouldn't expect it even from this rotten republic. The vulgar conspiracy, which showed unparalleled cowardice, was punished with such a light sentence, that this "offence" will do nothing but inspire the subhumans to yet more crimes.[38]

The SA took its revenge on Höhler. Soon after Hitler took power, the authorities began proceedings to reopen the case, and Höhler was brought for questioning to Berlin from a prison in Silesia. The Berlin police authorities refused to turn him over to the SA, knowing full well what his fate would be. But the SA, lusting for blood, nevertheless was able to get Höhler transferred to them, on the ruse that they were to return him to Silesia. Höhler was brutally murdered by an SA Rollkommando in the countryside to the east of Berlin, where his body was found. Answering a Gestapo inquiry into the details, Ernst Röhm replied that Hitler had given the order for the execution.[39]

Horst's memory inspired the SA poet Heinrich Anacker to write:

> Once, you yourself sang your song to us
> And the enemy raised his balled fist
> But in death your example has
> victoriously won their hearts;
> Now your song has power over us all!

> When you still fought under the flag,
> Which waves before us, radiant and pure
> We did not recognize the halo of eternity—
> You had first to pale in death,
> Before becoming immortal for us.[40]

Baldur von Schirach mused in his poem on Wessel, "You are bound to all, to all! Not a one, who does not name you brother."[41] For Gerhard Schumann, "Those who struck you down could not kill you. . . . And you gave form in glowing words and song to the silent waiting of the reawakened, who raise it high to the shining light of the standards."[42]

The myth of Horst Wessel was further refined over the next several years and reached its apogee on Sunday, 22 January 1933—Horst Wessel Memorial Day—when the fallen hero was elevated to the circle of Nazi Immortals. Goebbels staged a march of the entire Berlin SA to KPD headquarters, as well as a dedication of the Wessel monument in the St. Nikolai Cemetery and a Wessel memorial mass meeting in the Sports Palace with an address by Hitler.[43]

For several days before the march, the Berlin press warned of the dangers involved, and the communists called for a massive counterdemonstration. The police appeared in great numbers with storm units deployed with armored cars and machine guns. On the appointed morning, the SA columns marched through the Scheunenviertel toward the Karl Liebknecht Haus as if the district belonged to them. Hitler, Goebbels, and Ernst Röhm stationed themselves directly in front of the building, where the Brown Shirts passed in review. For the first and last time in party history, the Nazis staged a demonstration before huge photographs of Marx, Lenin, and Thälmann.

From the Bülowplatz, thirty-five thousand SA men made their way to the grave of Horst Wessel. A light snow had fallen, providing a colorful background for the sea of flags, inspiring the *Angriff* reporter to observe that they "shined forth their red like a bloody battlefield." In contrast to the actual burial in 1930, on this occasion most of the Nazi elite were present. Wessel's mother and sister, Lutheran clergy, singing cherubs of the Hitler Youth, hardened SS men, and fraternity representatives all joined the SA at the graveside.[44] An SA man removed a cover revealing a simple stone monument, crowned with a laurel wreath and bearing the inscription "Die Fahne hoch!" for Horst and "O Deutschland, teures Vaterland, ein Licht losch aus, das Dir gebracht!" for his brother Werner.[45] Then Hitler offered a remembrance:

> Every people which strives to purify and free itself from desperation and defeat brings forth its muse, who transmits in words what the masses are feeling deep in their souls. . . . With his song, sung today by millions, Horst Wessel has won a place in history which will last much longer than this stone and iron memorial. Even after millennia have passed, when there isn't a stone left standing in this huge city of Berlin, the greatest of the German freedom movements and its poet will be remembered. Comrades, raise the banners. Horst Wessel, who lies under this stone, is not dead. His spirit is with us every hour of every day, and he is marching in our columns.[46]

On that evening, the Sports Palace was decorated like a church on Christmas Eve. It was a veritable forest of fir trees, and the hall was darkened to transmit an aura of solemnity. Four huge candelabras cast an eerie light over a catafalque heavily laden with spruce boughs. A photograph of

Horst Wessel—crowned with laurel leaves and flanked by a huge swastika flag—smiled down on the gathered throng from its lofty perch.

Every nostalgic association of the martyr was conjured up during the ceremonies. Wessel's old crony from the Berlin SA, Richard Fiedler, was a featured speaker, and the *Schalmeienkapelle* struck up the Horst Wessel song as of old. After a tearful rendering of "Ich hatt' einen Kameraden," that most melancholy of songs from the Great War, the audience of twenty thousand people heard Otto Roloff of Storm 36 intone the lines of Theodor Körner's poem "Smoke of the Signal Fire": "Thrust your spear deep into your faithful heart! Let it open the way for freedom! Wash the earth, your German land, with your pure blood!"

Count Helldorf violently attacked the *Rote Fahne* for its villainous campaign against the noble Horst, whose life had served as a beacon of truth, strength, and justice for a downtrodden people. With the playing of the funeral march from Wagner's *Die Götterdämmerung*, the imagery of the epic Germanic hero Siegfried was seen to parallel the career of Horst Wessel. The way was open for Hitler, who observed that the party stood on the threshold of power because men like Horst Wessel had followed Zarathustra's call to greatness. He had won immortality with his blood sacrifice.[47]

The Horst Wessel saga became a centerpiece of the *Kampfzeit* blood mythology. On 9 October 1930—on what would have been Horst's twenty-third birthday—Goebbels gave thanks:

> A young man has shown the Movement how one can die, and if need be, must die. And a mother has given us a grand example of how one must ultimately bear pain that seems unbearable, without falling victim to desperation.[48]

By striking the motif of the nobly suffering mother and the martyred son— even for the nonbelieving an understandably poignant subject—Goebbels cleverly drew on a theme popular in Christian worship and cultic veneration. Variations on this motif took varied form.

In an article published on Mother's Day 1930 in *Der SA Mann*, Hermann Weiskopf rhapsodized on the love between mothers and sons in the fighting *Volksgemeinschaft*. It was well known that battle-weary veterans of the trench fighting in the Great War often cried out "Mother . . . Mother" in their mortal agony. It was this same devotion that informed the reawakened political soldiers of the SA, he claimed, and would one day inspire all German families joyfully to sacrifice for the nation. The German warrior always carried with him the spirit of his loving mother, and her eyes shone on him even in death. She had bid him farewell in the Spartan fashion as he went off to war, admonishing her son to be victorious or to go down fighting. Above all, she was "blood of my blood." "This is the real meaning of motherhood—blood loyalty," Weiskopf submitted, and all true SA men have such a mother.[49]

13. Hitler speaks at grave of Horst Wessel, 23 January 1933. (Bayerisches Hauptstaatsarchiv.)

Heinrich Anacker glorified this blood bond in his poem "Mothers of the Dead":

Do you know the mothers of our dead warriors?
Have you seen the women wan and transfigured by pain,
They bear their burdens nobly and quietly
Ever ready, to continue the efforts of the dead.
Pale transfigured Mary, Mother of Christ, lives in them,
She who mourned her own son at the Cross,
And his love, his holy service
United them in sacred humility.
So filled are they with the great memory,
That only one thing inspires them now: With pale hands
To fulfill for the sake of Germany
the noble legacy of their beloved dead.[50]

"The mothers," according to Josef Magnus Wehner, "are the great nameless ones of the Volk." Their "sacred grief, the tears of the widows and orphans, will lead to the pain of a new birth, and finally there will arise out of blood and death the new man, the Führer, on whose shoulders rests the construction of the future." The Reich would arise from the shattered bodies of the dead:

They died, that we might become. Without their sacrifice we would not have been transformed, our heart beats with their blood. The true meaning of their death is our resurrection in the Reich.

Their sacrifice was the fulfillment of Goethe's thought:

And as long as you do not have,
This die and become,
You are but a troubled guest,
Here on this earth.[51]

This nobility of sentiment had its counterpoint in the criminality of the Nazis' own behavior. The death myth embraced a murderous component, graphically illustrated by the tribute of Willi Ritterbusch for the fallen, entitled "The Political Sacrifice of National Socialism and Its Meaning." Ritterbusch queried: "Are these subhuman beasts, who rioted at the grave of Horst Wessel, really worth this kind of sacrifice?—This subhumanity certainly not; we don't want them at all, it really doesn't concern them, because they are an asocial element, which knowingly has left the human race." The Nazis' sacrifice was for a higher purpose, to mold a new nation, based on the *Volksgemeinschaft*.[52] The will to sacrifice to which Ritterbusch referred was displayed dramatically when Hitler visited the bedside of several wounded Brown Shirts in a Berlin hospital in 1931. According to Goebbels, who was present, "Right before his eyes one of them died with the words on his lips, 'Heil Hitler!' "[53]

The saga of Hans Maikowski, who took up the banner of the fallen Wessel, was skillfully exploited by Nazi propagandists. Sturmführer of the infamous Storm 33 in Berlin-Charlottenburg, Maikowski was killed following the torchlight parade at the Reich Chancellery on the night Hitler took power. His death presented Goebbels with a unique opportunity. By staging a magnificent state funeral in the Berlin Cathedral, he was able not only to eulogize a hero in the mold of Horst Wessel but also to lend the prestige of sovereign state authority to what had been purely National Socialist ritual. The Nazis alleged that Maikowski was shot by an enraged neighborhood gang of communist hooligans who ambushed the hero in the black of night. But the truth was more prosaic. In fact, the murder was not committed by the communists at all but by SA Truppführer Alfred Buske, a ranking member of Maikowski's own Storm 33. The bizarre tale combined elements of rivalry and internecine strife. It was a harbinger of troubles to come within the SA, which focused in part on differences over the party's mission to the suffering proletariat.

Hans Eberhard Maikowski was a native of Charlottenburg, the proletarian island in west Berlin called "Little Wedding." As a boy he had romped in the very streets that would lay claim to him in a less fortunate era. Although he was the son of a worker, Hans attended the Schiller Realgymnasium in Charlottenburg and hoped in vain for a career as an officer in the Reichswehr. He joined several nationalist youth organizations before finding his home in the Hitler Youth and SA. Maikowski, caught in the throes of the Weimar economic crisis, remained unemployed except for sporadic stints as a gardener on the staff at Charlottenburg Castle. For a proletarian boy, it took considerable boldness to join a small SA troop in a forlorn outpost surrounded by communists. He seemed destined to die young—he was nearly killed as early as December 1927 after being stabbed repeatedly in a melee with communists after returning from a Nazi rally in the Hasenheide. Although he never fully recovered from his wounds, he pursued a meteoric career as an SA Sturmführer. Lovingly called "Hanne Maiko" by his SA comrades, he came to be known as the "Horst Wessel of Berlin-West." He was the incarnation of the motto Goebbels had sewn on the flag of Storm 33: "Live loyally, fight fearlessly, die smiling!" ("Treu lebend, Tod-trotzend kämpfen, lachend sterben!").[54] It was fitting that he loved to sing the "Vikings' Song":

> If Wotan calls us, and our game is up,
> We'll gladly bear our breast to the sword.
> Don't stop our streaming hearts' blood from flowing,
> Eagles are already soaring toward Walhall.[55]

Maikowski seemed to be born for struggle, even if his unit of less than two hundred SA men went on the attack against thousands of communists in Charlottenburg. He was convinced that only Hitler could lead the way to true socialism. The fact that he was a native son of proletarian Charlottenburg, carrying the message to his own people, gave him added credence. The SA Home he founded on the Tegeler Weg housed and fed many homeless and unemployed workers, who in good times would have found work at the neighboring *Siemens Werke*. The SA pub Zur Altstadt on the Hebbelstrasse became a staging area for many bold attacks on the rival Red Front Fighters League. In February 1931, Maikowski personally earned the designation *Mordsturm* 33 for his unit when Red Front shock troops, gathered under the banner of the criminal Ringverein "Treue Freunde," invaded his SA pub. A desperate battle ensued, in which Maikowski shot and killed a communist. *Die Welt am Abend* decried the terror under the headline "Murder Eldorado in Charlottenburg: Result of the Fascist Blood Orgy, Two Dead, a Dozen Wounded in the Last Week."[56] Forced to elude a police dragnet, Maikowski fled first to Schleswig-Holstein and then abroad. He returned to Berlin in October 1932, only to be captured and imprisoned. He was released as a result of the Christmas amnesty of 1932.[57]

Maikowski loved the danger that came with battle to the death. Life or death was immaterial to him; what mattered was victory. He addressed the following communiqué to his unit following the murder of Herbert Gatschke of Storm 33 in August 1932:

> SA men of Storm 33! No other Storm has shown such unity as the 33rd in the battle for a German Berlin. The Charlottenburg *Kommune*, the elite of the criminal underworld, has met its match. The streets belong to us, but 20 members of our unit have been thrown into the prisons of the Republic. The Reds, reassured by this, set out to renew their regime of terror. We will never forget SA Man Gatschke, whom the Red murder pack shot in a cowardly attack on 29 August. Whom did these tramps shoot? Not a capitalist, not an exploiter, but an unemployed worker, who leaves a wife and three children behind. But we won't talk about it any more. For the 33rd there is only one motto: "Be silent and act." I order a state of mourning for Storm 33, until this murder of our comrade Gatschke is avenged.[58]

As the struggle for Berlin entered its final weeks, the situation in Charlottenburg became ever more brutal.

When Hitler was named Reich Chancellor on 30 January 1933, the communists of Berlin feared the worst. They held desperate meetings in several Charlottenburg pubs to prepare emergency plans to meet the crisis.[59] The KPD faced the immediate challenge of survival that first night in the face of what they knew was sure to come—an assault on the neighborhood by Storm 33. The communists, under orders to prepare an attack on the SA, made use of the instruction in armed insurrection given them by the war veteran Theodor Pohle. Leaders such as Kurt Rossel at Zum Hirsch (Wallstrasse) and Richard Hüttig at Tietz (Nehringstrasse)—to name just a few of the men and locales involved—organized the combined efforts of the Rote Frontkämpferbund, Kommunistische Jugendverband, Rote Hilfe, Sportverein Fichte, and five "apartment house protection staffs." The units were armed.

Tension rose as the district awaited the return of Storm 33 from their night of celebration. The pubs were teeming with people. At Döhrmann's on Krummestrasse, a speech on the theme "mobilizing the workers against National Socialism" was heard. With the hour of decision nearing, Gerhard Müller gave an impassioned speech to some seventy workers at the pub Werner:

> I'm taking command today. The Nazis are certain . . . to come down the Wallstrasse. Under no conditions can we let them enter the workers' district. . . . you can't be cowardly any more, it's deadly serious now. Whoever ditches and stool pidgeons on us, we'll take care of, whoever doesn't have the heart better stay at home.[60]

Riding a Harley Davidson motorcycle—an exciting new reconaissance vehicle in the *Kampfzeit*—two communists stationed themselves at the Gotzkowsky Bridge. From there and several other strategic points along Storm 33's parade route, the lookouts telephoned information of the enemy's position to the armed units and crowds of hangers-on in five Charlottenburg pubs, who were anxiously awaiting their call. Returning from the euphoria of a torchlight parade through the Brandenburg Gate, past the Führer and President Hindenburg—the fulfillment of years of longing and sacrifice—the Maikowski Storm did not take the most direct route home. Instead, they went out of their way to march through the nerve center of communist Charlottenburg and to intimidate the inhabitants. They took a route that ran through Moabit, down Helmholz, Dove, Galvini, and Guernikestrasse, past Lützow Square, where Maikowski had played as a boy, and over the Rosinen and Berlinerstrasse. As they entered the Wallstrasse shortly after 11:00 P.M., they were accompanied by Polizeiwachtmeister Josef Zauritz, who marched beside Maikowski at the head of the unit. A young woman who had attached herself to the marching column remarked: "You know, I think something's up here." In the ominous quiet, Maikowski gave the command for a song, and the refrain "Vorwärts an Geschütze und Gewehre, Auf Schiffen, in Fabriken und im Schacht, Tragt über den Erdball, tragt über die Meere, Die Hakenkreuzfahne zur Macht . . ." echoed through the darkened streets. Sensing immediately that an attack was imminent, Maikowski stationed three SA men at the door of each enemy locale. At once the shrill whistle of the communist Rollkommando was heard. Kurt Rossel commanded "Alles raus!" and the communists stormed out of the pubs like swarming bees. Screaming "Arbeitermörder! Nieder! Rotfront" and "Haut die Nazis raus!" they raised their fists defiantly and menaced the SA men marching by. A neighborhood woman, Marie Borchert, beside herself with rage, struck a Brown Shirt and received a cruel blow in return.

Maikowski attempted to maintain order in this wild situation, commanding his men "Eyes front! Keep marching!" Next, with Zauritz beside him, he ran to the end of the column to establish a rear guard. Within seconds, a shot was fired, and the policeman fell to the asphalt, mortally wounded. Next, Maikowski himself fell, the victim of another shot.[61]

At that point, pandemonium ensued. The SA broke ranks and carried Maikowski and Zauritz to the Spreestrasse; there they held the line until a police alarm unit appeared on the scene to restore order. Still alive, Maikowski was rushed in a taxi to the emergency room of Westend Hospital. Then the SA men repaired to their home base at Zur Altstadt, a few blocks away on the Hebbelstrasse. There they anxiously awaited news about their beloved Hans. Word was not long in coming. A witness described the scene in the SA den:

> Here we pass painful time; dead quiet hangs heavily on us . . . Our mood gets darker and darker. Then—it is already past midnight—the telephone rings. Everyone senses it: we'll know now, either he'll get better, or the worst has happened. "Truppführer Buske to the telephone!" Ped works his way with difficulty through the packed locale . . . dead quiet . . . 60, 70 men sit here, but they're all quiet; it's as if they are struggling to hear the voice on the other end of the line. Suddenly Buske lays the telephone back on the receiver; now we know it: Hanne is no more. Our throats choke up with emotion; we hear Ped's voice, even though it's as if through a deep fog: "Our Sturmführer is dead." We all lose our composure. Men who often enough have stared death squarely in the face, men who have become hardened after years of struggle, cannot hold back their tears any longer . . . dear, good Hanne, so you are dead, torn away from your delirious happiness; you, who have fought ten long years for a new Germany . . . Dear, dear Hanne.[62]

Der Angriff reacted with an enraged front-page article the next day:

> The horrible communist blood terror, which tonight cost the death of one of our best Sturmführer and a police officer doing his duty, can be halted only with absolute ruthlessness. These last unspeakable communist deeds of blood have started in motion severe countermeasures which no previous government even conceived of. The Muscovite murder rabble will be shown once and for all, that in the new *national Germany* there will be no place whatsoever for such activities. Informed sources have reported that the government is set to move

forcefully against the KPD. . . . Germany must be cleansed of the blood pestilence of the Moscow Foreign Legion.[63]

The state funeral, which the new regime staged in the Berlin Cathedral on 5 February 1933, was a propaganda *tour de force.* Just after midnight, the bodies of Hans Maikowski and Josef Zauritz were brought to the cathedral, where an honor guard was formed before the high altar by eight SA men from Storm 33 and eight Berlin police officers. The Prussian flag and a helmet and pistol lay over the body of Zauritz, while a swastika flag adorned Maikowski's casket, over which was laid his battle-scarred SA cap. Only a few garlands of flowers were permitted in the cathedral, to foil an alleged communist plot to hide bombs among the wreaths sent by high and low to honor the martyrs.

In the cold of that dark Berlin winter morning, forty thousand SA, SS, Hitler Youth, Stahlhelm and Schutzpolizei formed ranks in the Lustgarten, the scene of so much drama during the Weimar years. Huge crowds of silent onlookers were gathered there, people who had come by tram and subway from the four corners of Greater Berlin to witness the state funeral. The sonorous tones of the cathedral bells peeled over the square in honor of the dead. The sanctuary itself was filled with the party and administrative elite of the new Reich as well as comrades of the victims.

Hitler arrived at 1:00 P.M., wearing a simple SA uniform, and the signal was given for the ceremony to begin. The chords of Bach's Prelude in E-Minor rang through the cathedral, followed by the moving *Trauermusik* from Beethoven's Eroica, the Heroic Symphony. Pastor Hossenfelder, a Nazi party member, spoke on the theme of martyrdom for the nation, linking it to Christian beliefs: "No greater love can be shown, than by those who lay down their lives for their friends." To the accompaniment of the melancholy war song "Ich hatt' einen Kameraden"—Zauritz had served in the Great War—the bodies were carried slowly down the steps of the cathedral, toward the equestrian statue of Frederick the Great on the expansive Unter den Linden Boulevard. At that point an SA airplane appeared out of the clouds like an angel of death, circled the cathedral, and dropped flowers to the throng gathered below. The country at large was not denied the baroque imagery of the ceremony, which was carried in full over a national radio hookup. Fritz Otto Busch, a leading radio commentator reporting from the scene, remarked that he witnessed Frederick the Great dismount from his famous perch high over Unter den Linden, walk slowly to the caskets, and personally thank Hans Maikowski for his loyalty to the death. As Otto Lüpke of the *Völkischer Beobachter* noted "He who dies like this, has done it right!"[64]

With the parade formed, Maikowski's body was placed in an ornate black hearse, complete with a crown and crosses, drawn by four horses draped in black and led by retainers. The men of Storm 33 flanked the

14. State funeral for Sturmführer Hans Maikowski, Berlin Cathedral, 5 February 1933. (Bayerisches Hauptstaatsarchiv.)

hearse. To the sound of muffled drums, the funeral parade commenced its journey through the cold rain down Unter den Linden, to the Reichsehrenmal honoring the German war dead, past Berlin University, over the Spree Bridge, thence to Oranienburger Tor and the Invalidenfriedhof. En route, several bands accompanying the column played death marches. The streets were thronged nine and ten deep at some points. At length, the mournful crowd entered the cemetery where distinguished Prussian military heroes had been buried over the centuries. Hans Eberhard Maikowski was buried close to the resting place of the Red Baron, Rittmeister Manfred von Richthofen, in the shadow of Scharnhorst, Gneisenau, and von Moltke.[65]

Goebbels stepped up to the grave, briefly and poignantly to extol the life of the young Sturmführer. After graphically pointing to three legendary exploits in staccato fashion, Goebbels described the fulfillment Maikowski must have felt as he led Storm 33 through the Brandenburg Gate and past the Führer in his hour of triumph. But tragedy approached:

> And with the flush of the greatness of the hour rushing through his veins, this young Sturmführer marched as always, at the head of his troops, back to his own neighborhood and then was forced—afire with the joy and enthusiasm of the hour—to give up the ghost. Here we stand at his open grave, and this proverb surely fits the one we are about to return to the bosom of mother earth: Perhaps we Germans don't know much about living, but as for death—that we do fabulously! This young man knew how to die, this he could do fabulously. . . . Because of this, we want to raise our flags high up over this grave, and swear over the body of this dead comrade, that . . . one day a flame will arise from his grave, which will illuminate all of Germany.[66]

The truth regarding the death of Maikowski is diametrically opposed to the legend, which was circulated by the Nazi propaganda media and trumpeted again and again in ceremonies held at the murder sight during the first two years of the Third Reich. In fact, the communists had not killed him; instead, his own SA comrade Alfred ("Ped") Buske had committed the crime. The Gestapo protocol on the case was completed in the summer of 1933. Based on the testimony of three reliable witnesses, Standartenführer Hahn and SA men Deh and Lukas, it was destroyed in February 1943 on the orders of SS Oberstgruppenführer Kurt Daluege. But a few remaining documents survived. The first, written by Kurt Daluege— then a Ministerialdirektor in the Interior Ministry—was dated 12 May 1933 and was addressed to Oberregierungsrat Rudolf Diels, also at Interior:

> In the interest of an organized direction of the Maikowski murder case and that of von der Ahe, as well as what we have discovered to be the "Charlottenburg Circle," Kriminalkommissar Lipik from Section I will be named to head the Murder Commission. He will gather the evidence collected by Section I,

Section I, Feldpolizei and SS and will thereafter work closely with Nebe and SS–Section II, Sturmführer Rodde. Kriminalkommissaranwärter Glüss of Section I should also be detailed to him and where possible other officials, above all those who already have been working on the related murder cases.[67]

The second piece of evidence surviving in the Berlin Document Center was occasioned in 1943 by the tenth anniversary of the death of Maikowski. At that time it was suggested in a memorandum to Daluege that "the file on the murder Maikowski-Zauritz be destroyed":

> In the following documents you will find the testimony of the witnesses Hahn, Deh and Lukas on the murder of Maikowski. According to this testimony Maikowski and Zauritz were not shot by communists but by one SA-Mann Buske. The testimony was collected in July 1933 by the Geheimen Staatspolizeiamt. The witnesses had kept the secret for so long, because they did not want to harm the Movement.[68]

Very little is known about the murderer Alfred Buske. According to his NSDAP party book, he held the rank of SA Obersturmführer (first lieutenant), was a member of Storm 33, and was twenty years old when he committed the crime. His occupation was listed as worker. A photograph taken in the spring of 1932 shows him posing next to Hans Maikowski with an adventuresome band of SA men, gathered in a music unit called the Horst Wessel Schalmeienkapelle, which was traveling in Schleswig-Holstein.[69] The group seems the model of SA comradeship, but something went terribly wrong in Storm 33 as it did in so many SA storm units. The motive for the murder may never be known. It probably resulted from hostilities within the Charlottenburg SA, which led to the formation of the antileadership "Charlottenburg Circle." Tensions in Charlottenburg reflected the larger divisions within the SA itself, although the circle's links to the malcontents around Ernst Röhm are unknown. A significant number of SA men sympathized more with the workers, the communists, and their counterparts in the Red Front Fighters League than they did with the bourgeois crowd now calling themselves Nazis. There is every reason to believe that Alfred Buske was a member of this SA underground.

The manner in which the Nazis covered up the Maikowski affair—including the withholding of evidence in a major trial—demonstrated the lengths to which they would go to conform to an official myth, once it was promulgated. The Gestapo had known since the summer of 1933 that the killer was Alfred Buske. But the party sought to intimidate the communists in their strong neighborhood wards in the capital, with the hopes of eliminating potential opposition to the new state. As a result, the authorities went ahead with a sensational trial in the Schwurgericht I beim Landgericht, in the judicial chambers in Berlin-Moabit. The highly publicized proceedings against some fifty-four defendants arrested in connection with the

Charlottenburg disturbances of 30 January 1933 were conducted between October 1933 and January 1934. Despite an exhaustive search to locate the murderer among the accused, the state prosecutor's office was unsuccessful in pinpointing Maikowski's murderer. Left completely in the dark about the state secret in the matter, the writers of the court's judgment began with the revealing words, "Despite the most painstaking efforts of the Prosecutor's Office, it was not able to ascertain who shot these two men." Nevertheless, several defendants were sentenced for periods of up to ten years in prison. With the announcement of the judgment, the court noted: "While the new Germany was bathed in the shining dawn of *völkisch* renewal and the onset of a new era of liberation, the communists were bitter and thunderstruck."[70]

There was other evidence, widely discussed in the communist neighborhoods of Berlin, that the Nazis were attempting to blame the Charlottenburg communists for murders they did not commit. It did not go unnoticed in Stanni and the other Red locales that the memorial plaque to commemorate the exact location where Maikowski fell did not carry the inscription that he had been killed by communists; instead, it read, in part, "He died for Germany."[71] When the NSDAP was certain of something, they claimed it, as the wording of memorials across Greater Berlin in the period attested. Further, one hundred twenty SA men from various Charlottenburg units were taken prisoner by their fellow Nazis and incarcerated in the Charlottenburg police barracks on the Königin-Elizabethstrasse.[72] Many people also took note of the curious circumstances surrounding the shooting of SS Truppführer Kurt von der Ahe—a member of Charlottenburg Sturm 1—on the night of 19 February 1933.[73] This, too, was hushed up by the regime. Furthermore, on New Year's Eve 1934, an SA man was killed by a member of the SS in the Bamberger Hof on the Bismarckstrasse, a victim of an intraparty brawl. All the more curious did it seem that suddenly the name of Alfred Buske, a strapping proletarian lad, appeared in the obituary columns following the conclusion of the Maikowski show trial in January 1934. He was quietly buried in the Luisenstädtische Friedhof, in a section of the cemetery with twenty-one Nazi victims of the *Kampfzeit*.[74] Buske was not listed in the roll of martyrs in the effusive works of hagiography published during the Third Reich.[75]

Despite the evidence, the Nazis held firm to the myth of Hans Maikowski. On the first anniversary of the murder, 30 January 1934, a midnight torchlight ceremony was staged at the scene of the crime on the Wallstrasse. Toward the hour of Maikowski's death, church bells tolled throughout Charlottenburg, summoning the faithful to the ritual of remembrance. Then columns of torch-bearing SA men marched through the streets, bellowing their songs to intimidate the residents. They made their way to the memorial, where the uniformed elite of the Third Reich awaited them.

The notorious Edmund Heines, briefly assuming the role of the good shepherd, had dutifully escorted the parents of Hans Maikowski to the ceremony. Himmler, Göring, and Prince August Wilhelm looked on as the entire SA Standarte West listened to a memorial speech delivered by SA Chief of Staff Ernst Röhm. Ironically, Röhm himself would be gunned down in the "Night of Long Knives" just a few months later, on 30 June 1934.[76]

An identical ceremony took place on the Maikowski anniversary night in 1935, but the cast of characters changed. Goebbels and Victor Lutze, the new SA chief of staff, headed the list of notables who participated.[77] On anniversary day 1937, a small park was commemorated at the corner of Maikowskistrasse and Richard Wagnerstrasse. A larger-than-life statue of the hero was unveiled, as well as a fountain that featured a Siegfried motif. This tailored, green area seemed out of place, surrounded as it was by the drab tenements of proletarian Charlottenburg.[78] In future years, the Nazis gave very little attention to Hans Maikowski.

On the other hand, the image of Horst Wessel took on Homeric dimensions during the Third Reich. His legend was reinforced by the production of a feature film entitled *Hans Westmar,* which had its premiere in December 1933.[79] Based on the hagiographic biography by Hanns Heinz Ewers, and directed by Franz Wenzler, the film glorifies Wessel as a symbol of all SA men. The hero emerges as an exemplary figure, a god among the "Aryans." Emil Lohkamp, who played Wessel, was tall, fair-haired, and afire with enthusiasm. The character Hans, totally under the spell of Hitler and Goebbels, is prepared to be victorious or die in the attempt. Providence has called him to deliver Germany from the shame of Versailles and Weimar and to fight for a regime of law and order, racial harmony, and traditional values.

Above all, Hans is unselfish. He knows no class privileges; he knows only service to the Volk. In one notable scene, he attends a fencing duel with his fraternity brothers. Perched on a windowsill, he looks down to the street below where a ragged column of communists march past, following their leader Ernst Thälmann. The bleakness of their proletarian lives stands in marked contrast to the privileged world of his fellow students. Hans turns to his comrades and passionately declares:

> The real battle is out there, not here with us. The enemy is on the march. I tell you, all of Germany will be won down there, on the street. And that's where we must be—with our people. We can no longer live in our ivory towers. We must join our hands in battle with the workers. There can't be classes anymore. We are workers, too, workers of the mind, and our place now is next to those who work with their hands.

Thereafter he labors as a construction worker on Berlin's massive subway project, side by side with his proletarian brothers. His love of the Volk is so profound that he sublets an apartment on the Grosse Frankfurter Strasse and shares it with his lover, Erna Jaenicke, whom he has saved from a life of prostitution.

From the first to the last scene of *Hans Westmar,* one is reminded of the Soviet specter over Germany. Paul Wegener plays a convincing role as Moscow's agent in control of the German Communist party. A cynical creature of the underworld, he appears as a criminal conspirator, the antithesis of sunny, pure Hans. Viewing the agony of starving, unemployed Germans in their hovels, he utters through his tobacco-stained teeth: "Misery is our best ally." Surrounded by Russian Bolsheviks, Jews, women, and foreigners, he is successful in duping otherwise well meaning Germans. His jowly face framed by a huge hammer and sickle flag, he calls for unceasing political disturbances:

> We're coming down to the last battle. We've got to stage something new every day. Hunger demonstrations! Putsch in the welfare offices! Plunder stores! And then, Soviets in Russia . . . Soviets in Germany . . . and the world belongs to us. Heil Moscow!

It was inevitable that he would plot the murder of Hans Westmar.

Jews are subjected to a vicious attack in the film, most notably in the form of a KPD Reichstag deputy. A cowardly conniver—disheveled and intellectual—he is clearly the enemy of the German people. Having incited a riot by provoking Nazi discussants at a communist rally, he announces his immunity from arrest to the police, who proceed to cart the Germanic protagonist off to prison. The message is clear: international Jewry has joined with Soviet Russia to enslave Germany.

Whereas the fetid city was the Jews' natural milieu, the home of the true German was on the land. In another scene, Westmar is viewed leading his troops on maneuvers in the Prussian countryside. Girding themselves for the approaching battle—they are about to march across Berlin to KPD headquarters in a bold provocation—they strike up old Prussian army tunes as well as Brown Shirt songs of more recent vintage. The impression conveyed is that of a beautiful union of man and nature, featuring the rhapsodic delights of sunshine, fresh air, woods, and the blue sky of Mark Brandenburg. Westmar and his merry band would purify asphalt Berlin of its decadence, "Jewish putrefaction," and discordant materialism.

The real sin of the "Jewish-Bolsheviks" was that they fooled their German supporters. Camillo Ross, who symbolizes all non-Jewish German communists, is presented as a good German who falls victim to historical circumstances beyond his control. Although initially Ross warns Westmar that "proletarians can only be led by proletarians," gradually he realizes that his adherence to the Marxists has been misguided, and he joins the Nazis.

The storied hero's final days, his brutal murder, and his resurrection bring the film to a dramatic climax. Striking from their den of iniquity, a murderous gang locates Westmar in his apartment. The picture of innocence, he is discussing the movement with Jaenicke in the cosy domesticity of a mansard apartment. Upon answering the door, he is struck by a hail of bullets in the face and neck. Footage of the murderers swirling over Hans in a surreal sequence of delirium adds a horrifying touch of cruelty to the murder of this lamb of the Volk.

As Hans awaits death in the hospital, his only thoughts are of the party, his comrades, and the future of Germany. His most tender reveries concern Dr. Goebbels, whose visit to the hospital is the last great event of the Sturmführer's life. He is like a child when recalling Goebbels's words of encouragement: "He said my fever is like that of the Party's. For two long years it lay in fever, in crisis. But now it is healing and moving toward victory." As the last hope for recovery fades away, beloved comrades from Storm 5 tiptoe in stockinged feet past his room for a final glimpse of their leader. Westmar's eyes shine forth with idealism once more, and, summoning his last reserves of strength, he raises his arm in a final salute to his men. The last word he utters is a faltering "Deutsch . . . land!"

Hans Westmar concluded on a highly dramatic note, focusing on the burial of the hero. Following Goebbels's graveside address, a miracle takes place as the scene shifts heavenward, where a beaming Hans Westmar marches boldly to the music of his own composition, holding high the swastika flag, which waves in the ethereal breeze. Finally, the resurrected hero returns to earth and joins in step with the SA on their night of triumph, marching through the Brandenburg Gate and past Hitler on the balcony of the Reich Chancellery. The message of *Hans Westmar* is clear: "He is risen. He is risen indeed!" The nation has been delivered, the Weimar regime overturned, and a tragically divided people—washed in the blood of the martyrs—has become united once more and faces the future with confidence under the leadership of Adolf Hitler.

Goebbels was disappointed with the film. Above all, he felt that no film character could possibly live up to his mythical creation of Horst Wessel. He delayed the premiere of the film, sending it back for reworking and only reluctantly authorizing its release. Further, Goebbels—like so many other Nazis—found Ewers, the author of the book upon which the screenplay was based, a despicable man mired in perversion.[80] Ewers was over sixty years old when he joined the NSDAP, the result of a visit with Hitler and Hess in the Brown House in late 1931. According to Ewers, he was commissioned by Hitler to write the great SA novel on the life of Horst Wessel.[81] What the keepers of the grail did not know was that Ewers, a lawyer turned writer, was in fact a woolly-headed pornographer, whose works, such as *Alraune* and *Vampyr,* appealed mainly to an intellectual and cultural demimonde. According to Ewers, Goebbels banned his play *Stürmer*—adapted from his book on Horst Wessel—the day before it was to open in forty-seven theaters throughout the Reich.[82] Ultimately, all of Ewers's works were banned by the Reichsschriftumskammer, except for the life of Wessel and the controversial Free Corps novel *Riders in the German Night*.[83]

At the same time that Horst Wessel hagiography began to become a national growth industry, various groups found it necessary to defend publicly the good name of their beloved SA leader. At times this situation occasioned quite curious results. For example, Section 10 of the National Socialist German Students League staged a public meeting on 30 May 1933 in the Konzerthaus Clou in Berlin. Advertisements for the rally announced:

> In connection with the National Socialist revolution reports and books have been published abroad, which spread the grossest filth and lies about our Horst Wessel. We're going to take a stand in this matter and fight to get the truth across.

Several authors from abroad were scheduled to speak on the question, including Sefton Delmer (England), Captain Borelli (Italy), General Gantchew (Bulgaria), as well as "a representative from America." They would be joined by Horst's close friend, SA Oberführer Richard Fiedler, the student leader Kreisführer Fritz Hippler, who later became Reichsfilm-intendant, and Ewers.[84]

Part of the Horst Wessel propaganda campaign took place in the courts. Although they had been able to take revenge on Ali Höhler, it had long been a sore point among the Nazis that several of the accomplices to the Wessel murder had escaped the police dragnet in 1930. Accordingly, the Gestapo acted quickly upon receiving an informant's tip in 1934, arresting several individuals involved in the crime. Soon thereafter, a second major Wessel trial was staged, with great fanfare.[85] The communists Sally Epstein and Hans Ziegler, who had stood guard on the street in front of Wessel's apartment that fateful night, were sentenced to death and beheaded in Plötzensee prison.[86]

The myth of Horst Wessel was assiduously cultivated by the Propaganda Ministry.[87] The places where he lived and worked became Stations of the Cross. Shrines were established with appropriate ceremony at his birthplace in Bielefeld, in his Vienna and Berlin dwellings, at the Friedrichshain Hospital, and at his grave site. The KPD headquarters became Horst Wessel Haus, and Bülowplatz was changed to Horst Wessel Platz. The celebration of Wessel anniversaries were commonplace. The hero's mother served as an important stage prop at official ceremonies, and she even appeared with Mussolini on the fifteenth anniversary of the fascist *Miliz* in Rome.

Throughout the peacetime years of the Third Reich, the symbol of Horst Wessel remained a magnet for Nazi propaganda, which embraced all of the arts. On the anniversary of his death in 1936, the Berlin SA staged a ceremony at the Theater am Horst Wessel Platz (*Volksbühne*) before an audience including representatives of the party, the Wehrmacht, officers and men of Herman Göring's proud Horst Wessel Squadron, and relatives of several *Kampfzeit* martyrs. A pageant was presented, written by the SA poet Herybert Menzel, entitled "The SA Lives Forever," with musical accompaniment by Ernst Erich Buder. Following this mystical production, the SA formed up on the Lothringerstrasse under the command of Obergruppenführer von Jagow and marched to the hospital where Wessel had died. After laying a garland of red roses on his pillow, the Standarte marched to his grave in the Nikolai Cemetery to pay him honors. The entire ceremony was carried on a national radio hookup.[88]

On Wessel's birthday in October 1937, Goebbels took the occasion to address a rally of twenty thousand SA men formed on the Küstriner Platz, deep in Wessel's proletarian district of Friedrichshain. The *Völkischer Beobachter* gave a breathless account of the event, which was billed as a celebration "by the entire new Germany of Horst Wessel," staged in "the old battlegrounds in the east of the Reich capital where the immortal SA Sturmführer and standard-bearer of the nation campaigned and fought for Adolf Hitler." This was indeed an emotionally charged event, which was attended by Wessel's mother and sister. Goebbels claimed that he had received the inspiration of the Holy Ghost in the Wessel "death room" en route to the rally, and the participants had been roused by the playing of the festive *Signalhornmarsch* by the SA band. Following a spirited brass fanfare, Goebbels launched into a solemn yet ecstatic exaltation of the martyr. After an emotional recounting of the results of Wessel's sacrifice, Goebbels admonished his audience to hold high the banner drenched in sacrificial blood and to be ever mindful that only through virtuous and heroic struggle could the nation fulfill its potential under the leadership of Hitler. Goebbels could not resist gloating over the victory of his Berlin Old Fighters:

> I greet you in the heart of this once Red city, which we conquered with the Führer, a city which once was the reddest city in Europe after Moscow, and which we have made German once more! That's why we can so proudly say: This is our Berlin! It is your Berlin, SA men! We have won it! Today we can be proud to feel the love and support of the people in this city of millions, who loyally march under this flag, free of communist harassment.[89]

German youths were thoroughly indoctrinated with Wessel propaganda. The heroic warrior theme was an important component of German education, and the Horst Wessel saga was its crown jewel.[90] For example, the Munich *Jungvolk* meeting in the Dietrich Eckart Heim on the anniversary of the hero's death in 1938 heard spoken choruses extolling Wessel, punctuated by the Arioso by Händel and the "Song to the Dead" by Herbert

Böhme, scored for choir and orchestra by Erich Lauer. Poems were also read, including Hans Jürgen Nierentz's "How Men Died," "Choir of the Fallen" by Herybert Menzel, and "You left us, comrade!" by Heinrich Anacker. Finally, Gau Education Director Stölting delivered a speech on Wessel.[91]

The symbolic Wessel theme inspired artists and sculptors to mystic excesses in their creations. Ernst Paul Hinckeldey, winner of the Rome Prize and the *Grosser Staatspreis,* was commissioned to execute a sculpture of Wessel.[92] Hubert Netzer, sculptor of the Nornen Fountain on Munich's Karlsplatz, produced a "Young Siegfried" monument in honor of Wessel. The arms of the hero are raised in victory, holding high his sword. The *Münchener Neueste Nachrichten* noted of the work:

> The National Socialist world view and the symbolically configured world of Nordic-Germanic myth is more and more becoming the subject of the art of sculpture. We see in "Young Siegfried" the symbolic embodiment of the youthful hero and warrior, aflame with the fire of his convictions.[93]

Memorials to Wessel were often placed in beautiful and historic surroundings, most notably in the Teutoburg Forest, where a monument linked him with the heroes of the epic Germanic past. A description of the ceremonies at the Horst Wessel Monument on the anniversary of his death in 1936 carried the following account:

> The Horst Wessel Monument, which lies on the storied ground of the Teutoburg Forest, where long ago Armin freed the Germans from the Roman yoke and Widukind died fighting the French for religious and tribal freedoms, glowed in the red of the swastika flags, which was mysteriously reflected by the torches.[94]

Mystical exercises peaked during the SA's anniversary march for Wessel in the Teutoburg Forest in 1940. Lines from the repertoire of the nationalist worker and poet Heinrich Lersch featured a reincarnated Wessel calling to his men from the shadow of the living dead:

> Wanderer halt! I say to you, when you lie down to sleep tonight, and do not ask the dead soldier: "Who died for me today?" If your last thought is not of me but only of your own happiness, then I'll arise and come to you and kiss you with my mangled mouth and show you my bleeding wound.[95]

During World War II, the spirit of Wessel was conjured up from time to time with the hope of bracing the nation's capital city and the entire country for victory. One such event occurred on Sunday, 23 February 1941, when the Grossdeutsche Rundfunk carried a Horst Wessel memorial ceremony. Major figures in the SA spoke, including Graf Helldorff, as did

Wessel's comrades from the days of the battle for Berlin. According to the *Völkischer Beobachter,* they were all

> comrades who found their way to the Führer through him and who fought the Red subhumans at his side. Comrades who were with him daily and knew him best . . . "the hero of the Brown Revolution." His sacrificial death inspired and passionately inflamed millions who followed. The spirit of Horst Wessel is today the driving force behind the struggle for freedom of the armed services and the homeland of the Greater German Reich.[96]

Year after year SA Chief of Staff Viktor Lutze lauded the hero on his anniversary day, setting an example followed by Nazi literary figures such as Hans Zöberlein.[97]

In time, Horst Wessel memorial ceremonies became so commonplace that his sacred memory threatened to degenerate into a cliché. Goebbels was troubled by this, and he endeavored to retain the inviolability of his symbolic myth. Accordingly, in October 1939 he issued an order that forbade all Horst Wessel memorial ceremonies except those scheduled to take place on the anniversary of his death, 28 February.[98] Goebbels himself in 1940 marched with Storm 5 to the Dr. Goebbels Heimstätte—a home for aged SA warriors in Wessel's old Friedrichshain battlegrounds—where Ernst Paul Hinckeldey's sculpture was unveiled in the courtyard.[99]

Hans Maikowski was resurrected once more on the tenth anniversary of his death, 30 January 1943, at a time when the final pockets of the surrounded Sixth Army were about to surrender at Stalingrad. At that time, Otto Paust—a veteran of the Great War, the Free Corps von Klewitz, and the Berlin SA and author of the "German Trilogy," a series of historical novels on the history of Nazism—published a memorial to Maikowski that summarized the ethos of an entire generation of radicals. Paust's entire being embraced the ideas of comradeship, love of nation, and hatred for the scourge of Bolshevism. For Paust and many nationally minded youth, the fellowship symbolized by Wessel and Maikowski endowed life with its ultimate meaning.[100] The same spirit of the martyrs, they believed, which guaranteed victory in 1933, would once more excite the emotions of the true believers in their nation's hour of dire need. In his visionary memorial to Hans Maikowski, Paust focused on the communist threat and the final campaign against Nazism's hated enemy:

> Whoever knew you, Hanne Maiko, knew that you belonged among those who couldn't bear speeches even after they died. *Your life was the living deed!* And the fallen want to know that their lives live on passionately in their comrades, and that their spirit lives on in them and among those who follow. Hans Eberhard Maikowski, you are with the Great Army in the sky, transcending all that is earthly, and look down on Germany's fateful battle to the death. You can see

with other eyes than we, because you can already envision the victory for which we are fighting and over the din of the pounding guns, the clanging of the Panzers, and the whirling of the motors, you can already hear the symphony of the Peace of Europe . . . and the victorious outcome of our battle to the death against Bolshevism.[101]

V

The Death and Transfiguration
of Hitler Youth Herbert Norkus

Verrauscht sind die Schlachten . . . der Krieg
  ist aus . . .
mit kummerergrauten Haaren
tragen—wir—*Norkus* zum Hügel hinaus
ein Kind noch—von sechzehn Jahren!
Sein Traum war das Sehnen, die deutsche
  Nacht,
das Schicksal der Heimat zu wenden . . .
Darum—wurde—er—viehisch—umgebracht
von ruchlosen Mörderhänden!

Du deutscher Knabe! Du tapferes Kind!
Du fielst . . . indem du warbest
An deinem Grabe flattern im Wind
die Fahnen, für die du starbest . . .
Du fielst wie ein Held in tosender

                              Schlacht,

vom Geiste der Freiheit besessen!
Und wenn lange vergessen die deutsche

                              Nacht—

dich werden wir nie vergessen!

                   Pidder Lüng[1]

In the days of the *Kampfzeit,* no struggle was more fierce than that waged
between the forces of the communists and the Nazis, a battle that had its
counterpart among embattled youth organizations. Nationalist youths,
reared on the tales of heroism in the Great War, were anxious to prove
their manhood and political idealism. Leftists, schooled in the legends of
Lenin, Liebknecht, and Luxemburg, were aflame with enthusiasm and willingly entered into bloody confrontations to win victory for the German
proletariat. The struggle was fought nowhere more bitterly than in Berlin,
where the communists dominated many of the working-class areas of the
city and were determined to maintain their authority at any cost.

Red Berlin was an armed camp, and any group that challenged communist authority paid a blood sacrifice. An undeclared civil war was waged

in the streets and alleys of the city, though the Berlin police endeavored to maintain some sense of order in a period of political chaos. Tales of heroic deeds and legendary exploits arose from the bloodied asphalt of Berlin. The melancholy beauty of Heinrich Zille's sketches of Berlin's proletarian "milieu" gave way to the horror of repeated acts of murder in cold blood. Youth played a major role in this mercilous battle. No comet shone brighter than Hitler Youth Herbert Norkus, whose heroic death and transfiguration won a place of honor for him in the National Socialist pantheon of martyrs.[2]

The epic saga of Herbert Norkus celebrated the exploits of a model Hitler Youth and served to inspire millions of other young Germans. His behavior was seen as an exemplary fulfillment of the central tenet of the organization—that life is but a preparation for a noble warrior's death. Long-suffering, loyal, and devoted to the Führer, the Hitler Youth sacrificed twenty-one lives to blaze a trail for the Third Reich. Herbert Norkus became the standard-bearer of the youthful Immortals, and his blood drenched the magical Blood Flag of the Hitler Youth.[3] The appalling death of Norkus—butchered by a gang of young communists as he was distributing handbills for a party rally in January 1932 in Beusselkietz—lent credibility to Goebbels's demagogic claim that "Bolshevik subhumanity" was loose on the German land. Goebbels and von Schirach created a Norkus myth, whereby "Jewish-Bolshevik beastliness" would not waver even at the murder of a proletarian boy from drab, industrial north Berlin. A child of the Volk, he saw the star of deliverance shining out of the long night of agony, and he followed it across the abyss to greatness. According to the myth, the fighting, dying hero, worthy son and heir of the tradition of Langemarck, became the twentieth-century embodiment of a classic aphorism: "Whom the gods love, they call home at a tender age."

The child-martyr Norkus became a central theme of Hitler Youth propaganda. In the words of Reich Youth Leader Baldur von Schirach:

> This little comrade has become the myth of the young nation, symbol of the self-sacrificial spirit of all the young who bear Hitler's name. Many died in the battle of the young for the Reich; the name "Norkus" embraces all of them in the eternal comradeship of the Hitler Youth. Nothing binds us Hitler Youths together more closely than the knowledge of our brotherly link to this dead boy, nothing is more alive than this murdered one, nothing is more immortal than he who has passed away. I am more proud of this than anything else in my life: that Herbert Norkus belongs to us.[4]

The apotheosis of Norkus was the counterpart to the death, resurrection, and return of Wessel. Whereas the myth of Wessel was solely Goebbels's creation, the saga of Herbert Norkus resulted in great part from the enormously popular film *Hitler Youth Quex*.[5] This work, celebrating Nor-

15. Baldur von Schirach's annual New Year's Day speech to the nation from the grave of Herbert Norkus, Berlin, 1934. (Bayerisches Hauptstaatsarchiv.)

kus's life and death, influenced millions of young Germans to be prepared to sacrifice their lives for Führer, Volk, and Fatherland.

There was little in the background of the historical Herbert Norkus to presage his call to fame. Born in 1916, he was the eldest son of the grenadier Ludwig Norkus, a veteran of the Great War who joined Storm 6 of the Berlin SA in 1929. Norkus's father had lost what little savings he possessed to a confidence man and was employed as an oiler in the Chemisch–Technischen Reichsanstalt factory that lay on the Spandau Canal in Berlin-Plötzensee. His mother had died in a mental hospital in 1931 following repeated communist assaults on the milk store that she ran to help the Norkus family eke out a living in the unstable postwar economy. Herbert lived with his younger brother and father in modest quarters on the factory grounds, which offered them security in a hostile environment. Although he was the son of a worker, Herbert attended the Luisengymnasium on the Zwinglistrasse, the very street on which he was murdered.[6]

To live in Beusselkietz was to know the meaning of poverty and suffering. Life there—just as in the districts of Wedding, Prenzlauer Berg, Friedrichshain, and Neukölln—was difficult indeed. It was said that the sun never shone in much of this tenement complex, which was as depressing as any slum to be found in Europe. Hunger stalked the district, so sensitively reflected in Slatan Dudow's documentary production *Problems of Our Day: How the Worker Lives* (1930). One scene in this film shows an emaciated little girl gazing up at her mother and asking, "Mama, are there people who have warm meals every day?"[7] Unemployment, depression, and hopelessness were the daily fare there, a situation that led to drunkenness as well as physical and sexual abuse of wives and children. Zille, commenting on the situation, noted that "you can kill a human being with miserable living conditions just as easily as with an ax."[8]

Such was the world of Herbert Norkus. He, like the other youths in the area, never tasted the delights of childhood. For him, concrete and dirt fashioned a world of despair, punctuated only by the melancholy tunes of the proverbial organ-grinder making his rounds through the treeless courtyards of the neighborhood. The polluted Spree River snaked its way through the district, oily and disheartening. The Hohenzollern Canal, where commercial barge traffic worked the quays, seemed to be composed not of water at all but of a fetid brew of unsightly industrial sludge, lethal both to human and fish. Phil Jutzi's tragic film *Mother Krausen's Journey to Happiness*—featuring Alexandra Schmitt as the stooped and prematurely aged protagonist who found deliverance in a joint suicide with her child—was, Norkus knew, an authentic reflection of daily life in proletarian Berlin.[9] Youth sensed that radical times called for radical solutions, and the road to salvation seemed deceptively simple. The choice lay between the Soviet star and Ernst Thälmann and the black, white, and red swastika flag of Adolf Hitler.

Whereas the great majority of Moabit youth supported the communists, who ruled the district from the KPD party headquarters in the Karl Liebknecht Haus on Bülow Platz, Herbert Norkus joined the Hitler Youth in 1931. Initially the political *Weltanschauung* of the NSDAP was less important to this child of fourteen than the comradeship and adventure that the party offered. Charges of "Jewish-Bolshevik" betrayal of the Fatherland and attacks against the materialist decadence of the bourgeois Weimar system meant very little to him. Instead, the intensive group life drew him to the Hitler Youth as well as sports, hiking, singing, and play in the great outdoors. But the Hitler Youth's political message was inseparable from this ordered life of comradeship, and his later identification as a political soldier flowed from this source. The organization had the added attraction of being composed of youth and led by youth; youth promised salvation. In the words of von Schirach: "Holy Flame of youth, you are the light in the darkness! You will show us the path which leads to the morning's dawning, the way of loyalty, the way of Adolf Hitler."[10] The Führer guaranteed deliverance from the dark tenement world of depression Berlin and a grand future for the entire nation.

According to all accounts, Norkus was a devoted Hitler Youth. He delighted in the rhythm of daily activities in the organization, which afforded a structure to his life after his mother died. Pack meetings, rallies, propaganda work, music, and weekends in the country all provided a welcome relief from the tedium of slum life. His activities in the Naval Hitler Youth offered the opportunity for boating in the waters of Teltow Park in east Berlin. He was fascinated by contact with inspiring heroes of World I, such as Zeppelinführer Eisenreich, who captured his imagination with tales of air battles over France.[11] These were days of fulfillment for the lad. According to the chronicle of his unit leader Kameradschaftsführer Peter Mondt:

> Life was so rich and colorful, now that he was in the group. In the afternoon when he had the Bahnhof Beusselstrasse behind him and when he smelled smoke from the ships and breathed in the air of spring, and when he wound his way along the canal under the old trees, then he began to see images before him. He saw the group grow to a whole column, and he saw the misguided boys from the Commune fall in step and join in the singing, then he saw a huge, brown army of youth with a sea of flags and pennants, he saw the Führer, and he saw how his eyes danced and glowed in the knowledge that the nation's youth were united and marching in unison toward one goal.[12]

The joy of comradeship came at a high price. Violence, intimidation, and danger were a way of life for the Hitler Youth in Beusselkietz, where a mere fifteen or twenty boys faced what their commander called "a pack of hundreds of hoods from the Commune, criminals, pimps, and the assorted collected trash of subhumanity."[13] Crudely mimeographed flyers,

which the communists attached to walls and buildings in the district, reflected the nature of the threat:

> Anti-Fascists! Come forth! The S. A. bandits are planning a punitive expedition
> against the workers of Moabit Tuesday at 5:00. Let's put an end to the treach-
> erous deeds of this murderous rabble! Appear in massive numbers on Tuesday
> afternoon at 5:00 in front of the Nazi barracks at Huttenstrasse 3. Drive the
> murderous Brown plague out of proletarian Moabit.
>
> —The Revolutionary Workers of Moabit[14]

Often enough violence erupted into bloody confrontation. *Der Angriff*
headlined a report of one incident in its characteristically heated style: "Red
murder bands are on the loose!—The Red murder plague continues its
rampage!" According to the story:

> Eleven-year-old boy struck down by the Reds! Yesterday evening a large crowd
> of communist rabble gathered in Beusselkietz. The tramps loitered about the
> street awaiting the chance to pounce on unsuspecting National Socialists. They
> got their sights on the "Angriff" salesboy, who has a stand at the corner of
> Turm and Beusselstrasse. But there were police in the area, and they were
> reduced to voicing their hostile threats. But when they came across an eleven-
> year-old Hitler Youth on Huttenstrasse, the ragged pack fell upon him and
> bestially struck him to the pavement. They followed this up on the Beusselstrasse
> where they attacked an SA man, and mishandled him in the same way.[15]

Norkus knew the meaning of fear, but he took seriously the plea of the
Reich youth leader for a spirit of self-sacrifice among the corps during the
decisive phase of Germany's political crisis.[16] On many occasions his survival
came from luck and a pair of fast-running legs. Pursued by young communists, he would dash across the Jungfern Bridge and take cover in the
pine forest around Johannes Cemetery. At one point he was cornered and
given the choice of joining the Rote Jungfront within a week or of being
killed.

Ironically, the words of a song, which Norkus sang for his Hitler Youth
brothers, were strangely prophetic:

> There's no retreat for us,
> We'll stand man for man
> As firm as German oaks . . .
> And should out of our hot wounds
> Red blood come flowing forth,
> We'll die like Hitler Youths
> From Beusselkietz Berlin.[17]

The Hitler Youth of Beusselkietz grew under the leadership of young
Gerhard Mondt, and it was a constant irritation to the communists that the

group continued to operate despite their efforts to destroy it. As it turned out, Hitler Youth activities also threatened the renegade Nazis gathered under Captain Stennes—the same desperadoes who staged an intraparty coup in Berlin in 1930, trashing Goebbels's offices in the Hedemannstrasse. The Stennes faction was also determined to put an end to the Hitler movement. Strangely, it was a temporary alliance of the outlawed Rote Frontkämpferbund, the Rote Jungfront, and the Stennes faction organized in the National Sozialistische Kampfgemeinschaft Deutschland that led to the death of Herbert Norkus. His death involved a tangled web of conspiracy, treachery, and betrayal.[18] The events were shaped in the smoky neighborhood pubs of the proletarian district of Moabit, where unemployed workers lounged about drinking schnaps and mugs of beer for hours and days on end.

From his headquarters at Fleischmann's tavern on the Winterfeldtstrasse, Stennes cultivated his connections with the KPD Central Committee.[19] Stennes's section chief, Bernhard Lichtenberg, acting without the knowledge of his boss, provoked the crime when he called for an assault against the Moabit Hitler Youth on the morning of Sunday, 24 January 1932.[20] Lichtenberg had a link to the Stennes foot soldier Johannes Kuhlmann, who worked as a baker's apprentice at the Bäckerei Sorge with Gerd Mondt. For some time, Kuhlmann had been informing on the activities of Mondt's Hitler Youth section as well as SA Storm 32. Kuhlmann learned that the Hitler Youth planned a propaganda blitz through the heart of the 'Rostocker Kietz' at dawn the next Sunday. Kuhlmann tipped off the KPD section chief in Moabit, Georg Stolt.[21] Stolt was the leader of the forbidden Red Front Fighters League in the district, which operated throughout Berlin from its underground headquarters at the Kaffeesachse in Charlottenburg.[22] Kuhlmann promised Stolt's shock troops ten mugs of beer for the life of the Hitler Youth leader Mondt, and they shook hands to seal their agreement.

As a result, late on the night of Saturday, 23 January, Stolt put three communist units on alarm readiness. Some fifty young men and boys spent the night before the assault in the dingy rooms of Otto Marx's pub on Oldenburgstrasse, a KPD hangout. In these cramped quarters where the Rote Hilfe often met, Stolt instructed his men on the ambush. They were armed not with guns but with knives and the assorted fighting paraphenalia favored by street hooligans in the Weimar period. In the black of night, they departed in small groups from the rear of the tavern to avoid alerting the police, who kept the Beusselkietz area under constant surveillance. Fanning out throughout the district, they began to stalk their prey in the fog.[23]

At dawn, six Hitler Youths under the command of Scharführer Mondt moved rapidly through the tenements of the Beusselkietz, distributing flyers with the following message:

We are attacking! Public meeting of the Hitler Youth.
To speak: Pg. Edzardi, "Swastika or Red Star"
        Jg. Axmann
Theme: "What we want"
        Discussion
Thursday, 28. January, 8:00 P.M.
                Hansa-Säle, Alt Moabit 48
                Hitler Youth
                Beusselkietz-Hansa[24]

Within minutes Mondt sensed that something was wrong. Out of the darkness, a young man whom he recognized as a communist passed his group menacingly, riding his motorcycle with the lights off and speeding away. Mondt immediately commanded that Rostockerstrasse be avoided, one of the Reddest streets in Berlin and the scene of some of the worst fighting on "Bloody May Day" in 1929. Despite this diversion, within minutes the communists were hot on the heels of their foe. Mondt fired blanks from his pistol, which gave several of his boys the opportunity to get away.[25] Johannes Kirsch, who was paired with Norkus, was able to escape his pursuers by hiding behind an oversized garbage can in an apartment building.[26]

Herbert Norkus was not so fortunate. Dashing down the Gotzkowskistrasse, he turned into Zwinglistrasse. There he tried desperately to enter a wholesale milk establishment, but a night watchman refused him admittance. In no time some ten pursuers had pounced on him, and he fell to the pavement. Jumping to his feet, Norkus ran for his life. He tried without success to find a haven in several buildings down the street, including the Kirschner School, which he attended. Once more the communist band surrounded him, plunged their knives into his body, and trampled him mercilessly. Yet again he lunged to his feet and ran, leaving a trail of blood behind him. At Zwinglistrasse 4, he collapsed in the vestibule of a modest cleaning establishment. Marie Jobs, a working girl, testified that she was awakened by the commotion. Running to her door, she heard the victim say to her mother, "Help me. I've been attacked." She described the horrible scene that followed: "The young man lay right at our corridor door, his head lay on the entrance, his coat balled up at his feet. His little scarf clung to his coat. Once more he said to me in a weak, rattling tone, 'Help me.' "[27] He was rushed by taxi to the emergency room of the nearby Moabit Municipal Hospital, where he died shortly thereafter.[28]

The police immediately set up a dragnet throughout the Beusselkietz, searching for the murderers in the notorious communist pubs Lange (Rostockerstrasse 28) and Schall (Sickingenstrasse 4). The Polizeipräsidium sent the famed "Murder Commission" into action, which began an intensive series of interrogations among the communist street gangs, Hitler Youth, and witnesses. Within a matter of days the police had pieced together a fairly accurate description of the circumstances surrounding the murder. They posted wanted notices throughout the city offering a reward of five hundred *Reichsmark* for information leading to the arrest of the alleged perpetrators: Willi Simon, Bernhard Klingbeil, and Harry Tack. All of them were KPD supporters who had been spirited off to hiding places by the Rote Hilfe.[29] Several months later, a sensational trial took place in the Schwurgericht am Landgericht I in Moabit, which led to the sentencing of several of the individuals involved in the crime. Only years thereafter was it learned that Simon, Klingbeil, and Tack had escaped to the Soviet Union.[30]

On the morning of the murder, Goebbels was addressing a rally in the Sports Palace when the news arrived of the murder of Herbert Norkus. A shocked audience responded with bitter cries of "Revenge!". Goebbels— always a timely improviser—denounced the communists, and in the coming days he launched a vicious assault against his adversaries. He struck the leitmotiv of the Norkus propaganda in a tawdry, yet moving, lead story in *Der Angriff* that was a study in poetic imagery. Focusing on the corpse of Herbert Norkus, he wrote:

> There in the bleak, gray twilight, yellowed, tortured eyes stare into the emptiness. His tender head has been trampled into a bloody pulp. Long, deep wounds extend down the slender body, and a deadly laceration tears through his lungs and heart. . . . Yet it is as if life stirs anew out of pale death. Look now, the slender, elegant body begins to move. Slowly, slowly he rises as if conjured up by magic, until he stands tall in all his youthful glory right before my trembling eyes. And without moving his lips, a frail child's voice is heard as if speaking from all eternity: "They killed me. They plunged the murderers's daggers into my breast and mangled my head. . . . This happened only because I—still a child—wanted to serve my country. . . . *I am Germany*...one of you millions. . . . What is mortal in me will perish. But my spirit, which is immortal, will remain with you. And it . . . will show you the way. Until the Reich comes."[31]

The elaborately staged funeral for Herbert Norkus offered a vehicle for Goebbels to focus on the heroic death theme. For twenty-four hours the body was attended by a guard of honor of Moabit Hitler Youths at the mortuary of the Dorotheenstädtische Gemeinde on the Hannoversche Strasse. Remarkably, Norkus lay in an open casket, a cruel if effective dramatization of the brutality of his death. On the afternoon of 29 January 1932 the coffin, draped with the flags of the Hitler Youth and the Marine Jungschar, was moved with all honors to the New Johannes Cemetery in Plötzensee for burial. Tears of mourning alternated with declarations of triumph, as the party elite joined units of Hitler Youth, SA, and SS in the cortege that wound its way through the forest cemetery. There Goebbels engaged in rhetoric of pathos, calling for revenge and atonement while promising that the child's blood shed on Germany's road to freedom would be redemptive.[32]

Goebbels described the burial in his diary on 29 January 1932:

> We bury Hitler Youth Norkus in biting cold. I speak from the heart to the children and men who have gathered about the small casket. The father of this boy is brave beyond description. A simple worker, ashen gray with worry in his face, holds his arm high in a salute during the Horst Wessel Song, singing with a mixture of rage and bitter pride: "Die Fahne hoch!" Out in front of the gates of the cemetery the Red mob awaits its next victims. One day this rabble will have to be liquidated like rats once and for all.[33]

Despite the tragic circumstances of the death, it was a successful propaganda theme. Prince Friedrich Christian zu Schaumburg-Lippe, who served on Goebbel's staff, described the effect the graveside services had on those attending:

> It was in harmony with the desperation of the times and the danger of the moment. . . . The torches at the casket shone far beyond the borders of Berlin and burned in our hearts forever and ever. . . . I myself became a National Socialist by and through the death of Herbert Norkus. Such a death was far less a national than a socialist deed. Such a sacrifice meant that thousands and thousands came over to our flag, people who before were repressed by the chains of class and caste.[34]

The bourgeois press reacted with horror and condemned the murder, lamenting the continuing political crisis. With their own fallen to mourn, the KPD responded with unconcealed contempt. Willi Münzenberg's communist press trust geared up for a propaganda counteroffensive. Typical of the response was a feature in *Die Welt am Abend,* which described the murder as the result of a chance encounter. According to this report, a group of workers "happened to be passing by" when they were assulted by some twenty-five Nazi hoodlums who fired their revolvers in all directions. "Apparently the knife which struck Norkus was really meant for a worker."[35]

The Hitler Youth responded with fiery indignation and calls for revenge. *Der junge Sturmtrupp* decried the murder in an issue headlined "The Youngest Blood Witness for Hitler's Cause: Herbert Norkus Murdered!" Gotthart Ammerlahn mirrored the determination of the radical nationalist youth at its hour of destiny:

> What happened . . . is beginning to be the order of the day in this, the fourteenth year of November Germany: political lust murders of young German workers, bestially committed and financed by Moscow Jews. . . . If we want to live, this crowd must be annihilated! . . . Because we are Germany![36]

Ten days after the murder of Norkus, eighteen-year-old Hitler Youth Georg Preiser was killed in Berlin. This brought tension to a new high, and once again *Der junge Sturmtrupp* reaffirmed the determination of the Hitler Youth:

> We will fight on with proud courage! . . . *Can a people, can a Movement go to ruin, whose youngest fighters already know the meaning of dying for the Fatherland, like these two Berlin Hitler Youths have shown!* Comrades . . . prepare for the day of victory. Germany awake![37]

The communists were appalled that the ground had hardly settled over the grave of Herbert Norkus before it became a Nazi shrine. Within two weeks Hitler spoke to the Hitler Youth of Berlin at the Tennishalle im Westen, personally greeting the hero's Moabit comrades at a rally that featured combined units of Hitler Jugend, SS, and National Socialist students.[38] Baldur von Schirach placed the name of Herbert Norkus at the top of the list of the youthful Immortals, declaring 24 January as a national day of commemoration for all fallen Hitler Youths. Thereafter it became an important anniversary in the ritual calendar of the Third Reich.[39] The flag of *Schar* 2 (Hitler Jugend "Beusselkietz-Hansa") became the Blood Flag of the Hitler Youth. A commemorative tablet was later consecrated at the building where Norkus died, bearing the simple inscription "He Gave His Life For Germany's Freedom."[40] Thereafter, memorial plaques were erected throughout the country.

During the first weeks of terror after Hitler took power, two thousand Berlin Hitler Youth, protected by massed formations of police, staged a provocative march through Wedding and Moabit—two of the capital's strongest communist strongholds—en route to a memorial service at the grave of the martyr in Plötzensee.[41] Throughout the Reich countless ceremonies were held in honor of Norkus.[42] Every New Year's Day, Reichsjugendführer von Schirach appeared at Norkus's grave. From this hallowed place he issued marching orders to the Hitler Youth in a ceremony transmitted by all radio stations.[43]

The death of Norkus lent credence to the myth of reawakened German youth, which Hitler proclaimed at the Potsdam Reich Youth Rally in October 1932. Conjuring up the spirits of Norkus and his bloodied comrades, he called their sacrifice a "symphony of Germany's life source":

> What evil can befall a people whose youth sacrifices everything to serve the great ideal of National Socialism. . . . German youth is truest to its people when it finds itself in the greatest danger. German youth, what you glorify in your epic tales and songs, you yourselves must strive to become, so that one day your people will be worthy of a song of heroism. . . . It will be the happiest memory of your youth that as young boys you looked danger squarely in the face . . . and

that through your loyalty and readiness to go the limit you created the new Germany.[44]

The Norkus myth was popularized through both film and literature. Karl Aloys Schenzinger's novel, *Der Hitlerjunge Quex,* was a considerable success; it sold one hundred ninety thousand copies in less than two years and provided the basis for the screenplay of *Hitler Youth Quex.*[45] Far more than a tedious chronicle, the novel rendered historical reality into a sensitive morality play. The suffering of the Norkus family, the desperation of the unemployed father, and the suicide of Norkus's mother are credible themes, and Schenzinger skillfully wove a symbolic *völkisch* tapestry out of rather commonplace—if tragic—raw material.

The author treated Norkus (Heini Völker) as a modern child-redeemer.[46] His description of Heini's attraction to the Hitler Youth is at once lyrical and visionary. Forced by his father to attend a weekend outing with the Moabit communist youth, Heini was disturbed by the group's disorderly behavior. Their motley attire was but an outward sign of inner degeneration and stood in marked contrast to the orderly, colorful uniforms of the Hitler Youth. In Schenzinger's portrayal, alcohol, tobacco, and sex were the order of the day in this communist youth gang. Heini felt totally out of place among the ragtag clique, which proudly called itself "North Star" Moabit. What he longed for was the joy of wholesome comradeship and the purity of sunshine, forests, and lakes.

Heini escaped from the communist encampment the first night, and, creeping through the woods, he saw a great light. From afar he heard the stirring songs of nation and glory, and his heart pounded with excitement. Suddenly he saw boys and girls in uniforms, the picture of contentment and harmony. Their eyes were riveted on their leader, and Heini could hear the words "Führer" and "the movement" and "each giving his life to the other." He was ecstatic as what seemed to be a thousand voices struck up the passionate chords of "Deutschland über Alles." German youth on German soil, singing the most German of songs in a German forest! Henceforth he knew where his true home must always be—with these brave comrades.

Schenzinger lost no opportunity in his novel to emphasize the theme of social justice in the Hitler Youth, which he characterized as a bearer of the *Volksgemeinschaft,* transcending caste and class. The "young nation" was symbolized by the uniform of the organization. The day on which Heini Völker received his new uniform, he was happier than ever before in his life. The Bannführer—a model of "Aryan" purity and uprightness—spoke to him in nearly religious terms about its true meaning:

Heini, you have hundreds of thousands of comrades throughout the country. They all wear the same shirt you have on, the same insignia, the same stripes on the arm, the same cap. The uniform isn't some decoration or parade ground attire, my boy. It is the clothing of the community, of comradeship, of our ideology, of the unified organization! Do you understand? It makes us all equal, and gives the same to all and demands the same from all. He who wears such a uniform doesn't have desires of his own any more; he has only to obey.[47]

And obey he did. Heini was conscientious and industrious, ever ready and swift as Hermes. He was given the nickname "Quex" because he carried out orders faster than quicksilver. Heini was a good comrade and knew no fear.

Heini learned at first hand the joy of class unity when he visited the home of Fritz Dörries, a fellow Hitler Youth. The Dörries villa on the Altonaer Strasse in the Tiergarten represented another world when compared to Heini's crowded proletarian quarters. He was anxious, knowing that the Spree River, which he crossed at the Gotzkowsky Bridge, stood like a moat separating the rich and the poor. Instead of being patronized by this upper-middle-class family, Heini was received openly and as an equal. Frau Dörries's attitude signaled the dawn of a new era, and Ulla, Fritz's blond teenage sister, a member of the Bund deutscher Mädel, radiated a nearly divine, virginal glow on the young guest. But it was Fritz who won Heini over with his attack on wealth, the capitalist spirit, and elitist traditional education. Learning was needed, to be sure, but for a nobler purpose, for swift action:

I want to train myself, outwardly and inwardly, to become a model of courage. I want to feel my blood flowing, and that of others who are of the same blood. We have to develop an organic community again. Today we just have bastards. The word "Volk" has become a joke. We should be ashamed to show ourselves to a herd of deer or even elephants. They've got the sense to breed only with their own. . . . the zoo is the best university of all. . . . With us Hitler Youth there are no classes. There are only those who get the job done and parasites, and those we'll throw out.[48]

Heini was warmed by the comradeship of the Hitler Youth, and he became a paragon of good humor, courage, and devotion. "Castle Beusselkietz," the Hitler Youth lair, was his milieu, and he joyfully played piano accompaniment for the spirited songs of the movement, which proclaimed the light of the dawn in the east. Music had the effect of a tonic on Heini, encouraging him to serve the cause heroically. The song of the Hitler Youth, which called for self-sacrifice, had a special attraction for him:

Our flag waves before us
Our flag is the new era,
Our flag leads us to eternity,
Yes, our flag means more than death.[49]

Schenzinger reserved his most passionate description for the death of Heini, a thinly veiled parallel with the Resurrection. His Beusselkietz comrades gather around the bed of their dying friend:

> Finally they see the little face in the pillow, flushed, now and then wincing around his mouth and nose, sighing and groaning occasionally. So this is Quex, the Bengal. His friends are overcome with sympathy, and anger gives way to the call for revenge. There they stand . . . helpless before the incomprehensible. . . . has he already passed away? No, he's moving. Suddenly there is a scream. Heini is sitting up in bed, his eyes wide open. He is singing. They don't recognize the words, but they know the melody. It's the song they sing every day, every evening together, on every march. Everyone knows what it means— death is singing here.[50]

Not a soldier fallen in France, yet a soldier nonetheless. Heini Völker—a good comrade—had passed away.

The ennoblement of Herbert Norkus awaited the film devoted to his life. The *Ufa* (*Universum Film AG*) production *Hitler Youth Quex* was filmed in Neubabelsberg in the summer of 1933 and was released in September of the same year. Directed by Hans Steinhoff and employing Karl Ritter as production director, it enjoyed legendary success in the annals of cinema.[51]

Hitler Youth Quex was under the honorary direction of Baldur von Schirach, who put great store on the effect it would have as a symbol of heroism for the postwar generation.[52] A stellar cast joined Jürgen Ohlsen as Quex, and units of the Berlin Hitler Youth were also featured in the film. Heini's father was played by the massive figure Heinrich George, and his mother was sensitively portrayed by Berta Drews. Claus Clausen was a convincing Hitler Youth Bannführer, and Hermann Speelmans took the role of the sympathetic Beusselkietz leader, Stoppel. Karl Meixner, cast as the shadowy figure Wilde, was a Nazi version of the incarnation of the "Jewish-Bolshevik" will to destruction.

Hitler Youth Quex, a blend of historical fact and myth, contains all of the elements of a passion play: an innocent blond child; a desperate mother who attempts a joint suicide with her son; a drunken father drawn to communism for reasons beyond his control; the dark slums of starving Beusselkietz; German communists as tools of a foreign power; idealistic and heroic Hitler Youth; the redemptive death of a lamb of the Volk; and the promise of regeneration of the nation through Adolf Hitler. Schirach found the film a noble chapter in German history celebrating "eternal youth which knows neither darkness nor dawning," thus joining Goethe's Faust, Beethoven's Ninth Symphony, and the will of Adolf Hitler at the intersection of gods and men.[53]

Hitler Youth Quex reflects the theme of suffering and despair in the

Weimar Republic in a gripping manner, and its message is compelling. Both heartless capitalism and criminal Bolshevism are found wanting. The troubled Völker family is symbolic of the German nation as a whole. The father has been out of work for several years and is deeply depressed. The left-leaning actor Heinrich George gave vent to his true political instincts in this role, and he is at once a titanic and elemental force. Völker's brutal treatment of his wife and son clearly is not the result of faulty character; instead, his cruelty is caused by the miseries of the social system. He has become a fat, dissipated drunkard because the inequities of the capitalist system have made him a forgotten man, fated to stand in endless lines awaiting a minimal welfare payment. There never was a joyful Christmas in his tenement home, seldom a happy moment for lovable Heini and his mother.

Völker is a man conscious of his class identity—a proletarian to the core. In a singularly touching scene, he acknowledges Heini's manhood and makes an emotional declaration of his political creed. The time has come for Heini to declare for the party and to join the communist youth movement. Völker turns to his son and says:

> Look, there's a lot going on today that you can't understand, but we proletarians have to save our skin—that's what it's all about! Look how we live here, your mother and you and I—it wasn't always like this, there were better days—before. But my God, we've been derailed. I wanted to do more for you, and many was the night my head was spinning as I tried to find a way out for us (his voice breaking), but no work, no income for years, that wears you down. . . . And now you young ones must help. You must sign on with us, with us old ones! Otherwise we'll all be destroyed.[54]

Finally he gives Heini the keys to the apartment, signaling his acceptance of his son as an adult and a fellow communist.

Heini, caught in a dilemma, appreciates his father's love, yet he feels that his political solution is completely wrong. True to himself, he declares for the Hitler Youth. According to the Nazis, loyalty to parents must give way to political truth. One night his father overhears him singing the words of the Hitler Youth anthem to his mother, who has clung in desperation to the chimera that Heini would take the line of least resistance and join the communist youth. Fatherly love turns to rage, and Völker beats Heini, forcing him to sing the *Internationale*. In a pitiful scene, Heini—the battered victim of the battle of two world views—chokes out the hated refrain. His troubles are only beginning.

Heini's mother suffers even more than he does, being constantly subjected to brutal beatings and harassment by her husband. Undernourished, pale, and old beyond her years, she carries the weight of the world on her shoulders. Berta Drews is the quintessence of eternal motherly love in her role as a bearer of grief. She is a victim of the political and economic system, and her life is in shambles. She seems to live only to sacrifice for her beloved son. Sensing that young Heini might well be killed by the communists, she makes a decision in despair to commit suicide and kill him herself as an act of mercy. The orchestra strikes up a discordant, throbbing cacophony skillfully interwoven with the mother's love motif, preparing the audience for the haunting frames that follow. In an unforgettable scene, with the silver lights of the city giving an eerie cast to their skin, Frau Völker kisses her son goodbye and whispers, "Now everything will be all right." She turns on the gas of her stove, never to reawaken. Heini, on the other hand, is rescued from death only to meet a more terrifying end.

Hitler Youth Quex is striking in its focus on international communism. More than in any other film made in the Third Reich—including *Hans Westmar* and *SA Mann Brand*—the stereotype of the "Jewish-Bolshevik" presented in Steinhoff's film is devastating. The Communist party is viewed as a pack of marauding wolves with but one goal in mind—to destroy what they cannot control. Traitors and agents of the Soviet Union, they sing of human rights while dispatching their notorious Rollkommandos to carry out their nefarious deeds. They work only for the welfare of the Soviet Union, never for their own German nation and Volk.

When the devil took human form, he came as Wilde, and his followers are the gangsters and shadowy figures who compose the neighborhood KPD. His physiognomy is calculated to reflect an inner nature of decomposition; here, indeed, was a "subhuman," the product of miscegenation, venereal disease, and criminality. Unshaven, squint-eyed, and repulsive, he was the incarnation of Bolshevism. The gutter was his proper milieu. To see him gathered with his comrades in a smoky tavern beneath posters of Lenin and Stalin was to know a twentieth-century Judas. He led the assorted criminals who set out to destroy the Beusselkietz Hitler Youth, the noble vangaurd in the cause of Germany's regeneration.

Promiscuous sex is also a tool of the enemy, and the loose virtue of a communist street girl, Gerda, is boldly portrayed by Rotraut Richter. Her raw sexuality is devoid of Nordic refinement. Gerda seduces Hitler Youth Gundler, utterly ruining him for future work in the service of Adolf Hitler. She plies her erotic wares for the protagonist as well, but the purity of the future martyr remains unsullied. In young Völker's estimation the girls in the ranks of the Bund deutscher Mädel were much more desirable. Above all he is attracted to Ulla, whose close-cropped blond hair, gentle features, shining eyes, and enthusiasm for the cause stand in marked contrast to Gerda, the painted street girl, a walking catalogue of Berlin vice. On the other hand, what glory it was to behold sunny Ulla in command of her BdM unit. How proudly she took part in the pagan incantations over the crackling summer solstice fire! With such leadership the German nation was assured a heroic future.

Hitler Youth Quex presented Steinhoff and Ritter with a rare opportunity to romanticize the role of youth in the "rebirth" of Germany. Quex is the son any mother and father would have cherished. He unites in his person all of the best qualities of idealistic youth: courage, vision, unselfishness, and love. He is at once bold, ingratiating, and ever ready to serve. It was these qualities that endeared him to his comrades, and they demonstrated their love for him. After Heini's first brush with death, Fritz and Ulla lead a group of comrades to the hospital to visit their young friend. There they present him with a new Hitler Youth uniform. Star-struck by this show of acceptance, Heini thanks them, affirming that this is the happiest day of his life. Thereafter the Hitler Youth organization assumes the role of his surrogate family. He has need of the support of his fellows. He loses his mother, and his father sells the family's furniture to a secondhand dealer for a few marks and closes the apartment. The party is now the boy's only home.

Variations on this theme follow in a remarkable scene in the garden of a hospital, a study in contrast of the communist and Nazi world views as portrayed in the film. Heini's father and his Hitler Youth commander visit the boy simultaneously. Claus Clausen, who plays Bannführer Cass, is a model "Aryan"—blond and upright, pure of heart and soul. Reflecting on the eternal spirit of youth, with its wanderlust and love of adventure, he fascinates Heini with his enthusiasm. The question he asks is in fact directed to all German youth: "Where does a boy belong today? Two million boys volunteered in the Great War!" he continued. "They were all sons of a father and above all of a mother! And where did they belong?" Heini's turns the question around and asks, "Where do I belong then? With my class brothers, that's where. And where I belong, the boy belongs too!"

The next verbal exchange between the two leads to the conversion of Völker to National Socialism:

> Bannführer: "With your class brothers . . . with the
> Internationale you mean?"
> Völker: "Of course, with the Internationale!"
> Bannführer: "Where were you born?"
> Völker: "In Berlin of course!"
> Bannführer: "Well, where is that anyway?"
> Völker: "On the Spree!"
> Bannführer "On the Spree, right! But where? In what country?"
> Völker: "For heaven's sake, man. In Germany naturally."
> Bannführer: "In Germany, yes! In our Germany! Think
> about that."[55]

Viewers of the film are left with the indelible impression that the boy's only sensible alternative is to follow Hitler; to serve the cause of the red star is to be a traitor to the nation.

The struggle for the Fatherland led to Heini Völker's tragic death, yet at the same time it guaranteed him immortality. He becomes more active than ever in the cause of Adolf Hitler. The Bannführer withdraws him from the Beusselkietz sector, because he is on the communists' murder list. Yet Heini longs to return to the neighborhood where he knows every store and apartment, every street and alley. He confronts the Bannführer, playing on his sense of honor and duty: "You've always said that to be a Hitler Youth is to be a soldier, . . . and you were an officer in the war. . . . Did you forbid your soldiers from going into the front lines because there would be some shooting?" Cass relents and Heini beams at the prospect of participating in the battle for the Fatherland.

The scenes in connection with Heini's murder evoked an intense response on the part of great numbers of viewers who saw the film during the Third Reich. Not sensing that his end is near, Heini saves the day for the Nazi propaganda effort in Beusselkietz through quick-witted improvisation. He spends his few remaining marks for flyers to replace those the communists have cast into the Spree River. Racing through the district on his mission, Heini's smile of confidence and his joyous enthusiasm are juxtaposed to the dark and ugly world of sooty tenements that conceal the murderers who are stalking him. Precisely at that point the music of Herbert Windt and Hans-Otto Borgmann proved most compelling. The persecution motif gives way to the drums and trumpets of the Hitler Youth anthem, thus signaling the hero's imminent death.

The recurrent shrill double whistle—the communists' crude yet effective alarm system in the ghetto—rings out, and the Rollkommando swarms into the darkened streets prepared for action. A horrifying expression of fear crosses Heini's face, and he runs for his life. Finding all escape routes blocked, he dashes for the carnival field and takes cover in an amusement tent. The inhuman Wilde and his bellowing followers join in hot pursuit, finally discovering him there. An ungodly shriek pierces the ugly Berlin dawn, as the drunken, unsightly Moscow hit men carry out their evil deed.

In a final scene, Fritz and other comrades of the Hitler Youth rush to the side of the dying boy, whose eyes are fixed on heaven. As if already in a transfigured state, Heini strikes up the words of the song of the flag—"Unsere Fahne flattert uns voran!"—and dies. A heavenly scene of resurrection opens up, and several converging columns of marchers—the Immortals—take up the chorus of the song that Heini began. This baroque display is bathed in sunshine and gorgeous billowing clouds, a resplendent martial demonstration. Their spirits return to earth, and the martyrs join the columns marching toward victory below, fading out with the words "Our flag is the new era."[56]

The premiere of *Hitler Youth Quex* on 11 September 1933 at the *Ufa* Phoebus Palace in Munich took on all of the aspects of a Nazi festival. Long columns of Hitler Youth formed a ceremonial guard outside the theater, blowing trumpet fanfares to the delight of the crowd gathered to catch a glimpse of the Führer. The guests in attendance included many of the elite of the Third Reich: Göring, Hess, Ley, Röhm, and von Papen, as well as von Blomberg and other high-ranking generals.[57] Searchlights outside the theater added a dramatic touch, and the hall was aflame with the black, white, and red flags of party and nation. Flowers were banked in the national colors before the stage, featuring a raised floral swastika. Franz Adam and the Reich Symphony Orchestra played Anton Bruckner's Fourth Symphony. No touch had been overlooked for the celebration of the living dead.

Turning to Hitler and the guests of honor, Baldur von Schirach offered a brief testimonial:

> I want briefly to direct your thoughts to that young comrade . . . who can't be with us anymore, because he has lain buried for a year and a half. It was in the time of the worst terror, when I stood before 2000 Berlin Hitler Youth . . . and spoke to them of sacrifice, of Führer, and of heroism. An oppressive atmosphere lay over our meeting, and it was as if we expected something horrible to happen. I spoke of the bravery that everyone must show, and that there might be one of us out there whom I would never see again. And I said to him: thank you that you take this fate on your shoulders, that you have the honor among the millions to bear the name of Hitler Youth, to become a leader in the community which you embody. On the next morning, the Hitler Youth Herbert Norkus was butchered by Marxist murder bandits. As I stood at his casket, communists threw stones against the wall of the mortuary. Today a youth movement of a million and a half fighters stands where that little Hitler Youth fell. Every single one of them is wedded to this spirit of sacrifice, this comradeship. We want to fight on in his unyielding spirit. Heil Hitler![58]

After the playing of the Hitler Youth march, the director of the Bavarian State Theater, Hans Schlenk, read the prologue from Kurt Klawitter's "Ours the Victory—Ours the Power." The film itself was greeted with grand approval and boisterous shouts of "Heil!" At its conclusion Jürgen Ohlsen, who had played Quex, appeared on the stage in the company of Steinhoff and Ritter. Looking like the wandering Parzifal, he saluted Hitler who was standing with his entourage. Deeply moved, Hitler smiled approvingly, and, lost in memories of the *Kampfzeit*, he slowly returned the salute.[59]

The reporter for *Kinematograph*, Germany's oldest film magazine, described the conclusion of the ceremonies:

> The shouts and "Heils" were heard throughout the neighborhood, and they carried out into the dark blue fall evening. Blood, tears, and victory—the story of our times—were relived that night in the presence of those who gained the final victory. . . . *Hitlerjunge Quex* is a fanfare of German youth and of the German future.[60]

There is no question that *Hitler Youth Quex* fulfilled the mission assigned to it. It was at once a propaganda and an aesthetic success, an ornament to Goebbels's dream of using the best of modern technique in the service of the mythical National Socialist ideal. *Hitler Youth Quex* lent currency to Goebbels's affirmation that "film is one of the most modern and far-reaching means of influencing the masses."[61] It appealed to the propaganda minister because it was produced in the heroic key of National Socialism, because it was a felicitous union of political realism and art, and, most important, because it channeled idealism into action in support of the state. In a letter to Ernst H. Correll, director of production at *Ufa*, Goebbels praised the film, noting that "*Ufa* as well as all those involved have contributed significantly not only to the development of the film art but also to the aesthetic configuration of National Socialist ideology."[62]

The film had a remarkable appeal for young people in Germany. It was shown on both party and *Ufa* commercial channels, and its audience numbered well over twenty million.[63] Curt Belling, a senior official in the Goebbels film apparatus, referred to *Hitler Youth Quex* as "*the* film of National Socialist youth."[64] As late as 1942 it was being shown in the Youth Film Hours of the Hitler Youth, an important propaganda activity of the organization.[65]

There were many reasons for its success. Above all, *Hitler Youth Quex* was a film of youth, by youth, and for youth. As such, it both fascinated and inspired the young and met the requirements of the party elite. It set a standard for the other major propaganda films that followed: *Ich für dich—Du für mich* (Carl Froelich, 1934), *Kopf hoch, Johannes!* (Viktor de Kowa, 1941), *Jakko* (Fritz Peter Buch, 1941), *Himmelhunde* (Roger von Norman, 1942), *Hände hoch!* (Alfred Weidenmann, 1942), and *Junge Adler* (Alfred Weidenmann, 1944). From the point of view of the party, *Hitler Youth Quex* had the great merit of laying the foundation for the central motif of Hitler Youth martyrology. Further, it schooled a generation to prepare for a sacrificial death for Germany.

Norkus remained ever a model in Hitler Youth propaganda. Often in honor of their hero Hitler Youth would sing the stirring song "Fähnlein Norkus, tritt an!" by the National Socialist bard Hans Baumann:

> Norkus Squad, attack! Singing we carry
> the flag far and wide, Herbert Norkus
> raises it higher to the stars. Mounts it on
> every tower—Norkus Squad, attack![66]

Herbert Norkus was sacred among the fallen heroes of the Hitler Youth. *Die Jungenschaft* proclaimed in 1939:

The revolution of youth was fulfilled in your name. You will remain the model of the fallen Hitler Youth unto all eternity: unknown but yet our example, young but yet a man, dead but yet alive.[67]

The party and the Hitler Youth continued to celebrate the martyr in poetry, song, and ceremony well into the days of World War II.[68]

Norkus, like Horst Wessel, had taken up the banner of the martyrs of 1923. He had joined the noble band in *Walhall* among the heroes who, in Hitler's words, "have not died, but have been resurrected in us and live in us, as long as we ourselves shall live, and they live in our youth, as long as a German youth shall exist."[69] Blood of his blood, flesh of his flesh, Norkus had answered the call of destiny and had found the joy of eternal life. As Hitler said of his martyrs: "The blood that they have shed has become Holy Water for the Third Reich."[70]

The war brought a curious conclusion to the Norkus saga. In March 1943, Reich Justice Minister Otto Thierack dispatched a plea to the Führer's headquarters for mercy for Harry Tack, one of the murderers of Norkus.[71] Tack's letter to Hitler, written from Moabit Prison after he was sentenced to death by a special court in Berlin in January 1943, fully documented the tale of Tack's disillusionment with the Soviet Union after his flight there eleven years earlier. Soon after the underground network of the Rote Hilfe had spirited him off to Russia, Tack by his own admission learned the true meaning of the "Workers' Paradise." He was arrested and sentenced to hard labor in a Siberian concentration camp for allegedly spying and engaging in National Socialist agitation. Only a miracle spared him the fate of death in the camp. Released in early 1939, he managed to seek asylum in the German embassy in Moscow. Later that year, he decided to return to his homeland but was arrested by the German secret police at the border. Tack continued:

My Führer, I beg you to let me return to the German Volk community and to allow me to take part in Germany's heroic struggle. I want to fight for Germany, because it is a horrible thing for a German to be in prison, while our nation is at war. I know that we will be victorious under your leadership, my Führer.[72]

Martin Bormann, in a letter to Thierack, conveyed Hitler's surprising agreement to the request for mercy. Considering that Tack was only twenty years old when he committed the crime and had behaved honorably ever since—he had married a *Volksdeutsche* in 1939—Hitler granted him clemency. Further, Hitler ordered that Tack be released from prison, as long as the Minister of Justice was convinced that "his stay in Russia had cured him of his communism."[73]

After the war, when the thundering music and ceremony over the grave of Herbert Norkus had faded into memory, a strange quiet settled over the secluded forest cemetery in Plötzensee. Just a few short years before, the bells from Plötzensee Prison had been heard there day after day, tolling for the guillotined martyrs sentenced by Roland Freisler's Peoples' Court. Cemeteries tell their own historic tale, and the Neue Johannes Friedhof is no exception. Today a visit to that spot finds no trace whatsoever of Herbert Norkus. After the war the Norkus memorial was destroyed, and his body moved to a common grave reserved by law for those for whom cemetery maintenance fees were no longer paid. Herbert Norkus had truly passed into history.

VI

Gerhard Schumann

Elitist Poet of the Volk Community

> Und hingebeugt zu schwörender Verpflich-
> tung
> So knieten wir, blickhart und herzenweich.
> Und über uns im Licht der Dom, das Reich.
> Gerhard Schumann[1]

Gerhard Schumann was one of the Third Reich's most celebrated poets, whose career took him to literary prominence and influence in the cultural-political arena. He was at once an idealist longing for the rebirth of a German spiritual Reich and an intellectual aristocrat inspired by the towering giants of German literature. Schumann considered himself to be a German knight standing guard at the Holy Grail of German culture. He portrayed Hitler and Nazism in lyrical terms, forgiving many of the criminal acts of the regime. As a result, his poetry was often curiously out of harmony with historical reality. He did take satiric liberties to attack some of the political and cultural excesses of the Nazi regime. An insider, Schumann often chose to be an outsider who alienated even the highest state officials. For example, Goebbels decided that Hitler should award the twenty-six-year-old poet the National Book Prize in 1936. But the propaganda minister created a scene when he walked out on a gala Leipzig production of Schumann's play *Die Entscheidung* in 1939, sensing that he himself had been caricatured in the work.

Schumann held high rank in the SA; he was promoted to Standarten-führer in 1936 and Oberführer in 1942. He was a member of the prestigious Präsidialrat of the Reich Chamber for Literature and the Reich Culture Senate and ended the war serving in the Cultural Section of the SS Haupt-amt. His major works of poetry were standard fare in higher literary circles as well as in the propaganda publications of countless Nazi organizations. His choral productions were chanted and sung at major Hitler Youth ceremonies and festivals. Schumann volunteered for military service in 1939,

16. Gerhard Schumann as lieutenant and company commander, 1940. (Personal Collection.)

saw active duty on both the western and eastern fronts, and won the Iron Cross I.

What was the nature and background of this sensitive man, a self-styled elitist and comrade, theoretician and activist?[2] Born in 1911 in Esslingen on the Neckar River, Schumann enjoyed a happy childhood in his native Swabia. He came from a household steeped in classical Greek and German culture. His father, Albert Schumann, was a professor of education, whom Gerhard described as both Spartan and supportive. Albert Schumann was a passionate follower of Friedrich Naumann, whose dream of a Middle Europe led by Germany influenced young Gerhard. Schumann was also a pious Christian, which also profoundly affected Gerhard's life. Father and son—rucksacks on their backs—took many outings to Swabian cultural shrines, divining the historical and cultural images that would later inform Gerhard's writing. His mother, very artistic and loving, always had time for him. In later years, he wrote unashamedly that "as a child I simply could not go to sleep unless she came to my bedside, sang a lullaby and told a fairy tale, and later recited the ballads of Schiller and Uhland, which she knew by heart." His parents were devoted to the arts. Among Schumann's treasured memories of his childhood was "when father sat at the piano and our beautiful mother with her blond chaplet of plaited hair, sometimes leaning lightly on his shoulders, sang with all her heart the songs we loved so much by Schumann, Schubert, and Wolf in her clear soprano voice."[3]

Early on as a boy, Schumann joined the German youth movement. He delighted in wandering on extended summer trips through Franconia, rich in historic castles and churches. He felt a union with nature as the boys and girls hiked over hill and dale singing songs of the homeland. Above all, they dreamt and spoke of a renewed Germany, of "a new German man, of a liberated personality, of the Volk and Fatherland, of the world, art, and God."[4]

The young Schumann won a scholarship to study at Schöntal and Urach in the Swabian Alps, demanding preparatory schools supported by the Württemburg Protestant state church since the days of the Reformation. Schumann found his intellectual home in the princely baroque cloister at Schöntal in the Jagst valley. At Urach, the impressive Gothic church and the little town nestled in wooded heights provided an isolated setting conducive to contemplation and growth. In fact, he was in good company, because over the years these schools had produced thinkers such as Hölderlin, Mörike, Schelling, and Hegel. He responded well to the ordered life, to the austerity and discipline of the schools, and to the Christian humanistic traditions cultivated there. He found the masters both demanding and tolerant of the often-overzealous spirits of the youths charged to their care. Here Schumann went through his "Nietzsche period," learned to develop his mind, and, equally important for the future, became a comrade in a community of young men.

During the school vacations Schumann was catapulted from the ivory tower of traditional German humanism into the bleeding cities of Weimar Germany. The sensitive lad was appalled at the hunger, desperation, and political chaos he found there. Like so many of the young generation, he longed for what he later termed "the salvation of the Reich, and for the necessity of a strong Führer personality at the helm."[5] One of his earliest poems, written in 1930, dealt with Germany on the Cross:

Blood streams from a thousand wounds,
Suffering devours you, that fearful ghost . . .

Now that the entire globe has crushed you,
Aren't you too, guilty in your apathy?
Don't agonized prayers rise up
For the sacrificial purity of the Reich? . . .

Has God forgotten you?
Or have you betrayed yourself?[6]

To prepare for the struggle to right these wrongs, Schumann joined a paramilitary unit that engaged in secret exercises under the direction of the Black Reichswehr.

As conditions in Germany worsened, Schumann kept before himself a transcendent vision of the Reich, which served at once as solace and hope. He expressed this longing in a sonnet cycle entitled *Songs of the Reich.* In these autobiographical verses, Schumann joins a knightly circle of warriors, consumed by a spiritual reawakening that merges the individual with the Reich. The poet wanders in the lower depths and discovers the suffering Volk, longing to be united. But betrayal and a foreign ideology have taken root in Germany, nearly destroying it. Moved by the assuredness of innocent youth and armed with a Hegelian conception of freedom, he calls for a Führer to save the nation. But the road to freedom demands the shedding of sacrificial blood. The concluding sonnet brings the fulfillment of the Reich through the resplendent resurrection of the fallen hero.

Songs of the Reich reflected a poet concerned with the proper union of form and content. The sonnets are cast in a dialectical framework in which conflicting polarities give way to a synthesis in the glorious Reich. The battle lines are clearly delineated, pitting good versus evil and blood and soil against the dehumanized masses. It was perhaps the most important poem of his career and drew the attention of the *völkisch* novelist Hans Friedrich Blunck. In crisp and commanding language, Schumann began by surrendering himself to the whole:

I awoke from the icy dream,
Through which I walked in rags, proudly alone.
Yet I burst passionately from the ring,
Encircling me. Behold: there was a way out. . . .
And I was one. But one within a flowing whole.
And, lo, the newly forming wave surged high.
And in the current I felt good and strong

And filled with dedication I pushed through the bonds,
And gasping I broke through the dam and dike.
Lost myself and found the Volk, the Reich.

Continuing his grand pilgrimage to the holy city:

And a new dome, a new heaven arched
Its vault high across the rejuvenated,
German soil. . . .

With clear-cut force, in perfect towering layers
The staircase of all being, the new Grail.

> And bowing down in sworn commitment
> We knelt, our eyes transfixed, our hearts deeply moved.
> And shimmering high above us the cathedral, the Reich. . . .

Aflame with passion, the poet returned to the earth, saying, "I am coming home, O Mother, take me back once more." Germanic blood came alive again, as in the ancient days, "flowing through the veins, a brook of flame. And from blood and soil, the Reich began to grow anew." Everywhere he found suffering, hunger, and disunity. Mutineers and revolutionaries ruled the streets, filling the vacuum left by "the best, who bled to death on the battlefields." He shed tears of desperation, "because the destruction was immeasurable. And the sacred flag of the Reich torn to shreds." The final collapse seemed near, when new hope appeared:

> From a thousand eyes the last hope glimmered!
> From a thousand hearts a mute cry broke forth:
> *The Führer!* Make us into vassals! Lord, set us free! . . .

But the black of night set in anew. A noble hero arose to right the wrong, and he fought bravely for change:

> Until duty forced him to his knees.

> But as he arose the halo of the chosen one
> shone round his head. And as he descended
> He carried the torch illuminating the night.

> Millions silently revered him. Delivered.
> The heavens flamed up through the pale of morning.
> The sun rose. And with it rose the Reich.[7]

Schumann's longing for the Reich was consonant with much of the prevailing thought of the alienated political and intellectual elite of his generation. Fundamentally, Schumann longed not for the Third Reich of Adolf Hitler, based on racial elitism. Instead, he wanted the mystical conception of the Reich that stretched over thirteen centuries, from the days of Charlemagne and the Hohenstaufen emperors. Schumann conceived of the Continent united not under German dictatorship but under German political, cultural, and moral suasion. He and his circle of friends viewed this development as "infinitely more important than the Party platform of National Socialism." He was drawn to Hitler as the leader who would fulfill the idea of the Reich.[8]

At Tübingen University, where Schumann matriculated in 1930, he began the curiously antithetical union of humanist scholarship and Nazi party activity. There he was exposed to the Germanist Paul Kluckhohn and the Hegel scholar Theodor Haering. He found the lectures of the historian

Johannes Haller especially informative and on several occasions "had the honor of playing piano duets with him." According to Schumann, the fraternity to which he belonged, which traditionally had a heavy complement of students of theology, provided him a "noble tolerance" and a communal nationalist spirit. He appreciated the fact that his brothers valued intellect over class background and money. Like Horst Wessel at the University of Berlin, Schumann found the reactionary, class-bound attitudes of the traditional dueling fraternities out of touch with the "problems facing an industrial mass state." As a result, in November 1930 at the age of nineteen, he took a step momentous for his future career; he joined the NSDAP and was assigned the party card number 371,854. Commenting on his decision, he noted:

> For me and many of my friends it was almost a natural progression from the *Bündische Jugend* to the Christian-humanist-nationalist spirit of the preparatory schools, to the Movement, which at that time was the most uncompromising in meeting head-on the Bolshevik danger and the threatening Red revolution, and at the same time embraced a forward-looking ideology of reconciliation: the Volk community free from the shackles of caste and hate-filled class struggle.[9]

Schumann undertook an active role in the National Socialist German Students League. He moved in rapid succession from cell leader to Hochschulgruppenführer and Landesführer. Characteristically, Schumann agonized over what seemed the unbridgeable gap between party activist and poet. Describing his night of decision, he wrote:

> I saw two paths before me: either one hundred percent toward creative writing, which reflected my real nature . . . or the path toward political engagement, the duty of sacrifice for the Reich. Finally I decided on both of them! Writing and political engagement, dream and deed.

Another motivating factor was generational. Like so many young men of his age too young to have seen battle in the Great War, a sense of guilt overcame him whenever he saw a veteran wearing an Iron Cross. Now that guilt could be overcome; he would become a political soldier.[10] For Schumann, the armed fist of the nationalist intellectual belonged in the ranks of the Brown Shirts.

The young poet cast his lot with the SA in January 1931, joining Storm 10 at Tübingen. There Schumann moved rapidly up the ranks from Scharführer to Standartenführer and commander of the SA Hochschulamt. He was able to ward off some of the worst excesses of political and racial radicalism emanating from Berlin. Schumann successfully blocked his unit's participation in the notorious night of book burning that occurred in 1933, and he refused to take part in the nationally organized subscription campaign for Julius Streicher's scandalous anti-Semitic newspaper, *Der Stürmer*. These were exciting days for Schumann. In an autobiographical précis written for the NSDAP in 1937, he noted that it was really the SA—with its union of all classes and daily political battle—that had drawn him to National Socialism. Above all, he was moved by the concepts of "the *Volksgemeinschaft* and comradeship, which must be experienced to be understood."[11] Evidence of Schumann's idealism is reflected in one of his early poems, which he recited at a Christmas celebration of the Tübingen SA in 1931. It stood in marked contrast to the outrages being perpetrated by the SA in that period of crisis:

> All around us desperation makes lost hands reach up
> Toward blood-red skies of ghastly ruin.
> Our goal commands us to new deeds,
> Demands the harvest of our youth.
> But we shall rest just for an hour.
>
> Not one disgrace or agony have we forgotten,
> Yet do we kneel expectantly around this dream of God.
> And we all turn into silent vessels.
> Aglow with light . . .
>
> Hands draw together. The silent brotherhood closes its circle, each heart now shares the same emotion. We shall not flee. We are building new strength. The miracle will bind us like our blood united us.[12]

Ever the aesthete, Schumann was convinced that, because Christianity and National Socialism were fighting the same battles, the two could be merged. He was reinforced in this belief by the theologians and other academics at Tübingen, as well as his circle of friends. They longed for both a spiritual and a political renewal, a dream they hoped would be fulfilled in the coming Reich. According to Schumann: "In those days it seemed quite possible to unite this ideology of social justice with a community of the Volk, which would transcend class antagonisms and produce a Christianity of the deed."[13] When he married Margarethe Hausser, the daughter of the mayor of Tübingen, both Christian and Nazi symbols were in evidence.[14] At the time this did not appear incongruous. To be sure, the academic SA unit in Württemberg was a far cry from the rough and tumble of the urban wards, where blood was flowing in the streets in the SA's battles with the communists. This romantic and naive quality of the youthful Schumann was a trait of his character that followed him into manhood.

With the victory of Hitler in 1933, Schumann began a career as a party writer, which brought him great prestige. In 1934, he took a position in the Württemberg education bureaucracy, and thereafter he was called to high party cultural offices.[15] It was from this vantage point that he developed a theory of heroic art, which he employed both in his own writing and in the coercive system the Nazis constructed to purify German letters. As Schumann wrote in 1936:

> Poetry is the lifeblood of a Volk because the soul also hungers and thirsts and cannot be left barren. Poetry elevates the everyday into grand images transmitted to history and eternity. And beyond that today the creative arts have become important weapons in the ideological struggle for the peoples of the world. The Führer himself has shown us the path to take.[16]

According to Schumann's precepts, German poetry in the new era was to be inspired by elitist values, yet it was to be understandable to the Volk. Gone forever was the poetry of self-conscious isolation and "pathetic abstruseness" and the narcissistic snobbery of limp-wristed aesthetes and their cult of *l'art pour l'art*. These values, inspired by an epoch of selfish individualism, were consigned to the trash heap of history. Gone, too, "like chaff before the wind," were the *Asphaltliteraten,* the vanguard of Weimar cultural decadence. The Weimar crowd had emigrated, and they continued to purge the "sewer pipes of their souls," albeit now on foreign soil. But in their place Schumann lamented the appearance of the "knights of the market trends," literary opportunists who sprang up like mushrooms in a mossy forest after Hitler came to power. Suddenly one read nothing except paeans to the German landscape, references to the beautiful peasantry and the glories of barnyard and dung. He made it clear that the heroes of the SA had not gone to their deaths to prepare the way for an unholy desecration of Germanic values with cultural kitsch and pseudonationalist references to "the Movement," the "Führer," and the "*Volksgemeinschaft.*"

The work of German writers, he submitted, must be struck in the key of heroism, characterized by austerity, passion, martial values, and willingness for self-sacrifice. "The greater the subject, the more humbly must we fashion it," he warned. Writers had a holy calling, for they lived at a challenging time when the nation was returning to the greatness of its past. As a result, they were not to confuse the national community with theories about the equality of all Germans. Further, he advised, "Quiet hours of withdrawn contemplation are necessary for every person's soul," just as they were rewarding for the nation. The poet's task was to create heroic art that reflected the greatness of National Socialism and internalized the resounding march of the reawakened millions by drawing on their hearts and souls for strength.[17]

In the mid-1930s, when some Nazi writers and critics attempted to shackle their fellow writers with Stalinist cultural conformity, Schumann struck back in *Der SA Mann.* First he took aim at the source of the criticism, which he found located among a circle of "aesthetic pomade boys." These would-be guardians of National Socialist purity demanded that all writing deal with the party program and its history, the Führer, waving swastika flags, and a hodgepodge of blood, honor, and other party themes. Most of these writers, Schumann argued, had no practical experience in the party at all; they belonged to the same effete crowd that had cavorted with "the Impressionists, expressionists, futurists and dadaists and the liberal, Bolshevik, Semitic circles" of Weimar. And none of them had subjected themselves to the discipline of the SA, SS, or Hitler Youth. For these writers, National Socialism was purely a literary affair.

A National Socialist world view was the first consideration, he argued, not the choice of subject matter. The Third Reich was not the Soviet Union. Poets turn by nature to "life in all of its manifestations, not only the greatness of our heroic era but also the quiet of the German landscape, and the miracle of German men and women." Art was the organically developed fruit of the community. "Only in this connection," he submitted, "could the National Socialist artist be viewed as political, not as a tiresome dogmatist of a party program but as an impassioned herald of an all-embracing world view."[18] With the prestige Schumann enjoyed as a national literary figure and as a member of the Reich Culture Senate and the Präsidialrat of the Reich Chamber of Literature, his views carried weight in both political and literary circles. He was called to Berlin in 1938 to head the Writers' Section in the Reich Chamber for Literature. Schumann enjoyed a good relationship with its president, SS Brigadeführer Hanns Johst, who acted as his protector on more than one occasion. But as Nazi radicals demanding literary conformity insinuated themselves more and more into cultural politics, he resigned from this position within a year. He found the intrigue and dishonesty that surrounded him in Berlin unbearable.[19] Political reality had rudely intruded on his mystical vision of the Reich.

Schumann's own writing in the Third Reich was prolific. Besides nineteen books of poems as well as journal and newspaper articles, he published two plays and several scripts for NSDAP ceremonies for theater and radio. He held doggedly to his dream of a Reich free of imperfections.[20] He struck the leitmotiv for his later work in the poem "Germany, You Eternal Flame" (1932), which celebrated the struggle to renew the sacred Reich.[21] With Hitler's assumption of power he, like so many others, saw the Reich's incarnation in the Führer. The poem "Hitler" reflected the misguided idealism of those days:

In one will all the towering force
of millions living and dead. . . .

In one hand the brotherly greeting
of millions of outstretched hands. . . .

With the thunderous power of all the bells
his voice is ringing over the world.

And the world will hear.[22]

The realities of life in the Third Reich often fell short of Schumann's sacred vision for the creation of a mythical political community. Instead of burning zeal, he often found compromise and manipulation. Where once the flame of idealism burned, now often a bloated bureaucracy obstructed the path to greatness. In the face of these realities, the sensitive artist often despaired, turning to the sweet balm of poetry for renewed strength. The result was dangerous for Schumann, and he was suspected of being a member of the alleged Brown Shirt conspiracy against Hitler. His sonnet "The Purity of the Reich" was published in the spring of 1934, only a few months before the momentous "Röhm Putsch" of 30 June 1934.[23] Considering the fear and suspicion throughout Germany at the time, his poem was a bold statement indeed. "The Purity of the Reich" was an appeal for the rebirth of the virtues that had inspired the circle of Teutonic Knights and fired the passions of the SA.

Schumann first attacked the opportunists, who discovered National Socialism after the battles had been fought:

> After the victories appear those who celebrate them.
> Now they are great and the soldier is silent.
> They hand out glory in abundance and turn
> Our song of blood into ditties like organ-grinders. . . .

The upstarts had the nerve to patronize and seek to instruct those who had fought, who were "silently awaiting the command of fate, which rises like the red of dawn." But motivating the loyal and true was a call that "burns their hearts like fire, gushing forth the blood of the strangled, which bathed us in the battle for the flag." This was not the time to celebrate: "We are about the business of forging the New Reich." Worse yet was the tinny clang of the profiteers:

> They throw away sacrifices carved from ourselves.
> They put the blood of the dead on the market. . . .
> The dead did not die for that! . . .

Schumann conjured up the memory of the fallen, beckoning from afar:

> And those who wielded the weapons in battle,
> Feel out of place at celebrations and parades. . . .
>
> Sometimes they gather, vexed and angered,
> Homeless now in all the bustle . . .
>
> They look angrily at the commotion.
> And suddenly are quiet. Awaiting the command. . . .

Schumann concluded with a reaffirmation of victory, drawing on the secret source known only to members of the Order:

> Now there arises a band of the determined, . . .
> By night they dream of the blood that was shed, . . .
>
> And of the Führer, who carries the burden of fate,
> And of the fields, which cry out for our men,
> And of the river, flowing by on our borders,
> And of the brother, who forgives us our guilt.
>
> Nothing is kept secret from them.
> Their stern words are heavy as forged from steel.
> Their steps echo the call for ultimate judgment.
>
> In their souls they bear the Grail.
> Vassals of the Führer, keepers and avengers alike.
> Within them burns and with them grows the Reich.[24]

The executions related to the Röhm purge affected Schumann very deeply. Looking back on that event many years later, he remarked that "this was one of the worst days of my life."[25] It was inconceivable to him that Hitler would gun down hundreds of his brothers without a trial. "I was deeply wounded," he noted, "my political faith was absolutely shattered, and I cried when the unbelievable news came over the radio about the executions."[26] In this traumatized state, he wrote the poem "The Judgment":

> As the shots cracked through the night,
> Every bullet pierced the Führer's heart.
>
> As long as Germany lives, the salvos
> Will frighten people from their beds in the night.
>
> And blood-red will shine the heart of the man,
> Who killed his friends for the Reich.[27]

"This was an incredibly bold statement at the time," Schumann later noted.[28] It directly contradicted the propaganda line established by Hitler and Goebbels, whereby only a bold preemptive strike had averted Röhm and a clique of conspirators from committing high treason. Publication of the poem in *Songs of the Reich*, as well as reference to it by Professor Hermann Pongs in the *Stuttgarter Tagblatt*, drew fire from several quarters.[29] Radical Nazis, who had nursed their wounds after Schumann's attack on them in "The Purity of the Reich," had a new cause after publication of "The Judgment." His enemies collected letters of denunciation against him. As a result, influential friends stepped in to protect him. Schumann recalled that "E. Tschunke, commander of the Reichswehr in Tübingen and former adjutant to Field Marshall von Blomberg, called me to a meeting at this time and took me under his protection. The SS was about to arrest me."[30]

Early in 1935 Schumann was subjected to considerable harassment by the party bureaucracy. He was called to appear before Reichsleiter Philipp Bouhler at the Führer Chancellery to defend his publication of "The Judgment."[31] There he was asked to remove the poem from the recently published second edition of *Songs of the Reich*. He answered that "I could not do it: this tragic interpretation was the only way it made it possible for me to overcome these horrible events."[32] Soon thereafter Bouhler contacted Schumann, transmitting a request to him from Hitler that the poem be removed from the book. Remarkably, Hitler had affirmed that the time was not too distant when it could be published again. The author was deeply moved by this gesture, which caused some of his old faith and spirit to return.[33]

Despite these difficulties, Schumann continued to be successful. His chorale "Greatness of Creation" was carried over a national radio hookup when the Hitler Youth initiated the Sunday *Morgenfeier* series on 23 June 1935.[34] In the same year he won the Swabian Prize for Literature as a result of his collection of poems *Fahne und Stern*. Thereafter he received favorable attention in the press. Hermann Dannecker lionized him in the *Völkischer Beobachter* as an artist and a fighter who incarnated the true spirit of the "Revolution of 1933," a poet whose works inspired such a love for the homeland that the new German would willingly sacrifice his life for his country.[35] Even Goebbels took note of Schumann, calling him to membership in the Reich Culture Senate.[36] He was all of twenty-four years old when he attended his first meeting. Suddenly he was cast into the role of associating with people whom earlier he had admired from afar—composers like Richard Strauss and Hans Pfitzner, the playwright Hanns Johst, the actors Gustaf Gründgens and Heinrich George, the sculptor Arno Breker, and fellow poet Eberhard Wolfgang Möller. He was disappointed, however, that the Reich Culture Senate was not a working body but merely a cultural propaganda forum for Goebbels.[37]

Schumann was catapulted to national fame in 1936, with the publication of his volume of poetry *Wir aber sind das Korn*.[38] Goebbels honored the work with the National Book Prize.[39] It included poems of nature, love, and landscape, but the call to the heroic drew Goebbels to it. Schumann had been deeply moved by the midnight ceremonies of 9 November 1935 in Munich, when the bodies of the sixteen Immortals were bathed in torchlight within the Feldherrnhalle before being laid to rest the next morning in the Temple of Honor. The result was *Heldische Feier,* the lyric centerpiece for a festival meeting of the Reich Culture Chamber that Goebbels staged on 1 May 1936 at the National Opera in Berlin. Franz Philipp was commissioned to compose the symphonic score for the heroic cantata, which thereafter became standard ceremonial accompaniment for the Nazis' honor of their dead throughout the Reich.[40] State actor Lothar Müthel recited the verses of the three poems by Schumann that began the ceremony: "Marching Song," "German Solstice," and "Song of the Fighters." The National Opera Orchestra, directed by Artur Rother, struck up the resounding score of *Heldische Feier,* while SA men of the Standarte Feldherrnhalle recited the heroic verses and performed the cantata. With Hitler present in the Führer box, surrounded by the political and cultural elite of the Third Reich, a scene with spectacular dramatic effect was played out.[41] Scene after scene of the Feldherrnhalle passion recreated the blood sacrifice of those who had fallen on 9 November 1923. The work began with a prelude centering on the despair motif, followed by a call to Providence to send forth a new messiah as Zarathustra had been sent:

> For in that region, where thunder and lightning emerge,
> Whence stars plunge out of nowhere,
> And where the universe rages on its axis,
> One came to us, with haloed countenance. . . .
>
> Waving flag of light! . . .

Heldische Feier next broke into a rhapsody to death, while the orchestra plumbed the depths of passion, echoing Anton Bruckner:

> Death loves us, because we love life . . .
> But we are the grain . . .
>
> Threatened by darkness and a thousand murders
> We grew together into a secret Order . . .
>
> And although mothers stand with tears
> And reddened eyes, for the price they paid—
> Soon they are on their knees—and can hardly believe,
> How the souls of their sons arise from the graves
> To unfurl the red flag.
>
> Blessed be death, who called the swath to eternity
> With a harsh stroke of his scythe.
> Blessed be the silent comrades.
> Eternal life beams forth from their mute deeds . . .

The conclusion of the cantata, uniting the spoken word, chorus, and symphony, offered the sacrifice of the dead as a catalyst to the living. The message was clear: the goal was to construct the "Reich's Eternal Feldherrnhalle," organically to merge with it, and ultimately to die for their faith in the Reich. The cantata concluded on a note of mystical ecstasy:

The cathedral rises to stupendous heights . . .
For all the world a never-resting monument to the dead.—

And suddenly there arises over the cacophony . . .
Alone and grand in the sky that opened for it,
The image of the Feldherrnhalle bathed in red.

We are building the Reich's eternal Feldherrnhallen,
Whose steps lead to eternity,
Until the hammers fall from our fists.
Then you shall wall us into its altars.[42]

In his address to the Reich Culture Chamber, Goebbels pointed with special pride to the fact that a man from the National Socialist fighting cadres once again had won the National Book Prize. Schumann's works, he submitted, "born in the spirit of National Socialism," adorned the party's passionate struggle with elegant language and served as a didactic ideological achievement.[43] That afternoon the author was honored by Hitler at a reception in the presidential palace.[44]

On the next day, the poet received the following telegram from Viktor Lutze, successor to the murdered Ernst Röhm as SA chief of staff:

Dear Schumann! The entire SA is thrilled about your new honor and sends heartfelt best wishes. You are hereby promoted to Standartenführer. Now go forward with your work in the old spirit! Heil Hitler![45]

Consumed by his vision of the Reich, Schumann scorned the outrageous behavior of many party members. Armed with the increased prestige he enjoyed as a ranking SA man, he continued the course he had begun as the conscience of the party. A book of poems entitled *Herr Aberndörfer* (1937) was nothing less than a frontal attack on the little big men at the local level in the party, whose arrogance and recently acquired power so alienated the public.[46] It was perhaps the only book of antiparty satire that received the NSDAP imprimatur during the years of the Third Reich. Considering the widespread fear of the Nazi terror system, it was risky indeed for Schumann to publish this acid work, which was embellished with outrageous illustrations of a jackbooted provincial in his elevated milieu. With such titles as "Herr Aberndörfer and the Election of 1932," in which Schumann's Aberndörfer voted for the Democrats and Nationalists, and "The Year of the Heil 1933," in which his character reluctantly became a Nazi, *Herr Aberndörfer* was devastating caricature. Schumann was most effective when he ridiculed the pomposity of the parvenus. During the course of a lecture tour, the poet received cheers and applause that seemed never to end when astounded audiences heard the poem "Herr Aberndörfer and the Führer Principle":

He became a Blockwart. Oh what honor
flamed up in his flabby breast . . .

He was now a stern little man, a petty provincial satrap,
inspecting the block with patrician arrogance.
He knew the families, and all they had, down to their
kitchen pots and pans, everyone's sorrows and joys. . . .

Even the *Stammtisch* brothers didn't recognize him. . . .
The way he looked down on these insignificant men
none of whom could understand him anymore. . . .

When he went to and fro among his herd,
he expected a salute from everyone. . . .

And beside him like a ship under full steam,
there comes *Frau Blockwart:* "Good Morning, people!"
And all who'd had no interest in politics before,
would surely become born again fighters today.[47]

As might be expected, *Herr Aberndörfer* did not sit well with many threatened party members, and Schumann was denounced once more. Procedures were undertaken in the Reichsorganisationsleitung to punish the author and to forbid any further attacks upon the National Socialist leadership. After Lutze defended his SA poet, Hitler himself was forced to make the final decision in the matter. Ultimately the Führer deemed the satires to be "positive criticism" of weaknesses in the party, and the books on the Schumann affair were closed.[48]

Schumann was much truer to his own nature when composing poetry of praise. In a prolific outpouring of nearly religious sentiment, he conveyed the joy of an organic, productive Volk community. He focused on a renewed Germany and its bustling factories, on fields planted and harvested, and on a youth healthy and happy in the sunshine of the Third Reich. Schumann was consumed by the beauty of nature, where an individual could joyously surrender to the universal. Poems on the themes of work, duty, and loyalty cascaded from his pen as well. He celebrated the privilege of serving the living cathedral of the nation in *Wir dürfen dienen* (1937).[49] The titles of the poems in this collection reflect an interplay between joy and sacrifice: "The March of 30. January," "Celebration of Work," "Solemn Promise," "Harvest Thanksgiving," "Feldherrnhalle," "Winter Solstice," and "Song of the Dead." His cantatas *The Sacred Hour* and *Volk without Boundaries* celebrated the divine union of Providence and the Führer's will.[50] Schumann's fame as a muse was widespread, and he received praise from critics, writers, and academics alike.[51]

Hitler took further note of Schumann. Following the *Anschluss* of his Austrian homeland in 1938, Hitler included Stuttgart among those cities he visited on his euphoric progress through Germany. With an eye to the plebiscite on the annexation, he cast about for an appropriate song to highlight the propaganda campaign. Having read Schumann's hymn of praise for the *Anschluss*, the Führer called him to his hotel. The author pressed his way through the throng that was crying, "We want to see our Führer!" Somewhat overcome with the excitement of the experience, he was shown into Hitler's suite, where he found the composer, Hans Gansser, seated at a piano. Hitler soon appeared and asked Max Roth of the Württemberg State Theater to sing Schumann's song:

> After suffering the wounds of a thousand years
> Blood has returned to blood,
> Bursting through wall and dike!
> From the North Sea to the Brenner Pass
> Nothing but impassioned believers:
> One Führer, Volk, and Reich![52]

Schumann later recounted what followed:

> It was absolutely quiet. Then Hitler walked up to me, took my right hand in both of his, and looked deeply into my eyes for some time, as tears welled up in his eyes. I could hardly keep my composure. . . . Then he turned to Brückner, his adjutant, and ordered: "This song will be played over all German radio stations until the plebiscite."[53]

In January 1939, Schumann's play *Entscheidung (Decision)* premiered at the Altes Theater in Leipzig. Directed by Paul Smolny, it was well received by the public and after an interruption played well into the war years.[54] Set in the embattled Ruhr industrial area during the hectic days after the Kapp Putsch in 1920, the play was an aesthetic statement of postwar German nationalism and the warrior ideal. Although the battle lines between Nazism and Bolshevism were clearly drawn, Schumann accurately reflected the tragedy of the postwar era by assigning each *Weltanschauung* a protagonist in the form of a veteran of the Great War. Captain Friedrich Schwarz, commander of a Free Corps, remains faithful to the flag. On the other hand, Helmut Bäumler, who had saved his friend's life at the front, wavers and is swept up in the communist enthusiasm to create a more just society. Only the heroic death of Schwarz brings Bäumler home to the nation once more. The hero's sister, Anne, who is in love with Bäumler, is at once an intercessor and redeemer. Schumann, who traced his influences in the arena of drama to both Georg Büchner and Hanns Johst, recreated effectively the political and social turmoil of the tortured Weimar Republic.[55] *Entscheidung* featured some of the leading actors of the period, including Josef Zechell (Alex, commander of the Red forces), Georg Heding (Schwarz), Stig von Rauckhoff (Bäumler), Alice Warnke (Anne), Hans Finohr (the general), Albert Garbe (Reich commissioner), and Franz Kutscheras (propaganda chief of the Red Army).[56] Max Geisenheyner, reviewing the play for the *Frankfurter Zeitung,* praised it for giving "meaning to the tumultuous postwar years, which brought the breakthrough for the National Socialist idea." He noted that the audience, which included several powerful figures, "was captivated by the lyrical, dramatic movement of the production and by the brilliant conception of the work. It was no wonder that Gerhard Schumann was called to the curtain time and again with the actors and director."[57]

Schumann had a gift for the creation of bold political stereotypes. The confrontation between the Socialist Reich commissar, a cynic and opportunist, and the general, who submits the case for the Free Corps, sets the stage for the coming confrontation. In a simple farm cottage decorated with only a dagger and a picture of Frederick the Great, the patriot and Free Corps commander Schwarz argues the cause of the nation with Bäumler. Schumann showed sympathy for the plight of Bäumler, a good German who becomes a victim of historical forces beyond his control. Desperate, Bäumler cries out: "I just don't fit in here anymore. The Fatherland is dead. . . . The era of nations is over. The brotherhood of humanity has begun. A new order!" The Internationale was the only answer to a regime in which battle-tried German officers and men were forced to take orders from saddlers, herring salesmen, and scribbling journalists and in which gluttonous capitalists found their life's inspiration in money. "But we're all waiting for the revolution," Schwarz counters. The blood their comrades had shed in the war "could not have been shed in vain."

Schwarz, answering an inner call, expresses his zealous love for Germany: "There is only one thing that holds you together and nourishes you. Even if you don't know it and—betray it. The fallow German fields. The red blood in our veins. The poor, betrayed, loyal German men." But Bäumler holds fast to his new faith, imploring that "your companies await your command. *Lead the soldiers to the Volk! Let's destroy the old world!* Put yourself at the head of the revolutionary masses! Lead them to freedom!" There was no turning back for either man.[58]

Schumann drew a grotesque picture of the communist leadership. Brutal and cynical, they represented a "rootless subhumanity" set loose on German soil. Revolution for them was purely a technical affair, where criminality and murder were acceptable as long as the masses could be terrified into submission. In a devastating scene, Alex orders a hesitant Bäumler to ambush and murder his only friend, the Free Corps officer Captain Schwarz. For Furchheimer, the orchestrator of communist propaganda, the historical confrontation is important only as a source for headlines and manipulation.

Schuman employed a scene in a communist tavern as a vehicle for a frontal attack on what passed for culture in the Weimar Republic. In a smoke-filled den of iniquity, the communist political and military leadership has gathered for a night of illicit pleasure. A black jazz band blares forth its unsettling and raucous tunes, while an erotic *chansonette* sings her lurid songs. Fondling one of the heavily perfumed women of the night, Furchheimer shouts: "Broads in here, and our cannons and guns out there. . . . This is our bread and wine. These are the sacraments of the new era!"[59] Goebbels, who was attending the performance with Reichsdramaturg Rainer Schlösser, was so offended by the parallels between Furchheimer and himself that he stormed out of the theater.[60]

The final scene featured a heroic death for the nation. Captain Schwarz and his Free Corps march into the dawn with a joyful song of death on their lips: "The heavens are bloody red. We are the last guard. We want to die for Germany." Bäumler's conscience wells up as he lies in ambush, and he indignantly asks, "Who can be so arrogant as to say that he will redeem our brothers? Only he who went to the cross can do that." Upon hearing the approaching Free Corps with their song of death, he utters: "Death—that's it. . . . To want to die—that—is—life." Affirming his true self, Bäumler fires a warning shot into the air, provoking a burst of gunfire upon himself from the political commissar sent to guard him. In the melee, he is delivered to Anne, who dresses his wounds and saves his life. In an emotional denouement, Schwarz is borne into the room, carried on a stretcher from the battle with the Red Guards. Mortally wounded and consumed in the flame of Germany, his eyes gaze toward heaven and the first red of dawn. With his sister Anne looking on, he transfers command of the Free Corps to Bäumler, who has seen the light. The last words of Captain Schwarz are of nation and of Reich: "The new Führer is coming."[61]

With the onset of the war Schumann volunteered for the army, only to learn that he had been placed on the list of artists exempted from military service. To sit out the war would have amounted to a betrayal of all that he had stood for, and, after several appeals to Goebbels and Hanns Johst, he was permitted to serve at the front. Schumann saw action in France and Russia, was promoted to lieutenant, served as a platoon and company commander, and won the Iron Cross I.[62] He was severely wounded in Russia in August 1941. After an extended period of convalescence in the military hospital at Tübingen, he was appointed artistic director of the Württembarg State Theater as successor to Wilhelm von Scholz. He served in this capacity until late 1944 when, remarkably, he again volunteered for the front in the newly assembled SS Panzer Grenadier Division Horst Wessel. He saw the war to its conclusion as a member of the Cultural Section of the SS Hauptamt (Amt A I).[63]

With the coming of the war, Schumann felt an even greater urge to create poetry of meaning in Germany's hour of destiny.[64] He did not indulge in an excess of national enthusiasm, nor did his poetic works celebrate victories or mourn defeats. Instead, they reflected the tragedy of the human experience and took the form of prayers concealed as poetry—prayers for strength and courage, of praise of the Führer, of loyalty and steadfastness in the good fight, prayers for help to face the loneliness of the front, of thanks for the homeland, of the poet's native Black Forest, and of shimmering Lake Constance. There were prayers of mothers crying for their dead sons, of soldiers' longing for wives and loved ones, of the eyes of babies shining like candles in the night. But Schumann's most fervent prayers were for the dead. Indeed, the death motif ran through the entire corpus of his writing from 1939 to 1945, and it was around this theme that all his works coalesced.

Schumann spoke to the marriage of art and death in 1940, the year of *Blitzkrieg* victories:

> Always when Germany was winning her victories, sword and spirit went loyally hand in hand, songs provided accompaniment to the sword, and the eternal stars blazed over the waving flags. . . . Where could German men better learn the quiet, unexplainable power of a poem, which touches the soul like the soft, reassuring hands of a mother and thereby brings them closer to the great Mother Germany, than in the face of death, when they are prepared to protect this Mother Germany with their own heart's blood?[65]

Speaking at the annual Weimar Writers' Congress in 1942, Schumann went even further, assigning poetry in wartime the role of a holy sacrament. Ever the elitist, he warned of the dangers of kitsch, the "hurrah bards," the effete "Mommy poets," and matinee "paper heroes" who polluted true culture and weakened the war effort. This crowd, he submitted, might enter the anterooms but never the holy temple of German culture. "The all holy is not Luna Park and never should be permitted to disintegrate into it," he argued. But the danger was great:

> European culture must be saved from destruction at the hands of the Asiatic hordes from the steppes. We must defend the soul and majesty of the West with blazing swords against the satanic will to annihilation of a soulless demonic power, which has the goal of drowning the world in its own blood, and destroying the meaning of all history by establishing a subhuman reign of terror over the ruins of our grand human creation.[66]

Schumann's poem entitled "Führer" was an affirmation of total surrender to the great one come from above:

> We once swore an oath to you.
> Now we are yours forever.
> Like brooks, lost in a river,
> We flow into you.[67]

In the poem "Our Loyalty Is Our Thanks," victory was assured because Hitler was felt to be "fighting in the first ranks." Schumann also drew in this work on long dead heroes for support in the fighting:

The spirits of our heroic ancestors
Burst forth from their graves.
Unseen but with loyal power
They are out front when our flags attack.[68]

During the hours of stress at the front, Schumann felt the presence of the Führer. When strength had faded in the firestorm of battle, when friend after friend was killed and all seemed in vain, "We felt your eyes looking at us. . . . And all were silent. . . . That was the victory."[69]

Music also filled the lonely hours of anticipation before the next onslaught. "Song in the Night" conjured up the hopes and longings of men pressed to the limit after days spent pinned down by artillery fire. Out of the black of night, a song was heard from afar:

They listened. They heard: it was singing . . .
A sweet Psalm in the hell.

They sang of meadow and valley,
Of the homeland, of distant loved ones.
The sweet wound touched many
And tears welled up in their eyes.

And as the voices blended,
From the foxholes and trenches
There rose up—gleaming and reassuring—
The sound of a brotherly choir.

High above the ravished land,
That was consumed by the fires of death
In the horror of annihilation their
Song burned like a quiet prayer.[70]

Schumann's most famous war poem was a statement of determination to see the war through to victory. Widely distributed, and scored by Eugen Papst, "Soldier's Prayer" was sung far and wide and became standard propaganda fare in public ceremonials. Its message was simple, yet compelling:

O God, we are not much with words.
But please hear our prayer now:
Make our souls firm and strong.
The rest we'll do ourselves.

Protect my silent wife at home,
When she grieves in the dark of night

Light your star in the blue on high,
That its comfort might warm her heart.

Protect the Führer and the land.
Let the children rest in peace.
We place them in your hands.
The rest we'll do ourselves.[71]

Mothers were remembered as well, suffering and worrying on the home front. "To My Mother" was an unashamed acknowledgement of a son's awareness of his mother's love and compassion for his life's joys and sorrows and, if need be, her reluctant acceptance of his death. "There is nothing purer before God," he wrote, "than a mother's loving prayer."[72]

Schumann endeavored to teach his comrades who faced death to be cognizant of its deeper meaning. Although such poems contained elements of both poignant melancholy and stoic acceptance, they were suffused in the blessed assuredness of resurrection and the miracle of Easter. In the poem "For a Fallen Friend (H.P.H.)," he intoned:

Battle was embossed on your face. And you went
Unafraid into every danger and difficulty,
To offer yourself for your Führer.
Your whole life was like a flame.
And as you lived, so you proudly passed away.
. . . But in the blood-red shimmering ensigns
You march silently with us toward victory.[73]

When Schumann's brother Uli, a Luftwaffe officer, was killed in a mission over Malta, death struck Gerhard with a double force. At that time he wrote:

Your heart was as clear as crystal.
Your loyalty was
Like a mighty castle. . . .
I have borne many to their grave.
And my heart has bled.
But now that they have buried you
My fulfilled brother,
Young, silent German hero,
Some of my heart has been forever torn away.[74]

Many of Schumann's poems celebrated the final triumph of the fallen. Poems such as "You Dead Heroes," "Vision over the Graves," and "Triumph" point to a firm belief in the guarantee of deliverance from the realm of the dead to glorious eternity.[75] And in "Immortality" he affirmed his faith:

Nothing can disappear in God's universe of stars.
Death is only a quiet passage.
And all life is but a crossing over.
Be silent, listen, and hear: eternal law has become a
song.[76]

Schumann delivered an address on Heroes Memorial Day in March 1942, soon after he was released from a military hospital in Tübingen.[77] It embodied his belief in an eternal bond between those who had died for the nation and the mourning survivors on the home front. In a rhetorical flourish, he gave new life to the dream of his youth for the "great sacred Reich of the German nation." In a pastoral interplay between speaker and audience, the poet described this bond as he experienced it on a walk through a German town. In language of characteristic understatement, he elaborated on the courage shown in the face of suffering by a father, a mother, and a wife.

The father stood out from the crowd. "A German man with pure white hair" whose back "was bent as if weighed down by some great burden," he was somehow different from the rest. His eyes were focused within, and the lines on his brow testified to what fate had cast upon him. He wore a black ribbon on his coat. It was "a father whose son had died for the Fatherland."

Continuing through the town, the author caught sight of a woman in front of her house. Peering expectantly down the street, she seemed to be waiting for someone, but "she knows that the one for whom she waits will never return." Yet she could still hear his voice and see him waving his last farewell from the corner. Her hair is still blond, but you can see in her face a life lived for her loved ones and the sleepless, prayer-filled nights of war. Dressed in black, her eyes were moist and her mouth quivered. She clung to the door to support herself and after a time entered the house. "It is a mother whose son has died for the Fatherland."

Finally he crossed paths with a young woman, who was bending over her child. Her pale face looked like a beautiful rare flower, a stark contrast to her dress of mourning black. Her lips were pressed together, and "she seemed to be searching for something with her hands, something that she would never find again." Her eyes "reflected the icy loneliness of long nights alone." She drew her child nearer to her and looked into its lovely face, searching deeply into its eyes, seemingly joining souls with it. Tears began to stream down her face. Taking the child into her arms, she knew that she had seen the likeness of her husband in its innocent eyes, "her husband who fell for the Fatherland."

Schumann reflected on the reason for the bravery of these individuals, whose magnanimity was symbolic of the German people at large. What made them assume the role of "the silent inner guard of the soul of the sacred Reich and its holy mission?" They had learned that the fallen were not dead but instead lived on in their hearts. Their souls held communion one with the other. They had found immortality among that noble band of Germanic heroes, the eternal guard of the nation. This faith gave them comfort and strength, and "their faces reflected the splendor of fallen stars." Through their loyalty they united the nation in a family of common suffering and sacrifice. Schumann, ever the mystical idealist, concluded his speech with a romantic vision: "I see on this beloved German soil not only a living wall of men and machines, of hearts and steel. I see in a colossal circle a silent wreath of crosses, an awe-inspiring mound of graves." Together the living and the fallen would forge the victory.[78]

Schumann's last major work was the tragedy *Gudruns Tod*.[79] Based on an ancient saga, it premiered on the author's birthday in February 1943 and played with leading casts not only in Berlin and Vienna but also in theaters stretching from Stettin to Stuttgart.[80] The work was cast in classic form and influenced by Greek models, reflecting the death motif so characteristic of both Germanic myth and National Socialist ideology. Gudrun, the queen of the Hegelingen, is the incarnation of virtue and strength. Forced to choose between her love for the Norman king Hartmut and duty—she had been promised in marriage to Herwig, king of the Danes— she chooses instead redemptive death. The beautiful, self-sacrificing Gudrun answers the higher law of morality. She commits suicide over the corpse of King Hartmut, whom she passionately loves, and floats out to sea in a flaming black dragon ship, which bears the ill-fated pair to eternal rest in the fire and smoke of divine immolation. Opening only two weeks after the Stalingrad disaster, the message for wartime Germany was absolutely clear. Devotion to duty, if need be loyalty to the death, was a sacred moral obligation.[81]

Schumann took up this theme once more when he was installed as the first president of the Hölderlin Society in June 1943. Goebbels was the honorary chairman of the organization, and an elaborate ceremony was staged at Schumann's inauguration on the hundreth anniversary of Friedrich Hölderlin's death at Tübingen University in June 1943. In his address, Schumann referred to Hölderlin not only as a great poet and human being but also as a tragic hero. Through his depth of character, he had demonstrated the truth of the ancient affirmation that suffering ennobles. What held true for Hölderlin would have validity for the German people, Schumann submitted. Hölderlin's grand vision and heroic poetry had crowned the fighting zeal of the German soldiers with the moral force of the eternal word:

In the firestorm of all our battles your heart is with us and in your heart the heart of the Fatherland. We know:

17. Anna Dammann as Gudrun and Albin Skoda as Hartmut in Gerhard Schumann's *Gudruns Tod*. Deutsches Theater, Berlin, 1943. (Personal Collection.)

"The righteous strike, like a magician,
And their songs of the Fatherland
force the dishonorable to their knees."

And you will be with us also, when the battle is ours,
when victory rises like a silent star out of the
unending suffering and sacrifice.[82]

In the fall of 1944, with the imminent closing of the theaters throughout the country, Schumann was tapped by Obergruppenführer Gottlob Berger—who commanded the SS Hauptamt—to join the cultural section of his staff. Schumann received a commission as a first lieutenant in the Waffen SS because, according to Schumann, Berger "was in dire need of my talents as a poet in the hour of danger for both the fighting front and the homeland."[83] Sturmbannführer Dr. Heyd headed the culture section, which was situated at Berkenbrück on the Spree. For the next several months, Schumann engaged in a determined if hopeless attempt to strengthen the will of his compatriots through the arts. His office was ordered to evacuate to the legendary Alpine Redoubt, but he was taken prisoner by the Americans at Isny in the Allgäu. He was then transported westward, where he was incarcerated in an American internment camp at Marseilles.

One can only wonder at Schumann's selective morality and the compromise of his ideal vision of the German Reich. A keeper of the grail had lent his talents to a criminal organization, the vanguard of Hitler's brutal attempt to create a racially pure Reich. With the Holocaust reaching its tragic apogee, and the fires of Auschwitz illuminating the night, Schumann's efforts to defend the regime made a mockery of his life's work. He ended the war a tragic figure, unable to admit that his dream for a renewed German Reich was forever shattered.

After the war, Schumann testified to the shock he felt at the "horrible news of the death camps." In his memoirs, he expressed great disappointment at those responsible for the Holocaust, whom he deemed "a relatively small group of people given over to lawlessness and corruption, within a leadership driven by unparalleled delusions of grandeur in the final, truly apocalyptic zenith of the war."[84] Schumann failed to understand, however, that heroism by definition must embrace the concept of the antihero. *Poesie* and politics were merged in the regime. Through his misguided celebration of the "heroic"—Adolf Hitler, the "intrepid German soldier," the "brave German mother and wife," and the pristine German landscape—he provided the cultural and aesthetic trappings for the totalitarian state. Other, criminal hands drew racial variations on this heroic motif, with tragic results. The muses had thereby become the handmaiden to destruction.[85]

VII

Hans Baumann

Troubadour of the Hitler Youth

> Wir werden weiter marschieren,
> wenn alles in Scherben fällt,
> denn heute gehört uns Deutschland
> und morgen die ganze Welt.
>
> Hans Baumann[1]

Young Germans felt that they represented the nation reborn, and those in the Hitler Youth were perhaps the most radical of the post–World War I generation. They were absolutely assured that fate had chosen them for a special mission in league with their new messiah. Ideological education, rigorous physical training, and peer group cohesion reinforced their ideal of total commitment. Seemingly their entire program was put to music, in a form that delighted the young. No other genre expressed more clearly the emotionally assertive, if somewhat naive, ethos of the Hitler Youth. Pride swelled in their young hearts when the *Fanfarenzug* of pipes and drums stepped out smartly, blaring the good news of the New Age from town square to the parade grounds of Nuremberg.[2]

Music accompanied them on marches and outings in the countryside and brightened their pack meetings. The words of one song, "The sun never stops shining for us," accurately reflected the dawn of a new era. Music also excited their aggressive instincts, honed them for battle, and beckoned them to adventure. Although several individuals wrote poems that became songs of the Hitler Youth, only Hans Baumann combined remarkable poetic talents with an uncanny gift for conceiving musical scores for his own poems, which immediately became popular. His work was characterized by natural harmony, grace of style, and a marriage of adolescent enthusiasm with epic political goals. Baumann became the quintessential songwriter of the Hitler Youth.

Baumann was but a youth of nineteen when Hitler took power. He enjoyed a meteoric career in the Third Reich, which belied his simple background as a boy from the Bavarian Forest.[3] Baumann's poetic career developed over three distinct periods. During the halcyon days of the peacetime Third Reich, his poetry and song extolled the virtues of heroism,

18. Hans Baumann, 1944
(Personal Collection.)

manliness, and bravery. These rhapsodic works, based on both celebration and hope for the future, peaked during the era of Germany's *Blitzkrieg* successes. Phase two, which paralleled the fateful years from 1941 through 1945, reflected a curious ambivalence in the once self-assured author. Although he enjoyed continued popularity—even Gustav Gründgens recognized him by staging his play *Alexander* in Berlin in 1941—Baumann became ill at ease with the criminal regime even before the attack on the Soviet Union. Like many other writers, artists, and actors who had serious doubts about the system, he continued to support it with his propaganda. For example, on the occasion of Hitler's birthday in 1942, he published *The Saviour of Europe* in a propaganda pamphlet distributed to the Wehrmacht.[4] For the remainder of the war, he fought an inner struggle, guilt-ridden for the role he had played as one of Germany's leading cultural propagandists. More and more he withdrew into the world he had known as a boy, to a romantic, even escapist, poetic worship of nature. The final phase of his career began after the war, when he became a very successful writer of childrens' literature, with several national and international prizes to his credit.

There were many factors in Baumann's background that played a significant role in his development. Above all, he was joyfully uncomplicated as a young man, and it was this simplicity that made his works so popular in the Hitler Youth, where he was affectionately known as "Happy Hans" ("Hans im Glück"). Baumann revealed the source of his optimism in a biographical description that he wrote for a poetry anthology in 1934:

> The best mother in the world gave birth to me in 1914, in the nineteenth-century town of Amberg, in the middle of the *Steinpfalz*. A wild April storm was my first cradle song. When my father first came home from the war, I could already climb on his shoulders. That way I could nudge my head against his steel helmet. This iron helmet, a rusted pistol, some old hand grenades and soldiers were my first friends, since I grew up for seven years in an army camp. Last year I was a teacher in a logging village in the Bohemian Forest. Baldur von Schirach called me to Berlin. But the blood of the farmer in me simply gives me no rest. I'll work and work, until I own a piece of the good earth.[5]

Baumann's love of nation was molded by his father, who kept the spirit of the front alive after the Great War. He was an honorary regimental commander in Amberg, where he was also active in the local *Turnverein*. The values of young Hans were also molded by a former World War I pilot—Captain Filbig, nicknamed "Fliegerhax"—who served both as his teacher and his mentor in Baumann's youthful national zeal. Further, being raised far from the nervous city, he learned at an early age the beauty of growing up among the unspoiled people of the countryside. The result was an unashamed openness and naturalness. As Baumann observed: "If I had a gift, it was sincerity, and the ability to express clearly what others felt deep down in their hearts."[6]

Hans also was blessed with the joy of a loving family, which also accounted for his confidence. As he described it, "I was as happy as a bird in the nest," as part of a large family descended from peasants and iron miners. He had a very loving mother, who was an unpublished poet and first set an example for him with her mystic love of the German landscape. His grandmother was very sympathetic to the boy as well, and she taught him the meaning of simple country wisdom. Young Hans was a pious Catholic, and some members of the family hoped that he might become a priest. His favorite authors were Eichendorff and Mörike, while von Kleist and Körner nurtured his nascent interest in the union of art and nation. From time to time he would make cultural pilgrimages from provincial Amberg to beautiful Nuremberg, home of Albrecht Dürer and an entire school of German masters and craftsmen.

Baumann's secure world was shaken when the agony of unemployment reached his village in the 1920s. His own father was unemployed after the war. Thereafter he ran an inn and worked as a customs official, but the earlier secure family environment was disrupted.[7] Throughout the village, the sensitive boy witnessed the ravages of unemployment. In 1928, at the age of fourteen, he wrote the poem "Unemployed," bewailing the suffering around him.[8] Another poem that he wrote in this period, "Four Flights Up," testified to the sympathy he felt for a mother in distress.[9] Poverty and suffering became daily occurrences for young Baumann.

In his search for answers to the social problems of the day, Hans became active in Catholic youth activities (Katholischer Schülerbund Neudeutschland). In time it became evident that the hierarchy had marked him for future leadership in Catholic youth affairs. But his sensitive spirit could not bear the conflict he observed in the church between religious principle and political engagement. At a conclave in Haus Altenberg near Cologne, he resolved once and for all not to accept a political office. Nevertheless, he was about to embark on a career with cultural influence far beyond that of a provincial church functionary. He was soon widely known for his writing. Indeed, his first and most important song was written under the imprimatur of the Mother Church, and it became popular in the Hitler Youth almost overnight.

When in the film *Cabaret* a stereotypical blond and blue-eyed youth rises in a gorgeous Alpine setting to lead a group of boys in singing the seductive song with the refrain "Today Germany belongs to us, and tomorrow the whole world"—a scene often repeated in the Third Reich—he is singing Hans Baumann's song. Baumann had written it at the age of eighteen while studying for a career in education at a Jesuit academy for teachers in Amberg. His priest was so taken with this, and several other songs that Baumann had written, that he took the extraordinary step of approaching a publisher in Munich. The prestigious Catholic house Köselverlag brought out a collection of Baumann's songs in 1933 under the ironic title *Macht keinen Lärm* (*Make No Commotion*). Like many important songs of the day, the one in *Cabaret* had become popular in the youth movement repertoire long before it was taken over by the Hitler Youth. Ultimately it was published in the *Spielschar,* a publication of the Reichsjugendführung, which gave it official sanction.[10]

Entitled "Es zittern die morschen Knochen ("The Old Bones Are Trembling"), the song called for a violent end to the traditional German social system. It was not out of place in an era awash in theory about the "decline of the West."[11] Its swashbuckling attack on the moribund past and its apocalyptic call for destruction and renewal through war delighted many young Germans. Countless boys who sang it with such enthusiasm perished in the coming war, a struggle that fulfilled their affirmation with a vengeance:

> The old bones of the world
> are trembling at the sight of the red war.
> We've put an end to the terror
> It was a great victory for us.

Another verse proclaimed the victory of youth over the elders:

> And if the old should scold us,
> Just let them scream and yell
> and if the whole world were to oppose us,
> we'll still be the victors.

Finally, the song heralded the enthusiastic destruction of all that stood in the way on the road to the new era:

> Even if the whole world
> lay in ruins from our battle,
> we say what the hell
> and we'll build it up again.
>
> We'll keep on marching,
> even if everything is smashed
> because today Germany belongs to us
> and tomorrow the whole world.[12]

Baumann transferred his loyalty from Catholic youth activities to the Hitler Youth. He had become convinced that Hitler was a saviour, come to rescue the German nation from the mouth of the abyss. During the years of the peacetime Third Reich, he was engaged in a myriad of activities that influenced his songwriting, experiences that bore fruit in the publication of nearly one hundred fifty songs as well as several cantatas, plays, and shorter pieces.[13] He was a passionately devoted Hitler Youth leader, and his songs celebrated the joy of wandering over hill and dale and the beauty of comradeship in union with nature. He worked as a teacher during 1933–34 in a one-room schoolhouse near the logging village of Voithernberg in the Bavarian Forest. Although he was called to assume a role as a functionary in the Reichsjugendführung in Berlin—where he edited the publication *Jungenschaft,* headed the amateur theatrical section, and engaged in work for the radio—he was never really at home in the teeming capital.

The land always beckoned him, and he spent a period working it like the proverbial peasant. In a wistful autobiographical essay, he reflected on the joys of communion with nature in the countryside of Greater Germany. Revealing a deeply mystical strain in his character, Baumann wrote:

> I came to know Germany's streams and mountains, its heath and moor, its forest and fields, its castles and cathedrals. . . . During a hot summer in the Baltic, we dug a thousand-meter-long ditch through a swamp in Kurland. . . . We saw it [that is, beautiful Germany] in a blue autumn in Siebenbürgen, with its majestic castles Rosenau and Tartlau, and the Great Ring of Hermannstadt, the Black Church of Kronstadt, where Johann Sebastian Bach is resurrected each Easter.[14]

Everything about the reawakened nation seemed to thrill Baumann, even military service. He wrote:

> On 7 November 1935, when the new war flag of the Reich was first being raised, I stood in the Lustgarten at Potsdam, to take my military oath. I passed two happy years as a soldier in Potsdam and Göttingen.[15]

Baumann matriculated at the University of Berlin during the academic year 1938–39, where he studied history and literature. But his spiritual home remained the university of the soul, his classroom the forests and streams of the *Heimat*. Curiously, Baumann never bothered to join the Nazi party. It simply would have been out of character in a man for whom soil, homeland, and the cultivation of youth were true ideals rather than objects to exploit on the road to power.[16]

Taken together, the songs of Hans Baumann form a heroic tapestry embracing elements of romanticism, knightly concepts of bravery and loyalty, political religiosity, and heady nationalism. One sees traces of Eichendorff's idealization of youth, of Rilke's young hero called home at a tender age, celebrated in *Die Weise von Liebe und Tod des Cornets Christoph Rilke,* and of the worship of nature and the allure of a righteous death in Novalis.[17] The nationalistic excesses of both von Kleist and Körner are clearly evident as well. Ultimately, the poet set the stage for political destruction. The romantic imagery that he created had a seductive fascination for much of the youth of his era.[18] It was Baumann's belief that the young generation, in league with the Führer, would erect a shimmering castle on a distant hill from which would radiate a new city, freed from the shackles of caste and class. The actual result of this aesthetic vision was tragic.

On route to this new city, youths experienced the time of their lives. They thrilled to Baumann's verses:

> Now we're about to march
> We all know the cry:
> Youth marches for Germany. . . . [19]

This upbeat spirit took a bold cadence in "You Summoning Fanfares":

> And your trumpet calls
> will find all the young,
> ready to do battle against the old city wall.

Not mere destroyers, these:

> And your trumpet calls
> will lead us to the brave new city . . .
> sound your clear fanfares
> the world belongs to youth!

Nor would they be afraid:

> . . . your trumpet calls
> will find the dawn,
> will see us standing tall in danger
> keeping the faith in life and death.[20]

It was this sort of bravado that so captured the hearts of young Germans that they wanted to blare the new message from the rooftops. Baumann related the excitement he felt when as a young Hitler Youth leader—a mere boy himself—he "heard my compositions sung by sixty thousand Hitler Youth on the fields of Nuremberg."[21] How beautiful it was to live in such a time of change, to see the shining eyes of the red-cheeked and innocent young girls of the Bund deutscher Mädel as they passed smartly in review. How grand to march under the Führer's banners and see the swastika flag flying on high! The certainty that, like the Teutonic knights of yore, they were setting out to construct a citadel made the boys deliriously happy. Such impulses were enough to inspire them to sing:

> Now again there are new castles
> as always when Germany awakes:
> *Jungvolk* raises its flag
> like a tower in threatening night. . . .
>
> The walls stand firmly again
> built by our own hands. . . .
> *Jungvolk* raises its flags,
> no enemy can hold them back now.[22]

Baumann also employed the vision of Germany as a politically transfigured cathedral, drawing on symbolism important since the Gothic era. The song "Nun steht der Dom" celebrated this theme, as Germany was seen to have experienced the miracle of Easter under the Führer, Adolf Hitler:

> Now the cathedral is standing
> it's standing squarely in the light. . . .
> The suffering is gone, that tore our Volk apart . . .
> and our song makes us strong and sure. . . .
> The cathedral is standing there,
> it's standing squarely in the light.[23]

This vision of a new, holy city served as inspiration for the young guard to spread the faith. In his cantata *The New City*, the muses were once more called upon to serve the will to power:

The cathedral must be central once again,
inspiring all our hearts, the whole city,
where true life will dwell. . . .

As for the Hitler Youth and the party:

And priests will climb the steps of the temple,
proud and pure before almighty God . . .
because the Volk has sent them to pray there. . . .

In an obvious reference to Hitler, Baumann has the young sing:

And to one the truth is revealed.
Then the Volk listens with open hearts.
Then their faith burns with mighty candles,
and all doubt disappears from their great house.
You have peace that passes understanding
even as you wage war.
Germany, you high city on the hill.
Germany, you good castle.[24]

The cantata also featured the loyalty motif, a theme often found in
Baumann's work. Loyalty went hand in hand with comradeship, reinforcing
the simple yet profound obligation of "one for all and all for one," as well
as knightly faith to the death. Loyalty was a holy bond transcending all
other values:

And if we have loyalty
and nothing else in the world,
that is enough, then
no power can defeat us.
. . . nor can even the force of death
cut it down.[25]

Just as the epic Roland once harkened to the trumpet call in the Pyrenees,
fighting to the last for Christ and his noble lord Charlemagne, so now a
new generation took up the banner where it had fallen:

A new Roland is being raised.
And it is loyalty in all this land,
a quiet herald in this noisy world.
And for freedom he raises his hand. . . .
A new Roland mighty and secure,
To ensure that loyalty guards the gate to the world.[26]

Baumann conjured up the dead in his poetry and songs. He wrote:
"Our dead keep the faith even in death; they'll always be among the first

guard with the flag."[27] Wherever those in the Hitler Youth raised their voices in song or whenever a unit of them was deployed to meet the foe, they claimed that the spirits of long-dead comrades joined their march:

> And before us death rides in cadence,
> he has taken many from us. . . .
> But the dead stand by the flag,
> as long as we march on.[28]

The flag was the symbol of undying loyalty, binding the living and the dead in eternal unity:

> Where we are, there is loyalty,
> It commands our every step. . . .
> When we sing, loyalty keeps silent,
> it is greater than the song. . . .
>
> When we attack, loyalty is singing,
> and its song fires us on,
> and we are zealous like the flag,
> spurring each man on.[29]

Baumann's experiences as a manual worker in the East informed his songs, and their political message expressed a longing for expansion known for centuries as the "Drang nach Osten." One of the most notable examples among Baumann's works was a stirring cantata entitled *Call of the East,* published in 1936, which was nothing less than a trumpet fanfare to aggression.[30] The work admonished German Youth to take up the banners where the Teutonic knights had left them centuries before:

> Raise the banners in the East wind,
> for they wave so strongly there,
> they signal our departure
> and our blood hears the call.

The way would be hard:

> Make yourselves strong! Those who build in the East
> will face many an ordeal. . . .

In a format suitable for theatrical and radio productions targeted to the nation's young audience, individuals assigned roles as "Call" and "Answer" responded to themes describing the challenge of constant battle, the satisfaction of resettling and ploughing the good earth in the East, and the majesty of the reconquered homeland. *Call of the East* placed youth in harmony with nature and the flow of history. In this scenario, Germany became part of a mighty cosmic stream:

> Germany, you forceful stream . . .
> Stream flowing from the heart of God
> You once flowed here,
> this is your old course. . . .
> Germany, here is your stream bed
> into eternity.

In a rhapsodic finale, Baumann has the youth answer the "call from the East" with an affirmation that might well have been written by Hitler:

> Our morning stands in the East,
> this is Germany's future,
> cares of our Volk lie there,
> victory and danger await there.[31]

Shortly before the outbreak of World War II, Baumann enjoyed considerable acclaim for the success of his play *Rüdiger von Bechelaren,* which premiered in Passau in July 1939 amid much fanfare. The work was based on the saga of the Nibelungen, and Baumann's interpretation of the Germanic epic was notable for its use of music to convey the epic themes of the nation's warrior ancestors. The cast featured actors from across Greater Germany, including one Hans Baumann as Rüdiger (Chemnitz), Hans Kurth as Hagen (Breslau), Edyth Edwards as Kriemhild (Volksbühne Berlin), and Gotlinde, played by Maria Kindl (Graz). The setting of Passau was also significant, because it was situated at the confluence of the Danube—gateway to the East—and the Inn rivers. This was of no little meaning, considering that the play was staged only sixteen months after the *Anschluss* with Austria. According to Walter Talmon-Gros of the *Völkischer Beobachter,* landscape, hero, and song joined in a mellifluous union:

> The premiere of Hans Baumann's *Weihespiel* "Rüdiger von Bechelaren" provided a model for the outdoor theater. . . . The presence of Baldur von Schirach and several members of the Reichsjugendführung was an outward sign of the high regard our youth has for the work of the poet who marches in their columns. . . . The poet dared to stylize his material in as austere and monumental a way as did Sophocles or Aeschylus, as they fashioned the living myths of their people into eternal tragedies.

Those present could not fail to grasp the real meaning of the epic struggle between the Burgundians and the Huns, which concluded in bloody sacrifice:

> The applause of the audience came only gradually following the overpowering conclusion of the play. Deeply moved, the people wandered through the dark down into the town, past whose old walls flows the river so fateful for the Nibelungen.[32]

When the time came to complete the work of their Nibelungen ancestors with the onset of war, youths enthusiastically answered Hitler's call to arms. For his part, Baumann stood ready to provide poetic and musical accompaniment to aggression. In the song "Comrades, Raise the Banners" he focused on Hitler as field marshal:

Comrades, raise the banners,
let the drums thunder forth!
What the others only dream of,
will blaze in our hearts.

Führer, give the orders to march,
Which no doubts will countermand
By dawn's early light Germany
illuminates our souls.[33]

As the first blood was shed in the *Blitzkrieg* years, Baumann demonstrated a devil-may-care attitude about a soldier's death for the nation. In his poem "Oath of the Cadet Sergeant" he wrote:

Despite the trembling of brave men,
despite the distress in my heart
Afire with sorrow, I will raise the banner,
with hands that are no more.

When the skies suddenly explode,
when the stream stops flowing out of terror,
Though blown about by war, I will
sing with a silent voice.

Thousands die, thousands tower up
a mountain of bodies on the battlefield.
Though I am felled a thousand times,
I will get up on my knees and attack.[34]

On Heroes Memorial Day in March 1940, Baumann, now a lieutenant and company commander in Hitler's victorious Wehrmacht, gave a rousing address in the Schiller Theater in Berlin. Speaking on the theme "The Solemn Promise of the Young," Baumann hitched both the Greek and the German classics to the chariot of Mars. His address could stand as a model for National Socialist aesthetics. Baumann grounded his thought on the idea that "the German's link to the eternal comes through art." He admonished the young to honor the Reich's fallen with deeds, not words, submitting that beauty would flow naturally from timeless acts of heroism. Thus, the privilege of living in Germany's era of greatness called for the highest idealism, symbolized by the lines of Friedrich Hölderlin's "Der Tod fürs Vaterland": "The battle is ours! Hold high the banner, O Fatherland,

and do not count the dead! Beloved nation, not one too many has died for you."[35]

Baumann reflected on the impatience of the young to enter the fray, agreeing that a "baptism of fire" was every man's sacred right. Pure of heart and mind, Baumann's young knights would enjoy the protection of the Almighty only as long as their methods and goals remained firmly grounded in idealism. He argued that the nobility of the German stormers, graced by a nearly divine idealism, stood in stark contrast to the cynicism and slovenliness of the besotted French, whose perverted national consciousness inspired the posting of black colonial forces to occupy the Rhineland after World War I. Further, he submitted that it was a proud mission, indeed, to defend the culture of Goethe and Schiller against the English, who were inspired only by greed and materialism. "This," he predicted, "will be the last century for the merchants of the world." Facing the reactionaries were the singing youths of Germany, in harmony with the universal plan of Providence. Baumann testified unblushingly that "Germany's best young sons will die joyfully, that the nation might remain ever young."[36]

In a rhapsodic flight from reality, Baumann reminded the young Germans in the audience that their strength was based on a union with nature, with the beauty of the Alpine peaks, the eternally surging sea, the birch and pine. And where, he queried, does the soldier's mind wander at night? To the Linden trees of his village, rustling in the breeze. Thinking of his loved ones, his eyes peruse the heavens, coming to rest on the Big Dipper—Ursa Major—and the noble Orion. German culture was a sweet balm for the soldier as well, and Goethe, Mozart, and Kleist blessed his sacrifice. Baumann admonished the German soldiers of 1940 to look to Walter Flex and Gorch Fock as their models. These heroes loved the German union of intellect and power so deeply that they went to an early death for the Fatherland and were rewarded with eternal life. He encouraged them to heed the words of the Führer, which should inspire them all in the nation's hour of destiny: "Man becomes great through eternal battle."[37]

The realities of the war took their inevitable toll on Baumann, as they did on the German people.[38] With the spectacular victories of the *Blitzkrieg* campaigns of 1939–40 behind him, Hitler suffered defeat in the Battle of Britain and launched the invasion of the Soviet Union. There is little reason to doubt that Baumann had heard of the liquidations carried out by the SS Einsatzgruppen behind the lines. In October 1941, prior to the onset of what would become a cruel winter and defeat before Moscow, Baumann delivered a critical address at the Writers' Congress in Weimar. The tenor of his speech was worlds apart from that of the year before. His remarks were both philosophical and poetic, in marked contrast to National Socialist propaganda, and they offended Goebbels, who was present at the conclave held annually in honor of his birthday.

Baumann submitted that it is difficult for an experienced soldier to sing the praises of war; men who have been under fire for any length of time tend to advance wiser sentiments. The seasoned veterans had seen the agony of their comrades' deaths. They had heard their wounded brothers, captured by the Russians, crying out for help in the night from across enemy lines. They had witnessed the annihilation of an entire German regiment in a fire storm in a small sector of the eastern front. Yet he found personally that the war experience molds character in ways that are impossible in the ordered world of peacetime.

Baumann submitted that the horrors of war could be surmounted only through transcendence and the cultivation of noble character traits in one's inner life. Poets and writers, he noted, were blessed with the gift of fashioning eternal virtue into word and song. Through *Poesie,* the common soldier found the strength to endure the suffering and hell of war, and he was inspired by the belief that his cause was just, even unto death. Among all the virtues that he lauded, the most important was the cultivation of charity toward all mankind. He admitted that the "battle in Russia forces necessary severity on us, because a soulless instrument of power must be destroyed." Nevertheless, he concluded his address with a thinly veiled plea for a change of direction in Hitler's policies toward the eastern peoples. "War might be the father of all things," he noted, "but charity remains the mother of all things."[39]

There is other evidence that the war was forcing Baumann to rethink his loyalty to Hitler. The title alone of a volume of poems published in 1941, *War the Transformer,* demonstrated his ambiguity.[40] He also published the revealing poem "Inscription":

Few go to their deaths
with a smile on their face.
But the chosen bleed the future,
breathe their youth,
into their friends.[41]

The poem "Death and War" shows the inner struggle he was undergoing:

Swaying in the rain of steel, dazzled
by the luster of the weapons, death
nears and complains.

Who has put an end to summer, who
has felled the forests
and destroyed the fields by fire?

What happened to the larks' song,
to the whisper of the birches, the
streams' secret song? . . .[42]

It is ironic that Baumann's career in the Third Reich peaked at the very time that his agony of the soul had begun—with the premiere of his play *Alexander,* featuring the legendary actor Gustav Gründgens. Gründgens admired *Alexander,* which was published in 1941 before the offensive against Russia was launched. He wired Baumann that he wished to produce it at the Staatstheater in Berlin and to play the starring role himself. Delighted with this opportunity, Baumann worked closely with Gründgens on the production over seven hectic weeks. Mathias Wiemann played Hephaistion, and the ranking actors Lina Karstens, Lola Müthel, and Bernhard Minetti were also cast in leading roles. Premiering on 14 June 1941, the play received a great deal of attention.

The critic Karl H. Ruppel praised the work highly, noting that the author approached his composition through intellect, not the *Zeitgeist,* which was grounded in emotion. He contended that *Alexander* was a major contribution in the effort to maintain theater as an art form, not merely theatrical accompaniment to the events of the day. Ruppel found Gründens brilliant as Alexander:

> In appearance a Hellenistic statue come to life, face crowned with blond hair, half hero, half Apollo. . . . The Oriental traits of the historic Alexander take second place to the Hellenic genius of classic proportions. . . . The audience understood the grand moral and the achievement of the poet Hans Baumann. This play coming from the corps of youth promises great things for the future.[43]

On the night of its premiere, Gründgens received some twenty-five curtain calls. Although the Reichsdramaturg, Rainer Schlösser, was favorable to *Alexander,* Goebbels was offended by its political message, ordering the play closed after a run of only two nights.[44] Goebbels understood the deeper meaning of *Alexander*; the subtlety of Baumann's message did not escape him. *Alexander* was a barely camouflaged plea for Hitler to temper his harshness toward the conquered peoples of Europe with charity, a noble if totally unrealistic dream. In the world of Hitler, there was no place for an aesthetic vision that contradicted his fundamental ideological beliefs and policy directives. Baumann wrote:

> At that time I still believed in the Führer, but I had some serious concerns. I wanted to show not just Hitler, but anyone who would see the play how one should behave in war; that one cannot humiliate a conquered people, which just sows hatred, but instead should follow Alexander's example, to raise the Persians to the level of the conquerors and to consummate the "marriage of Susa."[45]

Alexander was in part a commentary on the political and moral choices that beset the conqueror. In his lust for power, Baumann's Alexander far oversteps himself. Yet his saving grace is the charity and gentleness he shows the conquered: "I am victorious because I love." Upon commissioning Hephaistion, one of his proconsuls, with the governance of several territories, Alexander says of him:

Hephaistion loves gentleness . . . the Reich is at peace, and the people of Asia are liberated from bondage. . . . We are not merely conquering territory; we are bringing order into a chaotic world.

Yet Alexander is consumed with an insatiable passion to conquer ever more territory. Scanning a war map, he expresses the desire to see all the territories of Rome, Carthage, and Syracuse "gloriously united in one Reich and unified for centuries." A driven man, Alexander opined, "Let us be contemptuous of the earthbound."

Despite his pragmatism and the fact that he placed the cultures of other nations on an equal footing with that of Macedonia, Alexander is beset with insurmountable problems. Many of his generals and admirals, as well as his foot soldiers, no longer support his policies of limitless aggression and want to return home: "The forests of our childhood are calling, calling us back with a great longing." Further, as the astrologer Aristander informs the emperor, "Your armies have won victory after victory, but they bear terrible guilt for their deeds." Many of his officers and men lose faith because "noble blood is wasted, a corps of youth is squandered at the height of its powers, firm in its loyalty, yet all for nothing." They revolt despite the emperor's impassioned plea:

Do you want to stop but halfway to the goal? May you rot! I must go to the end of the road dreamt of by the god of the Sun. The peoples of the world will be watching; I will mourn for my own people at the outer limits of the world.

There is considerable desertion from Alexander's armed forces, which leaves him in the lurch. The loyal Admiral Nearch remains, uttering the sentiment that "he who deserts Alexander, betrays truth."

Alexander the Great was beset with contradictions, just as was Baumann's vision of Hitler. Paralleling the denouement of Heinrich von Kleist's *Prinz Friedrich von Homburg,* the ethereal final scene of *Alexander* is played before the royal palace of Babylon at midnight. All signs point to the imminent death of the Great One. Alexander, surrounded by the ghosts of the slain Admiral Nearch and the souls of the fallen warriors of his once grand army, proclaims, "The Eastern peoples are now enjoying their hard-won freedom, purified in the flames of war." Charity has linked wisdom to power, thus setting the stage for a glorious imperial era. A voice calls out from the dark: "Suffering has set the stage for the future; sacrificial death was its seed." The "Choir of Becoming" answers, "Manly deeds result in eternal life."

In the final scene, a shimmering vision of beauteous heroic death announces Alexander's transfiguration and apotheosis. The astrologer Aristander recounts the vision of Alexander's final journey:

> Climbing the steps of eternal life, he stood before the gate of midnight, a godly halo shimmering over his head. He stood there bathed in the light of solitude. . . . I saw him striding through the harkening nations, through sleeping mountains, their summits aglow with his gaze, which was like the kiss of lightning, and his steps coiled like thunder; abandoned fields blossomed again as he passed; the song of the sea was born again.[46]

Striving, ever striving, Alexander's armies of the dead accompany him on this journey to the eternal. A foot soldier noted in wonder:

> Trusting, we marched loyally through the blowing sand to God's Island in the Egyptian desert; we carried the sun on our glimmering shields. . . . Eagles fanned down from the heavens to show us the way. . . . Only a few pilgrims had ever reached this sacred grove, and now an entire army stood to at its source.[47]

The glorious deeds of Alexander's troops had guaranteed them eternal life and the empire a noble future. The living and the dead were one in this grand community. But the future prosperity of the empire depended on their continued faith in the resurrection and return of Alexander: "He will be with us only so long as we believe in him. His legacy is awaited on all the coasts of the world." Baumann's dream of tempering the harshness of the Führer's policies through the medium of the theater was a hopeless exercise. But, considering what followed in the campaign against Russia, *Alexander* was indeed prophetic.

Baumann's last significant musical works glorifying Hitler and the Third Reich were written in 1941.[48] From time to time the old fires would burn anew when he wrote propaganda tracts for the Wehrmacht. In the spring of 1942, while serving as a company commander on the eastern front, he wrote one such essay extolling Hitler on the occasion of the Führer's birthday. Entitled *The Saviour of Europe,* it was widely distributed in the ranks.[49]

Early on, Baumann chose to continue to believe that Hitler was not personally responsible for the criminality and atrocities of his satraps and SS murder squads in Poland and the Soviet Union. But this changed with the growing evidence of the bankruptcy of the regime. He had personal reasons that wore on his soul as well. Baumann's brother, an artillery captain, had by chance visited the sight of the massacre at Babi Yar while traveling to Kiev and had told Hans what he had seen there. Further, Baumann's wife, the musician Elisabeth Zogelman of Munich, on a tour of the eastern front with an entertainment company, brought heartbreaking news to him. Her teacher, the violinist Lotte Harburger—who had sensed that Zogelman, a young woman of modest circumstances, had real promise as an artist and had taken her in and trained her—had been shipped off to be killed in Auschwitz. And Baumann's friendship with both Adolf Reichwein—a member of the Kreisauer Kreis who was executed after the abortive 20 July 1944 plot against Hitler—and Carl Friedrich von Weizsäcker turned him more and more against Hitler.

Baumann's role as the troubadour of the Hitler Youth and songwriter for the Wehrmacht was now behind him, and the heady days of victory gave way to resignation and defeat. Ultimately, he constructed a new reality for himself in search of both personal and moral survival. In the northern Russian village of Skugry near Ilmen Lake, officially a rest and recreation facility for German troops of the Sixteenth Army on leave, he directed a program in cultural understanding for German soldiers. There, even Russian works were performed, and Russian guests were allowed to attend the functions.[50] From time to time members of the resistance gathered at Skugry as well, a group that included Count Helmuth von Moltke, Johannes Popitz, Adolf Reichwein, and Colonel von Uckermann. Baumann had the good fortune of being transferred from the eastern front late in the war. After the downfall of the Third Reich, he was interned in France.

The German catastrophe changed Baumann fundamentally. After the war he became internationally acclaimed as a writer of children's literature, and his works were translated into some twenty-one languages. He won awards in West Germany, the United States, and Italy. *I Marched With Hannibal* (1954) and *Sons of the Steppe* (1960) were favorably reviewed in the West and perceived as allegorical accounts of Baumann's intellectual transformation.

Musing forty years after the collapse of Hitler's Reich, Baumann concluded, "Hitler was a star for us. Even such a man as Leonardo da Vinci said, 'Whoever ties himself to a star, never wavers.' But the more I realized that I had marched for a false Führer, the more guilt I felt." He added, "The great thing about having a long life is that one can correct his mistakes."[51]

VIII

Karl Ritter and the Heroic Nazi Cinema

Even the heroic deeds of a *Nibelungenlied*
fade compared to this symphony of heroism,
passion, courage, and contempt of death. In
fierce storms of steel the squadron flew victo-
riously to the sun, bearing death and destruction, where they assaulted the enemy.

Hermann Göring[1]

Karl Ritter, a pilot in the Great War and erstwhile artist in the alienated days of the Weimar Republic, became one of the two or three leading cinema directors in the Third Reich. He launched his career in Nazi film by heading the production staff under Hans Steinhoff in the highly successful *Hitler Youth Quex*. Thereafter his rise was rapid. He and Goebbels found each other mutually useful in the unscrupulous milieu of high politics among the new elite. Although Ritter was certainly not Goebbels's favorite director—the minister found his *Zeitfilm* genre intellectually unappealing while realizing its short-term effectiveness as propaganda—Goebbels helped him become one of the stars in the stable at *Ufa*, the most important film concern in Germany.

Ritter's nationalistic *Verräter* premiered at the Nuremberg Party Rally in September 1936 in the wake of the Olympic games. His World War I trilogy—*Patrioten* (1937), *Unternehmen Michael* (1937), and *Urlaub auf Ehrenwort* (1937)—drew enthusiastic audiences. With the release of *Pour le Mérite* (1938), a cinematic tone poem on the theme of heroism, despair, and resurrection under National Socialism, Ritter drew the favorable attention of Hitler. He dutifully set to work on *Kadetten,* an anti-Russian film based on the theme of the self-sacrifice of youth under Frederick the Great. Heavily loaded with anti-Bolshevik propaganda, *Kadetten* could not be released on schedule in 1939 because of the signing of the German-Soviet Nonaggression Pact. It premiered instead in December 1941.

Ritter's career fluctuated with the changing fortunes of German arms in World War II. During the heady days of *Blitzkrieg* victories, he soared with the eagles as he had in the Great War. A dream came true for Ritter when he directed *Stukas* (1941), a hymn of heroism, comradeship, and love of nation. With *GPU* (1942), he produced a heavy-handed, unrelenting assault on Bolshevism. The defeat at Stalingrad and the loss of North Africa compromised his next effort—*Besatzung Dora* (1943)—which was placed on the list of forbidden films. Finally, with disaster on the horizon, Ritter started shooting *Das Leben geht weiter* in 1945.

Little in the background of Karl Ritter presaged his future role as a luminary in Third Reich film.[2] An indication, however, of what was to come might have been divined by observing that Ritter united the talents of both artist and soldier, each of which was vital to the creation of National Socialist aesthetics. The arts played a major role in his upbringing, and Ritter's youth in Würzburg molded the nascent artist in him. His father was a professor at the Conservatory of Music in Würzburg, and his childhood, spent surrounded by the gorgeous baroque architecture of the city, was not without its permanent effects. Ritter attended the humanistic gymnasium in Würzburg. His wife, Erika, was a Wagner in a line descending from Albert, the brother of Richard Wagner. Ritter's father-in-law was a pronounced anti-Semite, and there is little reason to doubt that his *völkisch* mysticism and anti-Semitism influenced Karl.

With the coming of the Great War, Ritter became a Fahnenjunker in the Bavarian army and was posted to the Third Bavarian Pionier Battalion. He rose through the ranks, serving as infantryman, flyer, battalion commander of the Twenty-first Bavarian Infantry Regiment, and ultimately general staff officer. Like his fellow soldiers and officers, Ritter was devastated by the loss of the war and the onset of the Weimar Republic. He withdrew to the countryside at idyllic Grainau, which lay in the Alps at the foot of the Wetterstein. In the company of his wife and three sons—Heinz (1912), Hans (1915), and Karl Gottfried (1916)—he eked out an existence as an artist. After a stint as a Reichswehr officer training future pilots in Bavaria, he settled in Munich, where he became a graphic artist. There he heard Hitler speak and was thoroughly inspired by his forceful articulation of the political creed of the front soldier. Both Karl and Erika Ritter joined the NSDAP in October 1925.[3]

In 1926 Ritter began a career that would lead him to his future vocation as a cinematic artist. Employed by Südfilm (Emelka), he moved to Berlin and settled into the firm's offices on the historic Friedrichstrasse. There he was employed as a commercial artist, creating posters advertising new releases in the heyday of silent film. He soon became director of public relations for Südfilm and received experience working in both Paris and London. By 1930 he had taken on his first assignment as production director for the detective film *Der Zinker*. Very gifted in the technical aspects of cinema production, he received a host of offers in film production in the early 1930s. In 1933, *Ufa* offered him the post of production director of *Hitler Youth Quex*. Ritter's career was launched, and he remained with *Ufa* until 1945.

19. Karl Ritter directing *Pour le Mérite* at the *Ufa* Studios lot, Berlin, 1938. (Library of Congress.)

Ritter approached film directing in a manner radically different from his peers. He had nothing but contempt for traditional cinema, which he considered a form of high-priced hedonism. Instead, Ritter saw film as a propaganda medium in Germany's effort to win the ideological war being waged for the future of Europe. The result was *Zeitfilm,* that is, film that attains coherence through a cinematic telegram style, resulting in theatrical documentary film. Episodic in nature, the plots do not employ individual character development; instead, they deliver an ideological message through a series of fast-moving action scenes.

Ritter spoke on his theory of film to the prestigious film seminar of the Lessing Hochschule in Berlin in 1936. He contended on this occasion that "feature film belongs behind the lines in today's deployment of ideological fronts. *Zeitfilm* provides the shock troops, the tanks for the front." Contemporary film must be conceived, written, and produced in the National Socialist manner. "Today's film must reflect today's world," he submitted, and "should be optimistic, heroic, eager for battle and victory." It must be diametrically opposed to the Jewish productions of the Weimar era, which in his opinion took every opportunity to undermine the heroic nature of the true German. In this way, *Zeitfilm* would play a significant part in returning every German to the living stream of the Volk community. Further, by carrying out this role, writers, producers, and directors of German film would create works of which the Führer could be proud.[4]

Ritter received considerable attention as director of *Verräter*, a film produced under the artistic direction of Hans Weidemann, vice-president of the Reichsfilmkammer, which gave it a measure of official sanction. It had all of the elements of a major film—espionage, sex, dramatic tension, and ultimate victory of the forces of good over evil in the guise of an international conspiracy. Willy Birgel played Morris, the dapper boss of a spy ring operating in Germany, while Paul Dahlke was cast as a Jewish agent. Rudolf Fernau played Fritz Brockau, an engineer in a "T-Metal" factory vital to the German defense effort. By selling state secrets to the enemy, Brockau demonstrates the depths to which greed and lust can drive a man of weak character. He is mad with passion for Marion, a *femme fatale* played by the dashing Lida Baarova. Marion, a denizen of the white-telephone Berlin *Schickeria,* is taken only with champagne, glitz, and greed. She is the worst sort of holdover from the days of Weimar decadence. The spy ring succeeds in tricking even the eminently Germanic young tankman Hans Klemm (Heinz Welzel) and his fiancée, the attractive Hilde Körner (Irene von Meyendorff).

Ritter delighted in dramatizing the role of the Third Reich's elite organizations in ferreting out the ring of conspirators, who posed a serious threat to reawakened Germany. The Gestapo has a very positive role in *Verräter,* as do regular police detectives. The film draws to a climax in highly dramatic footage, as the Luftwaffe, the tank corps, and the navy are brought in to arrest the fleeing conspirators.

Ritter's next effort—*Patrioten*—began his immersion in film designed to prepare the youth of Germany to think heroically and to dream of glory in the next war.[5] *Patrioten* featured an outstanding cast headed by Mathias Wieman and Lida Baarova and took place behind the lines in France during World War I. Wieman played a pilot who is shot down, survives, and is hidden, nursed, and loved back to life by the voluptuous Baarova, a singer performing with a group of traveling entertainers. Although the two fall passionately in love—the pilot knows he owes his life to the torch singer—duty takes precedence over Eros. The German pilot never overlooks his duty as a soldier through the long period of his recuperation. Throughout his ordeal, the flame of Germany burns brightly in his soul, and, with the glorious image of the Fatherland illuminating his way, he ultimately forsakes his love to return to the German flying corps. *Patrioten* was but the first of Ritter's several films in the Great War genre released in 1937 and

1938, and it pales in importance when compared to the truly significant films that followed—*Unternehmen Michael, Urlaub auf Ehrenwort,* and *Pour le Mérite.*

Unternehmen Michael premiered at the Nuremberg Party Rally in September 1937. It was a film of major consequence, highlighting the character of German staff and line officers during the massive Ludendorff offensive in the spring of 1918. Based on the play of the same name by Hans Fritz von Zwehl (1932) and a script written by Karl Ritter, Mathias Wieman, and Fred Hildenbrandt, the film starred Heinrich George in a titanic role as commander of the Sixty-ninth Army Corps. Sharing star billing was Mathias Wieman as George's general staff officer Major zur Linden, a man of sterling qualities who, at a critical juncture in the offensive, carried out in the field the very plan he had conceived on the staff. He willingly sacrifices himself for his fellow soldiers and the nation. Other name actors in an entirely male cast were Paul Otto as Lieutenant-Colonel Hegenau, chief of the general staff; Ernst Karchow as Captain Noack; Christian Kayssler as the cynical Rittmeister von Wengern (corps adjutant); Hannes Steltzer as the earnest, boyish lieutenant Prince Erxburg; and the popular Willy Birgel as Major Graf Schellenberg of the general staff of the army high command.[6]

Unternehmen Michael takes place during a twenty-four hour period in late March 1918 on the French front, specifically in the Saint Quentin sector between Arras and LaFere. Ritter endeavored to present events and character development that were widely experienced during the war. While focusing primarily on activities at the headquarters of the Sixty-ninth Corps, Ritter also sought to demonstrate the brave fighting qualities of the battle-weary troops at the most critical juncture of the war. Through the magnificent acting of Heinrich George, he showed that commanding generals suffer right along with their men, whose fortitude in facing adversity had become legendary on both sides of the line.

Beginning in the late 1920s, many films, novels, and short stories celebrated the German front soldier. *Unternehmen Michael,* on the other hand, was devoted to the heroic image of the officer corps, leaders who were at once commanders and fighting men. This accorded well with National Socialist propaganda, which attacked claims from the left that the officer corps was a tool of monopoly capitalism. Further, the film dealt with the tension inherent in the staff-line duality. What emerged was a heroic tone poem that climaxed as the commanding general received word of the sacrificial death of Major zur Linden, his indispensable staff officer, while leading an engagement intended to prepare the way for the westward advance of the entire German front. Heinrich George gazed heavenward and uttered these enduring lines in stentorian tones: "A victory, which has been won at great expense with such sacrifices! I am sorry, zur Linden, but you know as well as I do: history will not judge us by the greatness of our victories, but by the nobility of our sacrifice!"[7]

Ritter used *Unternehmen Michael* as a vehicle to revise the popular notion that the world of the "green table"—the military headquarters staffs—was remote from the fighting man in the trenches. Heinrich George, drawing on talents refined during a distinguished career on the Berlin stage, presented the soldierly virtues of the general in a remarkable way. His command style reflects a leader who combines strategic brilliance with an acute sensitivity to human suffering. His Sixty-ninth Corps headquarters was a fighting man's command staff, its members composed almost exclusively of officers seasoned at the front. Although hardened by years spent as a professional soldier, he is comradely to his subordinates. He curses the pretensions of the supreme high command, which had often lost touch with the men in the field. He is the kind of leader with whom the front soldiers could identify. Clearly, Ritter was presenting the general as a model to be exploited by National Socialist propagandists.

One of the most notable scenes in the film occurs when Graf Schellenberg of the general staff, supreme army high command, visits the general's headquarters. The general reacts negatively to the arrogant assessment of the military situation presented by Schellenberg, played by the polished Willy Birgel. Schellenberg boasts that Operation Michael has brought unparalleled success in just five days, transforming a stalemate into a war of movement once more:

> The English southern army is as good as annihilated. The French are throwing their reserves into the gap. Only a miracle can save the enemy now, as in 1914 at the Marne. But that miracle will not be repeated. We know that Paris is in wild panic. Every half hour they are being shelled by our Wilhelm Battery. They are already storming the trains heading for the provinces. Clemenceau and Poincare are even considering the evacuation of Paris. Operation Michael will decide the war.[8]

The general responds characteristically, "When I hear talk of Paris and of the Channel ports, I get uneasy. The Supreme Command is breaking its head over how it will exploit the victory. Our problem is how to win it."[9]

Schellenberg called for a frontal attack against "the Labyrinth"—a blockhouse of cement and steel on a commanding height controlled by the English—which threatened to bring the entire offensive to a halt. He withheld, however, the requisite artillery reinforcements, claiming that they were indispensable in another sector. Upon hearing this, George rears back his beefy hulk and, with all the force at his command, responds:

> Here is where they are indispensable. Here, here, here. At no other spot between Ypers and Damascus. If at this moment any heavy artillery is deployed on another sector, it is a mistake. If as much as one battle-ready company is positioned anywhere else except with us, it is wrong! And for God's sake, turn

the fleet loose against the English instead of letting it rust in the ports. If we can be victorious here, then the war will be over.[10]

The general makes a final appeal for the artillery necessary to pave the way for a frontal assault. Then, contemplating the unnecessary loss of so many of his brave soldiers because of the bungling of the high command, he sheds tears of love for his men.

The character of the general shines through as he bids farewell to the death battalion in one of the most memorable scenes in Third Reich cinema. In a haunting vignette, George gives an impassioned and sensitive plea to the men of Storm Battalion 37 in the black of night from a veranda of his chateau, sensing that they can snatch victory from the jaws of defeat. The eyes of the general meet those of his men, which gleam with an indescribable determination and longing for victory, reflecting the agony of their long years of suffering at the front. He utters these words of farewell:

> Comrades! I can't pass up the opportunity to fulfill my heartfelt desire to speak to you as you take your rest here before leaving. You all know, my comrades, what the word "Michael" means. "Michael" is the concentrated fire power of the entire German army. "Michael" is the hope of ending this war in a battle of movement. Your brothers have burst forth from the stalemate of the trenches and have given the enemy hell for five days. Now it's your turn! The English have been able to take up positions in front of the Labyrinth once more! You are old soldiers; I can be frank with you. Boys! The storm on the Labyrinth will be tough work, and that's why I have chosen you for it. Why? Because I have no better troops to put in. You are my best troops. Get the job done boys— and God be with you![11]

As the general is speaking, Major zur Linden leaves the corps headquarters and assumes his place with the men of his command. After a threefold "Hurrah!" for their commander, the men set out for the front and almost certain death, striking up a hymn to the nation, "O Deutschland, hoch in Ehren."[12]

Major zur Linden assumes almost superhuman qualities in *Unternehmen Michael*. He is at once highly professional, gifted in strategic conceptualization, noble in bearing, and self-assured in command. In his person, he represents the conscience of Germany at its hour of destiny. Mathias Wieman was well cast in the role of Major zur Linden, the incarnation of the ideal military commander. Grounded in the classics, and schooled in the traditions of the general staff, he epitomizes those qualities that von Clausewitz sought in the officer class.

Zur Linden also personifies the tension between staff and line in the Great War. He is sorely troubled by the distance between himself and the foot soldiers of the Sixty-ninth Corps. He is very sensitive to the fact that staff headquarters are in a luxurious chateau, while the common soldiers

20. Mathias Wieman (center) in *Unternehmen Michael* (1937). (Library of Congress.)

suffer deprivation in the field. He sets out to reconcile the conflict between staff and line, determined that he personally can carry out on the line the plan he conceived on the staff.[13]

No other person with his talents is available to carry out the assignment. Furthermore, zur Linden's fellow officers are devoid of heroic qualities. The artillery staff officer, Lieutenant Weber, is adrift in doubt. The cynical corps adjutant, Rittmeister von Wengern, has lost his belief in victory and judges the carnage to be ultimately meaningless for both sides. Zur Linden admonishes Wengern sternly for his defeatism, as the adjutant crouches over a piano playing Chopin etudes, a cigarette dangling from his lips. Zur Linden, in contrast, adds a moral dimension to the sacrifice, affirming that "the unchangeable is never without meaning."[14]

With zur Linden's plan finally approved, the leitmotiv of heroism is sounded, and all subsequent scenes form variations on this theme. Upon reaching Beaurevoir, zur Linden orders his battalion into action. He is freed from all doubt, and the weight of the world is lifted from his shoulders. He immediately commences a fierce fight, but ammunition runs low. One after another, his comrades are killed. The hopelessness of the situation is immediately evident, and his only alternative is clearly charted. Zur Linden now knows that he must die for Germany in a violent firestorm to pave the way for victory.

In the final scene, knowing that death is near—he has dispatched the order for German artillery to begin a final concentrated barrage on his own position at "the Labyrinth"—zur Linden is transfigured. His countenance beams the ethereal light of the hero crossing over to eternal life among the gods. As the trumpets resound in celebration of this divine immolation, Herbert Windt's martial score changes from the minor to the major key and rises to a crescendo. The scene shifts to the corps headquarters staff, which is joyously moving out toward the west. Victory is in the air. Major zur Linden's sacrifice has been redemptive.

Unternehmen Michael premiered on 7 September 1937 at the *Ufa* Palast in Nuremberg. For the second year in a row Karl Ritter accepted the plaudits of the highly charged crowds at the Nuremberg rally.[15] In November 1937 during the Berlin premiere, Goebbels employed the film to bolster his rearmament awareness propaganda. Felix Dargel, writing in the *Berliner Lokal Anzeiger,* reported:

> This was the scene. As if made of iron, the Music Corps of the Berlin Wach-regiment appears on stage. At first in the dark you could see only the silhouettes of their steel helmets and the *Schellenbaum* high over their heads, with the ruins of a village in the background. Then one could hear the soft strains of the old song "Morgenrot," which in the Great War called so many to their deaths. Then suddenly there is bright light, and the great old marches resound, as the trumpets blast under the precise baton of Stabsmusikmeister Friedrich Ahlers. The drummers beat an ever-higher cascading whirlwind of sound, approaching symbolically the crashing of artillery, which during the war became a constantly recurring event at the front.[16]

Stage effects of this nature heightened the emotional experience of the film and appealed to the audiences' enthusiasm for the military. Concluding his ecstatic review, Dargel noted:

> One even forgets that they are actors. . . . They are all simply—*soldiers!* Whether they are generals, staff, or storm troop officers. This is the greatest compliment we can give them. And each one of them deserves our thanks.[17]

The premiere and release of yet another Ritter production, *Urlaub auf Ehrenwort,* was an important propaganda event of 1938. It was hailed in the press as a "major victory of German cinematic art," and Ritter was awarded a medal at the *Biennale* in Venice by fascist Italy.[18] The film was based on the autobiographical novella *Urlaub auf Ehrenwort* by Kilian Koll (pseudonym for Walter Julius Bloem), which appeared in more than one hundred newspapers.[19] Koll had entered the German army in 1915, and at the age of sixteen he was one of the nation's youngest volunteers. Wounded three times and rendered all but deaf, Koll had miraculously survived the firestorm in France. With this background, he produced a work that had widespread human appeal, focusing on weary, war-torn Berlin in the traumatic summer of 1918.[20]

It was from this literary source that Ritter fashioned a film of comradeship based on National Socialist ideals. It was generously larded with Ritter's simplified view of the world—anti-intellectualism, a clear juxtaposition of heroes and traitors, anti-Semitism, and a decided prejudice against organized labor in any form. Felix Lützkendorf and Charles Klein wrote the script of *Urlaub auf Ehrenwort,* using suggestions by Kilian Koll and his father, the novelist Walter Bloem.[21] Ernst Erich Buder's musical score was notable for its haunting songs from the Great War and its aggressive complement to the action. It lent credibility to *Ufa*'s advertisement for the film, which claimed that it was a "grand song of comradeship. Not blustering comradeship, but simple and spontaneous comradeship of the deed. Comradeship, born in the storm of steel of the front, meeting its greatest test in the lunatic asylum of a sick, politically incited metropolis."[22]

Urlaub auf Ehrenwort featured several individuals who became stars in later war films, most notably Carl Raddatz who debuted in the work. Fritz Kampers, who made a name for himself in G. W. Pabst's *Westfront,* played an important and convincing role, as did Berta Drews who had been cast as Heini's mother in *Hitler Youth Quex.* The film also provided a platform for Rolf Moebius and Ingeborg Theek, both of whom received major billing in *Ufa*'s very aggressive advertising campaign. As Oskar Kalbus of the *Ufa–Filmverleih G.M.B.H.* pointed out in a promotional letter to German theater owners, *Urlaub auf Ehrenwort* was an "outstanding film, which based on our wide experience gives us reason to hope that—just like *Verräter* and *Patrioten*—it will become one of the real hits of the season."[23]

From first to last, *Urlaub auf Ehrenwort* is a morality play based on the conflict between good and evil. As the first frame announces, "The action of this film takes place in the fall of 1918, when the homeland was already undermined with pacifist propaganda, while the field-grey front still held the line against the superior power of the whole world."[24] Good finds its home in the nobility of comradeship born in the trenches, which inspires national greatness. It is juxtaposed to forces of evil that appear in the form of Marxists, defeatists, pacifists, parasitical war-shirkers and profiteers, traitorous intellectuals, and hysterical women in political leadership roles. The outcome is never in doubt. Comradeship guarantees victory over the onslaught of the internal enemy, ultimately preparing the way for the rebirth of the nation under Adolf Hitler.

The intrepid Lieutenant Prätorius (Rolf Moebius) is young, tall and handsome and has the appearance of an officer of the old school. He emerges as a courageous leader with an intense sense of responsibility toward the men under his command. Ritter establishes this sense of comradeship in the first scenes, which reflect a blood bond between a natural leader and his men. This bond guarantees victory, come what may, and ennobles sacrificial death.

The film begins with a military unit being transported on a train rolling toward Berlin. Helmets and packs clang against the bulkheads, while melancholy music is heard in the background. The tone is pessimistic, because the soldiers realize that they are heading inexorably toward their death. The conversation—much of it in Berlin dialect—is sarcastic, raw, and sour. Sasse, a Marxist worker, announces that he will desert if the train passes through Berlin. He curses the whole notion of heroic death as nothing but Prussian elitism. His sentiments are echoed by the effete writer and parlor communist, Dr. Jens Kirchhoff.

As a counterpoint to this treachery, the loyalty motif is sounded. The musician Hagen and the nationalistic young lawyer Dr. Wegener discuss the bond between Hartmann and the lieutenant, pointing out that in 1916 Hartmann had saved the life of Prätorius by pulling him from the ruins of a bunker. This act set the stage for the dramatic turn of events that followed. Corporal Hartmann—streetcar driver, Iron Cross I, Silver Medal for the Wounded—enters the compartment of Lieutenant Prätorius—nineteen years old, Iron Cross I. There a situation unfolds that Ritter molded in the spirit of National Socialist ideology. Hartmann, requesting permission for a leave of but a few hours to see his wife and family in Berlin, initially receives a negative response. He protests vehemently: "Listen—wounded—military hospital, convalescent company—a week playing cards and then thrown again into the whole rotten mess! Without a leave! Do you think that's right? . . . Four years in the trenches, wounded three times—and . . . without a leave right back into the fray? . . . Who knows if I'll ever see my Anna and the children again!" But the lieutenant holds firm, saying, "Yes, Hartmann—such an old warrior like you. . . . We've experienced the whole mess together! . . . But you'll have to forget it, Hartmann. Think of the others."

Upon arriving in Berlin, Prätorius is ordered to march his men across town to the Potsdam Station, where they are to wait some five hours on the platform before entraining for Brandenburg. There they will link up with Infantry Regiment 435 for immediate transport to the front. The men become very restive as they march through Berlin. Groups of communists taunt them for their obedience to authority. Prätorius stares down the provocative Sasse, an outcome one would expect since, according to the script, Prätorius's "eyes show the superior power of the morally stronger man."[25] The lieutenant relents, realizing the cruelty of the situation. Despite standing orders against any such action, he grants a five-hour leave to each man in his unit. According to Prätorius, "I know my men . . . from the front," and therefore he takes the risk.[26] A musical motif of unrest and dissent gives way to harmonious chords, signaling the joy of the rightly ordered military life. The message is clear. An officer, certain of his authority, violates standing orders to answer the command of his heart. He thereby demonstrates the best spirit of the front soldier. As each man departs, he gives his word of honor that he will return on time; the bond between leader and men is sealed with a handshake, the camera closing in on this symbol of fidelity.

What follows is a dramatic overview of life in wartime Berlin. Vignette after vignette cascades before the viewer, reflecting the attitudes of the men, which range from idealistic to decadent. Despite their episodic nature—these scenes are by no means high art—taken as a whole they reflect the tempestuous capital in crisis. At times the portrayal of the mood of the Berlin "milieu" is so authentic that a viewer might confuse the scenes with Bertolt Brecht's *Three Penny Opera* (G. W. Pabst 1931).

Evil lurks everywhere in Karl Ritter's Berlin. The cancer of communism spreads its poison throughout the capital. Sasse heads directly for the Bouillonkeller, deep in proletarian Friedrichshain. In that smoky den, the meeting ground for deserters, small-time gangsters, extortionists, and prostitutes, a poster beckons the loungers to the next USPD rally of Karl Liebknecht. The wild cacophony of the musicians adds to the wretchedness of this low-life cafe. Sasse, who has traded his soldier's uniform for cylinder hat, silk scarf, and pungent cigar, seems amenable to the seductions of the easy money offered him as a deserter. Fritzi, a peroxide blond, offers the cheap sex that goes hand in hand with communism in Nazi film. When she calls for a tango—the epitome of sexuality in the 1930s—and takes Sasse into her arms, the possibility of his answering the call of loyalty seems remote indeed. Thereafter, in an orgy of drunkenness, a hooligan insults Sasse for wearing his Iron Cross, evoking a bitter response. He pounces on the young Bengal, beating and strangling him, and a grand melee ensues. Proudly, Sasse affirms to the pack, "Now you know how someone wins such a medal—you assholes!" The call to the nation has prevailed, even in this swamp of "subhumanity." Sasse climbs the stairs, leaving the darkness and eternal midnight of the cafe. Emerging into the light and sunshine, he sees his fellow soldiers marching by, a graphic contrast to the seedy Bouillonkeller. Reborn, he has come home to Germany, to the Reich.[27]

Yet another insight into the subversive world of the opposition comes when Dr. Jens Kirchhoff—described as "a *Literat*, a negative intellectual type"—has a rendezvous with Lulu Frey. Seductive and aggressive, she is a communist functionary operating from a plush apartment. She is presented as a social parasite, enjoying mounds of gourmet food while the real workers of Berlin go hungry. Hinting that he might desert the army and go to work for the Marxist cause as a propagandist, Kirchhoff joins Lulu at the notorious Romanisches Cafe on the Kurfürstendamm. There the elegantly clad Hektor Hasso Hellriegel, an arrogant writer with "the high-pitched voice of a castrato," is holding forth on his most recent "highly dangerous" bus trip to the front. Despite his sympathies for the left, Kirchhoff reacts negatively to the asinine pomp and defeatism of the chic arts and letters crowd. Remarkably, he even spurns the attractions of Lulu and races back to be with his comrades.

Ritter next staged a scene demonstrating that immoral Berlin was the breeding ground for treachery, poisoning the true German spirit. When the infantryman Dr. Wegener (Kurt Waitzmann), the epitome of racial and moral rectitude, searches for his beloved Vera Georgi (Ruth Störmer), he learns that she has moved out of her simple apartment. She has become the lover of a foreign sculptor, the debonair Professor Knudsen, and has moved into his apartment near the fashionable Reichskanzlerplatz. Wegener, upon entering the studio, is beside himself with rage as his eyes meet those of the voluptuous Vera; shame has rendered her mute. Beethoven's *Eroica* abruptly gives way to twelve-tonal dissonance. The contrast between Sybarite and loyal front soldier is graphically presented as Wegener confronts Knudsen. Ironically, Knudsen stands directly before a statue of a fallen soldier, which he has just completed. It bears the caption "For you!" Disgusted, Wegener storms out of the apartment. He, too, is happy to rejoin the loyal comrades of his company.

Stereotypes abound in *Urlaub auf Ehrenwort*. Anyone seeking the ideal of Germanic purity and Nordic beauty, as well as a homily on the proper relationship between the sexes, need look no further than the scenes of Lieutenant Prätorius and his fiancée, Nurse Inge, played by the elegant Ingeborg Theek. Cast as "a pure, intelligent, beautiful, quiet, and kind girl," she contrasts vividly with the communist women of the night. Inge is the model of rectitude and self-sacrifice; hers is a selfless love of race and nation. We first encounter her succoring the patients in a military hospital. Now writing a letter for a wounded soldier, now hurrying here and there helping suffering and lonely men far from home, she is the quintessential sister of mercy. She is idealized by the wounded, representing for them surrogate lover, mother, and entreating Virgin Mary.[28] Secretly engaged to Walter Prätorius, she appears with him on the platform of the Potsdam Station, where the innocent pair exchange sweet nothings, dream of peace, and dance to the strains of a popular waltz. Inge's beauty casts a Raphaelite glow on the otherwise drab surroundings. Seldom in the history of cinema has misguided idealism been married to fantasy with such seductive skill.

The film also demonstrates that Ritter, despite his anti-intellectual nature, did not denigrate the use of art, properly applied, in the service of national goals. An intense young composer, Wilhelm Hagen (Heinz Wilhelm König), returns to the home of his soul, the Berlin Academy of Music, to direct his own composition. Professor Greisenkopf, conducting Beethoven's Eroica in the Temple of the Muses, surrenders the podium to his favorite student, now both hardened and refined by the *Kriegserlebnis*. Hagen takes the podium to direct his piano concerto, displaying a nobility belying his tender years. Overcome with emotion, he reveals to his fellow musicians that "the war is in this work."

The character of Corporal Hartmann is sunny and uncomplicated, and Ritter delighted in his direction of Fritz Kampers who played the role with verve. Hartmann is a good comrade and a devoted family man. Cast opposite Berta Drews, who played his wife, Anna, Kampers as Hartmann is at once ebullient and sensitive. He is a very loving father to his four children—Erna, Emil, Fritz, and Gretel. In a memorable scene on a streetcar, he surprises Anna, who has replaced him for the duration of the war as a driver. When they return to their garden cottage, they enjoy a festive family meal. Having overslept, Hartmann's friends commandeer a truck, fill it with the entire family, and race through the countryside of Mark Brandenburg to overtake the speeding train. Upon catching up with it, his comrades welcome him with delirious enthusiasm and spirited military music.

In the final scenes Prätorius, very uneasy because three of his men have failed to return, contemplates the court martial that might well result from his comradely behavior. At the Brandenburg Station, the last two men arrive, not too late to vindicate the lieutenant. Honor has won the day. Differences of class, background, and political affiliation have been overcome, as the entire unit—officers and ranks alike—merge into the Germanic whole. As the train pulls out of the Brandenburg Station and begins to traverse the Havel landscape, signaling the end of this wondrous day, a grenadier strikes up the chords of "Argonnerwald." Comradeship was indeed the sweetest influence.

Urlaub auf Ehrenwort premiered at the *Ufa* Palast am Zoo on 19 January 1938 in a gala setting. Several leading political, military, and cultural figures attended as Goebbels's guests of honor.[29] Joachim Brenner's review in *Das 12 Uhr Blatt* was typical of the acclaim that followed:

> The applause of the deeply moved audience that greeted the lead actors who were present went on for a quarter of an hour, and would know no end. This film, which in its aesthetic conception, incisiveness, and execution was absolutely unique, can be considered a meaningful turning point in the history of German film. The premiere will send a message to the world henceforth as to what exactly constitutes cinematic art.[30]

Ritter could celebrate his achievement, and Goebbels honored him by sending the director his photograph framed in silver with the following dedication: "To the director Karl Ritter in grateful recognition of his exemplary pioneering work for German film on the occasion of the great success of his film 'Urlaub auf Ehrenwort.' "[31]

The success Ritter enjoyed with his next film, *Pour le Mérite*, was remarkable. It was not by chance that the presence of Adolf Hitler at the Berlin premiere of *Pour le Mérite* in December 1938 turned yet another opening into a political extravaganza.[32] Indeed, with this work Ritter had reached the apogee of his career in Third Reich cinema. Given the honorary title Professor, and appointed to the Präsidialrat of the Reich Film Chamber and to the Reich Culture Senate, Ritter now found himself lionized both in the film world and in Nazi propaganda.[33]

Pour le Mérite was a military and political biography of a flyer from World War I and a cultural statement of decline, suffering, and resurrection that paralleled the career and cultural outlook of the front soldier Adolf Hitler. It was Ritter's final prewar propaganda film, and it inspired German youths to emulate their elders in worshiping at the altar of Mars. Hitler sent a telegram of appreciation to Ritter for his achievement in this film, and the director's response reflects the fulfillment he felt in working for the ideals of National Socialism:

> My Führer!
> I want to express my heartfelt and humble thanks to you for your congratulatory telegram after seeing my film *Pour le Mérite*. I can hardly express to you how pleased and happy your words of appreciation have made me. I can assure you, that this time just as always in the conception and direction of my films I have thought only of your judgment, with the hope of being able to contribute even in a small way to your wonderful and grand work.
> There is no greater inducement to further creativity for the artist than your praise! I feel this now more than ever, grateful and deeply moved. It is an overwhelming experience to see that under your leadership fate has blessed me to fulfill the oath that I made twenty years ago on the march home from France.
>
> Heil mein Führer!
> Your grateful,
> Karl Ritter[34]

Pour le Mérite appealed to Hitler and Goebbels because it was the consummate cinematic statement of their heroic world view. It delivered what they considered the most important elements of National Socialist ideology through the medium of a film employing both historical documentary form and traditional film drama.[35] They also observed that Ritter made use of current advances in technical effects, which increased the dramatic intensity and appeal of the work. Both leaders understood that, with such films, the party could gain far more adherents than through the turgid prose found in the *Völkischer Beobachter* and so many of the wooden National Socialist publications. The magnetic appeal of film art—especially in films such as *Pour le Mérite*—was an excellent complement to their own grandly evocative public ceremonies. Karl Bodenschatz, an adjutant in the original Richthofen Squadron and later chief adjutant to Field Marshal Hermann Göring, explained the reason for this when he extolled the virtues of the young flyers of the Great War. He reminisced about the "last knights," youths of eighteen, nineteen, and twenty years of age:

> When the war broke out, the limitless strength of youth and the purity of their souls welled up passionately in them. They summoned up everything that their minds and bodies could give, and they embraced Germany heart and soul, with such zeal that the nation was almost overwhelmed with its enthusiasm for these young men. . . . Because they were an entirely special race of young men, they went where the war had a romantic appeal. They went to the aerodromes. And as they saw the rawness and agony of this romanticism in the field, they were united in one thought more than ever. They were in the right place! They formed an elite in the wonderful group of young men from all the fighter squadrons of the field army. They learned to fight in an entirely new style, and they learned how to die in this style, which had no precedent.[36]

Pour le Mérite was a labor of love for Karl Ritter, and in its production he received the full cooperation of the air ministry and Generalluftzeugmeister Ernst Udet.[37] From the first to the last reel, the film rests on the presupposition that there are two forces at work in the history of twentieth-century Germany. The force of evil—Jewry, communism, and social democracy—plots to stab the nation in the back in its great hour of need during World War I and succeeds. The force of good, represented by all God-fearing adherents to the German nation and its traditional elites, goes down to defeat and destruction. The way is open for the corrupt Weimar Republic, which glorifies not generals but general directors and materialistic businessmen devoid of moral values.

Ritter was able to gather an outstanding cast for *Pour le Mérite,* drawing some of the lead actors from *Ufa.*[38] The aristocratic Paul Hartmann, a veteran of the Berlin and Viennese stage and screen and every inch the hero, was cast as Rittmeister Prank. Lieutenant Gerdes, a fanatical and sullen flyer, was played by Herbert A. E. Böhme, and Albert Hehn took the role of Fabian, the reserve lieutenant who is transformed from a spoiled schoolboy into a hero. The gentlemanly and sophisticated Major Wissmann, commander of several squadrons, was played by Paul Otto, a regular in the Ritter war films. Heinz Welzel played Lieutenant Romberg, who finds an early death. The stunning blond Jutta Freybe was cast as Isabel, a Potsdam socialite who grows in virtue through her association with her husband, Rittmeister Prank. Gerda, Fabian's fiancée and bride, was played by Carsta Löck, whom Gustav Ucicky first discovered as an unknown actress at the Nollendorf Theater in Berlin. Chacteristically for Ritter, Gerda was described as "the best type of female comrade, a sincere and genuine blond German maiden." To round out the casting in the female roles, Gisela von Collande played Frau Moebius, a "healthy, independent young farm wife." Willy Rose as Private Krause and Josef Dahmen as Sergeant Zuschlag remain the eternal optimists, ever loyal to their officers.[39]

Moving through three stages of history—from the war, through the republic, to the Third Reich—Ritter located the soul of the nation in its young heroes, the flying youths epitomized by the holders of the highest military award for valor, instituted by Frederick the Great, the Pour le Mérite. In their uprightness of character, these noble flyers, tested in the skies over France, keep the faith in the ignoble era of Jewish liberalism following the defeat. They emerge victorious in 1933, resurrect the nation, and form the vanguard of the new German Luftwaffe under Hermann Göring, which stands ready to defend German interests under the leadership of Adolf Hitler. The flyers of *Pour le Mérite* have returned honor to the German war flag once again. At each stage the musical score of Herbert Windt provides appropriate crescendo and decrescendo to accompany the swiftly moving, often-episodic action on the screen. The elite young guard becomes symbolic of Germany itself, guaranteeing final victory against the world enemy.

Ritter delighted in molding the image and spirit of the front flyers in the war, and nowhere did he do so with such subtlety as in his development of the character of Rittmeister Prank. Paul Hartmann played a convincing and nuanced role as Prank, the quintessential knight of the air. He is both spirited and mature, an inveterate fighter and the model of chivalry. The Rittmeister sets a standard of bravery and heroic conduct that is emulated by his men. He cuts an impressive figure aloft in his command aircraft, where he demonstrates the agility of an eagle. He appears to be nearly superhuman, having mysteriously bridged the great chasm lying between men, women, and the beyond. Ritter's air battle scenes are very realistic, showing Prank's squadron engaged in breathless combat, now swooping, now careening wildly, before dashing in for the kill ("Kreuze und Kokarden im wilden Kurvenkampf"). A man's man to the core, Prank is the consummate fighter pilot.

The Rittmeister also manifests the gentlemanly behavior and knightly chivalry characteristic of a military elite whose traditions persist even in an age of technological warfare. For example, his behavior toward a downed English ace, Captain Cecil Brown, is exemplary. It parallels the memorable scene in Jean Renoir's *The Grand Illusion* in which Erich von Stroheim treats a captured officer with grace, according to the ancient chivalric code. The richness of the dining room in the French chateau is magnificent, replete with Gobelin tapestries, paintings, heavy drapes, fine Oriental rugs, and table service that would be a source of pride in a royal house. Prank's gentle words of greeting as he introduces Brown to his colleagues at dinner reflect the nobility of the *Pour le Mérite* set:

> The circumstances under which we meet Mr. Brown are not fortunate for him but for us they are—such is war. I have the honor of welcoming you as the most famous ace of the British Royal Flying Corps, and I wish to express my satisfaction that Captain Brown has not been wounded. Gentlemen, please rise and drink with me a toast in honor of our guest.[40]

The fact that Brown manages to escape that same night does not diminish the respect accorded him by his peers. Brown, after all, had not been asked to give his word of honor that he would not try to escape. Such conduct was expected of prisoners of war.

Lieutenant Romberg also demonstrates nobility of character in the film. Romberg is something of a *Schmerzenskind*. In the midst of an air battle, he withholds his fire when the machine guns of his English prey become jammed. Chivalry has won out against any temptation of a cowardly victory in this world of knights. When the clean-cut, youthful idealist finally gains his first victory—it was the squadron's five-hundreth kill—his celebration is short-lived. Romberg himself is killed on his next sortie, but he is remembered for his character and bravery. In a fascinating burial scene, the Rittmeister offers a homily on heroic death to his officers, who are solemnly gathered in a French village cemetery:

> Thus we say goodbye to the youngest of our comrades, Lieutenants Romberg and Lagwerth. Our hearts are filled with both sadness and pride. There is an old saying, which is especially suitable to us fighter pilots: Whom the Gods love, they call home at a tender age. Both of our friends died as youths, but have entered *Walhall* as mature and fulfilled men.[41]

On the periphery of the cemetery, a French girl is seen crying for her beloved, while the gathered flyers earnestly look on, reflecting sadness yet gratification in the thought that their future deaths will be redemptive.

Above all Prank loved the Fatherland, and he would accept nothing short of devoted spirit and brave conduct from the men of his squadron. When morale begins to decline in 1918, leading to a mood of depression and resignation, the Rittmeister is indignant. Calling his officers together for a meeting, he severely dresses them down for questioning the victory. To lose faith in the final victory would separate them from the German national community, the fountainhead of morality for the warrior:

> Men. It cannot go on like this any longer. At any rate not under my command. I understand that your nerves are on edge. Mine are on edge, too. But I demand from each of you that you show enough self-discipline to rise above these ir-

ritations. I will ruthlessly expel any man from my squadron who does not do his duty in this crisis.[42]

Then, to set an example for the others, he discharges a whining complainer on the spot.

When the collapse of the German Reich comes, Rittmeister Prank and the officers and men of Fighter Squadron 12 are determined to defy the order to surrender their beloved aircraft to the English. They follow their leader to the homeland, landing on an aerodrome held by a Soldiers' and Workers' Council. The confrontation of the virtuous pilots, still aflame with their love of nation, and the Bolsheviks at Darmstadt is notable. Ritter cast the commander of the Reds as a Jewish intellectual with wire-rimmed spectacles, a man who has never spent a day at the front. He is surrounded by a ragtag crowd of disorderly, disheveled communists, many of them front soldiers seduced by a foreign ideology and "Jewish-Bolshevik" leadership. Despite the pilots' best efforts, the aircraft of Fighter Squadron 12 go up in flames, and the young warriors are cast out into the broken and insecure postwar world.

Ritter delighted in employing every negative stereotype about the hated Weimar Republic. He presented it as a world where business and money are king, where criminals and prostitutes, stock market racketeers and manipulators, parasitical Jews and wirepullers have all joined hands with corrupt politicians. The knights of the air are totally alienated in this world of soulless corruption, materialism, and hedonism.

It is not by chance that the young eagles who had flown closest to the sun go asunder in the swamp of Weimar. Rittmeister Prank is nearly destroyed, wandering aimlessly from job to job. He fails as the owner of a Berlin auto repair shop, and little wonder why. In one scene, an overweight, cigar-chomping speculator and his painted consort berate Prank for the price of repair work. He stomps off, declaring that he will seek better service on the notorious Kurfürstendamm. Another vignette contrasts the hero with the collected menagerie of Weimar business and demimonde circles gathered at a swank Berlin nightclub. There, in dense clouds of tobacco smoke, Prank and his beautiful wife, Isabel, are in the process of concluding a wholesale wine contract. With the orchestra bellowing its satin tunes in the tingle-tangle of the glittering club, a thoroughly offensive crowd of parvenu businessmen in tuxedoes and their women of the night rollick and cavort over champagne and caviar. Nausea wells up in the soul of the protagonist, whose heart now and always remains with the men of Fighter Squadron 14 and who is simply unable to close a lucrative business transaction.

Ritter displayed many of his antiurban prejudices in the film. All that is decent, clean, and good comes from the pristine land and Germanic countryside, while corruption and immorality are rooted in the city. This is nowhere more evident than in scenes of the Rittmeister and Isabel, along with the doggedly loyal mechanics Zuschlag and Krause, vegetating in a seedy hotel on the Friedrichstrasse in Berlin. All seems lost in this decayed world of alcohol and cigarettes in the fetid, asphalt capital. Suddenly, as if heaven-sent, Moebius appears from the country, offering deliverance to his former comrades. He invites them to join him on a large estate in the east, where the soil of the *Heimat* guarantees renewed spiritual and physical health, as well as prosperity in a racially unified and organic community. Soon enough, the chaos and racial miscegenation of strident Berlin will be but an ugly memory. The transition is made doubly dramatic when, upon arriving in the country, Moebius secretly takes Prank to a secluded barn. There he presents him with the finest gift any man could give his former commander—Prank's own Fokker aircraft from the good old days at the front. The Rittmeister becomes starry-eyed as he comes face to face with this physical link to his men and a happier day, when love of nation and self-sacrifice were unchanging ideals. Just to see once again the mementos of his victories emblazoned on the fuselage of his aircraft is to know life's fulfillment. Later he turns to his wife and affirms, "My plane, Isabel. Now life has meaning again."[43] It is all the more bitter for him when the Fokker is burned in a shootout with communist revolutionaries. Shortly thereafter, Prank and his comrades are sentenced to prison for violating the strict weapons laws. Prank's hatred and contempt for the Versailles system knows no bounds, and, upon being released, he goes abroad. He could follow no other course:

I'm getting out, going abroad, where there is some action, where I am needed as a soldier once more. To fly again, to fight, to experiment with real planes, with real motors. And I'll return one day with what I learn."[44]

At home the battle for a renewed German spirit continues. Several of Prank's comrades are involved with flying schools, while others continue a propaganda barrage against the hated republic. Some of them work to destroy it from within, most notably Major Wissman, who has a position in the Reich transportation ministry. When other despairing comrades see no way out except to go abroad, Wissmann warns them of the danger to the nation. He tells the men of Fighter Squadron 12:

I serve a government that I know is taking Germany to its ruin. But it will not succeed. One day a miracle will happen. If I didn't believe in this, I wouldn't be here. And besides we are not alone. There are others, better men than we, who believe in this miracle and are fighting for its realization. Just as in the old days I am now issuing you an official order: stay in Germany.[45]

The final scenes of *Pour le Mérite* bespeak the joy of the resurrection of Germany under Adolf Hitler. Darkness gives way to dawn; depression and pessimism, to belief in a limitless future. Ritter employed every available device to announce that the chains of Versailles and Weimar had been broken. Windt's musical score gives rhythmic accompaniment to Hitler's pageant of joy, to scenes of swastika flags snapping briskly in the breeze, to new aircraft in Hermann Göring's proud Luftwaffe flying into the wild blue yonder. The nation has awakened from the dark night, and factories are humming with work. The rearmed country is on the move once again, and honor returns to Germany's once-tattered and shamed battle flags. Kampers as the folksy Moebius, beaming in his SA uniform, marches out confidently, flanked by sunny Hitler Youth and girls of the Bund deutscher Mädel. Seemingly the entire nation responds ecstatically to Goebbels's announcement of German rearmament.

Major Wissmann, now a general in the Luftwaffe and a high official in Göring's air ministry, has called the old boys together once more. The Jagdgeschwader Richthofen has been reborn and is stationed at a new aerodrome at Döberitz. Rittmeister Prank has sailed from South America to Hamburg, where he is met by his comrades. Upon planting his feet on German soil once more, he exclaims, "Boys, there's no place like the home-land!"[46] A grand surprise awaits the Rittmeister. He is taken to the aerodrome where the old team is gathered, turned out smartly in review before the humming motors of their aircraft. Some are in the immaculate uniforms of Göring's dapper Luftwaffe staff; others are officers and men of the Jagdgeschwader Richthofen. Overhead, a unit of vintage planes from the western front appears, tipping their wings to Rittmeister Prank who represents the reborn spirit of the Red Baron. On this beautiful day of national and personal fulfillment, General Wissmann turns over command of the squadron to Rittmeister Prank on the orders of Hermann Göring. Prank simply cannot believe that the miracle has indeed come to pass. The resurrection motif is struck, and the film fades out with a closeup of a radiant *Pour le Mérite* medal. The spirit of the front had never died, and through their faithfulness the youth of 1918 had contributed significantly to the rebirth of the nation.

It was evident that *Pour le Mérite* was Karl Ritter's personal testament. He spoke to this theme in December 1938 in connection with the premiere of the film:

> It was exactly twenty years ago when we marched home. It was ice cold. We marched past Laon, through the Ardennes and the Eifel to the Rhine. We had lost the war after all. When we arrived there, we almost had the feeling that we had become lost on the way. Germany had changed so much. I swore at that time that one day I had to tell the story about these impressions that we had and how we suffocated at the cursing and indifference. It just wasn't right to carry that around inside oneself for years. I had to get it out. I wanted to

write a book. Years went by, ten years, twenty years. Life itself drove me to this film.[47]

Pour le Mérite received rave reviews. *Filmwelt* referred to it as "the best film of contemporary German history," a "ballad, a song of the storm, an epic, a heroic song." Waxing ecstatic, the editors exclaimed:

> When in these days and nights the wild song of the big motors resounds over us, when the fighters and bombers, the steel guardians of the heavens, circle over German territory once again, then Germany can thank all those men featured in this film: the eternal soldiers of the Fatherland, who kept their faith alive like a battered battle flag through the darkest night of our history.[48]

The *Schwarze Korps*, the newspaper of the SS, lauded Karl Ritter in its Christmas issue of 1938, praising him for showing conclusively that the film community did not have to be a world unto itself. Instead, there need be nothing mysterious at all about it, if it had the two ingredients Ritter brought to *Pour le Mérite* and all of his films: the dedication of the political soldier and the technical and aesthetic qualities of a good film director. The *Schwarze Korps* concluded, "We never doubted that the *best German film* could only be produced by a National Socialist."[49]

In 1939 Karl Ritter turned his talents to the production of *Legion Condor*, detailing the exploits of the German intervention in the Spanish Civil War. Begun in early August, filming was broken off with the onset of the war against Poland. *Legion Condor* was never completed. Similarly, production of the anti-Russian film *Kadetten* was concluded in 1939, but its release was delayed because of the signing of the German-Russian Nonaggression Pact in August 1939. It premiered with considerable fanfare in December 1941.[50]

Ritter was convinced that, if Germany were to win the next war, the nation must depend upon a youth schooled in heroism to see the struggle through to victory. He was certain that the absence of a spirit of self-sacrifice had caused defeat in 1918 and the subsequent Spartacus revolution. Accordingly, he set out to contribute to the education of youth through the medium of film by turning to the era of Frederick the Great and the Seven Years' War. A little-known episode during the campaign with Russia celebrated the Prussian ethos, teaching German youth to view death in the service of the nation as more beautiful than life itself.

Ritter was impressed with Alfred Menne's historical account of the bravery of a Prussian cadet corps, whose conduct epitomized the values Ritter sought to inculcate in German youth—a sense of honor, proper military spirit, heroic conduct, and "youthful courage that impresses men." In concert with Alfred Lützkendorf, Ritter wrote the script by hand, and his style is evident throughout the production.[51]

The veteran actor Mathias Wiemann was cast in the role of the Prussian Rittmeister von Tzülow. Born in Russia and able to conjure up the stereotypical features Germans had come to expect in representatives of the "barbaric East," Andrews Engelman played the role of the Cossack leader Colonel Goroschew. Theo Shall was cast as Captain Jupow and Erich Walter as General Graf Tschernitschew. The Frisian Carsta Löck played the lovable Sophie ("Küchenmädchen im Kadettenkorps"). Klaus Detlef Sierck (Cadet von Hohenhausen) was the only professional actor among the cadets who played in the film. The rest were chosen by Ritter and Wieman from the corps of cadets at the Napola Potsdam. Ritter sensed that there were dangers involved in using the cadets as amateur actors. He was fearful of lessening their zeal to become soldiers for the Fatherland, and he required that each cadet-actor take an oath not to pursue a film career after playing in *Katetten*.[52]

The historical episode on which the film was based took place in October 1760. Frederick the Great had concentrated his army in Silesia, which left Berlin vulnerable to attack. The weak Berlin garrison retreated to the fortress of Spandau, leaving young cadets—boys ranging from 9 to 12 years of age—at the Royal Academy at Berlin-Lichterfelde. There they were captured by the invading Russians, who treated them brutally and, in the film, tried to break their spirit. Viewers of Ritter's film watch as the cadets are dragged around eastern Germany like roped cattle, kicked and hounded by the Cossack horde. They are mocked by prostitutes and camp followers and endure the agony of cold and hunger throughout the winter. But the cadets are gallant, reflecting not only their noble blood line but also the virtue of their Prussian training. These are boys of whom even "der alte Fritz" can be proud. They are aided by the sweet ministrations of Sophie, a true "mother of soldiers," who offers balm to their suffering. Brave and true, she joins the cadets in their black winter of despair, firing their dreams of freedom.

Klaus Detlef Sierck played a grand role as Cadet von Hohenhausen, demonstrating that noble character is not a function of age; rather it flows naturally from a Prussian source. The future cadet officers set an example of courage that inspires even hardened veterans. The young soldiers, the scions of the Prussian nobility, refuse to bend to the demands of the enemy. Even Colonel Goroschew, bereft of moral instincts, is impressed by their will to sacrifice. Their bravery inspires Rittmeister von Tzülow, a former Prussian officer unjustly cashiered by Frederick the Great, who has gone over to the enemy. He sees mirrored in them the power of the Prussian spirit, which lies hidden in the innermost recesses of his soul. He comes home to Prussia through the example of the cadets.

The bravery of the boys is symbolized by the spirited musical score, which features the *Kadettenlied:*

Ich habe Lust, im weiten Feld
zu streiten mit dem Feind,
wohl als ein tapfrer Kriegesheld,
der's treu und redlich meint.[53]

Scored for the film by Herbert Windt, the martial tune inspires the cadets in their direst need as well as in their hour of victory. They hold true to its admonition to show the courage of brave warriors: "The flag waves nobly for them, who loyally stand by her!"

Seldom in the cinema of the Third Reich were the "horrors" of the Slavic "subhuman" presented with such graphic clarity as in *Kadetten*. The Cossack leader, Colonel Goroschew, is a veritable beast in human form. This satanic creature seems more an animal than a man, and his Mongol physiognomy alone makes a sinister statement of racism, consonant with Nazi ideology. Goroschew's drunkenness, his intolerable crudity, and his lecherous conduct with a harem of prostitutes from the steppes stands in marked contrast to the purity of the blond, blue-eyed Prussian boys from Company 4. Further, juxtaposed to Mathias Wieman—a model northern German reared in the pastoral surroundings of Osnabrück in Westphalia— is Andrews Engelman, a horrendous figure from the nightmarish east. Ritter left little doubt in the mind of his audience that the character and racial traits of Goroschew had their twentieth-century equivalent in "Jewish-Bolshevism."

The virtue of the dauntless young warriors is ultimately rewarded. The lads arm themselves surreptitiously, take positions in a fortress, and make a stand against the storming Cossacks. Having commanded the youths to hold out to the last, Rittmeister von Tzülow finds a sacrificial death, giving his life for his young Prussian comrades. Several of the cadets also shed their blood for king and country, lending credibility to the affirmation of the Hitler Youth that "the deeds of the glorious dead are eternal!"

With their flags flying, and the band striking up the *Kadettenlied*, Company 4 marches home to Potsdam. They are the pride of the officer corps in Prussia's great hour of need. With such a noble human reserve from which to draw, surely the laurel crown of victory will adorn the battle flags of the House of Hohenzollern. By inference, the same blood that flowed through the veins of the Prussian cadets now nourishes the minds and bodies of the Hitler Youth.

In the context of 1941, Ritter's message was clear. Hitler's success was assured in his struggle to the death against the international conspiracy aligned against Germany. Wilhelm Utermann reviewed *Kadetten* for the *Völkischer Beobachter*, noting that only a master like Ritter could have turned the untrained enthusiasm of the cadets into a sophisticated and moving testament to the fighting spirit of the German nation. Ritter demonstrated his bond with the cadets when he took the plaudits of the crowd on the stage of the *Ufa* Palast in Berlin at the premiere, surrounded by the boys.[54] Along with *Hitler Youth Quex*, *Kadetten* was at the top of the list in the number of films for youth that Goebbels sponsored throughout World War II.[55]

The heroic vision that Ritter portrayed in *Pour le Mérite* found its fulfillment in the extraordinarily successful deployment of the Luftwaffe in Poland and France. These victories were an inspiration to Ritter, nicknamed the "Old Eagle," who stood ready to glorify the mission of the second generation of young heroes. *Stukas*, his 1941 release, was a hymn of devotion to the intrepid warriors of the air, joining elements of power, intellect, and idealism. By employing the heroic poetry of Hölderlin, Ritter made a dramatic testament to the cult of death. The film also launched a popular song, the *Stukalied*. What was remarkable about *Stukas* was that it delivered its message without any mention of Adolf Hitler or even the Nazi party. Instead, attention was devoted entirely to the beauty of comradeship in the corps—often in scenes of boyish enthusiasm—to the love of the good fight, urging surrender to the higher morality of eternal life through death for the nation. The result was a film that was praised by the authorities as a significant achievement in the war effort.[56]

Featuring many actors from his earlier films, *Stukas* fulfilled Ritter's dream of seeing the Luftwaffe play a major role in a campaign. Focusing on the experiences of a Stuka unit in the Battle of France in 1940, the film reflected his adolescent enthusiasm for the flying corps and his joy in battle itself. Carl Raddatz heads the cast in the role of the squadron commander, Captain Heinz Bork. O. E. Hasse, a veteran of the Max Reinhardt School at the Deutsches Theater in Berlin, made a remarkable contribution to the aesthetics of National Socialism in this work. He plays the sensitive chief surgeon, Dr. Gregorius, who gives universal meaning to the motif of *Heldentod*. The *Illustriertes Filmprogramm* commented on the heroic milieu of the flyers:

> At an aerodrome on the western front the Stukas return from a battle. The chief surgeon, Dr. Gregorius, and the *Stabsfeldwebel* pour wine from a generously laden table as the flyers take their dinner at a long table in a French chateau. The mood is boisterous. . . . Good spirits abound—a brief moment of peaceful rest—until they take off in their Stukas once more, climb into the sky, and launch into an attack moments later. A corporal and six men push a piano into the tent barracks, and when Commander Bork lands, the strains of Siegfried's "Rhine Journey" rise in full intonation over the airfield. It is like an echo of the battle they have just finished and at the same time an overture to a new effort.[57]

Heroic action is but a gateway to immortality, blessed by the gods.

The ultimate meaning of *Stukas* is not revealed in the heat of military action. Rather it flows from a thoughtful discussion between Captain Bork and Dr. Gregorius, when they ponder a letter written by the mother of a youth from the squadron who died in battle. A true Prussian mother, the woman has made the point that, instead of sadness and melancholy, she feels pride and a sense of fulfillment that her son had the privilege of dying a heroic death. With a grand Wagnerian accompaniment, Hasse, drawing on his considerable talent for philosophical nuance, comments, "If a mother accepts the news like this, then death suddenly has lost its sting." Raddatz answers, "Yes, one does not think about their death, but instead about what they have died for, and remembers them like the young gods that they are." With violins providing a tone of pathos, the camera moves into a closeup of the staff surgeon, who thoughtfully removes his glasses. Gregorius solemnly quotes the passionate lines of Hölderlin's "Death for the Fatherland":

O take me, let me join that circle,
so that I will not die a common death!
I do not want to die in vain; but
I would love to perish on a hill of sacrifice

for the Fatherland, to bleed the blood of my heart,
for the Fatherland—and soon it is done! To you,
dear ones! I come, to join
those who taught me to live and to die!

And heralds of victory come down: We have
won the battle! Live on high, O Fatherland,
and do not count the Dead! For you,
sweet one! not one too many has died.[58]

With these words of dedication and self-sacrifice finished, the captain and the surgeon, Bork and Gregorius—representing the union of power and intellect, the state and the muses—turn to the piano and strike up the chords of "Siegfried's Death," perhaps the most euphoric lines Wagner ever penned on the theme of heroic death. The men of the unit converge on the scene through the French doors, moved by the call to greatness. How beautiful it is to live a life with meaning! God and man have joined over the body of a fallen hero. Compared to this moving scene, the visit of a commodore to present Captain Bork with the *Ritterkreuz* as a symbolic tribute to the fallen men of his unit seems almost routine.

Gregorius demonstrates anew that man does not live by bread alone, when he observes that one of the flyers, Lieutenant Wilde, played by Hannes Stelzer, will not heal completely from his wounds, despite a total physical recovery. Only the experience of drinking at the source of the Germanic spring offers the opportunity for a total psychological transformation. Nothing, it seems, can bring this fine comrade to his senses, including the ministrations of a beautiful nurse. In the final scenes, the monumental *Gesamtkunstwerk* of Richard Wagner—experienced at the Festspielhaus at Bayreuth on the suggestion of Gregorius—proves redemptive for Lieutenant Wilde. Once more, the muses are the handmaiden to miraculous healing.

The lieutenant's recovery is evident even from his reaction to the trumpet fanfares for *Siegfried,* blown from the balcony of the theater to the throng gathered on the veranda—framed by the beautiful Franconian countryside—beckoning them to the ritual of holy mystery. The nurse accompanying him has to restrain her patient in the theater, so consumed is he with memories of fire fights over the Channel with English Spitfires. He insists that he must return to his comrades immediately. What fulfillment, what joy! Lieutenant Wilde literally races to the train to return to the home of his reawakened soul—to the company of his comrades. What delirious happiness to be able once more to fly his Stuka, to join the fellows again in the clouds, and to look death squarely in the face. With France defeated, there was but one thing on his mind—to punish England.

In the final scene of hysterical nationalism, Wilde has joined his unit flying off into the sun to launch the Battle of Britain. Victory, it seems, is assured with such fine young men to lead the vanguard against the enemy. The men of the unit strike up the lusty strains of the *Stukalied,* written by Geno Ohlischläger and scored by Windt:

> We are the black Hussars of the air,
> The Stukas, the Stukas, the Stukas.
> Always prepared, when the call to battle comes,
> The Stukas, the Stukas, the Stukas.
> We dive from the clouds and press the attack
> We're not afraid of hell and never relent,
> Till the enemy is destroyed,
> Till England, till England, till England is crushed,
> The Stukas, the Stukas, the Stukas.[59]

Stukas premiered in late June at the onset of the offensive against the Soviet Union. Curt Belling, reviewing the film in the *Völkischer Beobachter* on 29 June 1941, considered it a monument to the heroism and comradeship of Germany's young warriors. *Stukas,* he wrote, was a living testament to both the fighting and the home fronts, linking them in a blood bond. It spoke the language of the front and would inspire millions of German soldiers and citizens. *Stukas,* he submitted, showed the deft hand of Karl Ritter, who was deployed along the Channel coast for several months in 1940 as a Luftwaffe major. The result of Ritter's efforts was a film that joined art with experience and reflected the spirit and ethos of the young eagles of the sky.[60]

With the start of the war against the Soviet Union, Ritter launched his production of the anti-Bolshevik film *G.P.U.* He thereby contributed to the psychological warfare waged by Goebbels and the propaganda ministry against "the "Jewish-Bolshevik" specter. Anti-Bolshevism had been a constant theme in Nazi propaganda since World War I, interrupted only by the signing of the Nazi-Soviet Nonaggression Pact in August 1939.[61] And film had been used with considerable success since the onset of the Third Reich to convey the image of "Jewish-Bolshevism." *Blutendes Deutschland* (Deutscher Film-Vertrieb, 1933), *Flüchtlinge (Ufa*, 1933), *Henker, Frauen, und Soldaten* (Bavaria Film, 1935), and *Friesennot* (Delta, 1935) had all dealt with this theme. Joined to Goebbels's relentless assault on the Soviet Union, the image of the Russians that emerged was horrifying indeed. The "Jewish-Bolshevik subhuman" was a parasite, the source of all evil. He only appeared to be a man; in reality he was a form of swamp human. He knew only filth; German cleanliness was totally foreign to him. He shunned real toil like the Devil avoids Holy Water. The "Jewish-Bolshevik" had no soul, was devoted to the acquisition of gold, and was a culture destroyer. The asphalt of the modern city was his milieu. There the conspirators flourished, directing international crime, drug traffic, stock fraud, prostitution rings, and the syndicate. In the Soviet Union, the cancer had spread to the countryside as well. Now, in the battle of Russia, the German Wehrmacht and its allies were facing the world enemy in a struggle to the death.[62]

Karl Ritter collaborated with Andrews Engelman and Felix Lützkendorf on the script for *GPU*, which dealt with the machinations of the Soviet terror organization in the Baltic and in Western Europe early in World War II.[63] From the first frame, the GPU is presented as an organization devoted to carrying out its regime of horror, panic, and destruction. Nikolai Bokscha, played by Engelman, is the stereotypical Bolshevik. His behavior as commander of a mobile killing unit in the Baltic in 1919 reflects a murderous character. He personally executes the members of the innocent Feodorowna family, which sets the stage for the horrible scenes to follow. Bokscha demonstrates that he is typical of all members of the international "Jewish-Bolshevik" conspiracy; he engages in murder and destruction ruthlessly and without remorse. Worse still, he serves only himself. After directing for years an operation stretching across Europe, he is ready to betray his own cause and to enjoy the fruits of his sinful life.

Juxtaposed to Bokscha is an irresistibly beautiful and sensitive figure, the loyal Olga Feodorowna, played by Laura Solari. She bears the call for revenge in her heart every waking moment. True, steadfast and pure, she joins in her person all of the best features of the "Aryan" woman. To see her playing the violin in the Riga cultural center is to know beauty itself. Contrasted to the confused liberal bourgeoisie gathered in the communist-front Women's League for Peace and Freedom, she is the very model of probity. Her virtue is evident once more in Göteborg, Sweden, where Olga dances with Mr. Spiegelglas, a Jewish communist agent. As a jazz band blares its throbbing cacophony, a bust of Stalin surveys the glittering scene.

The message is clear: the purveyors of international conspiracy may wear the glitzy silks and satins of the *Schickeria,* but the conniving Jew lies hidden behind the facade. Compared to these sad creatures, sunny Olga appears as radiant as Mary, Mother of God. She remains true to her convictions unto death. As the German Panzers and infantry race to liberate Western Europe at the conclusion of the film, the band plays the freedom motif from Beethoven's *Fidelio.* The forces of Adolf Hitler have arrived to return Europe to its senses once more and will eradicate the curse of the GPU.[64]

G.P.U. was perhaps Karl Ritter's weakest film. The episodic nature of the script and the gruesome subject matter contributed to an altogether leaden production. The result was that Goebbels's apparatus ignored the film. The public found it tedious as well, a thoroughly understandable reaction. In their rare moments of rest, audiences sought relief from fear, suffering, and tension in the fourth year of World War II.

The gradual decline of the influence of Karl Ritter as a film director paralleled the increasingly poor fortunes of the German Wehrmacht during the period from 1942 to the collapse in 1945. There were deeper reasons, however, for Ritter's lack of success in the waning years of the Third Reich. His film style, which united dramatic reporting and documentary components, was suitable to the atmosphere of frothy German success during the years 1936–39. It was also consonant with a period of *Blitzkrieg* victories, when Ritter's approach to film provided more of a continuation of the breathless weekly newsreels than true cinematic art. As Goebbels often said, victory makes its own propaganda; defeat, on the other hand, calls for creative genius. The difficult conditions and continuous blows to the Reich after the fall of Stalingrad in February 1943 demanded film of some depth. Above all, Goebbels sought works that would create aesthetic accompaniment for his own "total war" propaganda. Ritter possessed neither the temperament nor the ability to create films of this nature, which reached their apogee in the 1945 release *Kolberg,* directed by Veit Harlan.

Ritter's decline into obscurity, which began with *G.P.U.,* continued with his next major effort, *Besatzung Dora* (1943). Filmed in North Africa, in France, and on the eastern front, *Besatzung Dora* was yet another glorification of the flying corps. Focusing on the adventures of the crew of a reconnaissance aircraft, it starred Hannes Stelzer, Hubert Kuirina, Ernst von Klipstein, and Clemens Hasse. Carsta Löck, Suse Graf, and Charlott Daudert played romantic accompaniment to the heroism of their men at the front.[65]

Ritter went to great lengths in *Besatzung Dora* to present authentic scenes of the Luftwaffe in action. He described the experience:

I spent six weeks as a soldier with a reconnaissance unit before I wrote one line of the script. Thus, it was under these conditions that the plan arose to present to our people the authentic front experience, and not to film one scene at the studio, but instead right at the front with real flyers and their officers. Only the main roles were played by actors. . . . We had our whole staff with the men in the West who are flying against England, we were outside of Leningrad on the Eastern front and we were in the heat of the South. I think you can feel that when you see this film. Just as I had hoped, it conveys the fresh air of the front.[66]

The release of *Besatzung Dora* was forbidden in November 1943 for several reasons. A third of the film took place in North Africa, but by the spring of 1943 the Wehrmacht and their Italian allies had surrendered the last German positions there. Further, in two scenes played in Berlin—where the flyers are on leave enjoying the company of their sweethearts in a fashionable rooftop cafe—references are made to establishing farms after the war in Russia, which was to become a German colony. Finally, Goebbels made it clear to Karl Ritter through his intermediary, State Secretary Leopold Gutterer, that *Besatzung Dora* was simply not a National Socialist film.[67]

The last film that Karl Ritter directed was *Sommernächte*, a work of little consequence. In 1945 he worked under the eminently successful director Wolfgang Liebeneiner on *Das Leben geht weiter* (*Ufa*), which dealt with the bravery of the Berliners under the strain of the bombing of the capital. It remained uncompleted at the conclusion of the war.

True to his character, Ritter ended the war as a Luftwaffe major. He was captured by the Russians but was able to escape and make his way to Bavaria. After undergoing de-Nazification proceedings in the French zone, he emigrated with his family to Argentina in 1949. He reemerged briefly in the early 1950s as a director with Eos-Film in Mendoza, Argentina. He even attempted a comeback in West Germany as a director, filming *Ball der Nationen* with Zsa Zsa Gabor and Gustav Fröhlich. He died in Argentina in 1977 at the age of 89.[68]

IX

Hitler, Heroes, and *Heldentod*

The Myth of Death in World War II

> In der Hingabe des eigenen Lebens für die
> Existenz der Gemeinschaft liegt die Krönung
> alles Opfersinnes.
>
> Adolf Hitler[1]

With the coming of World War II, National Socialism had come full circle. Born in the trenches of the Great War, the will to battle had ever been
the essence of the party and its Führer. This spirit of combat embellished
the epic myths of heroism during the *Kampfzeit* and was the leitmotiv of
the peacetime Third Reich. With the launching of the *Blitzkrieg,* myth once
more became the handmaiden to Mars.

Initially the treatment of the theme of death in World War II was
considerably different from that experienced during the Great War.[2] The
nationalist euphoria that accompanied the call to arms in 1914 presented
a marked contrast to the reserved posture of the public in 1939. The bloody
trench stalemate was not forgotten.[3] It took the victories over Poland and
France to engender the war fever that Germany experienced in 1940. At
that stage of the war, the astounding German successes totally oversha-
dowed considerations of death. Such overconfidence proved a brief phe-
nomenon indeed, and, in time, death loomed ever larger in the German
experience.

The early victories offered fulfillment of the most remarkable dimensions. With Poland defeated in some four weeks time, the feat of German
arms was praised to the skies. With the occupation of Denmark and Norway,
and the stunning victory over France in a matter of weeks, the Wehrmacht
seemed invincible. As a result, extravagant exaggeration dominated the
propaganda front. Goebbels claimed at the height of the battle in France
that the Wehrmacht had delivered "the greatest military victory of all times."
To win this victory, individuals had devoted themselves to the greater good
of the whole: "The German Reich idea and the national ethos of the German racial community have received the most noble consecration and the
ultimate glorification through the fighting, dying, and victory of the German soldier."[4]

During this period, the genre of heroic film controlled the commanding heights. More than any other medium, film offered graphic and dramatic testimony to the devastating effect of the German onslaught. Nazi cinema— always a unique blend of myth and reality—took on a special character. It celebrated the Führer, sent by Providence, who had delivered Germany from the shame of Versailles and was setting about the difficult task of reordering Europe for the next millennium.[5] Hitler's mission was a racial one, and the film propagandists reiterated time and again that Nazi Germany had achieved a racial cohesion never before equaled in its tortured history. From this point on, the coalition of Bolshevism with the "international Jewish parasites" would be pursued unto death.

The men of the Wehrmacht were lionized as the armed fist of reborn Germanic man, at once brave and self-sacrificing. With the racial stereotypes of Leni Riefenstahl's *Triumph of the Will* as their model, film experts in the propaganda ministry and the Wehrmacht high command went to great lengths to convey the image of the German soldier as a racially pure, loyal, and courageous warrior. He knew no fear and was imbued with but one idea—to serve the Fatherland. He represented more a type than an individual. In *Sieg im Westen* (1940), the apogee of this genre was reached. Line after line of blond and stocky figures in the prime of young manhood conjured up images of the finest sculptures of Praxiteles and classic Greece, a culture devoted to the heroic warrior theme.[6]

Nazi propaganda conveyed the message that no armed forces in the world could compete against the Wehrmacht's new fighting machine. In *Der Feldzug in Polen* (1939), *Feuertaufe* (1940), and the newsreels of the period, the Wehrmacht seems to be riding the crest of an elemental force, cascading toward inevitable victory. German dead were seldom shown, only beaming troops with the dust of the field on their faces, often bursting into lusty songs to case their burdens. They were absolutely assured of success. Footage of Panzers, the new strategic arm of the military forces that had revolutionized warfare, delighted audiences. In film after film, tanks were seen rushing toward classic victories of encirclement, pushing eastward into Poland or westward through the Ardennes Forest, toward Amiens and the Channel, toward Dunkirk and victory.

Repeatedly film commentators pointed to the role of the Wehrmacht in avenging the pain of defeat in the Great War, the "stab in the back of 1918," and the Versailles *Diktat*. The machinations of the Jews remained a central theme as well. Hitler was clearly the architect of victory, and he was often seen studying the huge war maps in the situation room with his military advisers. When he appeared at the armistice ceremony at Compiegne, the spirits of his comrades from 1914–18 were present. When the soldiers of the Wehrmacht occupied Verdun, it appeared as if there never had been a fortress there. When German tanks rushed over the gently undulating hills of Flanders, they were on sacred ground. The message was clear: honor had been returned once more to the German war flags.

Film specialists followed Goebbels's lead in placing the German victories in ideological perspective. The Reich, it was argued, was engaged in fighting "English plutocrats" and their "Jewish-Negroid bedfellows" in France, and the German mission was claimed to be of world historic importance—to save the Christian West from the "parasitic culture destroyers," the tools of the "international Jewish conspiracy."

The newsreels of the French campaign were hard-hitting propaganda vehicles. One of them shows German troops occupying Domremy, the birthplace of Joan of Arc. A memorable scene features the virgin saint beckoning to the soldiers of the Wehrmacht, as if entreating them to save Christian France from abuse at the hands of the purveyors of Jewish-Negroid putrefaction. Footage of St. Joan was juxtaposed to scenes of escaping Jews, forced to abandon their stylish cars loaded with booty. A nattily dressed black, shown lighting a cigarette on a street in Paris, seemed to symbolize everything that the invaders wanted to liquidate. The ringing of church bells across Europe after the victory demonstrated anew the Reich's cultural mission. *Sieg im Westen* shows German soldiers solemnly entering a Gothic church "bombed by the enemy." An enlisted man, moved by the greatness of the hour, strikes up the chords of Bach to lend a new dimension to the profound truth that the battle of France was a struggle for civilization itself.

The myth that bound the whole was the cult of the Führer, the leitmotiv of all Nazi ideology and propaganda. Hitler emerged as the greatest military commander of all times. He is seen reviewing the parade in Warsaw, as the victorious field-gray columns pass in review in October 1939. Footage of the Führer's triumphant return to Berlin after the battle of France is highly emotional material by any standard, replete with scenes of Bund deutscher Mädel girls bearing flowers, swooning women, and an absolutely beaming, boyish Hermann Göring. Bells and music accompany the ecstatic scene, as wild crowds gyrate in the streets, while the Führer receives their plaudits from his balcony at the Reich Chancellery. A propagandist's dream, the victory over France was the last such success the Germans would celebrate in World War II.

The poetry of SA Sturmführer Heinrich Anacker was characteristic of the nationalistic bravado of this period. Having joined the Schlageter Company of the SA as a student in Vienna in 1924, Anacker was widely published and a leading Nazi poet. His pen re-created the frothy excitement of his experiences as a Storm Trooper, reflecting a sometimes raw authenticity. *Die Trommel* (1932), *Der Aufbau* (1938), and *Wir wachsen in das Reich hinein* (1938), all published by the Zentralverlag der NSDAP and priced at three marks a copy, were widely distributed.[7] Anacker glorified "the unknown fighter" and "reawakened youth"; at the same time, he spoke to the emotions of the common man—workers, farmers, and artisans. He captured the excitement of the era in his works, which often seemed more like lyrical editorials than poetry. Many of his poems were put to music and worked their way into popular culture. For Anacker, it was only natural to shift from glorifying the grand agony of the *Kampfzeit* to exalting the nation at war. The steady stream of victories only intensified his romantic spirit, and his euphoric poems appeared continually in the press.

Above all, Anacker reflected the zeal of the troops during the days of *Blitzkrieg* glory. In "Seaman's Song," he captured their emotions accurately:

> The day was gray, the day was bad,
> And the sea was terribly rough.
> But it's clearing now from the west . . .
> Inspiring golden dreams in me—
> Antje, my blond baby!
> Don't you hear our accordian from afar?
> Antje, this song sends you my greetings!

Death seemed to hold no sting for a seaman:

> If the sea should claim me one day,
> Don't take it too hard!
> Everything happens, as God wills it,
> And there's plenty of other sailors out there. . . .
> Another one will come, to ask for you,
> Antje, my blond baby![8]

From the icy campaign in Norway, the Alpine Corps was not to be outdone:

> From Stavanger as far as Trondheim Germany's
> proud flag waves, storm-tossed.
> Even on Narvik's steep rocky throne
> The true sons of the Ostmark stand guard.

Death seemed but a matter of course when the corps sang farewell to its fallen comrades:

> When a comrade dies a hero's death,
> The snow blooms red as an Alpine rose. . . .
> And for him, who died so far from home,
> We sing this song as our farewell:
> "From Steiermark and from Tyrol,
> From the Kärntner Mountains we hail.
> Fighting in snow and ice far in the north
> Hitler's Alpine Corps the Edelweiss!"[9]

The arrogance conveyed in Anacker's "Artilleryman's Song" can be understood only in the context of 1940:

> Each for each and all for all
> The battery!
> Shot for shot we send
> The enemy an iron greeting—
> Yes, the cannons thunder
> And resound bum bum![10]

Hatred for England was a major theme of the period, and Anacker wrote with the verve of a naval man who had not forgotten the indignities the officers and men of the German fleet suffered in the Great War. In "Quiet Before the Storm," he wrote:

> Full steam ahead! The flags wave on the masthead!
> Nor will our sword be returned to its scabbard,
> Until Britannia's power is broken![11]

Contempt for Jewry came second for Anacker, who lamented the cost in German blood of fighting such despicable enemies as the English:

> The dead, the women with tear-stained faces
> Raise their lament and sit as a court,
> Which announces its judgment before history:
> England is guilty![12]

The English "sea robbers" would pay a heavy price for their arrogance, Anacker boasted. The dramatic mission of Lieutenant Günter Prien, commander of U-47, who sank the battleship *Royal Oak* in the harbor of Scapa Flow in October 1939, promised to be just the beginning. England's once-mighty empire, he wrote, would itself "sink like the Royal Oak."[13] Anacker warned that the same fate awaited any and all ships that attempted to enter English territorial waters. "Black flags are beckoning," because "the star of England is sinking."[14]

The campaign in France presented Anacker with the opportunity to celebrate Hitler as the "greatest military commander of all times," while glorying in the memory of the fallen of World War I. He was honored when his *Frankreichlied* became the official song of the battle of France and was heard throughout the campaign. Its melodic cadences—put to music by the prominent bandleader Herms Niel—became very popular:

> Comrade, we're marching in the West,
> Together with our bomb squadrons—
> And though many of our best will die,
> We will strike down the enemy!
> Forwards! To the fore! To the fore!
> Over the Meuse, over Scheldt and Rhine
> We march victoriously through France—

We march, we march
Through France![15]

The return of the field-gray columns to Flanders caught Anacker's imagination. German troops were passing over land once drenched in the blood of their fathers. Conjuring up the ghosts of the fallen, he wrote:

On the broad fields of Flanders,
The poppies bloom so red . . .
The fields of Flanders surely
Know of the death of soldiers!

But at this historic juncture a new celestial constellation had formed, and the laurel crown of victory awaited the Germanic warriors:

There rages anew in Flanders
A bloody hard-fought battle.
The victory won in spring's splendor
Greater Germany, young and strong,
Brings in the harvest of the dead
At Ypres and Langemarck![16]

Anacker delighted in the image of the Führer as commander-in-chief, and he celebrated him in a poem of adoration entitled "The Gray Coat."[17] Whereas the Führer was at the front with his men, sharing the dangers of battle, the members of the English cabinet dispatched death orders for their countrymen from the safety of distant headquarters.[18] Hitler's very presence guaranteed victory:

Now as commander of Greater Germany's Army he leads
It to victory from the Argonne Forest to the sea
Motors thunder and roar—
Announcing the triumph of German arms
In the Forest of Compiegne.[19]

According to Anacker, the world understood the historic importance of the victory. Both the conception and the execution of the plan had depended on the brilliance of the Führer, the first soldier of the Reich:

Unseen the eagle of eternal glory circled . . .
Everything that happened was conceived by Hitler
Who, weighed down with care, leads us to the dawn![20]

Surely, such a Reich and its Führer were worth fighting and dying for.

Hitler was convinced that death for the ideal of the Reich guaranteed eternal ennoblement for the warrior. On Heroes Memorial Day 1940, he elaborated on this theme in remarks delivered at the Berlin Armory. The

Führer placed the individual soldier's death within the context of the flow of nature, which demands sacrifice to bring about new life, as well as pain to heal a nation's wounds. An individual called to heroic death was thereby "furthering life itself," because he was answering the injunction of Providence, which demanded a struggle of world-historic proportions. Immortality in the Eternal Hall of Heroes was a precious reward for the ultimate sacrifice in the service of the *Volksgemeinschaft*, guaranteeing that the two-thousand-year chain of life of the Germanic people would not be broken. Conjuring up the images of the fallen, Hitler continued:

> The witnesses of an unparalleled glorious past speak to us from the sacred halls of this grand building. It was won and washed in the blood of countless German heroes. We would have no right to enter these halls, unless in our hearts we were determined to be just as brave as those who went before us. . . . We are now fighting for the same thing for which they once struggled. What was noble enough for them—if necessary—to die for, should find us ready to emulate at all times. . . . As Führer of the nation, as Chancellor of the Reich and as Commander-in-Chief of the German Wehrmacht I live today for only one goal: to think of victory day and night and to struggle, work and fight for it, and if necessary not to spare my own life, knowing that this time the future of Germany will be decided for centuries.

The Führer concluded by addressing the spirits of his fallen comrades from the Great War:

> As a former soldier of the Great War, I have but a single humble request to direct to Providence, that it may give us all the grace to conclude the last chapter of this great world struggle for our German people with honor. Then the spirits of our fallen comrades will rise from their graves and thank all those who by their courage and loyalty have at last avenged the horrible crime once committed against them by our people in an hour of weakness.[21]

With the outbreak of Operation Barbarossa—the invasion of the Soviet Union—both Hitler and Goebbels radically altered the central themes of Nazi propaganda. Thereafter, blatantly racist propaganda of savage intensity was focused on "Jewish-Bolshevism." Long before the attack began, it was evident to many what lay ahead. During the delicate period of *rapprochement* between Germany and the Soviet Union—from August 1939 until June 1941—Goebbels ordered his film administrator, Fritz Hippler, and the head of the Bolshevik desk in the propaganda ministry, Eberhard Taubert, to produce a film on the Jewish question. The result was the devastating production *The Eternal Jew*, which accomplished in documentary form what Veit Harlan had achieved in his remarkable feature *Jud Süss*. Jewry and Bolshevism were equated, and both were marked for destruction.[22]

Hitler's proclamation at the outset of the campaign against the Soviet Union clearly set the tone for what was to follow:

The hour has come in which it becomes necessary to move against the plot of the Jewish-Anglo-Saxon warmongers and of the Jewish rulers of the Soviet Union. German people! At this moment a movement of troops is taking place which in its scope and expanse is the greatest the world has ever seen. . . . The German eastern front stretches from East Prussia to the Carpathians. . . . The task of this front is no longer to protect single countries but to ensure the security of Europe and thereby save them all.[23]

Once again German newsreels graphically revealed both the ongoing campaign and its deeper meaning. Film treatment of the astounding victories of the Wehrmacht in the summer of 1941—featuring battles of encirclement at Bialystok, Minsk, Smolensk, and Kiev—was euphoric. Emphasis was placed on the total superiority of the German war machine and the inevitability of victory. Panzer columns were seen moving through the "Stalin Line" with ease, rushing eastward with crushing momentum, spreading their net around the baffled enemy in strategic pincer movements that would have astounded the great field commanders from Hannibal to Napoleon. In these films columns of troops merrily sing the song of the Russian campaign. These men—light of hair, dashing, and racially pure— were the best examples of the Reich's new manhood, indeed the "best soldiers in the world." Drums, trumpets, and spirited march music accompanied the film image of this onslaught, and the dark shadows of Panzers amid the rich colors of ripening wheat and sunflower fields left the impression of a somber majesty that belied a brutal reality.[24]

Scenes of Hitler flying to be with his men were remarkable. Strongest of the strong, bravest of the brave, he was hailed by his men as one of their own. What a joy to do battle at the Führer's side! How beautiful the life of the German soldier! How sweet the taste of victory against the Bolsheviks! How noble the sacrifice for Führer and Reich! One fascinating scene shows men of the Waffen SS gently walking through gorgeous fields of wild flowers in full bloom, picking one here and one there, to form a garland worthy of honoring their brave comrades who had fallen in battle that day. Although their friends were buried in the soil of Russia, their souls had risen and returned to inspire their comrades until the final victory.[25]

Film reports wove variations on the Crusader motif, which Goebbels had sounded in a major article in *Das Reich* at the beginning of the campaign. Just as their ancestors were involved in a struggle to the death against "Islamic anti-Christ," so these twentieth-century Crusaders were engaged in a battle to the death against "Soviet barbarism." Seldom in world history had the lines between good and evil been so clearly drawn. Film propaganda throughout the Russian campaign focused on the theme of Europe united against Bolshevism, demonstrating that the Continent had come to its senses and was intent on exterminating the Jewish bacillus at its source. Footage showed Franco's "Blue Division" leaving Spain for the East, Mussolini reviewing departing troops, and Cossack SS regiments dashing across the steppes freeing their Ukrainian Motherland. Eager young men from Denmark, Belgium, France, Slovakia, and Croatia don the uniform of the Waffen SS.[26] The message was forthright: Europe would not rest until the last Bolshevik had been liquidated.

The image of the "Jewish-Bolshevik" that the Nazis presented was horrifying indeed. The *Untermensch* was a parasite, the source of all evil. He had never worked for a living but was a trader and middleman, shunning real toil. The "Jewish-Bolshevik" had no soul and was completely devoted to the quest for gold. The species flourished in the city, acting as a catalyst to cultural disintegration, polluting all that was sacred, just, and moral.[27]

The weekly newsreel offered Goebbels the opportunity to propagate the myth of the "Jewish-Bolshevik" in continuous episodes. Brutally treated Russian Jews became mere stage props in the hands of the war reporters organized in army and SS formations. The Nazis employed radical language in referring to their enemy. Epithets such as "Jewish Soldetska," "hordes," "beasts," and *"Flintenweiber"* alternated with "G.P.U. murder beasts," "butchers," and "devilish murder lust." Often groups of undernourished, diseased, and unshaven Jewish prisoners were photographed and presented as stereotypical "subhumans." Well-fed, tailored officers and men of the SS were juxtaposed to these pitiful prisoners of war, many of whom perished.

In an ironic turn of fate, the Nazis made the crimes perpetrated by the Soviets a major theme in their propaganda. The newsreels often featured scenes of unearthed corpses, "victims of the murderous G.P.U.," with women and children mourning over the bodies of their dead. "Bolshevik criminality" was treated in the documentary films *Soviet Paradise* and *Europe Fights Bolshevism*, but the best example of this genre was the 1943 documentary release *In the Forest of Katyn*.[28] As the fires of Auschwitz were burning, the cynical Nazis called in neutral journalists to view the remains of twelve thousand Polish officers murdered by the GPU in the Katyn Forest near Smolensk. This was followed by the viewing of the graves of thousands of Ukrainian nationalists "butchered for their heroism" and artifacts such as photographs of wives and children, Bibles, and crucifixes. Only Adolf Hitler and the Wehrmacht stood between this murderous horde and the people of Western Europe. It was taken for granted that the protection of cultured Europe from the scourge of subhumanity would exact a heavy toll in blood.

Goebbels struck the leitmotiv for the ensuing propaganda of heroism in a major article entitled "The Fulfilled," which he published in *Das Reich* (27 December 1942).[29] He compared Germany's struggle to climbing a towering mountain, a metaphor for the mission of *Grossdeutschland*. At the same time he linked the theme of *Heldentod* to Greek heroism and German idealism. Those who had given their lives for the Fatherland had been freed from the chains of earthly existence and were at one with the heroic rhythm of historic necessity. The fallen were now free and had already crossed over the mountain. The survivors, on the other hand, had to continue the climb and to endure the vicissitudes of fate.

Goebbels turned to an image that all of his readers could understand—the memory of the beloved dead. His late adjutant in the propaganda ministry, an SA Führer and Luftwaffe officer, was the embodiment "of the new German manliness." He was loved and respected by his colleagues. But, with each passing week, he became sadder that he was not fighting at the front. Finally his hour came, and, according to Goebbels, he went into combat "like he was taking Holy Orders." He died in the assault on Crete, a striver for the good. He lived on in the memory of those who loved him, and, as Goebbels described it, "one already began to see the dead soldier in the glow of transfiguration." His was the glory of "fulfilled fulfillment." When his comrades studied the painting of him in the adjutant's room in the ministry, "we stood," Goebbels wrote, "before a harmonious union of idealism and reality, which would forever be out of reach for the rest of us."[30]

Those who continued to shed tears for their loved ones, long after an acceptable period of proud mourning, were accused of engaging in narcissism. They were instructed instead to ponder the beauty of their fate, because the dead had already transcended the zone of mere earthly suffering. The blood that once flowed through their veins would flow anew in happy, healthy children who would colonize the Germanic East. The nation honored its mothers and wives who mourned the loss of their sons and husbands. Theirs was truly a difficult personal fate. But the German Reich was not a collection point for individual fates; rather, the responsibilities of continental leadership had been thrust upon it. "The dead have earned more than our tears," Goebbels claimed. "They form the national conscience and admonish us to demonstrate the same zeal and fanaticism in both work and battle that they themselves have shown."

Goebbels concluded with a visionary statement, as he reflected on the difficult climb ahead:

We bury our dead along the edges of the steep path. They fell in the first ranks, and all who march after them, must pass by them. . . . Like silent directional markers, they point toward the peak. When we finally reach the crest, we will lay garlands along the path to the heights; only then will the dead show us their warmest and most transfigured faces. . . . Then the new century will open its gates wide for our entry, and the same bright light of transfiguration that shines on us will also beam on the unknown dead soldier, for whom his comrades dug a grave at twilight after a hard-fought battle, in a distant, shimmering light. In

21. Field burial in Poland, September 1939, SS Leibstandarte Adolf Hitler. (Klaus Weill, snapshot album presented as gift to Hitler, Library of Congress.)

this way our fallen enter the mythology of our Volk for all time; they are no longer what they were among us, but instead the eternal models of our epoch. . . . We are the searchers; they are the fulfilled.[31]

The soldiers of the SS were the model for the National Socialist "fulfilled" generation. The fighting spirit of the Waffen SS resulted in part from their adherence to the mythical ideological precepts of Nazi ideology, which combined racism and elitism with medieval concepts of loyalty.[32] Loyalty, honor, unconditional obedience, and readiness for self-sacrifice were the hallmarks of this ethos.[33] The SS celebrated their warrior ancestors, whose exploits had been exalted in the *Edda*, the epic poem that glorified the heroic vanguard of the Teutonic mission: "I know but one thing which is eternal; the glorious deeds of the dead." Reichsführer SS Heinrich Himmler stressed continually the importance of loyalty, that noble bond that obligated the SS man always to remain true to the Führer and the Reich ideal, to his comrades, and to the Volk. "My Honor is Loyalty" had been the motto of the corps since 1931. Further, it was customary that the *Treuelied der SS* was sung at most gatherings of the Black Order, and loyalty to the death was its theme:

> When all others are disloyal, then we
> will remain loyal,
> so that there will always be
> a guard for you.
> Comrades of our youth, you images
> of a better time—which dedicates us
> to manly virtue and to love death.[34]

Sacrifice for the German people was not to be feared. "Death holds no sting for us," Himmler affirmed, because "individuals die, while the Volk lives on." Because the men of the Germanic SS were more concerned about the future of the Volk than about their individual destinies, members would "willingly and bravely seek death, wherever that is necessary."[35] Life was embraced in death, death in life. Nature itself was the great teacher of political ideology; one needed only to observe the annual cycle of the seasons to ascertain God's meaning for man. The new life of spring was embraced in the death of November. The warrior's affirmation of heroic death carried with it the obligation to procreate new life, to ensure that the eternal chain would go unbroken. The future of the race depended not only on victory in battle but also on the birth of great numbers of healthy, racially pure children. Thus, each SS man had the duty to father as many children as possible. Women had a dual role in partnership with their husbands. They were to be beautiful and loving wives, while at the same time brave in undergoing the life-threatening dangers of childbirth. As a result, the loyal SS wives, theoretically equal members of the "blood-bound Order," faced death on the home front just as their husbands did on the battlefield.

It was a sacred duty of the SS that heroic death be rewarded with a burial appropriate for heroes. Accordingly, Himmler issued strict orders that standards of unerring military precision were to be the hallmarks of all SS burials.[36] The state funeral that Hitler ordered to honor SS Obergruppenführer Reinhard Heydrich, commander of the Security Police and the SD, following his assassination in May 1942 in Prague, became the standard against which all future SS burials were judged. Following elaborate ceremonies at the Hradchin Palace in Prague, a special train was dispatched to Berlin with the body of Heydrich, accompanied by an SS honor guard. At noon on 8 June, two days of elaborate pageantry began. The Anhalter railway station was decorated for the occasion, as the highest officers of the SS awaited the arrival of the mortal remains of their comrade. Himmler and his paladins saluted the casket, which was bedecked with the Reich war flag and borne by Waffen SS noncommissioned officers to its

22. Field burial in Poland, September 1939, SS Leibstandarte Adolf Hitler. (Klaus Weill, snapshot album presented as gift to Hitler, Library of Congress.)

caisson. Following the playing of the Präsentier March, the motored cortege—a staff of honor, a company of elite SS troops, and two SS men bearing velvet cushions displaying Heydrich's medals like pieces of the True Cross—slowly made its way through the streets of Berlin toward the notorious Prince Albrecht Palace. Large crowds of true believers and the curious alike struggled to catch a glimpse of the somber cavalcade of black automobiles carrying the cream of SS officialdom. As the body reached SS headquarters, it was received by sixty officers of the Reichssicherheitshauptamt, who had formed ranks before the building to receive their leader appropriately. Heydrich lay in state in the conference hall throughout the day and night, attended by six SD officers.

A state funeral took place the next day in the Mosaic Hall of the new Reich Chancellery, an opulent and imposing setting for the ceremony, which was broadcast live over the *Grossdeutsche Rundfunk*. Heydrich lay on a raised catafalque flanked by flaming urns, and a huge black and silver SS rune flag was hung directly behind the body. His helmet and dagger lay on a swastika flag draped over the coffin, which was banked with flowers. Every conceivable ranking party and Wehrmacht personality was in attendance. Hitler and Himmler entered the hall together at 3:00 P.M., taking their places next to Heydrich's two boys, Klaus and Heider. Wagner's funeral music from the *Götterdämmerung*—announcing that the noble Siegfried had been martyred by the ignoble Hagen—set a majestic yet profoundly melancholy tone to the ceremony.

Himmler delivered the funeral address, which characterized the life of Heydrich as a heroic symphony of loyalty, bravery, purity of character, and obedience to the Aryan racial imperative. His life had given new meaning to the motto of their Nordic warrior ancestors: "Stirb und Werde" ("Die and Become"). According to Himmler, Heydrich was both efficient and determined in every position he occupied, from deputy protector of Bohemia and Moravia to commander of the SD and Security Police. He had even flown as a fighter pilot on the Russsian front, where his bravery won him the *Frontflugspanne* and the Iron Cross I. Himmler praised Heydrich for his role as a model family man, noting that Frau Heydrich could not attend the funeral because she was heavy with child. Reflecting his belief in the myths of the SS, Himmler concluded that the hero had not died but lived on in the Order of the SS. Prophetically, the Reichsführer resolved that Reinhard would inspire the men of the SS when they carried out the most difficult assignments for the Führer and Reich. His memory would enable the men of the SS to keep the faith, to attack ruthlessly, and to form the final guard at the hour of destiny. Henceforth, the Sixth Infantry Regiment of the Waffen SS would bear the name Reinhard Heydrich, an elite unit in the struggle to the death against Bolshevik subhumanity.

Hitler then solemnly took the podium. He referred to Heydrich as one of the best National Socialists, one of the strongest defenders of the German Reich, one of the greatest opponents of all the enemies of this Reich. He died as a blood witness for the preservation and security of the Reich. As Führer of the Party and of the German Reich I award you, my dear comrade Heydrich . . . the highest decoration, which I have to give: the "Oberste Stufe des Deutschen Ordens."[37]

With that Hitler pinned the medal to one of the velvet cushions bearing Heydrich's decorations and gave his final salute. A long column of mourners fell in behind the honor guard and coffin as the funeral parade, accompanied by the beat of muffled drums, made its way through the streets to Heydrich's last resting place in Berlin's cemetery of heroes, the Invalidenfriedhof.

SS Sturmbannführer Richard Wolf (SD) was so moved by the death of Heydrich that he wrote the poem "The Führer's Wolves" soon after the ceremony. It was the same desperado spirit and savage love of violence that inspired the units of the Waffen SS to fight to the bitter end:

The lead wolf was killed—
The pack huddled together
And forms—still fired up from battle—
With their bodies alone
A ring of loyalty around the chief
Who chose the pack to protect him.
The strongest wolf springs up again!
He bravely surveys the field with flaming eyes—
And full of rage strikes his fangs into the heart of the enemy,
While the pack forms up around the knoll.

No matter what you might plot
In vileness from your cowardly ambuscade—
You creatures will not stop the avalanche.
No matter who else might fall victim to your
base hatred, It doesn't matter to us!
We trust in our star and hold firm to the command!
And our battle cry remains: "Das Reich!"[38]

There were many variations on the theme of *Liebestod* in SS propaganda. Freiherr von Wangenheim's *The Last Roll Call: The Deeds, Dream, and Brave Death of SS Oberjunker Radewitz* was the quintessential front novella, a genre that had gained respectability after the Great War but had fallen into disrepute under the Nazis.[39] Fritz von Radewitz dies while leading a storm unit against a Bolshevik bunker in the black of night. His comrades find him with a smile on his face, surrounded by a mound of Russian dead, as if he had already entered that "heaven of the brave" of which he had dreamed.

23. Hitler delivers eulogy for Reinhard Heydrich, Mosaic Hall of Reich Chancellery, 9 June 1942. (Bundesarchiv.)

It was this kind of literature, exuding the nauseating perfume of parlor heroism, that so repelled many front soldiers. One Lieutenant Hasser would have no more, and he protested in the strongest possible terms. The German soldier, he said, was sick of being misrepresented by propagandists, who invariably wrote descriptions of the "warrior's countenance," of "eyes gleaming forth from his steel helmet," of his "boldly placed chin reflecting energy and ice-cold determination." This supersoldier seldom spoke, but his few chosen words would do justice to any philosopher, military thinker, or geopolitician. At breakfast he faces the strafing of low-flying enemy fighter planes, at lunch a shattering artillery attack, and at dinner a major assault of crazed Bolshevik infantry. Hasser ridiculed the notion that only a dozen of these heroes could destroy an enemy division, before launching into several choruses of popular military songs, steeling their will for the morrow. He called for an end to the characterization of the German soldier as having steel and granite instead of blood in his veins.[40]

Reports about lives based on historical authenticity were no doubt better received. One such example was the death of SS Brigadeführer Fritz Witt, commander of a division on the Normandy front in June 1944. Thirty-six years old at his death, Witt had enjoyed great success in the SS. He had been chosen by Sepp Dietrich as one of the original 120 members of the Leibstandarte Adolf Hitler, the vanguard of the future First SS Panzer Division. Awarded the *Ritterkreuz* and the *Deutsche Kreuz in Gold* for action in France and Russia, he was a model officer. In 1943 he was commissioned to command a new unit, the Twelfth SS Panzer Division Hitler Jugend. By all accounts, he was beloved by his men for his modesty and brotherly solicitude to their needs; he acted according to his conscience, wherever that would take him. He fell on the front lines while defending Caen, the victim of a heavy naval barrage.[41]

Letters from the fighting front to relatives in the homeland also became a propaganda stock in trade. There is little reason to question the authenticity of a letter from a fallen SS man to his parents, which appeared in the December 1943 issue of the *SS Leitheft*. For "Werner," living a noble life meant returning to the Russian theater once more to continue the good fight. "If this had not been possible," he said, "something would have eaten away at me my whole life." The only real concern he had was for the suffering his family might endure should he perish. As for himself, "should I die in battle at the front, in the company of my comrades until the last minute, then this will be the ultimate fulfillment of my life." He asked his family to be joyous in his fulfillment as well. If depression were ever to raise its ugly head, and should his dear mother worry in vain about her son—wondering how he died and where he had perished in the wastes of Russia—she should "take a walk into the fields, up to the Glössberg and look down at Kallich. No price was too high to preserve our beautiful Sudetenland and the German Reich!"[42]

The "final will" of the SS man "Heinz H." was not consoling; rather it read like an SS textbook. Heinz stressed that he gladly offered himself in "sacrifice" for the victory of Germany and that his death would be the fulfillment of his life as a soldier. His body was to remain where his heart was—with his comrades in the soil of Russia. His family was admonished to show no outward signs of mourning but rather to be joyous in his sacrifice. His wife was to remember her duty of bearing children for the eternal life of the German people, and his daughter was told to follow this same path. His son was to be raised by his brother, and he was to be educated with a fanatical will to serve the Reich. In an accompanying letter to his wife, Heinz noted that "it is unimportant whether we live; what is important is that Germany lives."[43]

Herbert Lange's *The Bridge between Life and Death: A Fallen Soldier's Diary*, a booklet distributed widely to Waffen SS troops, gave eloquent testimony to the ethos of the Order.[44] It expressed at once romantic love of *Heimat*, family and ancestors, and the gods of German culture, while celebrating an SS man's biological fulfillment in the arms of a tender maiden of the Volk. Death under such conditions was beautiful, because the future of the race was guaranteed by the hero's divine transfiguration.

The Bridge between Life and Death begins as the protagonist, SS man Schröter, entrusts his diary to an army surgeon shortly before his death in the East. Although his patient's hours were numbered, the surgeon was certain that "there would be no death for him" because he was so brave and self-assured in the final hours of his life. The diary recounts the indescribable joy Schröter felt upon returning home and visiting his beloved mother. He attended a performance of Beethoven's *Fidelio*, whose theme of universal longing for freedom renewed him "like the water of a healing spring." He thrilled to the touch of the leather-bound works in his library. Turning to the profoundly moving poetry of Rainer Maria Rilke, he was convinced that the master's *Duineser Elegie* exalted young martyrs, from whose blood flowed greatness, overshadowing the temporary pain and loneliness felt by their survivors.

Sexual passion also welled up in Schröter's breast, and after a week with mother he journeyed to a neighboring village to visit his beloved, Veronika. They spent a grand afternoon in the hills bordering a majestic forest, an outing made more dramatic by a violent rainstorm. That night—as the radio played Bach's Concerto for Two Violins, signaling ecstasy and spiritual struggle—the fever of love overcame them. As Schröter described it, theirs was the physical embodiment of eternal German culture; beauty and duty to the Volk had been joined, guaranteeing victory. Before returning to the Russian front, Schröter visited the grave of his father, where he rejoiced that the family would live on in the fruit of his union with Veronika.

Within two weeks, he lay mortally wounded in a Waffen SS field hospital in the East. Sensing that "God had commanded him to his great army,"

Schröter committed his final thoughts to his diary on 12 July 1942. Although his future child would never know him, he was reassured by the knowledge that Germanic blood would determine the course of its life. His child would become a bridge between life and death, thus bringing eternal life for the Volk. He instructed that should Veronika bear a daughter, she was to follow the customs of her ancestors and become a mother. A son was to set his sights on colonization of the eastern territories, cultivating with the plow what the sword of his father had won:

> As our blood sacrifice flowed, now sweat should stream from your brow, because only peace gives a higher meaning to war, and productive work alone transforms the horrors of death into victory. Never forget that we died in the service of life.[45]

Schröter's last words to his mother and wife consisted of a quotation from Walter Flex.

SS propagandists went to great lengths to give meaning to the death of the men of the Order, and support for the families of fallen SS men was a sacred obligation. The *SS Leitheft* published a letter from a mother, which was illustrated with a photograph of her surrounded by her three radiant, blond children. The caption read, "My husband is not dead. He lives on in my children." She testified:

> My husband volunteered in 1939 and was killed in the line of duty in 1940. When I received the news of his death, at first I was terribly depressed, but when the children came to me and hugged me, suddenly I was given the strength, the strength to bear what was necessary. That very night I brought the little girls to my side. Our little boy, then only eight weeks old, was in his carriage by my bedside. All of them, life of his life, have made me so strong. I now have a very worthwhile life goal, to raise the children in the spirit of my husband and to educate them as good and strong Germans in his memory.[46]

An SS widow who had lost her husband in Russia told of the comfort she felt one day in her garden, as she bathed in the beauty of a delightful spring morning. She saw her husband everywhere. She saw him in the beauty of nature and heard him in the wind, but, most important, she saw her beloved in the ray of sunshine he gave her in their child. Rejoicing, she expressed the hope that her simple words might lift the spirits of other SS widows, that they might see the real meaning of the death of their husbands:

> Your blood in the earth,
> your soul in the light
> your nature in our child—
> you have not left me![47]

For Goebbels the problem of the suffering of the loved ones of the fallen was no mere subject for romantic rhetoric and poetry. It was an important component of morale on the home front, and as a result he gave this theme a great deal of attention. The longer the war lasted, the more sensitive the subject became. Accordingly, in August 1940 he informed all Gauleiter and Gau propaganda leaders that a new approach must be taken toward the survivors of soldiers killed in action.[48] In Germany's battle for existence, wives, parents, children, and relatives were suffering horrible personal torment as the result of the death of their husbands, sons, brothers, and fathers. Because of their sacrifice, they had a right to the personal and moral support of the German people. At no time was evidence of the comradeship of the *Volksgemeinschaft* more important than at the critical moment when relatives first learned of the death of their loved one. It was at that point that the loyalty of the Volk should be demonstrated.

For Goebbels, proper treatment of the theme of the dead was more than an expression of personal concern. He understood that properly orchestrated propaganda on this motif could become a major force in uniting the fighting and home fronts. Expressions of sadness presented in the minor key of melancholy were out of place. Instead, the blood and body of the dead should inspire the German people to turn the black night of death into the shining dawn of final victory. Therefore, Goebbels wrote, commemoration of the traditional memorial days for the dead—9 November and Heroes Memorial Day—should be seen by all party offices as only part of their larger responsibility.[49]

Survivors on the home front were to be made to feel that they were not alone. Each Ortsgruppenleiter of the party was given the responsibility of either appearing personally or dispatching a representative to the home of the bereaved to announce the heroic death of a family member. In many cases, he carried with him a letter from the loved one's military unit commander. Ideally this conformed to the strategic high command's standing orders regarding condolence letters, which directed those responsible to convey with sensitivity details of the *Heldentod* and burial of the hero. When this went according to plan, there was generally a feeling of gratitude on the part of the bereaved. When it did not, however, complaint was known to reach as high as the Führer's headquarters. Martin Bormann, who headed the party chancellery, took a personal interest in this activity and had the authority necessary to coordinate its functioning. If problems arose, they often were traceable to the unit commander; these officers, quite understandably, were not always able to write an appropriate letter. They were soldiers, not writers. Nor were they all suited to this endeavor, either by temperament or background. As the war progressed, there were so many dead that it was impossible for unit commanders to carry out this function adequately. In such cases, the bereaved often wrote to comrades of their loved ones in the field to learn more details, a situation that was detrimental to morale and a source of irritation to both the party chancellery and the OKW.[50]

There is evidence that most letters were appreciated by those who received them. One such letter was written from the Russian front on 5 July 1941 by a company commander. Addressed to the mother of the fallen, it detailed the last news about the heroic death of "Hans M." The lieutenant described how his company—which was among the vanguard of the division—was pinned down near the village of Krupki on the Minsk-Moscow highway. The lieutenant himself was wounded and all seemed lost for the company when Hans, who led a reserve unit, heroically crossed the river and took the enemy position from the flank under heavy fire. Acting independently, he saved the day and encouraged the company to press the attack once more:

> When we found him later, he still had a smile on his face. He died without pain—a shot to the heart tore him from this world at the moment of victory. For us soldiers there is no more beautiful death. We buried your son in the center among 14 other comrades, very close to the place where he died.
>
> Dear Frau M., you are not alone in the deep and indescribable grief you feel for your son. All of us, who knew him and for whom he gave his life, are deeply saddened at the loss of our friend and comrade Hans. But even in your suffering you can be proud of your son; he died victoriously, brave and loyal. You have spared many other German mothers the same fate through your suffering, because we owe our lives to your son. I greet you in deepest sympathy.[51]

Inappropriate letters caused Goebbels great anguish, and he was appalled at missives being sent to the bereaved from priests and chaplains at the front. Walther Tiessler forwarded to Goebbels a particularly offensive letter from a divisional priest to one Herr Bayer, the father of a dead soldier (10 September 1941). It outlined details of his son's "horrible facial wound," which none expected him to survive, and the long hours of his suffering. Toward the end, he could not be understood but was earnestly attentive to the death sacrament. According to the priest, "Just as I said, 'Into your hands, oh Lord, I commend his spirit!' he died." According to the chaplain, the family would be comforted to know that the sacraments of the Mother Church accompanied Johann on his journey to the "blessed Resurrection."[52]

Goebbels would gladly have responded as Himmler did under similar circumstances. Upon hearing that some SS officers had begun speaking at marriages and funerals in violation of his standing order permitting only immediate superiors this privilege, the Reichsführer SS wrote to one of them to set an example for all. It was not the goal of the SS, he contended, to create a new "SS priesthood":

Should I ever again hear that you or any other SS leaders have spoken to SS men in an SS ceremony, before those who are not under your immediate command, I will strip you of your rank and lock you up for years for trying to found a new priestly class.[53]

Goebbels, on the other hand, fought a losing battle with the church, whose traditional influence far outstripped that of the party when it came to dealing with the pain of death.[54] According to the confidential morale reports of the SD, the party simply could not compete effectively with the church, whose priests arranged timely meetings with the bereaved and could promise an early reunion in the great beyond. The party, on the other hand, had to be content with affirmations about the beauty of death for the Reich. Furthermore, the church was able to stage special ceremonies and masses for the souls of each individual, at a time soon after death. As one SD report noted, "The opinion was often expressed that the supreme sacrifice of every German soldier was worthy of a dignified separate commemoration." The church was prepared to do this, but it went far beyond the capability of the party to accomplish.[55] Infrequent National Socialist observances, commemorating large groups of dead in one ceremony, were no substitute for personal services, and they were poorly regarded by many people. Often families resented the intrusion of the party into matters of religion, and they took matters into their own hands. In one area, Nazi liturgical flaming urns were removed at night and replaced with the Cross.[56] Many overburdened party officials themselves were unenthusiastic about being forced to appear at ceremonies held continuously in their districts, and there were reports of insensitive grumbling. With the mounting losses at the front, party bureaucrats were simply unrealistic about what they expected their subalterns to do at the local level.

Hitler's paladins were outraged when Nazi party members themselves took part in Christian services. The SD noted that in one town, the Ortsgruppenleiter, who had lost his only son in Russia, staged and participated in a memorial mass for him. Some party members and supporters purposefully integrated both Christian and Nazi elements into their beliefs and practices. For example, the parents of a former outstanding Hitler Youth leader in Wels, who had been attached to the elite guard at the Reichsjugendführung headquarters in Berlin and was later killed in Russia, demonstrated that, in time of real need, Jesus, not Adolf Hitler, was the sweet balm for the sorrowful. The family's memorial card read, "In anticipation of his resurrection in Christ Jesus Herr (x) of the Regiment Grossdeutschland, died a hero's death on 6 March 1942 in the Soviet Union in his 23rd year."[57] The memorial card of SS Rottenführer (x), *Kreissachwalter* in Grieskirchen, killed in Russia in May 1942 at twenty-three, featured a photograph of the deceased in the uniform of the Allgemeine SS on one side with a representation of Christ on the Cross being pierced by the lance of a Roman captain on the other. The caption read, "Truly, this man was the Son of God (Mark 15:29)."[58]

If the Nazi apparatus showed weakness at the local level, Goebbels made every effort to compensate for this by his orchestration of propaganda for the war dead. Elaborate instructions were disseminated by the Reichspropagandaleitung for the proper functioning of memorial ceremonies for the fallen. Model programs were organized according to the size of the community involved, from Gau capital cities to villages. A premium was placed on National Socialist taste in ornamental decoration, with emphasis on simplicity, manliness, and soldierly virtue. The Iron Cross of 1939 was central to all ceremonies. The practice in use after World War I, with steel helmets and rifles arranged on altars as stage effects, was to be avoided, because it was seen as reliquary worship. Instead, "true symbols," such as the flags of honorary party and military formations, were to be employed. Color played an important role as well; black and silver—denoting death—were to give way to natural hues. The ceremonies were to assume a tone not of mourning but of national celebration and affirmation of final victory. They were to be worthy of the sacrifice of the fallen and were therefore to avoid sentimentality and theatrical flamboyance. The sites chosen for the ceremonies were to be dignified. City squares flanking the monuments of the Great War, which were found in every town, were deemed most appropriate for this function, although concert halls were often used as well.

Music and heroic poetry were important components of these events, which in large cities began with a trumpet fanfare in honor of the dead. Poems were then read, such as "To Our Dead" by Gerhard Seeger-Ahlert, a former Hitler Youth who died in Poland:

> This is how the Volk has been fulfilled
> And for a few moments
> The hearts of the strong become tender.
> Now raise the banners higher!
> Germany can wait no longer
> Stand firm, you sacred Reich!

Poetry by Walter Flex ("We died for Germany's glory. Flower Germany, as our death garland") and Herybert Menzel ("The Guard") was also frequently heard. Massed choirs sang Eberhard Wolfgang Möller's "Germany, Sacred Germany" or H. Gebhard's "Honor of the Dead" (Kurt Eggers). Ranking party officials spoke of the Führer's mission and the place of the fallen heroes in guaranteeing the future of the Reich. The fallen were then honored, as "Ich hatt' einen Kameraden" was played. Lines from the epic poem *Edda* were often read, followed by poetry in honor of bereaved mothers and wives. Ceremonies ended with the earnest singing of the Old Netherlands Hymn of Prayer.[59]

Goebbels viewed the annual observance of Heroes Memorial Day as an important date in the Nazi liturgical calendar, and it took on great importance during the war. In preparation for its observance on 21 March 1943, he ordered all propaganda offices to focus on the sacrifice at Stalingrad, which would serve for all time as the ultimate example of heroism in the history of the great German military tradition. The ceremony, he continued, was not to be one of mourning; rather, the spirit of the heroic Sixth Army was to steel the resolve of the nation for the coming battle for the life or death of the Germanic Volk community.[60]

Preparations for the ceremonies throughout the Reich were well organized, and every conceivable party and state organization was called into service. During the morning hours, the party and Wehrmacht laid wreaths at war memorials throughout the country. At 1:00 P.M., Hitler spoke at a *Staatsakt* in the Berlin Arsenal, which was carried on a national radio hookup.[61] Later in the afternoon, every locality held observances in honor of the fallen. Special attention was given to the relatives of the dead, who received personal invitations to the ceremonies and were accompanied by members of the Wehrmacht and the party.[62] The young women of the Bund deutscher Mädel fanned out to decorate the graves of the war dead in every corner of the Reich. Representatives of the Nationalsozialistische Volkswohlfahrt honored the war wounded in the hospitals, while the Deutsche Arbeitsfront decorated the memorials to the fallen in the factories throughout the country. Other groups taking part in the collective effort were the SA, the Hitler Youth, the NS Kriegsopferversorgung, the Studentenbund, and the NS Reichskriegerbund.[63]

Despite extensive preparations, Heroes Memorial Day ceremonies did not always go according to plan, and the party admitted that mistakes were made. Reports were received that party functionaries in some cases missed the point of the ceremony entirely. One Ortsgruppenleiter, for example, had the temerity to add a coda to the prescribed speech on military heroism. Acting like a priest concluding his Sunday morning homily, he spoke on such compelling issues as potato deliveries and the imminent collection of bottles in the village. Other speakers carried out their assignment very poorly, boring their audiences with pedantic recitals of German military history from the Great Elector to the present. Still others irritated audiences by programming dull poetry readings, forgetting that many people were suffering terrible grief. The limit was reached when a Nazi party bureaucrat featured the singing of Schubert's *Ave Maria*, a catalyst to tears and sadness at any time. Not only did this give a confessional tone to the event but it also violated Goebbels's basic rule that Heroes Memorial Day ceremonies not be exercises in melancholy but inspire the population to make increased sacrifices for the Reich.[64]

There is no question that personal attention offered to the bereaved by party members was a good deal more effective than public ceremony. Accordingly, small books of consolation were published for the functionaries to take with them as a gift when first visiting the homes of the relatives of the fallen. The Central Cultural Office of the Reichspropagandaleitung reported that wives and mothers responded very positively to this gesture. Grief knows no politics, and there is little reason to question that these books achieved their purpose despite their blatantly propagandistic nature.[65] One such work, Friedrich Wilhelm Hymmen's *Briefe an eine Trauernde,* demonstrated the author's ability to offer spiritual comfort to individuals in a state of shock and desperate for reassurance.[66]

Hymmen was a young writer serving at the front. He was no stranger to suffering himself; both his brothers had been killed, Hermann in Poland (1939) and Paul on the Don front in Russia (1942). His letters, written to "Lena" from the East in the fall of 1942, offer comfort and consolation to a widow, while framing her loss in the dialectic of history. Hymmen structured his book cleverly; widows and loved ones could read his homilies in five sittings. The result was the equivalent of a symphonic tone poem dedicated to the life-affirming power of heroic death. He wove variations on this theme, dealing in turn with the motif of death as the guarantor of eternal life, the ongoing inspirational spirit of the fallen at home and at the front, the legacy of the dead warrior to the living, and the proper behavior of a German soldier's wife.

Commencing with the annunciation of death, Hymmen reassures Lena that Gerhard is not really dead but is at her side at all times. He had never feared death in battle; he perished with a "confident smile" of contentment on his face. The virtuous character of her loving husband could not be buried with him; he is "nearer to us now than he ever had been." Gerhard's only fear concerned how Lena—whom he loved so much—would adjust to his death. The last thing he said to his friend was, "Write to her, so that she will be brave and live a full life." It was important that after a period of "brave mourning," she find joy once more as a mother and German woman.

It was imperative that Lena guarantee his fulfillment. Gerhard's heroic death, "in the rhythm of history," was part of nature's grand plan. On the one hand, it guaranteed personal immortality for him. More important, he had contributed to catapulting the German Reich to its destined role as the leader of Europe for the next thousand years. The oak sapling that his friend, Friedrich Wilhelm, had planted over Gerhard's heart, next to two other fallen comrades, would grow into beautiful maturity, nourished by the spirit of the heroes. Lying in the soil of Mother Earth, Gerhard was at home in nature.

Hymmen also testified that Gerhard's spirit lived on in the regiment and was decisive in winning many hard-fought engagements. In a passage clearly inspired by Homer, he recalled:

As we were positioned near the industrial city of Mogilew on the Dnjepr, I learned for the first time very clearly how the dead can decide a battle. The regiment on our flank became bogged down, and because of several snafus we were wedged into a precarious position and seriously outnumbered by the enemy. I was attached to the battalion staff as a messenger and heard the concerned deliberations of the officers, who considered the option of escaping the disaster that threatened by pulling back into our takeoff positions from that morning. . . . I heard the commander say, "We will stay here because of our dead." We remained solely for this reason and held the position until nightfall. On the next morning, and this was an uncanny confirmation of the fact that morale alone is decisive in this war, the enemy had withdrawn from the positions on the other side of the railway embankment. They did not have the strength to throw the honor of their dead into the scales as the ultimate weapon.[67]

Gerhard also lived on in the children of the nation, who laughed and played amid Germany's beautiful fields, mountains, and streams, as well as its bustling cities and productive factories. The flowers blooming in the gardens and parks, the fruit maturing in Germany's orchards, all bespoke the nation's mission. It was surely worth dying to preserve these rich blessings of Providence. Optimism, not tears and sadness, was the only behavior worthy of the dead: "Our cheerfulness is the most beautiful flower on their grave." The author advised that at those moments when Frau Lena was tempted to take refuge in sadness and melancholy, she should hum very slowly the melody of the *Deutschlandlied*. She would thereby affirm that "Soldiers may perish but they do not die."[68]

The final letter is one of celebration. Lena has decided to volunteer for the war effort as a nurse's aide in a military hospital. Upon hearing word of this, one of Gerhard's former comrades said, "We soldiers are proud of such women." She had seen the vision of Gerhard in that great tower in the sky, which was formed by the transfigured war dead. With such women standing behind their men on the home front, Germany's final victory was assured.

Other booklets delivered by party members to the bereaved on their initial visits of consolation cleverly exploited the relatives of national heroes. No less a figure than the mother of the revered Luftwaffe ace, Colonel Werner Mölders, lent her services to the cause. A national hero with 101 air victories to his credit, in July 1941 Mölders received the distinguished Knights Cross with Oak-leaf Cluster, Swords, and Diamonds from Hitler. Following Mölders's death in Russia in November 1941, he was buried in the Invalidenfriedhof in Berlin, next to the most distinguished flyer of World War I, Manfred von Richthofen. Within weeks, the Central Cultural Office of the Reichspropagandaleitung approached Frau Mölders, who agreed to lend a hand. The result was a booklet in appealing format, featuring a painting of Mölders gazing determinedly from his aircraft before takeoff. Wreathed in fresh laurel, an affirmation by Reichsmarshall Hermann Göring carried the message "A nation with such heroes is assured of victory."

Frau Mölders demonstrated her stolid Prussian background in her letter, which epitomized traditional military virtues. Writing to the mothers of the German dead on Mother's Day, she noted that a common grief and pride bound them together:

> All of us—no matter what our names—are mothers of heroes, but it would be dishonorable for us to claim that this realization can end our pain and grief. We are mothers. And we know that we have returned to eternity some of our own life spirit with a beloved child, whom we once gave life and whom we have lost to death. He is gone. And he will never return.[69]

Frau Mölders noted that, like so many others, this was not her first experience with sacrifice for Germany. Her husband had died in the battle of the Argonne Forest in the Great War. She understood that men are called to fight—and sometimes to die—for a noble purpose: "As long as the world exists, women will hate war and love the warrior, precisely because the best warrior is also the best man."[70] Therefore, she claimed, courageous grief must be distinguished from improper mourning. Courageous grief was to be channeled into creative and happy activity, and she reassured each mother that she was not alone but was one with the entire nation that supported her and felt the pain that she felt. The words of the immortal war poet Walter Flex, she wrote, were as true today as they were when he died on the island of Ösel in 1915:

> Give your dead the right to return home, you the living, so that we might live among you and be present in both good and bad times. Don't cry for us, so that even friends cannot mention our names. Act, so that our friends have the courage to talk about us and to laugh, let us come home, just as we did when we lived.[71]

The annual observance of Mother's Day was an occasion when the party exploited a tradition with considerable popular appeal. In the Nazi world view, mothers were exalted as bearers of future soldiers, and they were the object of a great deal of sentimental propaganda, poetry, and song.[72] Even during the period of the *Kampfzeit*, battle-hardened veterans unashamedly had turned their thoughts to their mothers. Some party leaders even wrote poetry on the subject. Baldur von Schirach focused the attention of youth on the beauty of motherhood when he wrote:

> If there is something good in me,
> Then it is because you are my mother.
> Even if I am so terribly far away
> I can still see you, you silent star.

24. Colonel Werner Mölders (1913–1941), the Luftwaffe's leading ace, prepares for takeoff. (Painting by Wolf Willrich, Grosse Deutsche Kunstausstellung 1941 im Haus der Deutschen Kunst in Munich.)

Even though you are in Heaven and I am only here
My life is but a path to you.[73]

During the years of the peacetime Third Reich, a veritable cult of the
fertile and adoring mother emerged. Hans Baumann dedicated a song to
his and all mothers, which curiously almost overnight became a permanent
addition to the Christmas repertoire. The last stanza of "Hohe Nacht der
Klaren Sterne" intoned:

Mothers, for you all fires,
all stars burn brightly,
Mothers, deep in your hearts
beats the heart of the whole world.[74]

Eberhard Wolfgang Möller, winner of the National Book Prize for
1934–35, wrote in *Letters of the Dead:*

My dear mother, you will receive
this last letter, when I am in the earth,
which endlessly called me home,
I will be lying with my other comrades.

My dear mother, you must love
this simple earth, which devoured my life
Oh what I would give, if just once more,
I might caress you.

The mother for her part had answered, "Oh, we would gladly bleed in
your place, when you are wounded."[75]

Hermann Gerstner, poet, teacher, and archivist at the Bavarian State
Library in Munich, had lost his older brother, Valentin, in the battle of the
Somme in 1916. Sorely troubled, he wrote *Requiem for a Fallen Soldier* and
To the Mothers of the Dead Heroes in his memory.[76] Like many young men
of his generation—he was born in 1903—Gerstner and his mother were
consumed with the memory of the beloved fallen. His poem "A Mother in
a Military Cemetery," recalling their journey to Valentin's grave at Saint
Quentin Cemetery, offered poignant evidence of the suffering of mothers
and sons alike. Solemnly approaching the memorial to the fallen, his mother
reached the column and saw the bronze plate bearing the name of her
beloved son. Gerstner described his mother's emotions at this sacred moment:

You raise your hand for all the dead
and bless the column in the tomb,
which once formed a sworn death storm.

In the light you breathe deeply the sweet smells of
spring, and you listen intently, wondering if at the
gates of heaven one doesn't stand and call for you.[77]

In "Sacred Ground," Gerstner himself speaks to his brother:

Now you rest forever and are united with
those friends, who shared your fate.
You do not know, that near the dark tomb
of eternal sleep a loving mother weeps.[78]

Finally, in 1940 Gerstner wrote "A Talk with My Baby Daughter," in which
he left a literary testament to his daughter and wife.[79]

During World War II a genre begun in the trenches of the Great War
blossomed anew—poetry linking the fighting and home fronts, focusing
on the soldier and his mother. Sentimental poems and letters home were
not viewed as demonstrating weakness; instead, hardened Nazis felt that
they reflected their strength as real men. Such love deepened the warrior's
sensibilities and steeled him for the brutality of combat. It reminded him
of the greatness of his mission and of the privilege of serving the Führer.
He saw his place clearly in the eternal chain of life; death was an impos-
sibility if one perished in the service of the Volk. According to Friedrich
Kaiser, "the soul of the warrior raced to the heights of danger, his heart
beating accompaniment as he approached the final great test, commanded
by fate."[80]

The soldier and poet Bodo Schütt showed anew the bond between the
fighting man and his mother, when early in the war he published the poem
"To Mothers":

O mother, guard and increase
Our noble blood!
The years of the sword are reaping a
Terrible toll of our dearest treasure,
and fathers and sons boldly
die, like heroes.[81]

Agnes Miegel (born 1879), an East Prussian poet of *Heimat,* forest, and
stream, spoke for many women during the war who were less concerned
with party and ideology than with the pain of wartime separation and the
fear of the death of their beloved sons. Memories of a happier past haunted
them, of days when in the circle of their beloved family they could take
their little boy into their arms and look deeply into his eyes. Saint Anthony's
Chapel at Garmisch-Partenkirchen, framed by the beauty of the Alps—but
one of thousands of cemeteries and memorial chapels in wartime Ger-

many—spoke eloquently of a mother's passion at the loss of her son. There row upon row of photographs of young men in the uniforms of all of the services stared out upon the visitor. Handsome young men in the spring-time of their youth testified to the agony of loss. Often two brothers from one family perished, doubling the pain and sorrow, and in some cases three. One mother placed a poem she had written next to the photograph of her boy. Entitled "Vermisst" ("Missing-in-Action"), its lines spoke of searing pain, standing as mute testimony to the loss of an entire generation. Agnes Miegel felt this same pain when she wrote "From Mothers to Sons in the War." The poem reflects the emptiness all mothers feel when facing the loss of their own flesh and blood. Sending packages from home to the front was itself a relief, because it seemed that their boys were only away on an extended vacation, just like in the halcyon days of their youth. But the truth always returned to haunt Miegel.

> But then the heart aches and knows again the great, bitter word
> and knows, he went as his father went before him!
> And we are brave, just like we were then,
> and ready again, to wait patiently for news!
>
> But this makes it so hard: that you are protecting us, no longer we
> protecting you, you dear boys!

How beautiful was the memory of having them close as little ones, how bearing and caring for them was all the fulfillment a woman ever needed. And finally, as night fell:

> And we shut our eyes, tired from work and cares,
> feeling one with you and united with all mothers,
> grateful, we are so proud of you,
> saying—oh how sweet comes sleep—:
> My child is also at the front![82]

National Socialist ideology and pedagogy were based on the principle that life is but a preparation for a noble death for the Führer and Volk. In his last letter to his mother, written before his death on the western front in 1940, Hitler Youth officer Ernst Nielsen tried to prepare her for the loss of her son. When the news arrived, he warned, she was not to grieve; rather, she was to affirm the nobility of the cause:

> When the final chord is sung one day,
> they will say of the German youth:
>
> That just like the heroes of our epics
> they rallied to the Führer's flag,

that Germany revealed itself in us,
Germany, which we carry deep in our hearts.

If I die, mother, you must bear it,
and your pride will conquer your pain,
because you have the privilege of offering a sacrifice
that is what we mean, when we say Germany.[83]

Such was the euphoric will-to-death of some elements of the true believers in the Hitler Youth.

For years Mother's Day had served as the forum for Goebbels's "victory of births" propaganda, with mothers of five to seven children receiving a bronze, silver, or gold medal respectively for their prodigious service to the Fatherland.[84] With losses at the front rising at a frightening rate after the onset of the battle of Russia, it became imperative that success in biological reproduction be recognized and that German women be encouraged to bear children.[85] Mother's Day ceremonies were also a joyous celebration of the coming of spring, after the widespread depression attendant on a long winter. Accordingly, Goebbels annually issued instructions for the holiday. Operating in cooperation with the party chancellery, he delegated responsibility for its organization to the Central Cultural Office of the Reichspropagandaleitung.[86]

Party leaders issued orders for Mother's Day long before the annual event itself. Boys of the Hitler Youth, girls of the Bund deutscher Mädel, women of the N. S. Frauenschaft and functionaries of the N. S. Volkswohlfahrt, the national relief organization, were mobilized across the Reich. Their work began in the family. Mothers were to be relieved of the drudgery of housework for two days, as young women were dispatched to their homes to assist them. Here even the youth sections of the Reichsarbeitsdienst were employed. All children were put on notice that they were to make Mother's Day a happy day for "Mutti," and they were expected to put themselves at the family's disposal throughout the day. Women who lived on farms were to be relieved of the chores of milking, feeding livestock, and preparing meals. Women who had jobs in war industries often found flowers at their workplaces, courtesy of the Deutsche Arbeitsfront. Further, during the week after Mother's Day, all women and mothers were to receive an invitation from the local Nazi leader to attend a concert, film, or theater performance. The sick and infirm, the lonesome and elderly, were delighted to be visited in the hospitals and old folks homes by girls of the Jungmädel, who sang folk songs to them and presented them with flowers. Many a mother in the twilight of her life was brought to tears by this experience. In the countryside, young mothers who had borne a child during the past year found a wreath or a festively decorated runic life symbol attached to the doors of their homes. In the Sudetenland, these mothers were treated to a song as well, as the traditional musical celebration of spring's arrival reached their doorsteps. In this way, especially in the south and in Catholic regions of the west, the worship of Mary, Mother of God, long a tradition in May, was grafted to the party's policy of honoring mothers and attempting to increase the birthrate.[87]

The Mother's Day ceremonies were meticulously planned. Because of the importance of breeding new soldiers to fight future wars, it was mandatory for party members to be present. Many of the party elite and rank and file attended, as well as representatives of the Wehrmacht. The war wounded were considered indispensable participants at the ceremonies, as were mothers who had given birth to a child during the war. All mothers and wives of the war dead were invited, as were mothers who had lost children or relatives in the devastating bombing raids. To stress the importance of the day, and to show proper respect for the mothers, they were escorted from their dwellings to the ceremonies and back home again by beaming boys and girls of the Hitler Youth and BdM, Pimpfe, and Jung-mädels. By all accounts the children were on their best behavior for the occasion. Women who could not attend the ceremony because of extenuating circumstances were paid polite visits in their homes, where they were given a garland of flowers as a gift from the *Volksgemeinschaft*. Mothers who had lost a husband or son at the front were often visited by a Nazi official, accompanied by a member of the N. S. Kriegsopferversorgung.[88]

The tone of the ceremonies was not to be characterized by grief or sadness at the great losses suffered by the mothers; rather, it was to be joyful and happy, in harmony with the season. As a result, bright flowers and evergreen garlands adorned the halls and outdoor settings for the ceremonies. As late as 1944, in directives for what would be the last Nazi Mother's Day, Karl Cerff of the Central Culture Office noted:

> The ceremonies of the NSDAP for Mother's Day this year should have a happily meditative character consonant with the great losses suffered in this war. Within these parameters . . . they should not be mourning ceremonies or memorial ceremonies for the fallen, but instead they should give German mothers a brief time for relaxation and moral invigoration.[89]

A typical ceremony in a city commenced with an orchestra playing a Beethoven overture, while in the villages a brisk Hitler Youth trumpet fanfare called the faithful to attention. Next a speaker briefly cited the Führer on the mother's role in the German Reich:

> There are two worlds in the life of a Volk: the world of the woman and the world of the man. Nature has provided a correct division, in which the man is the master of the family and has the added responsibility for the protection of the Volk, the whole. The world of the woman, if she is happy, is the family, her husband, her children, her home. We see in the woman the eternal mother

of our Volk and the partner of the man in life, work, and battle. Taken together, these two worlds form a community of interests, in which a Volk can live and survive.[90]

After a spirited choral rendering of C. Bresgen's "Let's Sing a Song for Our Mother" and an aire from Johann Sebastian Bach's Suite No. 3, Theodor Scheller's poem, "Mother's Hands" was read. Next cherubs from the Jungmädel stepped forward, shy yet very excited about the important role they were about to play, and honored their mothers with folk songs. A speaker read from "A Heartfelt Experience of Little Andreas" by Wilhelm Pleyer, drawing a moral lesson from a simple tale about a mother and her son. Any distinction between this Nazi ceremony and a Protestant or Catholic May Day service was blurred when those present sang the optimistic and joyful song "Praise the Mountains" by G. Blumensaat. The high point of the ceremony was reached as the ranking party functionary briefly addressed those present and commenced his priestly function of decorating those mothers who had won five to seven "victories of birth." As he moved down the line smiling and congratulating the mothers, a comely BdM girl attended him bearing colorful blue and gold medals, while a member of the N.S. Kriegsopferversorgung presented each mother with a bouquet of flowers.

The speaker wove variations on the theme of idealized motherhood, tailored to wartime conditions. "Mothers," one claimed, "you are the soul of the nation. The happiness of the family rests in the hands of the woman; she is the bearer of happiness and peacefulness, sacredness and thoughtfulness in the lives of her loved ones, making the house a home with the warmth of her motherliness." When the fighting men at the front, he continued, pause to consider their noble mission, they think of Germany. And when they think of Germany, they think of the German woman, who often carries the double burden of working in industries essential to the war effort while at the same time maintaining a proper German home. They also reflect on the bravery of the women who place their lives on the line by undergoing the dangers of childbirth. They know that mothers who have given birth to a child during this sacred war for Germany's future have guaranteed that the mission of the fallen has been fulfilled; they have given the gift of life, the link to eternity. They, too, are true soldiers, guaranteeing the nation's future.[91] They are keeping a stiff upper lip, he claimed, even while traumatized, as they see their beloved German homeland being battered beyond recognition by the "barbaric terror bombers, the gangsters of the air." Nevertheless, the German woman knows that, "if there is to be a Fatherland, then this must be a childrens' land!" The "brave grief" of the mothers who have given the lives of their sons to the nation is an example for all to fight on to the final victory.[92] Only in that way will Germany repel the scourge of the Bolshevik beast. The Führer, Adolf Hitler, knows and understands the trials and tribulations of the noble women of the Volk community.

The speaker concluded by reading the letter of a young German front soldier to his mother, extending congratulations on her birthday. It testified to the Nazi perception of the true German mother:

> Dear Mother! I am coming to you today from afar with a warm heart and deep gratitude. What is it, mother, that leads a son to his mother? It is true and deep love, which I receive day after day and which is returned from me to you. Especially now, when I am standing guard at the front, you are the source of all the joy and strength that I need. On your birthday, mother, I only want to say, that you are the revelation of the godly for me. You see, we are so near, that we both now have one and the same fate, mother and son. Therefore, celebrate your birthday joyfully. Dear mother, remain strong at my side. I need your support now more than ever as a soldier.
>
> Faithfully your thankful son[93]

The war front was brought home in the form of the devastating Allied bombing of Germany, which exacted a very high toll in lives.[94] Early in the war, Goebbels endeavored to present accurate casualty reports on the bombing war. This brought him into conflict with the strategic high command, which was concerned about providing the enemy with useful information.[95] He understood that to camouflage the truth would cause credibility problems, because the German people could verify the news for themselves. Subsequent events proved Goebbels correct.

Germans in the western provinces—especially after the great Cologne raids of 1942—resented Berliners deeply, until the Reich capital underwent heavy bombing. There were also many cases of problems in credible reporting, a situation that was inevitable considering the overlapping jurisdictions and constraints on telling the truth. For his part, Goebbels made every effort not only to steel the nerves of the suffering population but also to instill in them the will to sacrifice. To this end, early in the war he declared the home front a fighting front and began to cultivate the mythology of the fighting, dying home-front warrior.[96] Goebbels was most impressed by Churchill's propaganda during the Battle of Britain, where the minister discerned a mythical heroization of the English people. As a result, he called for major coverage of brave conduct in burning German cities, with heroism being awarded the Iron Cross and, in exceptional cases, the Knights Cross.[97]

The bombardment of Germany came as a surprise to an overconfident nation, mesmerized too long by Göring's unrealistic and irresponsible boasts of invulnerability to air attack. When the major raids began in earnest, Goebbels had a problem of immense proportions on his hands. Shock gave way to cries for revenge, as a sense of impotence and helplessness overcame the victims. Hitler was certainly correct in his assertion that the "hundreds of thousands of people who have been bombed out form the avant-garde of revenge."[98] This bitterness was reflected in a poster that appeared in Frankfurt am Main after a major raid by the "plutocratic gangsters of the air":

> We survivors stand with clenched fists at the graves of our fallen. Above the tumult of explosions, collapsing walls, and wildly burning flames, we swear not to be cowardly and give in. Our hearts grieve for our loved ones and for our possessions. But our minds are filled with boundless hate for the inhuman and barbaric air pirates, and our voices cry out for revenge against the English: "May God take pity on you!"[99]

Goebbels made many journeys into bombed cities after major air raids, where he carried the propaganda battle to a weary people. In the Ruhr and Rhineland he drew on his own background, claiming that a people who had known how to bear the scourge of Versailles and the French occupation of their homeland would courageously face the terror from the air. And it was clear who was responsible; the Jews were the force behind the British and American raids. While awaiting the great miracle weapon that would turn the tide in the war, he admonished the German people to hold the line just like their husbands, sons, and brothers were doing at the front.[100] Personal sacrifice demanded by the air war was also a favorite subject of his weekly editorial in *Das Reich*. Early in 1944 he wrote:

> There is no crime against humanity, culture, and civilization that the enemy has not committed in this war. They are so morally corrupt, that they even brag about it. . . . They murder women and children in droves because they hope by this godless barbarism to weaken their husbands and fathers in their will to fight. They view the sacred cultural endowment of two thousand years as nothing more than plunder and set fire to it with bombs and phosphorus canisters. . . . Who has the right to speak of war crimes? We or the enemy?[101]

Because of the trauma from loss of life on the massive scale caused by the air bombardment, rumors were rife. In the summer of 1943, when the Berlin authorities evacuated many school children from the capital, reports spread throughout the provinces that the government was evacuating the city. Berliners received letters from their loved ones urging them to evacuate immediately. Following the devastating firestorm raids on Hamburg in July and August 1943, wild rumors spread that one hundred fifty thousand people had been killed in the attacks. This had repercussions not only at home but also at the fighting front. The tables were now turned, as soldiers on the eastern front received mail rife with rumors about the safety of their loved ones at home, news that must have profoundly unsettled them. These reports were of such a serious nature and so deleterious to the war effort that Goebbels acted decisively to counter them. A propaganda bulletin was issued to all Gauleiter, as well as all Gau and Reich propaganda leaders and propaganda units throughout occupied Europe and Russia, informing them that eighteen thousand five hundred people had perished in flaming Hamburg. The inflated body count claimed by the enemy was challenged with vigorous counterpropaganda.[102]

There was often a wide divergence between propaganda about the unified *Volksgemeinschaft* engaged in a struggle for the life or death of the German nation and the reality of an often selfish and cruel people looking out for their own interests. When it came to offering food and shelter to air raid victims, who were fleeing the cities by the hundreds of thousands, many members of the Volk community simply did not wish to be inconvenienced. Some areas were so bitter about the intruders that they referred to the evacuees as "gypsies." When refugee women informed their husbands serving on the fighting fronts about the treatment they had received, their reports were very poorly received in the companies.[103] Hitler was undoubtedly irritated about this situation, because the party chancellery issued a memorandum whereby individuals who refused to take in the wandering homeless faced punishment and possible imprisonment for their offense.[104] Nevertheless, many Nazi party members, even those in high leadership positions, refused to shelter refugees in their own homes. Responding to widespread complaints about this sensitive subject—there is no evidence that a single refugee darkened the door of the homes of Goebbels or Göring—the party distributed a warning letter in December 1943 that party members should extend themselves to the homeless.[105]

The pain that civilians endured in the bombing raids was profound, as hundreds of thousands of people lost their lives in the raids. The trauma suffered by survivors, who discovered that members of their families had burned to death or been melted down like eggs in flowing lava, was indescribable. In many cities there were no effective shelters, as concrete bunkers became coffins for the victims. Undergoing even one night of intense bombing was enough to lend credence to Goebbels's claim that the home front had also become the fighting front.

The experience of Georg Grabenhorst is informative, because it was identical with that of hundreds of thousands of other people. Shortly after the war, he retold his tale in a vignette entitled "Sacrifice in the Homeland." During a bombing raid on Hanover on the night of 29 November 1944, Grabenhorst lost his wife and daughter. "I can see the face of my dear wife before me," he wrote, "her beautiful big eyes smile at me from her face, heavy with grief. Poor creature, just like game to be hunted down! And how brave! And my daughter, seventeen years old, whom I called the dream of my youth with her charming grace and enthusiasm for life."

It all happened so suddenly after the radio warned that heavy bomber units had penetrated Lower Saxony and were flying over the Steinhuder Lake in the direction of the Gau capital city. With no bunker close by, the neighbors hurried to the Grabenhorst cellar to seek shelter, as they often did. On that fateful night, fifteen people were gathered there. And then the hell began: "The first wave passed over, without hitting us. But I knew that we were next. I heard the bombs hitting one after another. The house had already collapsed, burying us underneath. Burning coals and ashes poured down from above." Grabenhorst desperately tried to free his son who was trapped next to him, as the other wounded cried out for help. He himself became faint, as he choked for air. Finally, there was an eerie quiet as the horrible realization came over him that a wall had caved in, crushing his wife and daughter. He wanted to yell to them, but he could not utter a word. With the help of soldiers who freed him, Grabenhorst was able to get the living to safety, but nine of the fifteen people in the bunker had died that night. In total shock, he laid the bodies of his wife and daughter on a truck that took them to the cemetery. He and his son ran for their lives to a nearby woods. "We will not forget," he admonished. "No one who experienced this war on the heartland of our nation, on our wives and children, and on the noble endowment of Western culture, can or should forget."[106]

The poet Wilhelm Pleyer took note of the strange marriage of the living and the dead in the streets of burning Germany when he wrote "Amidst the Ruins":

> We hurry amidst the ruins by night and day,
> Knowing corpses are in the debris, yet look away
> Chatter a bit and laugh and conceal the wounds,
> Utter something harmless, and suppress a scream. . . .
>
> Everyday life and the dead . . . death and life in a bright
> and dark meander. Are we ourselves but half alive?[107]

How was God to answer his people in a firestorm, when even his churches burned? A young soldier, Oskar Gitzinger, wrote from a military hospital bed late in the war:

> He blew it up in a thousand screams
> and carried it into the sky
> and in the firestorms it became a sea
> of desperate prayers. But there is one less
> place for quiet retreat here. The stones
> transform this destruction into hope
> alone. But what are we expecting . . . ?[108]

Despite the hopelessness of Germany's situation by 1945, the party tried desperately to shore up the strength of the German people to fight through to the "final victory" or perish in the attempt. Mass funerals over common graves and memorial ceremonies for victims of the air war became commonplace. In these commemorations, the party stretched the limits of credibility in its effort to offer consolation and meaning to the loss felt by the mourners. The propaganda ministry used the ceremony of one major city as a model for other communities seeking to honor the victims of the air war. Beethoven's Coriolan Overture and the reading of a Führer quotation bewailing "the many murdered men, women, and children in the homeland" set the proper tone for the memorial service. This was followed by the party speaker, who castigated the "air gangsters" for their cowardly attack on the innocent. In no uncertain terms, the speaker placed the loss within the context of Goebbels's central theme during the final months of the war: the "Jewish Bolsheviks," in league with the Allies, planned to carry out the liquidation of the German people:

> Once more the *Volksgemeinschaft* of our community have gathered together to bid farewell to the countless dead of the merciless air terror who have joined the great invisible throng of those who have fallen for the fatherland. Amidst the ruins of this heavily damaged city we say goodbye to the many men and women, whom a cruel fate has torn much too early from their families. . . . We say goodbye also to the many children, whom a degenerate enemy has murdered. . . . Our enemies have made it absolutely clear that they want not only the destruction of Germany but also the biological annihilation and liquidation of the German people.

What possible consolation could it have been in the traumatic days of 1944 and 1945 to hear a party speaker promise that "in the knowledge of a common fate you are not alone in your grief, but the people of our community enfold you in their arms, as do those of the Gau and, yes, the entire German people"?

Goebbels had said that help was on the way in the form of the long-promised miracle weapons, which would snatch victory from the jaws of defeat:

> Our consolation in this hour of remembrance is our unalterable faith, that one day the shining hour of victory will rise up from the graves of our dead, our noble fallen. This victory will be crowned with the miraculous blessing of the sacrifice of these men and women, for whom we grieve today.

In the hour of the nation's most pressing moral and spiritual need the cry went out for an even greater blood sacrifice:

> The heart of the dead is not silent, but continues to beat, especially in the youth of Germany, who cannot wait to avenge the great sacrifice of your loved ones with an eye for an eye and a tooth for a tooth. The hour of revenge has begun! We must see inscribed over the caskets of our fallen the old call to action: Germany must live—even if we must die.[109]

Ultimately Goebbels, like Hitler, took refuge in the mythical corpus of National Socialist ideology, which viewed noble death as the moral equivalent of victory. It was not by chance that he turned to cinema as the most eloquent expression of the heroic ideal. In the film *Kolberg* (Veit Harlan 1945), he offered the German people a call to heroic death in technicolor. The film featured many of Germany's great stars, including Heinrich George as Joachim Nettelbeck, hero of the defense of Kolberg in 1807 against the forces of Napoleon. Kristina Söderbaum played his niece, Maria Werner, a beautiful Nordic stereotype representing traditional virtues, who assumed the mantle of the redemptive woman for the proud Hanseatic town of Kolberg. Horst Caspar, with the noble features of the Bamberg Rider, played von Gneisenau, an authenic hero who recognized that only a peoples' army could redeem Prussia and bring the final victory against French tyranny. The veteran actor Paul Wegener was cast in the role of the reactionary Prussian fortress commandant, Colonel Lucadou, hopelessly tied to the ideas of the past that if unchanged, guaranteed the destruction of the nation.[110]

Kolberg reflected Goebbels's resolve that the nation must arise at the hour of destiny in 1945 to strangle the "Jewish-Bolshevik" beast on the sacred soil of Prussia. When Gneisenau utters the stirring lines from a poem by Theodor Körner, "Now rise up nation, and let the storm rage!" ("Nun Volk, stehe auf, und Sturm brich los!"), he was employing the exact reference that Goebbels himself had used at the climax of his famous "total war" address in the Sports Palace after the fall of Stalingrad. When Kolberg writhes in flame and smoke and the town is flooded to block the invaders, the clear reference is to the suffering undergone by the home front in bombed-out Germany. Nettelbeck's admonition that "they can burn our houses but not our soil" echoed Hitler's demand that Germany must be defended to the last bullet. With Nettelbeck setting the stage by exclaiming that "it is better to be buried under the ruins than to capitulate," Gneisenau strikes up the *Heldentod* motif when he joyously asserts, "Now we can die together." Their lines might easily have been spoken by Goebbels in one of his many speeches during the last months of the war.

At the conclusion of the film, the stirring Netherlands Hymn of Prayer accompanies the brave citizens of Kolberg as they gather among the dead in the ruins of their beloved city to celebrate a magnificent triumph of the will. They have stayed the course, and through their willingness to die, they have guaranteed the rebirth of the nation. Gneisenau offers his benediction to a Volk worthy of the name: "A regenerated people will arise from the ashes, a new Reich." The majestic effect of the victory is crowned when Nettelbeck offers the finest praise that a National Socialist woman could hear in 1945. Turning to his niece, the comely Maria, the Volk hero says, "You have been victorious, too, Maria."

When all was lost for the Third Reich, Goebbels left *Kolberg* as his testament to heroism for the German people. He might well have quoted from General von Gneisenau's farewell to the citizens of Kolberg on 8 August 1807. In that message, the peoples' general contributed to the mythology of death, which was later exploited by the National Socialists, and played no small role in the configuration of the German tragedy:

> The beautiful memories of the courage, patriotism, charity, and sacrifice of the Kolbergers will remain with me forever. I leave you with a heavy heart. I will do everything possible for a city where virtue still lives, at a time when it is rare elsewhere. Pass this spirit on to your children. This is the most valuable legacy that you can give them. Your loyal devoted commandant, N. v. Gneisenau.[111]

Epilogue

The Nazi "heroic era" has passed into history. It is difficult to imagine the frenzied rituals of nationalism that became commonplace during the Third Reich. Euphoria and romantic pageantry were the order of the day and took many forms. The fields of Nuremberg resounded with the shouts of devoted Hitler Youth, bronzed SA, and SS, and zealous Nazis of all hues proclaimed the dawn of a new era. Parade grounds were illuminated by the "cathedral of light," signaling deliverance by a national saviour. Every fall Hitler climbed the "sacred hill" at Bückeberg, weaving his way past an adoring peasantry gathered to celebrate the harvest in a "liberated homeland." The "Horst Wessel Song" was treasured as a national anthem, celebrating the resurrection of a symbolic German youth cut down by "murderous Bolsheviks at the nation's hour of destiny."

Every effort has been made to obliterate the physical remains of the Third Reich and its fallen heroes. Nazi shrines have been removed from postwar Berlin. In communist East Berlin, the red flag flies over the Brandenburg Gate and adorns the Unter den Linden Boulevard. Heroes Memorial Day is no longer celebrated. The Schlageter Memorial on the Golzheimer Heath outside Düsseldorf has been razed. The Königsplatz in Munich has been returned to its traditional form. Grass adorns the square there, not cobblestones reverberating with the march of jackboots. November 9 is just another day once more; "martyrs" no longer stand guard for the German Volk community at the Temple of Honor. The graves of Horst Wessel and Herbert Norkus, earlier sacred shrines, have disappeared. Hans Baumann, Gerhard Schumann, and Karl Ritter, important in the development of National Socialist aesthetics, are forgotten figures. For school children born after the war, the heroic ideal has as much relevance as the epic warrior tales of Homer. The Third Reich is but a haunting memory.

From the perspective of the postwar world, it is not naive to ask why the German idea of heroism developed as it did. Most countries have heroes, and there are martyrs for every conceivable religion and nation. What was unique about the German experience? Why did the German idea of heroism ultimately lead to criminality on such a massive scale? Why did the German image of the heroic Nordic ideal carry with it the demand for an antihero in the form of Jewry? Why did the German obsession with the Jews lead to the Holocaust, the "Final Solution of the Jewish Question"?

Historically, the development of a national image of heroism has often resulted from a sense of inferiority and hopelessness. Heroes have offered redemption, a way out of tribal, racial, or national despair. The need for heroes often derives from suffering, tension, and threatened annihilation. The political, social, and economic trauma of the early years of the Weimar

Republic set the stage for the victory of racial mythology. The Germans were condemned for causing the outbreak of World War I, and they were convinced that the Treaty of Versailles had robbed them of their honor. A sense of shame was exacerbated by communist insurgency, devastating inflation, and misguided Allied occupation policies. The high unemployment that accompanied the depression further poisoned the political climate. Out of this hopelessness, the myth of the hero as the force for national regeneration was born.

Germany could serve as a model for heroic mythology based on national despair, which differed fundamentally from the form of heroism celebrated by the English, French, Russians, and Americans during the Great War. When an Englishman died in Flanders, he was protecting king and country and a national way of life. But, when a German soldier died at Langemarck, his blood took on the properties of the blood of Christ. The death itself was seen as redemptive, washing away the sins of the fathers and offering the promise of national resurrection. The German philosophy of death was thus linked to the hope for national regeneration.

The German predilection for the celebration of death has deep historical roots. When, in the year 9 A.D., Hermann the Cherusker led the Germanic tribes to victory in the Teutoburger Forest—decimating the invading Roman legions—the myth of the fighting, dying Germanic warrior was born. In the epic saga of the *Nibelungen*, death is ever present, a counterpoint to the heroic themes of loyalty, courage, and steadfastness to the last. A noble gloom hangs over the land of the Nibelungen. Siegfried, the ideal Germanic youth, pure of body and spirit, is cruelly murdered by the ignoble Hagen. Goebbels, the impresario of the well-staged political funeral, observed that the German people were obsessed with grieving, and took a macabre satisfaction in it. Hitler made a point that the death of the Nazi Immortals was not to be the subject of grief; rather, the march to the Feldherrnhalle and the Temple of Honor was to be celebrated as symbolic of the rebirth of the nation. Death was viewed as the guarantor of renewed life for the German people.

In its most radical form, a cult of heroism can unleash the demonic in man, calling for the annihilation of the antihero. Such was the case in the Third Reich. The postwar trauma set the stage for Nazi and radical conservative propaganda focusing on world Jewry. The Nazis hated the Jews with an irrational hatred and contempt that knew no bounds. According to this propaganda, the Jews were the beginning and end of all that was evil and were inspired by the Devil himself. The Jewish parasite drained the blood of the Volk and was intent on destroying the German nation. German troops had not been defeated in the field of battle in 1918, it was claimed; instead, a "Jewish-Bolshevik conspiracy" caused the downfall of the Reich's noble cause. It was this racial mythology, based on the dualism of the Germanic hero and the "Jewish-Bolshevik" antihero, that determined the climate of opinion that led to the Holocaust. Although Hitler was the spokesman for radical anti-Semitism, he was joined by a rabid Nazi leadership that transformed myth into a brutal reality.

During the Third Reich, the arts embellished the mythically based world view of the Nazis. National Socialist aesthetics served not only as ornamentation but also as an integral part of life in Hitler's Germany. As a result, the pursuit of the beautiful—the ultimate goal of the arts—ultimately supported ignoble ends. Rallies and monumental architecture, painting and sculpture, poetry and song, grand theatrical productions, and feature films and newsreels all played a role in buttressing the Nazi state. The often-lyric quality of the artistic presentations at once concealed and distracted the German people from the brutal agenda of the party elite. Heroic man was on the march and would be victorious or perish in the attempt.

It is regrettable that this work could not be more comprehensive in its depiction of National Socialist aesthetics. The demands of space, however, have limited a broader sweep of the subject. Separate chapters might well have been devoted to the sculptors Arno Breker and Josef Thorak, whose colossal works adorning the entrance to the Reich Chancellery and the Berlin Olympic grounds so impressed Hitler. The architectural conceptions of both Paul Ludwig Troost (the Brown House, the Temple of Honor, and the Haus der Deutschen Kunst in Munich) and Albert Speer (the Nuremberg Party Rally grounds and the new Reich Chancellery) gave neoclassical and monumental architectural form to Hitler's conception of German greatness. The career of the artist Adolf Ziegler—President of the Reichskammer der Bildenden Künste and organizer of the infamous "Decadent Art" exhibition in Munich in 1937—would illustrate an important chapter in National Socialism and the arts. Ziegler's paintings, as well as his effectiveness in removing the expressionist art of "Jewish-Marxist subhumans" from German galleries, won him the esteem of both Hitler and Goebbels. The career of Eberhard Wolfgang Möller—dramatist, poet, and winner of the National Prize for Literature—also deserves thorough exploration. Möller, more than any other creative artist, demonstrates the link between National Socialist aesthetics and the fires of Auschwitz. It was Möller, a highly successful dramatist, who wrote the film script for the most powerful of all Nazi anti-Semitic feature films, *Jud Süss*. *Jud Süss* was so persuasive that Reichsführer SS Heinrich Himmler ordered that every SS man view it.

There are many other individuals who contributed to the Nazi aesthetic, and an ideal study would embrace each significant artist. All of them, in one form or another, wove variations on the theme of heroic accomplishment and noble death for the German nation. The evidence, however, is convincing that the conclusions of this work would have remained the same.

Abbreviations

BA   Bundesarchiv Koblenz
BayHStA   Bayerisches Hauptstaatsarchiv, Munich
BDC   Berlin Document Center
B/R, SLM, StAM   Bürgermeister und Rat, Stadtrat der Landeshauptstadt München, Stadtarchiv München
DIFW   Deutsches Institut für Filmkunde, Wiesbaden
GFD/MPS/LOC   German Film Documentation, Motion Pictures Section, Library of Congress
GStALgB/LAB   Generalstaatsanwaltschaft bei dem Landgericht Berlin, Landesarchiv Berlin
IfZ   Institut für Zeitgeschichte
LOC   Library of Congress
NA   National Archives
NSDAP/HA   Nationalsozialistische deutsche Arbeiterpartei/Hauptarchiv
OKW/WPr   Oberkommando der Wehrmacht/Abteilung für Wehrmachtspropaganda
RFB   Roter Frontkämpfer-Bund
RFSS/SSHA   Reichsführer SS/SS Hauptamt
RKK   Reichskulturkammer
RMfVP   Reichsministerium für Volksaufklärung und Propaganda
RPL   Reichspropagandaleitung
RPL/IIKA   Reichspropagandaleitung/Hauptamt Kultur
SD   Sicherheitsdienst
SF   Schlageter File
VI/SO   Vertrauliche Informationen/Sammlung Oberheitmann

Notes

INTRODUCTION

1. Philippe Aries, *The Hour of Our Death,* p. 213.
2. Konrad Jarausch, *Students, Society, and Politics in Imperial Germany,* pp. 394–96.
3. See Martin Broszat, *Hitler and the Collapse of Weimar Germany,* pp. 15–16.
4. On the theme of youth and the *Zeitfilm* genre, see David Welch, "Educational Film Propaganda and the Nazi Youth," in David Welch, ed., *Nazi Propaganda,* pp. 78–79.

I. THE MYTH OF LANGEMARCK

1. Adolf Hitler, *Mein Kampf,* p. 183.
2. Walter Flex, *Der Wanderer zwischen beiden Welten. Ein Kriegserlebnis,* p. 110. On the theme of the glorious dead, see George L. Mosse, "National Cemeteries and National Revival: The Cult of the Fallen Soldiers in Germany," *Journal of Contemporary History,* 14, 1 (January 1979), pp. 1–20. See also Konrad H. Jarausch, "German Students in the First World War," *Central European History,* 17, 4 (December 1984), pp. 310–29.
3. The Free Corps leader, Gerhard Rossbach, discussed the philosophy of death in *Mein Weg durch die Zeit,* p. 42. For an analysis of the theme of heroic death in the arts, see Werner Rittich, "Heroische Plastik," *Die Kunst im Dritten Reich,* 10 (December 1937), pp. 28–34.
4. See Robert Weldon Whalen, *Bitter Wounds: German Victims of the Great War, 1914–1939,* pp. 21–31. Uwe-Karsten Ketelsen was on the mark (*Heroisches Theater,* p. 138) with his observation: "Der heroische Held ist nicht auf den Sieg, sondern auf den Untergang bezogen." See also Hans F. K. Günther, *Ritter Tod und Teufel. Der heldische Gedanke.*
5. *Völkischer Beobachter,* 24 February 1938.
6. Emil Alefeld, Munich, writing from Strassburg on 8 October 1914, in Josef Magnus Wehner, *Langemarck. Ein Vermächtnis,* p. 23. Compare Ernst Jünger, *In Stahlgewittern,* pp. 154–55, who claimed, "In the course of four years, the fire fused an even purer, braver fighting force." On the idealism of German youth, see Robert Wohl, *The Generation of 1914,* pp. 42–60.
7. Will Decker, *Kreuze am Wege zur Freiheit,* p. 17.
8. Franz Brüchle, 1. Vorsitzender der Angehörigen ehem. K.B. 6. Res.-Feld.-Art.-Regts., "Allerheiligen 1914, Langemarck-Wytschaete," *Völkischer Beobachter,* 1 November 1939, Langemarck File, Slg. Personen 2778, Sammlung Rehse, BayHStA.
9. *Mein Kampf,* pp. 180–81. Willi Rehkopf, a veteran of Langemarck, fervently denied the veracity of the myth. He asserted that ordering the young regiments into battle without artillery preparation was totally irresponsible on the part of the leadership. There was no singing in his sector, nor did he ever meet a single Langemarck veteran who either sang or heard singing. See Willi Rehkopf to Archivrat Dr. Jochen Meyer, 13 February 1985, Bestand Willi Rehkopf, Deutsches Literaturarchiv, Schiller Nationalmuseum, Marbach am Neckar.
10. Ruhet, ihr Knaben vor Langemarck
    und wartet den Frühling ab, . . .

Wenn nur die Wolken nach Osten stehen . . .
Werdet ihr Deutschland wiedersehn
und die Wälder, für die ihr starbt. . . .

blüht ihr dann im Gerank
und der Sommer darüber singt
euern Ruhm und unsern Dank.

Eberhard Wolfgang Möller, *Berufung der Zeit*, p. 74.

11. Rudolph G. Binding, *Deutsche Jugend vor den Toten des Krieges*.

12. Binding wrote in "Mourning," "What would victories be without the death of heroes?" Rudolf G. Binding, *Stolz und Trauer*, p. 44.

13. See Kuratorium für das Reichsehrenmal Tannenberg, *Tannenberg. Deutsches Schicksal–Deutsche Aufgabe;* George L. Mosse, *The Naticnalization of the Masses*, pp. 69–71.

14. See *Vorwärts*, 11 November 1929, Langemarck File, Slg. Personen 2778, Sammlung Rehse, BayHStA.

15. Ernst Jünger, *Im Stahlgewittern;* Josef Magnus Wehner, *Sieben vor Verdun;* Hans Zöberlein, *Der Glaube an Deutschland;* Heinz Steguweit, *Der Jüngling im Feuerofen;* Franz Schauwecker, *Aufbruch der Nation*. For analyses of the nationalist literature of this period, see Hermann Pongs, *Krieg als Volksschicksal im deutschen Schriftum;* Arno Mulot, *Der Soldat in der deutschen Dichtung unserer Zeit;* William K. Pfeiler, *War and the German Mind*.

16. Film section, LOC; Alfred Bauer, *Deutscher Spielfilm Almanach 1929–1950*, p. 77. There were several films released as an antidote to *All Quiet on the Western Front*, which the nationalists considered to be a scandalous attack on their ideals. These included *Kreuzer Emden* (Louis Ralph, 1932) and *Morgenrot* (Gustav Ucicky, 1933). For an excellent analysis of the firestorm waged over the image of the front soldier, see Modris Eksteins, "War, Memory, and Politics: The Fate of the Film *All Quiet on the Western Front*," *Central European History*, 13, 1 (March 1980), pp. 60–82.

17. "Günter Kaufmann: Einführung der Jugend in den Frontkämpfergeist," in Hans-Jochen Gamm, *Führung und Verführung. Pädagogik des Nationalsozialismus*, pp. 358–59.

18. See Alfred Baeumler, "Der Sinn des Grossen Krieges," *Männerbund und Wissenschaft*, pp. 1–17.

19. *Langemarck. Ein Vermächtnis*, "Worte von Josef Magnus Wehner, am 10. Juli 1932, zur Stunde der Übernahme des Gefallenen-Friedhofs in Langemarck durch die Deutsche Studentenschaft, gesprochen an allen deutschen Hochschulen, verbunden mit Briefen Gefallener."

20. Hanns Johst, *Langemarck. Bekenntnis zu Josef Magnus Wehners Rede, Münchner Neueste Nachrichten*, 4 August 1932.

21. "Langemarck," *Der SA Mann*, 12 November 1932.

22. Wilhelm Dreysse, "Die Deutschen von 'Langemarck,' " 22 October 1935, Langemarck File, Slg. Personen 2778, Sammlung Rehse, BayHStA. See also Wilhelm Dreysse, *Langemarck 1914. Der heldische Opfergang der Deutschen Jugend*.

23. Herbert Böhme, *Rufe in das Reich*, p. 114. See also Böhme's poem "Langemarck." Ibid., p. 16.

24. Kurt Fervers, "Langemarck Leben," Langemarck File, Slg. Personen 2778, Sammlung Rehse, BayHStA. See also Sigmund Graff, "Langemarck," *Unvergesslicher Krieg*, pp. 35–40.

25. See *Breisgauer Zeitung*, 27 November 1933, cited in Guido Schneeberger, *Nachlese zu Heidegger*, pp. 158–60.

26. Christa Kamenetsky, *Children's Literature in Hitler's Germany*, pp. 195–96. See also Günter Kaufmann, ed., *Langemarck. Das Opfer der Jugend an allen Fronten;* Her-

mann Thimmermann, "Der Sturm auf Langemarck," *Kampf. Lebensdokumente deutscher Jugend von 1914–1934*, pp. 14–16; Gerhard Scholtz, *Tag von Langemarck;* Werner Beumelburg, *Von 1914 bis 1939. Sinn und Erfüllung des Weltkrieges.*
    27. See Geoffrey J. Giles, *Students and National Socialism in Germany*, pp. 242–43; Nationalsozialistische Deutsche Studentenbund, *Die Bewegung*, 28 January 1941, p. 8.
    28. See, for example, Walter Haur, "Die von Langemarck. Von einem alten Langemarckkämpfer," *Völkischer Beobachter*, 8 December 1934; W. Ehmer, "Kriegsfreiwillige Berliner Jugend: Das Sterben von Dixmude," *Völkischer Beobachter*, 28 October 1934; "Die erste Kampfform des 'Wir,'" *Kyffhäusser Wehrkorrespondent*, 1933, in Langemarck File, Slg. Personen 2778, Sammlung Rehse, BayHStA; "Langemarck–Ewiges Symbol heldischen Einsatzes," *Völkischer Beobachter*, 12 November 1939.
    29. *Deutsche Passion 1933* was aired over all German radio stations on 13 April 1933. Richard Euringer, *Deutsche Passion 1933*. For other radio coverage of the theme, see Gerhard Hay, "Rundfunk und Hörspiel als 'Führungsmittel' des Nationalsozialismus," in Horst Denkler and Karl Prümm, *Die deutsche Literatur im Dritten Reich*, pp. 366–81.
    30. Baldur von Schirach, *Revolution der Erziehung*, pp. 26–29.
    31. Baldur von Schirach, "Langemarck Feier der deutschen Jugend," Munich, 10 November 1935, ibid., pp. 29–32.
    32. Hitler left his headquarters at Bruly-le-Peche on 2 June and visited Langemarck, Vimy Ridge, and the French monument on the heights of Loretto. See Max Domarus, *Hitler: Reden 1932–1945*, p. 1519. A photograph of Hitler visiting the Langemarck memorial appears in Heinrich Hoffmann, *Mit Hitler im Westen*.
    33. "Das andere Langemarck," *Völkischer Beobachter*, 2 June 1940. Günter d'Alquen, editor of the SS organ *Das Schwarze Korps*, wrote: "We would have nothing today were it not for the sacrifice of those lying here in countless graves who are celebrating a proud resurrection and to whom we offer fervent gratitude, deeply humble yet proud. Langemarck is not far from here. Perhaps many of us without knowing it are passing over fields once soaked with the blood of our fathers. . . . Our columns move forward along the broad highways toward their last victories for the great Reich." See "Auf dem Kemmel," *Völkischer Beobachter*, 5 June 1940.
    34. Günter Kaufmann, "Einführung der Jugend in den Frontkämpfergeist," Gamm, *Führung und Verführung*, p. 360. Hitler established the Twenty-seventh SS Freiwilligen Grenadier Division Langemarck, which served in Russia. D. S. V. Fosten and R. J. Marrion, *Waffen-SS*, p. 38.
    35.   "Vom Blut der Helden Schlägt
             Das Herz der Welt".

    Ihr sollt nicht weinen und nicht traurig sein,
    denn unser Opferblut ward Lebenswein.

    Gott hat dem Leben Bruder Tod gesellt:
    Vom Blut der Helden schlägt das Herz der Welt.
    Wir schritten euch voran durchs dunkle Tor
    und strahlten eurer Auferstehung vor.
    Drum feiert uns mit hohem, hellem Klang,
    ein Siegeslied sei unser Grabgesang.

    Lebendig glüht der Trauer edler Stein,
    der Tod ist kurz und ewig währt das Sein.
    Erhebt euch hoch und schreitet stolz ins Licht:
    Schon küsst die Freiheit euer Angesicht!

Cited in *Der Gute Kamerad,* "Die 'Grauen Hefte' der Armee Busch," Schriftenreihe zur Truppenbetreuung, Heft 21, p. 71.

II. THE MARTYRDOM OF ALBERT LEO SCHLAGETER

1. Schlageter's motto was "das Banner muss stehen, wenn der Mann auch fällt." Rolf Brandt, *Albert Leo Schlageter,* p. 103.
2. Otto Paust, "Das Lied vom 'Verlorenen Haufen,' " in Friedrich Glombowski, *Organisation Heinz,* p. 6.
3. Schlageter to Rektor Matthäus Lang zu Konstanz, 30 March 1915, in Albert Leo Schlageter, *Deutschland muss leben,* p. 8.
4. Ibid., p. 8.
5. Brandt, pp. 7–10. Schlageter, letter to Rektor Lang, 4 November 1916, in Schlageter, p. 18.
6. Schlageter, pp. 27–28.
7. Schlageter to parents, 24 February 1918, ibid., pp. 35–36.
8. Schlageter to parents, August 26, 1918, ibid., pp. 39–40.
9. Brandt, p. 9.
10. Wilhelm Hügenell, *Schlageter,* pp. 9–10.
11. General von Cochenhausen, "Deutsches Soldatentum im Weltkriege," in Hans Roden, ed., *Deutsche Soldaten,* pp. 29–31.
12. Compare Ernst Jünger, *The Storm of Steel,* pp. 318–19, and Ernst Jünger, *Der Kampf als inneres Erlebnis,* pp. 47–54.
13. Ernst von Salomon, *Die Geächteten,* pp. 37–38.
14. Edwin Erich Dwinger, *Wir Rufen Deutschland,* pp. 277–79. Compare Ernst von Salomon, "Die Gestalt des deutschen Freikorpskämpfers," in *Das Buch vom deutschen Freikorpskämpfer,* pp. 11–14, and Robert G. L. Waite, *Vanguard of Nazism,* pp. 22–32. For a broader perspective of German youth and the war, see Robert Wohl, pp. 42–84, and Michael H. Kater, "Generationskonflikt als Entwicklungs-faktor in der NS-Bewegung vor 1933," *Geschichte und Gesellschaft,* 11 (1985), pp. 217–43.
15. See letter of 16 March 1919 from Schlageter to his parents, Schlageter, pp. 43–44. On the economic prospects for students, see Michael H. Kater, *Studentenschaft und Rechtsradikalismus in Deutschland 1918–1933,* pp. 43–73, 95–110.
16. Manfred Franke, *Schlageter,* pp. 24–26.
17. See Schlageter, p. 45; von Salomon, *Das Buch vom deutschen Freikorpskämpfer,* p. 479. See also "Gefechtsbericht des Detachements Medem," 23 May 1919, in von Salomon, *Das Buch vom deutschen Freikorpskämpfer,* pp. 165–70, and Erich F. Berendt, *Soldaten der Freiheit,* pp. 84–92.
18. Having lost their beloved Pastor Eckhard to a Bolshevik firing squad, the citizens of Riga responded to the moving ancient chorale "We Thank You, God" with tears and wails of joy. Schlageter to parents, 19 October 1919, Schlageter, p. 45. See also Brandt, pp. 15–16, and Hügenell, pp. 11–12.
19. Waite, p. 236; von Salomon, *Das Buch vom deutschen Freikorpskämpfer,* pp. 480–81.
20. General von der Goltz, in analyzing the importance of the campaign, con-cluded that "God did not allow the Baltic warriors to achieve all of their goals. Our nation—rotted by the November Revolution—was not mature enough to see that then. But we have saved Germany from Russian-Asiatic Bolshevism, a world-historic development, the importance of which will be realized only years from now." Von der Goltz, "Baltikum," in Roden, p. 100.
21. See Lieutenant General Freiherr von Watter, "Die Bedeutung der Frei-korps," in Roden, pp. 75–77.

22. Hügenell, pp. 14–15.

23. Glombowski, pp. 84–85. In the 1928 trial of Lieutenant Edmund Heines, Hauenstein testified that the Spezialpolizei were responsible for the deaths of some two hundred people in Upper Silesia. *Berliner Tageblatt,* 25 April 1928, cited in Waite, pp. 226–27.

24. Hügenell, pp. 16–17; Brandt, pp. 22–47.

25. Cited in Lieutenant General von Hülsen, "Freikorps im Osten," Roden, pp. 110–16. See also Berendt, pp. 92–95. When all of the Free Corps were disbanded on the orders of Reich President Ebert soon after their victory, the men were dumbfounded. For a moving description of their response, see von Salomon, *Die Geächteten,* p. 289.

26. *Wer war Schlageter?* pp. 7–8.

27. Brandt, 58–67. Despite his distaste for spying, Hohenstein valued the experience his men gained for their future deployment as shock troop commanders. He often gained important intelligence that aided his clandestine operations in the undeclared war in the frontier areas. Glombowski, p. 51.

28. Schlageter was listed on the 1922 membership list of the NSDAP, Ortsgruppe Berlin, as a businessman living at Friedrich Seestrasse 107. Hauenstein also appeared on the rolls, living at Linkstrasse 15, which was also the address of the import-export business. A partial 1922 membership list of the NSDAP, Ortsgruppe Berlin, appears in Glombowski, p. 109.

29. Von Salomon, *Die Geächteten,* pp. 231–32.

30. Decker, pp. 76–77; Berendt, pp. 96–114. See "Unsern toten Kameraden," a poem of fiery nationalism written after the murders at the Krupp plant, in *Rote Erde,* 10 April 1923, p. 10. The suffering in the Ruhr was remembered with sweet revenge at the height of the German onslaught against France in 1940. On the anniversary of the death of Schlageter, the *Münchener Abendblatt* (25 May 1940) published a memorial to him, with accompanying details on the murder of 137 Germans and the wounding of 600 others.

31. Brandt, p. 72.

32. Brandt, pp. 72–75.

33. Schlageter to Hauenstein, Werden Prison, Schlageter, pp. 49–51.

34. Schlageter to his parents and family, Düsseldorf, 22 April 1923, Schlageter, pp. 53–54.

35. H. O. Hauenstein, "Severing gegen Schlageter," Schlageter File, Slg. Personen 3796, Sammlung Rehse, BayHStA.

36. Karl-Heinz Harbeck, ed., *Akten der Reichskanzlei,* pp. 550.

37. Franke, p. 61.

38. Hans Sadowski received a sentence of hard labor for life, while the other accomplices drew prison terms ranging from five to twenty years. See Glombowski, pp. 155–60. See also *Albert Leo Schlageter. Seine Verurteilung und Erschiessung durch die Franzosen in Düsseldorf am 26.5.1923,* and Gustav Ritter und Edler von Oetinger, *In Ketten vom Ruhrgebiet nach Saint-Martin de Re.*

39. Schlageter, p. 59.

40. Schlageter, pp. 57–58.

41. *Rote Fahne,* "Das Düsseldorfer Todesurteil," quoted in Berendt, pp. 133–36.

42. This article was passed by the British censors. See Brandt, pp. 92–93.

43. According to Constans Heinersdorff, a Red Cross delegate who visited with the prisoner several times before his death, Schlageter refused to hear of any further plans for his escape. He submitted that he did not want to implicate innocent German guards or to cause his kindly French military guards unjustified punish-

ment. See Constans Heinersdorff, "Die letzten Stunden Schlageters," Schlageter File, Slg. Personen 3796, Sammlung Rehse, BayHStA.

44. Schlageter, pp. 62–66.

45. Several of these letters were pierced by rifle bullets and were found on the victim's body. Schlageter, p. 67.

46. Schlageter, p. 69.

47. Gefängnispfarrer Fassbender, "So Starb Albert Leo Schlageter," *Der Angriff*, 26 May 1933.

48. Hans Weberstedt and Kurt Langner, *Gedenkhalle für die Gefallenen des Dritten Reiches*, pp. 17–21; Decker, pp. 72–75.

49. Franke, pp. 80–87. For documentation on the participation of youths in the ceremonies, see *Albert Leo Schlageter. Ein deutscher Freiheitsheld*, pp. 27–28.

50. Schlageter, pp. 30–31.

51. Sturmabteilung Schlageter, *Albert Leo Schlageter. Dem deutschen Helden zum Gedächtnis*, pp. 6–7. This pamphlet, dating to the period 1923–24, contained strong doses of Nazi propaganda. The outside cover carried the following recruiting material: "Deutsche Jugend! Deutsche Männer! Ehrt das Andenken des für uns alle ermordeten Helden. Steht nicht abseits in der Pflicht für unser liebes Vaterland und den teuren toten Helden des Weltkrieges. Rafft euch auf zu dem Entschluss, Gut und Blut einzusetzen für die Befreiung Deutschlands aus Knechtschaft und Schande. Werbet Streiter wie Schlageter und gedenkt stets seines Wahlspruches: 'Alles für's Vaterland!' Sturmabteilung Schlageter der N.S.D.A.P." For other early literature on the hero, see Wilhelm F. von der Saar, *Der deutsche Martyr 'Schlageter' und der Französische Sadismus an Ruhr und Rhein* and Erwin Friedrich Kern, *Albert Leo Schlageter und seine Heimat*.

52. Hügenell, pp. 32–37.

53. Hügenell, pp. 37–39.

54. Hügenell, pp. 39–41; Franke, pp. 80–87. The *Kölnische Zeitung* carried a story on 16 June 1923 headlined "Das Hakenkreuz am Totenwagen," which lamented the Nazi excesses along the train route. At Freiburg, an inflammatory Nazi speaker had said, "Ehe Deutschland zugrunde geht, wird ganz Europa in Flammen aufgehen." The paper also regretted the impression that the swastika must have made on the Jewish students present that night. Schlageter File, Slg. Personen 3796, Rehse Archiv, BayHStA.

55. "Heldenehrung auf dem Königplatz, Gedächtnisfeier für Albert Leo Schlageter," ibid.

56. Ibid. Following the ceremony, a memorial mass for Schlageter was performed by Abbot von Emmaus at the St. Bonifazius Kirche. Flanking the altar were the standards and banners of the Vaterländische Kampfverbände. See "Trauerfeier in München," in *Albert Leo Schlageter. Dem deutschen Helden zum Gedächtnis*, pp. 13–15. Hitler often referred to Schlageter in 1923. See the text of his speech at the Sängerhalle in Augsburg, 6 July 1923, NSDAP/HA, Roll 2, Folder 59. There is a good deal of evidence that the Nazis attempted from the outset to lay exclusive claim to the Schlageter legacy. See the call for SA participation at the dedication of a Schlageter Cross at Campen bei Langgries (Tölz), in "SA Verfügungen," Das Oberkommando der SA, Der Chef des Stabes, Hoffmann, Mitteilung an alle SA Bez. Führer, Munich, July 20, 1923, NSDAP/HA, Roll 16, Folder 296.

57. Berendt, pp. 133–36.

58. *Bergisch-Märkische Zeitung*, 20 June 1923, pp. 1–2.

59. Carl Severing, *Mein Lebensweg*, I, pp. 402–11.

60. See Dr. Walter Luetgebrune Akten, 4, in Records of Private German Individuals, T-253, Roll 1, NA. Severing sued August Wilhelm Silgradt, editor of the *Bergisch-Märkische Zeitung* (Elberfeld), for libel in the III. Schöffengericht, Straf-

kammer I des Landgerichts, Elberfeld. Severing lost the case, which was decided on 17 October 1923, in part because Silgradt was defended by a leading trial lawyer for the nationalist cause, Walter Luetgebrune. See Trial Record 4J 1089/23/21, T-253, Roll 1, 1453005–46, NA. See also Severing, I, pp. 402–09, and Alfred E. Cornebise, *The Weimar in Crisis: Cuno's Germany and the Ruhr Occupation*, pp. 254–55.

61. For the official record of the trial, which was concluded on 12 July 1928, see Generalstaatsanwaltschaft beim Schwurgericht, Landgericht Berlin, Rep. 58, 2046, Acc. 399, Band 6 (Alfred Götze), Landesarchiv Berlin.

62. Harbeck, *Akten der Reichskanzlei*, p. 550. See also "Gerhard Rossbach an Reichskanzler Cuno," Leipzig, 15 June 1923, R 43 I/2678, ibid., pp. 570–72.

63. "Der Preussische Minister des Innern (Severing) an Staatssekretär Hamm," 8 June 1923, R 43 I/213, ibid., pp. 550–51. For Severing's protest to Gessler, see "Der Preussische Minister des Innern an den Reichswehrminister," 14 June 1923, R 43 I/416, ibid., pp. 557–68. See also Severing, I, p. 404; Otto Braun, *Von Weimar zu Hitler*, pp. 50–52; Cornebise, pp. 255, 281.

64. Karl Radek, "Leo Schlageter, der Wanderer ins Nichts," in *Schlageter. Eine Auseinandersetzung*, pp. 1–4. See also Warren Lerner, *Karl Radek*, pp. 120–21, and Ben Fowkes, *Communism in Germany under the Weimar Republic*, pp. 96–97.

65. See "Schriftwechsel der BüLtg des *Schlageter-Gedächtnis-Bundes* mit den einzelnen Untergruppen," NSDAP/Gauarchiv Südhannover-Braunschweig 1924–1945, Hann. Des. 310 I, H, Vols. I–XII, Staatsarchiv Hannover. See also Jeremy Noakes, *The Nazi Party in Lower Saxony, 1921–1933*, p. 34.

66. The Schlageter-Gedächtnis-Bund was outrageously anti-Semitic. Posters ran such lines as "Germans! Have you joined the Schlageter Memorial Union yet? Rescue Germany from the clutches of the Jews! Join the National Socialist Storm Sections!" Schlageter File, Slg. Personen 3796, Sammlung Rehse, BayHStA.

67. Gustav Lauterbach, Hanover, "Gründer und Hauptgeschäftsführer des Schlageter-Gedächtnis-Bundes e. V.," "Schlageter zum Gedächtnis!" ibid. The Bund symbol was a modified Iron Cross centered on a swastika, wreathed in laurel leaves. When the dream for a Third Reich was fulfilled ten years later, the Schlageter-Gedächtnis-Bund merged with the Reich. As the Bund surrendered its standards to Hitler at the 9 November ceremonies in 1933, the Führer was presented with the Ten Year Medal of Honor of the Bund. Throughout that year of victory, the leaders of the organization made much of their trailblazing work for National Socialism: "Among the ranks of our Bund from the beginning only pure National Socialism was taught, even as we were forced to march separately because of the ban on the Party. We belonged among the first warriors for Adolf Hitler." See Heinrich Haselhorst, Bundesführer/Gustav Lauterbach, Bundesschriftführer, 12 August 1933, Schlageter-Gedächtnis-Bund e.V., Bundesleitung Hannover, "10-Jahres Ehrenzeichen des Schlageter-Gedächtnis-Bundes e.V.," ibid.

68. "Turnerschaft 'Schlageter' Berlin," "Fest-Ordnung für den Grossen Deutschen Abend," Berlin, 22 October 1924, ibid.

69. The program included the admonition "Werd jeder ein Schlageter! Adolf Hitler braucht Euch!" " 'Treuschaft Hitler' der National-sozialistischen Deutschen Arbeiter-Partei in Thüringen—Gruppe Weimar, Trauerfeier," including "Gedächtnisrede des Führers der 'Treuschaft Hitler,' Parteigenosse Otto May," ibid.

70. Franz Müller, *Drei Sturmtrupplieder zur Deutschen Freiheitsbewegung. Dem Helden Schlageter gewidmet*.

71. Schlageter File, Slg. Personen 3796, Sammlung Rehse, BayHStA.

72. "Albert Leo Schlageter," "Melodie: Zu Mantua in Banden," ibid.

73. Walter Eberhard Freiherr von Medem, "An Schlageters Bahre," *Deutsche Allgemeine Zeitung*, Reichsausgabe Nr. 262/263, ibid. See also "Am Grabe Schlage-

ters," *Münchner Neueste Nachrichten*, 24 May 1924, ibid. For a notable memorial article published after the death of Schlageter's mother in 1925, see Teresa Mohr, "Die Mutter des Helden Schlageter, eine Alemannenfrau," ibid.

74. "Dem Gedächtnis Schlageters, Weiherede bei der Schlageterfeier auf der Deutschherrnwiese zu Nürnberg am 26. Mai 1924, gelegentlich der ersten Wiederkehr des Todestages Albert Leo Schlageters, gehalten von Rudolf Kötter," *Fränkische Kurier*, 26 May 1933.

75. Ernst von Salomon, *Fragebogen*, pp. 174–75.

76. Joseph Goebbels, *Das Tagebuch von Joseph Goebbels 1925/26*, p. 44.

77. Hans-Peter Görgen, *Düsseldorf und der Nationalsozialismus*, p. 14. The site of the original oak monument on the Golzheimer Heath was a magnet for political troublemakers and was vandalized in March 1929. See "Gemeine Schändung der Schlageter-Stätte," 16 March 1929, Schlageter File, Slg. Personen 3796, Sammlung Rehse, BayHStA.

78. "Einweihung des Schlageter-National-Denkmals," Düsseldorf, 23 May 1931, in *Essener Volks-Zeitung*, 24 May 1931.

79. Görgen, p. 97. Willy Münzenberg's communist press empire responded vehemently to the building of a monument for Schlageter, whom they termed a "Landsknecht adventurer" and "patriotic scum." Das Andere Deutschland, *Wer war Schlageter?*, pp. 6–20.

80. Friedrich Christian Prinz zu Schaumburg-Lippe, *Als die Goldne Abendsonne. Tagebücher 1933–1937*, pp. 130–31. For comparative purposes, see Robert R. Taylor, *The Word in Stone*, pp. 182–218.

81. Hubert Schrade, *Das Deutsche Nationaldenkmal*, p. 107.

82. Hanns Johst, *Schlageter*. At Goebbels's direction, *Schlageter* opened simultaneously in sixty theaters throughout the country.

83. Franke, pp. 9–11; Joseph Wulf, ed., *Theater und Film im Dritten Reich*, p. 189.

84. The quotations are from Johst, pp. 19–20, 26, 35–36, 48, 81–85, 134–35.

85. *Der Angriff*, 21 April 1933, p. 5. By most accounts, Richard Weichert's production of *Schlageter* in Munich's Residenz Theater was a *tour de force*. H. W. Geissler, writing in the *Münchner-Augsburger Abendzeitung*, found Hans Schlenk to be a brilliant actor in the role of Schlageter. Josef Magnus Wehner noted in the *Münchner Neueste Nachrichten* that Weichert's *Schlageter* was far better than the Berlin production. See "Pressestimmen: *Schlageter*" in Schlageter File, Slg. Personen 3796, Sammlung Rehse, BayHStA.

86. See Gauleiter Florian, "Der Sinn der Schlageter Gedenkfeier," ibid. See also Wilhelm Frick, Der Reichsminister des Innern an die Herren Reichsminister und Preussischen Minister, Berlin, 8 May 1933, I A 2200/5.5., "Betrifft: Schlageter-Feier," Schlageter File, BDC.

87. The band of the SA Standarte Schlageter No. 39 and the National Socialist Chorus of Düsseldorf provided the music, which ranged from Wagner to battle music from the Peasants' War. See "Ruhrkämpfer-Appell 1933," "am Vorabend der Schlagetergedenkfeier," Schlageter File, Slg. Personen 3796, Sammlung Rehse, BayHStA.

88. *Der Angriff*, 29 May 1933, p. 1; Görgen, pp. 98–99.

89. Mosse, *Nationalization of the Masses*, p. 206.

90. *Breisgauer Zeitung*, 27 May 1933, p. 9, quoted in Guido Schneeberger, *Nachlese zu Heidegger*, pp. 47–49.

91. *Der Angriff*, 26, 27, 29 May 1933.

92. It is probable that Reichsführer SS Himmler made the final decision in a case of such importance to the party. Otto Schneider had returned to Germany from Canada in 1933 with the intent of clearing his name, and Alfred Götze was

engaged in the same effort before his arrest. See Götze and Schneider, "Der Fall Schlageter," Götze files, BDC. This is a forty-two-page documentation of the history of their case, presented to the Gestapo on 23 January 1934 following their release from prison.

93. See SS Tgb. Nr. 5590, 8 November 1934, naming Götze to the rank of SS Sturmbannführer, ibid.; see also Sturmbannführer Alfred Götze, "im Stabe des Reichsführers SS," to SS Hauptamt, SS Standartenführer Schmidt, 2 February 1935, ibid.

94. In this connection, see Geheimes Staatspolizeiamt, II-1 H 2-24527-(172/34), Berlin, 19 October 1934, to Ministerialdirektor Daluege, Preussische Ministerium des Innern, which declared Götze and Schneider free of guilt in the case.

95. See *Volksparole*, Düsseldorf, 26 October 1934, headlined "Verrat um Schlageters 'Verräter'/Götze und Schneider völlig unschuldig an dem Verrat/Opfer der Systemregierung," Götze files, BDC. See also *Der Angriff*, 3 November 1934.

96. See "Vereinigung ehemaliger Angehöriger des Sturmregiments und der Organisation 'Heinz' " to the membership, "Betrifft: Götze und Schneider," Berlin, 28 October 1934.

97. Pordom, Hauptmann a.D., Schlageter-Gedächtnis-Museum e.V., to General der Landespolizei Daluege, Berlin, 28 October 1934, Götze files, BDC.

98. See H. O. Hauenstein, "Entwurf" (draft letter) to Alfred Götze, 28 October 1934, Götze files, BDC. Hauenstein's acid attack concluded with a warning: "Um Ihnen Gelegenheit zu geben, sich in aller Öffentlichkeit zu rechtfertigen, erkläre ich hiermit ausdrücklich, dass ich Sie und Schneider auch weiterhin als gemeinen Verräter bezeichnen werde und dass ich die Absicht habe, in Vorträgen und in Presseartikeln Sie auch weiter in dieser Weise zu bezeichnen."

99. Reichsführer SS to Alfred Götze (SS Nr. 245 685, z.b.V. RFSS), 2 August 1935, "Ich stosse Sie mit sofortiger Wirkung aus der SS aus," Götze files, BDC. See also Reinhard Heydrich to "Oberste SA-Führung zu Hd. d. Stabschefs Lutze," 27 July 1935, MA 847, pp. 8850–53, Institut für Zeitgeschichte, cited in Franke, pp. 117–18. The curious divisions within the party were demonstrated anew when Gauleiter Ernst Bohle intervened with Himmler in 1938 on behalf of Otto Schneider, who was living in abject poverty. See Ernst Wilhelm Bohle to Reichsführer SS Heinrich Himmler, "Persönlich!" 11 March 1938, Schneider files, BDC. This did not conclude the saga of the two adventurers. As late as August 1943, an undisclosed matter concerning Götze received the attention of Himmler (Der Reichsführer SS, Persönlicher Stab, Tgb.-Nr. 22/33/43, Feld-Kommandostelle, 4 August 1943, to Obersturmbannführer Bender, Berlin, Götze files, BDC). In 1944, Götze volunteered for service in the Waffen SS (Der Reichsführer SS, SS Hauptamt to Herrn Generalstaatsanwalt bei dem Landgericht Berlin, 26 August 1944, BI 4c–Az. 21e Bra/Rie, Generalstaatsanwalt bei dem Landgericht Berlin, Rep. 58, Acc. 399, Band 2046 (Alfred Götze), Landesarchiv Berlin. Götze was still trying to clear his name as late as the early 1950s (Dr. Drumm, Rechtsanwalt, Koblenz to Oberstaatsanwalt bei dem Landgericht Berlin, 22 July 1951, Generalstaatsanwalt bei dem Landgericht Berlin, Rep. 58, Acc. 399, Band 2046 (Alfred Götze), Landesarchiv Berlin. The irrepressible Götze emerged after the war as a member of the board of the German League for Human Rights, having passed himself off as a member of the anti-Nazi resistance. He was discovered, expelled from the organization, and once again convicted for fraud. See also Alfred Götze, Berlin-Wannsee, to Gustav Kreutlein, 1. Vorsitzenden, Freiheitsbund e.V., Landesverband Berlin, 28 October 1953, Götze files, BDC.

100. Karlheinz Schmeer, *Die Regie des öffentlichen Lebens im Dritten Reich*, p. 25.

101. See "Sie starben für das Dritte Reich," Schlageter File, Slg. Personen 3796, Sammlung Rehse, BayHStA. See also "Schlageter-Gedächtnisfeier 1936: Grosskund-

gebung der Gaupropagandaleitung Baden," Schönau, *Völkischer Beobachter,* 19 May 1936. For other examples of the genre, see "Gedenkfeier der Hitler Jugend vor dem Schlageter Kreuz auf der Golzheimer Heide," *Münchener Illustrierte,* 24 May 1934.

102. For examples of this literature, see Franz Kurfess, *Albert Leo Schlageter. Bauernsohn und Freiheitsheld;* Erika Mann, *School for Barbarians,* pp. 62, 90; Kamenetsky, pp. 196–98, 272. When Schlageter's father died in 1938, Hitler sent a wreath and telegram of condolence to the family. The eighty-four-year-old party member was buried in the family plot at Schönau, next to his wife and son. His funeral was attended by comrades of Albert, and the Baden Gauleiter Robert Wagner headed the list of official representatives. See "Abschied vom Vater Schlageters," *Völkischer Beobachter,* 13 November 1938.

103. Von Schirach address, Schlageter Memorial, Düsseldorf, "Schlagetertag," 27 May 1934, NSDAP/HA, Roll 18, Folder 336.

III. SACRIFICE AT THE FELDHERRNHALLE: THE NAZI IMMORTALS OF 9 NOVEMBER 1923

1. "Am 9. November vor der Feldherrnhalle zu München" ("On 9 November at the Feldherrnhalle in Munich"):

God isn't showing himself
in the old ways.
But you can feel his presence,
where the flags
of our faith wave: on the scaffold.

There, where the devils cry out:
'Recant, you dog or die!'
That for which they once built cathedrals,
for us the steps of the Feldherrnhalle
are an altar.

Baldur von Schirach, *Die Fahne der Verfolgten,* p. 32.

2. Hitler quotation of 1936 in Hans Frank, *Im Angesicht des Galgens,* p. 213.

3. Hitler address, Bürgerbräukeller, 8 November 1933, *Völkischer Beobachter,* 9 November 1933, p. 1.

4. Harold J. Gordon, Jr., *Hitler and the Beer Hall Putsch,* p. 270. See also James M. Diehl, *Paramilitary Politics in Weimar Germany,* pp. 142–51.

5. Some of the men from the front ranks yelled, "Don't shoot! Hitler's coming. Ludendorff's coming, comrades. Germans don't shoot Germans!" See "Auszug aus dem Bericht von Pg. Johann Aigner, München, Lämmerstr. 1/3. vom 15.12.1937," in NSDAP/HA, Reel 5, Folder 116.

6. Ibid. Compare Karl A. Kessler, *Der 9. November 1923 in München,* NSDAP/HA, Roll 5, Folder 116. Field Marshal Ludendorff was deeply moved at the shooting of his orderly, who had been loyal unto death. In his memory, Ludendorff erected a memorial column at his graveside in the Waldfriedhof Solln outside Munich. Its simple inscription read, "Zu Ehren von Kurt Neubauer gefallen an meiner Seite am 9. November 1923 zwischen *Feldherrnhalle* und Residenz in München. Er kannte nichts höheres als sein Vaterland! Ludendorff." *Abendblatt* (München), 31 October 1933.

7. Hauptmann a.D., Richard Kolb, SS Hauptsturmführer, "Bericht über den 8./9. November 1923," undated, in NSDAP/HA, Reel 5, Folder 116.

8. Heinrich Wilhelm Trambauer, "Der 9. November. Der Markstein meines Lebens," NSDAP/HA, Roll 53, Folder 1278.

9. See report of Adolf Rottenberger, Geschäftsführer der SS Oberleitung, "Erklärung: Blutfahne vom 9.11.23," NSDAP/HA, Roll 53, Folder 1278. During the mid-1930s, the Nazi Party Archive undertook an extensive investigation to document accurately the circumstances surrounding the Blood Flag. This involved both official oral and written testimony, focusing mainly on exactly who carried the original Blood Flag. A heated controversy ensued, involving several offices, including the Adjutantur des Führers (Obergruppenführer Wilhelm Brückner), the Hauptarchiv der NSDAP (Dr. Uetrecht), and the Amt für den 8./9. November 1923 (Christian Weber). See Georg Wiborg, Gruppenführer der 6. Kompanie der SA der NSDAP to Pg. Kallenbach, Munich, 6.10. 1935, NSDAP/HA, Roll 5, Folder 116. See M. Sesselmann's report, 1 November 1935, Munich, NSDAP/HA, Roll 5, Folder 116. Wiborg stated in his deposition entitled "Die 6. Kompagnie der S.A. der NSDAP am 8. und 9. November 1923" (NSDAP/HA, Roll 4, Folder 93): "The Storm Flag of the Sixth Company, which is drenched in the blood of the fallen (Andreas Bauriedl) was saved—a member of the company tore it from the pole and hid it under his uniform—and in 1925 was given to the Führer by the former sergeant of the company, party comrade Eggers. The Storm Flag of the former Sixth Company is the Blood Flag of the movement." See also Der Reichsführer SS, SS Gericht, Munich, 23 October 1935, "Betrifft: Blutfahne," to Pg. Damann, Archivstelle, Barerstrasse 15, München, calling for information regarding police confiscation of NSDAP flags on 9 November 1923. Damann answered that several flags had been taken by the police but that the actual Blood Flag was not (NSDAP/HA, Roll 4, Folder 93). See also Amt für den 8./9. November 1923, Munich, 22 May 1939, to Dr. Uetrecht, Hauptarchiv der NSDAP, "Träger der Blutfahne am 9. November 1923 während des Marsches zur Feldherrnhalle und an der Feldherrnhalle," NSDAP/HA, Roll 4, Folder 93, and Dr. Uetrecht, Leiter des Hauptarchivs der NSDAP, Reichsamtsleiter im Stabe des Stellvertreters des Führers, to Amt für den 8./9. November, Munich, Rezidenz-Kaiserhof, 4 July 1939, "Blutfahne," NSDAP/HA, Roll 4, Folder 93. See also Uetrecht's letter to the editors of the *Deutsche Allgemeine Zeitung*, 12 November 1940 (NSDAP/HA, Roll 4, Folder 93) castigating them for their error of naming Hans Grimminger as the bearer of the Blood Flag in 1923. Uetrecht noted that after an extensive investigation, the legend that Andreas Bauriedl had carried the flag was disproved. It had been incontrovertibly demonstrated that Heinrich Trambauer had served as the standard-bearer. The exacerbated archivist complained that, by pointing to Grimminger, the paper had only confused the issue.

10. Karl Richard Ganzer, *9. November 1923. Tag der ersten Entscheidung*, pp. 69–70. Compare Gordon, pp. 475–85.

11. Ganzer, pp. 69–70.

12. See NSDAP, *9. November 1923–1933*, memorial brochure, p. 5, IfZ, 5138.

13. Weberstedt and Langner, pp. 33–43. Compare Decker, pp. 108–11.

14. See Max Erwin von Scheubner-Richter File, BDC. Compare Walter Laqueur, *Russia and Germany*, pp. 58–68.

15. Theodor von der Pfordten File, BDC. See also Hans Frank, *Theodor von der Pfordten*, which includes chapters entitled "Principles of Authoritarian State Leadership," "The *Völkisch* State Principles," "The Philosophy of von der Pfordten," and "Hero of Law."

16. See introduction to Hitler's *Mein Kampf*, p. xxix, in which he charged that "Sogenannte nationale Behörden verweigerten den toten Helden ein gemeinsames Grab."

17. Those buried in Munich cemeteries included Dr. Max Erwin von Scheubner-Richter, Felix Alfarth, Theodor Casella, Martin Faust, Karl Laforce, Claus von Pape, Lorenz Ritter von Stransky (Waldfriedhof); Andreas Bauriedl, Oskar Körner, Theodor von der Pfordten (Nordfriedhof); Anton Hechenberger, Karl Kuhn, Wilhelm

Wolf (Ostfriedhof). See "Der in den Städt. Friedhöfen Münchens befindlichen Grabstätten der Gefallenen vom 9. November 1923," in Bürgermeister und Rat 512, Stadtrat der Landeshauptstadt München, Stadtarchiv München. The three remaining dead were buried at locations outside Munich.

18. Mantel, Polizeidirektion München, 2011/VId, 2 November 1925, to Geschäftsstelle der NSDAP, Schellingstr. 50/I Rg., NSDAP/HA, Roll 4, Folder 89.

19. Hitler address, Munich, 8 November 1927, NSDAP/HA, Roll 2. Dr. Buttmann, who also spoke at the Bürgerbräukeller rally, noted, "Once again this year we have placed wreaths on the graves of the dead of 9 November in the Munich cemeteries. We are forbidden from glorifying them. But hooligans have destroyed these wreaths and torn the insignias from them." Ibid.

20. See Baldur von Schirach in Die Fahne der Verfolgten, p. 32.

21. "Erschlagener Kamerad," ibid., p. 29.

22. For a general description of the place held by 9 November mythology in Nazi propaganda, see Schmeer, pp. 101–05. Compare Friedrich Heer, Der Glaube des Adolf Hitler, pp. 266–67. For a discussion of the symbolism of the 9 November pageant, see Klaus Vondung, Magie und Manipulation, pp. 155–71.

23. Morgenpost, Munich, 7 May 1933, headlined "Das Künftige Ehrenmal in der Feldherrnhalle: Ein Blick in die Werkstadt des Künstlers."

24. Ibid.

25. See "Der 'Blutorden' der NSDAP," in Gutachten des Instituts für Zeitgeschichte, pp. 322–23, and Jürgen Brinkmann, Orden und Ehrenzeichen des "Dritten Reiches," p. 43.

26. For press coverage on the functions of Christian Weber, see Völkischer Beobachter, 25 August 1938. For humorous accounts of his pranks, see Der Spiegel, 21 March 1951, pp. 23–24. The stories concerning the indelicate behavior of Weber were such that even the Nuremberg 8-Uhr Blatt ran a voyeuristic series on him (1–27 July 1953).

27. See Rudolf Apel, "Bestimmung über Verleihung des Ehrenzeichens vom 9.11.23.," NSDAP/HA, Roll 16, Folder 301. Certain members of the police and Reichswehr who had joined the NSDAP were also given the honor.

28. Völkischer Beobachter, 3 November 1933.

29. Gaupropagandaleiter, NSDAP, Gau München-Oberbayern, to Oberbürgermeister Karl Fiehler, 16 October 1933, B/R 458/2, SLM, StAM.

30. The schedule of the Stosstrupp Hitler 1923 for the morning of 11 November 1933 began with a Frühschoppen (Weisswurst) at the Restaurant Grosser Rosengarten. Punctually at 12:20 P.M. the members were to appear for photographs with their party comrade Mayor Karl Fiehler at the Munich Rathaus, where they were to sign the official Golden Book of the City of Munich. Thereafter they retired to the Ratskeller for a banquet as honored guests of the city. See SA der NSDAP, Stosstrupp Hitler 1923, Munich, 3 November 1933, "Programm für den Ehrentag der Alten Garde, 7.-9. November 1933," R/R 458/2, SLM, StAM.

31. See Polizeipräsident Schneidhuber, Munich, 6 November 1933, B/R 458/2, SLM, StAM. See also J. V. Lang, Polizeidirektion München, "Ortspolizeiliche Anordnung für den 9. November 1933," 6 November 1933, B/R 458/2, SLM, StAM.

32. Münchener Zeitung, 8 November 1933, p. 8.

33. Völkischer Beobachter, 9 November 1933. Dr. Friedrich Weber paid homage to the sixty-one men of the Bund Oberland who sacrificed their lives. Gerhard Rossbach, commander of the Free Corps Rossbach, remarked that the flag his unit surrendered that day was the very one carried by the Battalion Heines in the first ranks on the march to the Feldherrnhalle in 1923.

34. See "Der Stabschef übernimmt die alten Freikorpsfahnen," Völkischer Beo-

bachter, 9 November 1933. For film coverage of the flag transfer, see *Der 9. November in München*, Agfa, 1933, Mag. Nr. 192, BA.

35. See "In der Stunde der Freikorpskämpfer," *Völkischer Beobachter*, 10 November 1933.

36. See "Begrüssung der Freikorpskämpfer," *Münchener Neueste Nachrichten*, 7 November 1933.

37. *Völkischer Beobachter*, 9 November 1933.

38. *Der 9. November in München*, Agfa, 1933, Mag. Nr. 192, BA.

39. *Völkischer Beobachter*, 9 November 1933.

40. See the program directives by Günther Wissmann of the Reichsrundfunk Berlin in Wolfram Wessels, " 'Der 9. November,' Weihvollster Tag im Dritten Reich," in *Studienkreis Rundfunk und Geschichte: Mitteilungen* 10 (1984), pp. 88–90.

41. Ibid. See the fascinating chapter "Der braune Blutkult" in Hans-Jochen Gamm, *Der braune Kult*, pp. 127–50.

42. *Studienkreis Rundfunk und Geschichte: Mitteilungen*, 10 p. 90. Günther Wissmann's directives were quite explicit. He called for appropriate music to accompany the day's events, noting that the Christian mass offered the best opportunities. See "An-und Absagen für den 9. November," "Der historische Zug," R78/2298, BA, cited in ibid., p. 91.

43. Victor Dobbert, Reichssendeleitung, Abt. Alb, "Zum 9. November," *Nationalsozialistische Hörberichte*, R78/2298, BA, ibid., pp. 91–94.

44. Ibid., p. 93.

45. *Völkischer Beobachter*, 10 November 1933.

46. Ibid.

47. *Völkischer Beobachter*, 9, 10 November 1933.

48. *Völkischer Beobachter*, 10 November 1933.

49. Ibid.

50. Ibid.

51. Hitler, however, did return to Munich for his traditional speech at the Bürgerbräukeller. At that time he remarked that "we have only one regret, that all those who marched then are no longer with us, that sadly a number of our very best, most loyal, and fanatical fighters did not live to see the fulfillment of the goal for which they were striving. But they are also here with us in spirit, and in the great beyond, they will know that their struggle was not in vain." *Völkischer Beobachter*, 10 November 1934.

52. See Dr. Armand Dehlinger, *Architektur der Superlative: Eine Kritische Betrachtung der N.S. Bauprogramme von München und Nürnberg*, MS 8/1(a) and MS 8/2(a), IfZ, and Hermann Giessler, *Ein Anderer Hitler. Bericht seines Architekten Hermann Giessler*, pp. 144–81. Giessler had been appointed by Hitler as the Generalbaurat München.

53. Gerdy Troost, ed., *Das Bauen im Neuen Reich*, I, pp. 15–16. Compare *Die Kunst im Dritten Reich* 2 (January 1938), p. 37.

54. *Völkischer Beobachter*, 10 November 1935. See also Karl Arndt, "Filmdokumente des Nationalsozialismus als Quellen für architekturgeschichtliche Forschungen," in Günter Moltmann and Karl F. Reimers, *Zeitgeschichte in Film und Tondokument*, pp. 48–52.

55. The directives consisted of a script of sixty-eight pages and is an important source in understanding Nazi propaganda. See "9. November 1935 in München," NSDAP/HA, Roll 4, Folder 103. For a shortened version, see Gaupropagandaleitung München-Oberbayern, "Vorläufiges Regie Programm für den 8./9. November 1935," B/R 458/2, SLM, StAM.

56. Gaupropagandaleitung München-Oberbayern, "Vorläufiges Regie Programm für den 8./9. November 1935," B/R 458/2, SLM, STAM, p. 8. The con-

ceptualization of the march was quite explicit: "The route from the Bürgerbräu to the Feldherrnhalle should—as in 1933—symbolize the sacrifice of the National Socialist Movement. The way from the Feldherrnhalle to the Temple of Honor should symbolize victory and the resurrection of the fallen of 9.11.23 in the year of freedom. The bands, which will have taken their positions at the Odeonsplatz and in the Brienner Strasse, will play selections during the march which convey the joy of the resurrection (ending with the *Deutschland Lied*)."

57. Ibid., p. 11.

58. *Völkischer Beobachter*, 10 November 1935.

59. For documentary film coverage of the proceedings on the night of 8 November 1935 as well as the ceremony at the Königsplatz the next day, see NSDAP/RPL, *Ewige Wache*, 1936, Mag. Nr. 68, BA; *Ufa* Wochenschauaufnahmen, *NS-Feiern und 9.November 1933–1938*, Mag. Nr. 273, BA; *8. und 9. November 1935* (Arbeitskopie von Wochenschauaufnahmen), 1935, Mag. Nr. 781, BA.

60. For the parade in 1936, this system involved hookups at thirty-one points. See Gaupropagandaleiter Wenzl, Propaganda/Hauptstelle Rundfunk, NSDAP/Gauleitung München-Oberbayern to Oberbürgermeister Fiehler, 28 October 1936, B/R 458/2, SLM, StAM. More than ever, the marchers appeared as a unified band. According to explicit orders, they wore Brown Shirts without any insignia except the "armband of 1923" and turned out with neither hat nor coat. The only medal allowed was the Blood Order of 1923. *Völkischer Beobachter*, 3 August 1935.

61. *Völkischer Beobachter*, 10 November 1935.

62. See NSDAP, "9. November 1935 in München," NSDAP/HA, Roll 4, Folder 103. The ceremonies in November 1937 went even further in some areas. At the Gauleiter's command—"Ewige Wache—raus!"—the martyrs were to rise from the dead and assume their positions as the Eternal Guard. See SA der NSDAP, *Gruppe Hochland*, Der Aufmarschleiter, "Feier auf dem Königlichen Platz," Munich, 5 November 1937, B/R 458/3, SLM, StAM.

63. *Völkischer Beobachter*, 10 November 1935. On 8 November, von Schirach had addressed the youth on the meaning of their oath in the Festival Hall of the Löwenbräukeller on the Stiglmeier Platz. The hall was decorated with sixteen candles for the event, as well as the traditional Nazi affirmation, "You were victorious after all!"

64. The place of youth in the ceremony was graphically illustrated in the official program for 1936. Nazi youths were described as "torchbearers of the future" who "would take fire from the blazing flame of their sacrifice and the spirit of Adolf Hitler will live on in them. . . . Youth is the direct inheritor of the heroic sacrifice; with pure hands and hearts youth will carry the torches of freedom and racial inheritance into the future." See NSDAP, Traditionsgau München-Oberbayern, *Zum 9. November 1936* (Munich, 1936).

65. In order to be visible to as many people as possible, Hitler rode in his open Mercedes and retraced the entire parade route in reverse.

66. *Völkischer Beobachter*, 9 November 1935.

67. NSDAP/RPL, *Für Uns*, 1937, Mag. Nr. 77, BA. The march presented in the film took place on 9 November 1936. The meaning of the ceremony was reiterated in the Bavaria Wochenschau, *Im Geist der Alten Garde*, 1936, Mag. Nr. 252, BA. In a 30 January 1936 speech at the Lustgarten in Berlin, Hitler made it clear that in the future National Socialism would call for a blood sacrifice. Theirs was not, he said, an "ethos of sloth but of battle, not an ideology of bliss but of hard work and struggle." Domarus, pp. 569–71.

68. Stosstrupp Adolf Hitler 1923, Munich, 12 October 193, to all members, B/R 458/3, SLM, StAM.

69. Christian Weber, "Der Ausschuss des 8./9. November 1923," "Dienstliche

Mitteilung: Richtlinien für die Berechtigung der Teilnahme am 8./9. November," Munich, 1 July 1937, NSDAP/HA, Reel 54, Folder 1291.

70. *Völkischer Beobachter,* 8 October 1937.

71. Hermann Kriebel to Rudolf Hess, 12 July 1938, NSDAP/HA, Reel 5, Folder 116. Hermann Kriebel had been an important figure in the putsch of 1923 and was among those sentenced to serve a jail sentence at Landsberg with Hitler. Kriebel did not receive a position of importance in the Third Reich. He served as German general consul in Shanghai until his death in 1941.

72. Ibid.

73. See Ernst Schulte-Strathaus to Leitgen, 11 August 1938, NSDAP/HA, Reel 5, Folder 116, and Ulrich Graf, "Ratsherr der Hauptstadt der Bewegung," to "Reichsminister Pg. Hess," Munich, 16 August 1938, ibid. Graf won the minibattle. Photographs of the 1938 march show him at Hitler's side. See *Völkischer Beobachter,* 10 November 1938.

74. Oberbürgermeister Karl Fiehler, B/R 458/2, SLM, StAM.

75. Dr. Friedrich Weber, Ministerialdirigent im Reichsministerium des Innern, Berlin, 14 November 1935, to Oberbürgermeister Karl Fiehler, Munich, ibid. One senses the excitement of the occasion when reading the response to the gracious invitation from just one "Old Fighter." Gerhard Hoff, at the time a book dealer in Wuppertal-Elberfeld, wrote the mayor on 6 November 1935: "Ich freue mich schon sehr auf das Wiedersehen mit Euch alten Kameraden. Bis dahin grüsse ich Dich recht herzlich in alter Kameradschaft. Mit Heil Hitler!"

76. Stosstrupp Adolf Hitler 1923, Munich, 1 November 1938, B/R 458/3, SLM, StAM. The membership was instructed that "am 8. November fährt der Stosstrupp nach Landsberg am Lech zum Besuch der Festung. Abfahrt um 9 Uhr vom Ratshaushof mit Fahrzeugen der Stadt München."

77. Adolf Lenk, Munich, 16 October 1936, to Oberbürgermeister der Hauptstadt der Bewegung, Pg. Karl Fiehler, B/R 452/2, SLM, StAM.

78. *Germania,* 9 November 1937.

79. See the invitation from Rudolf Hess to Mayor Fiehler, B/R 458/3, StAM. Göring spoke in the Congress Hall of the Deutsches Museum on the morning of 8 November 1937. At noon the party leaders repaired to the Altes Rathaussaal for a luncheon.

80. See SA Gruppe Hochland file, B/R 458/3, SLM, StAM.

81. *Völkischer Beobachter,* 11 November, 1938.

82. Ibid.

83. For complete plans for SS participation, see Der Reichsführer SS, Berlin, SS-HA/IA/A, 12/21.10.38, 21 October 1938, "Vorläufiges Programm, 8/9 November 1938," B/R 458/3, SLM, StAM. Compare Der Reichsführer SS, SS Personalkanzlei, P 5 Wu/Schl., Tagb.-Nr. 456/37, Berlin, 30 October 1937, "Programm für die Veranstaltungen am 8./9. Nov. 37 in München," ibid.; Der Chef des SS-Hauptamtes, IA/A Az. 10 c 12/30.10.37, Berlin, 30 October 1937, ibid.; Gaupropagandaleiter Pg. Wenzl, "Vorläufiges Regie-Programm für den 8./9. November 1937 in München" (pp. 20), ibid.; SA der NSDAP, Gruppe Hochland, Abt.: Fl Br. B. Nr. 3877, Der Aufmarschleiter, "Feier auf dem Königlichen Platz," Munich, 5 November 1937, ibid.

84. See Anton Hoch, "Das Attentat auf Hitler im *Bürgerbräukeller,*" *Vierteljahrshefte für Zeitgeschichte* 17 (October 1969), pp. 383–413, and Johann Georg Elser, *Autobiographie eines Attentäters. Aussage zum Sprengstoffanschlag im Bürgerbräukeller, München am 8. November 1939,* ed. Lothar Gruchmann.

85. *Völkischer Beobachter,* 10/11 November 1939. See also Jay W. Baird, *The Mythical World of Nazi War Propaganda, 1939–1945,* pp. 64–66.

86. *Ufa* Ton Woche 480/39, November 1939, BA.

87. *Völkischer Beobachter,* 12 November 1939.
88. Martin Bormann, NSDAP-Parteikanzlei, Führerhauptquartier, 16 October 1942, Rundschreiben Nr. 156/42, Nov. 1942, NSDAP-Reichsring f.V.und P.-Hauptamt Pro., T-81, Roll 675, 5483725, NA. Compare Friedrichs, NSDAP, Stellvertreter des Führers/Stab, Munich, 1 November 1940, to Oberbürgermeister Fiehler, "Feierlichkeiten am 9. November 1940 in München," which included the following passage: "On the express wishes of the Führer, the Leadership Corps on the invitation of Gauleiter Adolf Wagner must take part in the wreath-laying ceremony in the Temple of Honor." B/R 458/3, SLM, StAM.
89. F. Geisselbrecht to Stosstruppkameraden of Stosstrupp A.H. 1923, 7 November 1940, B/R 458/3, SLM, StAM.
90. See Gauleiter Wagner, "Feierlichkeiten des 9. November 1941," B/R 458/3, SLM, StAM; Gauleiter Paul Giesler, "Feierlichkeiten des 9. November 1942," NSDAP/Reichsring für Volksaufklärung und Propaganda/Hauptamt Propaganda, T-81, Roll 675, 5483692, NA. Compare the plans for 9 November 1940 in Gauleitung München-Oberbayern to Oberbürgermeister Karl Fiehler, 20 October 1940, B/R 458/3, SLM, StAM.
91. Goebbels to all Gauleiter and Gaupropagandaleiter, Berlin, 21 October 1942, Der Reichspropagandaleiter der NSDAP, NSDAP/HA, Roll 16, Folder 291. See also accompanying orders from Walter Tiessler, Reichspropagandaleitung/Hauptamt Reichsring, 27 October 1942, ibid. In November 1942 Goebbels made political capital for himself by giving a gift of money to survivors of the party's dead. Immediate family members of the martyrs of the NSDAP each received RM 100. Party members wounded in the *Kampfzeit* received monetary awards on a sliding scale from RM 50 to RM 500, depending upon the number of children in their families. Goebbels, "Rundschreiben an alle ämtliche Reichspropagandaämter," 1 October 1942, Reichspropagandaleitung/Hauptamt Reichsring, T-81, Roll 675, 5483729.
92. *Völkischer Beobachter,* 9 November 1942.
93. Max Domarus, ed., *Hitler. Reden und Proklamationen 1932–1945,* p. 2160. In 1943, Gauleiter Paul Giesler oversaw the formalities at the Feldherrnhalle and the Königsplatz. See "Regieprogramm für den 8./9. November 1943," Gauleiter Dr. Müller, 1 November 1943, B/R 458/3, SLM, StAM.
94. Horst Überhorst, *Elite für die Diktatur,* pp. 226–30.
95. Wolfram Sellg, ed., *Chronik der Stadt München 1945–1948,* p. 43.
96. Ibid., p. 65.
97. Ibid., pp. 65–66.
98. Ibid., pp. 231, 233. The Bavarian minister of culture Franz Fendt, acting on the command of the American military government (JCS Directive 1067), ordered that every monument in Munich was to be de-Nazified by January 1947. See "Amtsblatt Nr. 9 der Bayerischen Ministeriums für Unterricht und Kultur vom 9.12.1946," in Friedrich Prinz, *Trümmerzeit in München,* p. 80.

IV. GOEBBELS, HORST WESSEL, AND THE MYTH OF RESURRECTION AND RETURN

1. Raise the flag! The ranks are closely formed!
The SA is marching in clipped cadence,
Comrades, shot by Red Front and Reaction,
March along in spirit in our columns.

Clear the streets for the brown batalions,
Clear the streets for the Storm Section man!

Millions already look with hope to the swastika
The day of freedom and of bread is in sight!

The Nazi party anthem "Die Fahne hoch!" composed by Horst Wessel essentially became the second national anthem during the Third Reich.

2. For a general background, see Karl D. Bracher et al., *Die nationalsozialistische Machtergreifung,* pp. 830–55; William Sheridan Allen, *The Nazi Seizure of Power: The Experience of a Single German Town, 1922–1945;* Diehl, pp. 199–292.

3. This caption was frequently quoted in references to Horst Wessel.

4. For relevant literature on the SA, see Peter H. Merkl, *The Making of a Stormtrooper,* pp. 164–74, 231–43; Michael H. Kater, "Ansätze zu einer Soziologie der SA bis zur Röhm Krise," in Ulrich Engelhardt et al., *Soziale Bewegung und politische Verfassung;* Otis C. Mitchell, *Hitler over Germany: The Establishment of the Nazi Dictatorship, 1918–1934,* pp. 103–93, and, by the same author, "Criminals of the Dream: Nazi Storm Troopers during the Drive to Power," in *Nazism and the Common Man,* pp. 7–42; Richard Bessel, *Political Violence and the Rise of Nazism: The Storm Troopers in Eastern Germany, 1925–1934,* pp. 75–96; Eve Rosenhaft, *Beating the Fascists? The German Communists and Political Violence;* Conan Fischer, *Stormtroopers.* For an excellent analysis of Nazi heroization of an SA martyr in the provinces, see Lawrence D. Stokes, "Der Fall Radke. Zum Tode eines nationalsozialistischen 'Märtyrers' und die Folgen in Eutin, 1931–1933," in Erich Hoffmann et al., *"Wir bauen das Reich". Aufstieg und erste Herrschaftsjahre des Nationalsozialismus in Schleswig-Holstein,* pp. 41–72, and, by the same author, *Kleinstadt und Nationalsozialismus. Ausgewählte Dokumente zur Geschichte von Eutin 1918–1945.*

5. For examples, see *Der unbekannte SA Mann; Der Angriff,* 7 November 1927; Joseph Goebbels, *Der Angriff. Aufsätze aus der Kampfzeit.* For an analysis of the heroization of the death motif, see Mosse, "National Cemeteries."

6. Goebbels, *Michael.*

7. See Nachlass Goebbels, 19 January 1930, NL 118/62, BA.

8. Ingeborg Wessel, Horst's sister, edited two hagiographic works about her brother entitled *Horst Wessel. Sein Lebensweg, nach Bildern zusammengestellt* and *Mein Bruder Horst.*

9. See letter of Horst Wessel, 27 November 1924, to his Bismarck Bund commander bewailing the weaknesses of the leadership and the passivity of the organization, NSDAP/HA, Roll 53, Folder 1280, and Ingeborg Wessel, *Mein Bruder Horst,* pp. 13–53. Photographs show Horst proudly wearing the Viking uniform while on maneuvers. See Erwin Reitmann, *Horst Wessel: Leben und Sterben,* p. 17. Another photograph shows him in trench-fighter fashion posing with rifle, uniform, and shepherd dog. LC-USZ 62–42896, LOC.

10. *Hans Westmar* (Franz Wenzler, 1933), the feature film on Wessel's life, was especially effective in portraying his restless student days at the University of Berlin.

11. For a convincing discussion of the pressures on students in the era, see Kater, *Studentenschaft und Rechtsradikalismus,* pp. 80–114, and Giles, *Students and National Socialism in Germany,* pp. 1–100.

12. According to Giles (*Students and National Socialism in Germany,* pp. 17–18), "The elite of the fraternity world was to be found in the so-called Corps, above all in the *Kösener Senioren-Convent Verband,* which retained an aristocratic air." Alumni of this distinguished corps controlled 20 percent of the highest-ranking government positions in Prussia in 1928. While studying in Vienna in the winter semester of 1928, Wessel was affiliated with the *Alemannia* chapter of the fraternity.

13. Reitmann, pp. 11–15, and Hanns Heinz Ewers, *Horst Wessel.*

14. Horst Wessel, undated autobiographical sketch, NSDAP/HA, Horst Wessel File, BDC.

15. Wilfred Bade, *Die SA erobert Berlin*, pp. 182–83.

16. Horst Wessel fits into the schema developed by Peter Loewenberg in his masterful essay, "The Psychohistorical Origins of the Nazi Youth Cohort," *American Historical Review*, 76, 5 (December 1971), pp. 1457–502. See also Kater, "Generationskonflikt."

17. Reitmann, p. 45.

18. Berlin Police Presidium, I. A. III. 1., Bericht, Horst Wessel, Horst Wessel File, BDC. Berlin Police, Inspektion II, and Kriminal Kommissar Walther Teichmann, who was assigned to the Wessel case, were included in the team that composed this assessment of the career and character of Horst Wessel. See also Reitmann, pp. 16–18, 22–23, 65–67; Bade, *Die SA erobert Berlin*, pp. 188–89; Z. A. B. Zeman, *Nazi Propaganda*, p. 15.

19. Reitmann, pp. 65–67. For a summary of Wessel's activities in this period, see SA Obersturmbannführer J. K. von Engelbrechten, *Eine braune Armee entsteht. Die Geschichte der Berlin-Brandenburger SA*, pp. 87–112.

20. See von Engelbrechten, pp. 94–97.

21. Ewers, p. 121; Ernest K. Bramsted, *Goebbels and National Socialist Propaganda, 1925–1945*, p. 41. Wessel's connection with Jaenicke was mentioned neither by his sister in her two works nor by the SA chronicler J. K. von Engelbrechten. On the other hand, his party biographer Reitmann (pp. 27–28) noted that "extreme idealism" had motivated Wessel to live with Jaenicke, "whom he succeeded in extricating from communist circles."

22. The character of Jaenicke was a source of controversy at the time. Jaenicke claimed at the Höhler trial that she and Wessel were to be married, that she was no longer engaged in prostitution, and that she was working as a seamstress. This was reaffirmed in a report of the Berlin Police, I. A. III. 1., Bericht, 15. June 1931, "Horst Wessel," Horst Wessel File, BDC. The report stated: "Jainichen was a prostitute before, but Wessel took her out of these circles." The communist defense lawyer Fritz Löwenthal attempted to prove that Jaenicke continued to ply her trade after moving in with Wessel, but she vehemently denied the charge. Imre Lazar, *Der Fall Horst Wessel*, pp. 148–52. An émigré news service reported from Paris, 20 July 1934, that the Höhler defense lawyer, Dr. Apfel, recalled that Jaenicke had admitted under oath that she had engaged in prostitution while living with Wessel. The trial documents do not confirm this allegation. See "Spezialdienst," Horst Wessel File, BDC.

23. After they came to power, the Nazis destroyed the police files on Wessel as well as all official materials relating to the Wessel trial. Listed as "missing" at the Landesarchiv Berlin is GStALgB, Rep. 58, Lfd. Nr. 11, 1 J 126/30, "Rubrum: Höhler und Andere, Sachverhalt: Ermordung des Studenten Horst Wessel, Urteil." *Kriminaldirektor* Werner Togotzes (born 1899), who served with the Berlin police in those years, observed in an interview in 1962 with the Vassar historian Hsi-Huey Liang that the police "treated the case as a political crime. Who among the IA people at that time—when the Nazis were so close to reaching power—would have dared to contradict Nazi propaganda and declare this murder to be a sordid affair among pimps and prostitutes?" Liang, letter to author, 7 September 1980.

24. *Völkischer Beobachter*, 14 June 1934; Lazar, pp. 134–44. See the story in the *Vossische Zeitung*, 23 September 1930, headlined "Wer ist schuld an Wessels Tod? Der richtige und der falsche Arzt."

25. Lazar, pp. 122–34. Max Dombrowski testified to making this warning in the second Wessel trial in 1934. *Völkischer Beobachter*, 13 June 1934.

26. See the testimony of Salm in Lazar, pp. 126–27. Salm testified that Jaenicke was not engaged in prostitution, nor was Horst Wessel a pimp; instead, she noted,

both worked for a living during the period when she was able to observe them closely (October 1929–January 1930).

27. See *Neue Badische Landeszeitung*, 24 September 1930. See the story under the headline "Höhepunkt des Wessel-Prozesses: " 'Ali' klagt an," *Tempo*, 24 September 1930.

28. *Völkischer Beobachter*, 13 June 1934.

29. *Tempo*, 24 September 1930. Compare Lazar, pp. 138–42.

30. *Tempo*, 24 September 1930.

31. *Der Angriff*, 27 February 1930. Although scholars and writers have often pointed to Goebbels's cynicism, this was not the case with the murder of Wessel. His recently discovered diary for this period shows his deep sorrow and concern for Wessel. Reflecting on his visit to Horst's bedside on 19 January 1930, he wrote: "I drive to the hospital and look at him for a minute. . . . he stares at me, his eyes fill with tears, and then he slurs: 'We must hold out! I am happy.' I am close to tears." On 21 February he noted: "I talk with him for a half hour and raise his spirits somewhat. He simply cannot give up the will to live. I hope that Fate keeps him with us." On the day of Wessel's death Goebbels wrote: "When I announce the news in the theater, the men start to sob. It is simply too tragic." On 28 February, he added, "I stand at the coffin of H. Wessel and make a solemn oath." See Nachlass Goebbels, NL 118/62, BA.

32. Reitmann, pp. 29–31; Ewers, pp. 257–62. For documentary films of the burial, see NSDAP/RPL, *Begräbnis Horst Wessel*, 1933, FAA 1084, LOC; NSDAP/RPL, *Jahre der Entscheidung*, 1939, FAA 1084, LOC; NSDAP/RPL, NS-Ton-Bild Bericht Nr. 2, 1933, BA. For a photograph of the funeral procession, see "Die Beisetzung des ermordeten SA-Mannes Horst Wessel in Berlin, am 1.3.1930: Der Trauerzug unter polizeilicher Bedeckung," A-B-C Nr. 9303, Horst Wessel Collection, Photographs Section, BA.

33. There is conflicting evidence regarding Hitler's curious absence from Wessel's funeral. Goebbels was livid that he did not appear, complaining that "Hitler is not coming. I explained the situation to him completely on the telephone—and he actually declined. Well then!" He also submitted: "I talked to the chief on the telephone again, who—while Wessel was being buried—was staying in Berchtesgaden, and one has to say I made the earnestness of the situation absolutely clear. Göring and Lippert are traveling tonight to Munich, to have one last talk with Hitler tomorrow. I am very skeptical about it, he will back out as always, but now I am ready for anything; I will not fight him but instead will resign. Then he can find his marionettes somewhere else." See Nachlass Goebbels, 1930/47, NL 118/62, BA. Ernst Hanfstaengel, a far less reliable witness, claimed that at a strategy session in his home on the evening of 24 February 1930—attended by, among others, Hitler, Göring, and Goebbels—it was decided that Hitler should absent himself from the funeral for reasons of personal safety. Hanfstaengl, *Zwischen Weissem und Braunem Haus*, pp. 204–05.

34. Bade, *Die SA erobert Berlin*, pp. 200–01. See also Nachlass Goebbels, 1930/47, NL 118/62, BA.

35. *Der Angriff*, 27 February 1930. In his *Angriff* article of 6 March 1930 entitled "Bis zur Neige," Goebbels referred to the taunts and yells of the communists as "wild shrieks of the subhumans." For a lively account of the funeral as experienced by a Berlin "Old Fighter," see Wilhelm Lut, "Als wir Horst Wessel die letzte Ehre erwiesen. . . . Eine Erinnerung an den Tag seiner Beerdigung," *Völkischer Beobachter*, 12 February 1934. Dr. Werner Naumann, Goebbels's protégé and later state secretary in the propaganda ministry, has described the excitement the burial of Horst Wessel caused not only in the Berlin SA but also in the provinces. For an account

of his own speech to the Görlitz SA on the evening following the burial, see the unpublished Naumann memoirs in the possession of the author, Vol. I., p. 5.

36. For a lively account of how the Wessel martyrdom inspired one youth to join the Nazi ranks, see Fred-Erich Uetrecht, *Jugend im Sturm: Ein Bericht aus den schicksalsschweren Jahren 1917–1933*, pp. 122–27.

37. For an example of the genre, see Hans Richter et al., "Erinnerung an unseren Kameraden Horst Wessel," in Bert Roth, ed., *Kampf. Lebensdokumente deutscher Jugend von 1914–1934*, pp. 234–37.

38. Lazar, pp. 154–55, 158.

39. For the Gestapo director's report, see the memoirs of Rudolf Diels, *Lucifer ante Portas*, pp. 220–23.

40. Heinrich Anacker, "Horst Wessel," in *Wir wachsen in das Reich hinein*, p. 31.

41. Baldur von Schirach, *Die Fahne der Verfolgten*, p. 33. See also "Am Grabe Horst Wessels," in Baldur von Schirach, *Vom Glaube der Gemeinschaft*, p. 6.

42. See "Horst Wessel," in Gerhard Schumann, *Schau und Tat. Gedichte*, p. 58. Compare "Horst Wessel" by Hans Flut, *Der SA Mann*, 8 October 1932, which included the stanza:

> Kamerad Wessel, wir ehren dich . . .
> Tief zur Erde die Fahnen wir senken;
> Hoch nach Walhall die Blicke wir lenken,
> Schaudernd, als wenn ein Adler entwich—-
> Kamerad Wessel, wir ehren dich!

43. Joseph Goebbels, *Vom Kaiserhof zur Reichskanzlei*, pp. 246–47, and articles headlined "Adolf Hitler am Grabe Horst Wessels auf dem Nicolai-Friedhof" and "20,000 deutschbewusste Berliner grüssen im Sportpalast die Kameraden des gefallenen Sturmführers," *Der Angriff*, 23 January 1932. For documentary film coverage of the events, see NSDAP/RPL, *Begräbnis Horst Wessel*, 1933, FAA 1084, LOC. For an excellent still photograph of Hitler in the Nikolai Cemetery on 22 January 1933, flanked by Goebbels, Graf Helldorf, Brinkner, Röhm, and von Tschammer-Osten, see Wessel Collection, A-B-C-Nr. 2306, BA.

44. Little did the true believers gathered that day realize the trouble Horst's mother had caused Hitler and Goebbels. By appearing thirty minutes late for the ceremonies, Frau Wessel—understandably saddened by the loss of not only her husband but also two sons—was beginning a series of tantrums and confrontations with the hierarchy that would end in a total break. Ultimately, she even expected royalties for the Nazis' use of the "Horst Wessel Song" and filed suit in court to this end. Goebbels wrote in his diary (23 January 1933, Nachlass Goebbels, NL 118/62, BA): "Sie ist unerträglich in ihrer Arroganz. Unsere Toten gehören der Nation."

45. "Die Feier auf dem Friedhof," *Der Montag*, 23 January 1933.

46. Domarus, p. 181. Heinrich Anacker celebrated the occasion by publishing the poem "Der Horst-Wessel-Tag," which concluded with the following lines: "Bald ist's in Berlin und ganz Deutschland so weit, Dass keiner mehr Heil Moskau' schreit! Bald holen wir aus zum letzten Schlag, Zum letzten, grossen Horst-Wessel-Tag!" Anacker, *Die Fanfare*, p. 55.

47. *Der Angriff*, 23 January 1932.

48. Joseph Goebbels, "Horst," in *Wetterleuchten. Aufsätze aus der Kampfzeit*, pp. 29–30.

49. Hermann Weiskopf (Munich), "Sinn und Opfer der Mütterlichkeit: Den Müttern unserer S.A.-Männer in Verehrung zum Muttertag 1930," *Der SA Mann*, 10 May 1930. Compare J. Frenck's article on heroism, *Der SA Mann*, 19 November 1932, which concluded with the following admonition: "Lasst uns treu sein, wie sie waren, treu bis in den Tod!" J. Berchtold's article, in *Der SA Mann*, 10 August 1932,

headlined "Mörder und Pharisäer: 14 Jahre Rotmord–14 Jahre ohne Schutz; 430 Tote und über 46,000 Verwundete SA Männer," was a model of the genre.

50. Heinrich Anacker, *Die Trommel. SA Gedichte*, p. 30.

51. Und solang du dies nicht hast,
Dieses Stirb und Werde,
Bist du nur ein trüber Gast
Hier auf dieser Erde.
—Goethe

Josef Magnus Wehner, "Stirb und werde," *Illustrierte Beobachter*, 30 September 1933.

52. *Der SA Mann*, 3 May 1930. One *Totensonntag* issue of *Der Angriff*, 9 November 1932, carried a full page of photographs of funerals and gravesites of many of the Nazi heroic dead. For other examples of the genre, see Thor Goote, *Kam'raden, die Rotfront und Reaktion erschossen*. The cover of the book featured a photograph of Hitler placing flowers on a row of graves, and another photograph showed the corpse of Hans Maikowski.

53. Nachlass Goebbels, 8 June 1931, NL 118/62, BA.

54. *Sturm 33: Hans Maikowski*, "Geschrieben von Kameraden des Toten," pp. 51–54; J. K. von Engelbrechten and Hans Volz, *Wir wandern durch das nationalsozialistische Berlin. Ein Führer durch die Gedenkstätten des Kampfes um die Reichshauptstadt*, pp. 113, 181. Maikowski once wrote to Standartenführer Werner Hahn: "Ich glaube kaum, dass wir uns wiedersehen werden, denn ich habe nicht mehr lange zu leben. Ich will froh sein, wenn ich 30 Jahre alt werde, denn älter werde ich bestimmt nicht; und ich will noch froher sein, wenn ich das Dritte Reich noch erleben könnte, denn ich weiss, dass ich verhasst bin wie selten jemand. Bis jetzt scheint noch keine Kugel für mich gegossen zu sein, doch eines Tages hats auch mich. Am liebsten würde ich dann für meinen Führer vor meinem alten Sturm 33 sterben." *Sturm 33: Hans Maikowski*, p. 57.

55. Und ruft uns Walvater, ist Fall uns beschert,
Bieten wir freudig die Brust dar dem Schwert.
Hemmen nicht hellroten Herzblutes Lauf,
Schweben gleich Adlern nach Walhall hinaus.

Engelbrechten and Volz, p. 58.

56. Facsimile in *Sturm 33: Hans Maikowski*, p. 35.

57. Ibid., pp. 32–34.

58. Engelbrechten and Volz, p. 116.

59. The following account is based on records of the trial (October 1933–January 1934) of fifty communists or communist sympathizers involved in the melee on the Wallstrasse in Charlottenburg on the night of 30 January 1933. See Schwurgericht I beim Landgericht, Urteil (500) 1. pol. b K.10.33 (53.33), File 30 (Zauritz), GStALgB, LAB.

60. Ibid.

61. Ibid. For a communist version of the murder, written by a witness, see the remarkable memoirs of Jan Petersen, *Unsere Strasse: Eine Chronik Geschrieben im Herzen des faschistischen Deutschlands 1933/34*, pp. 39–41.

62. *Sturm 33: Hans Maikowski*, pp. 72–73. Compare Walter Röling, "Hans Maikowski," in Bert Roth, ed., *Kampf. Lebensdokumente deutscher Jugend von 1914–1934*, pp. 263–66. When the news of Maikowski's death reached the Tietz pub, there was general satisfaction with the turn of events. One communist said mockingly, "Jetzt brauchen wir nur noch dem langen Hahn die Federn auszurupfen." He was referring to the former Sturmführer of Storm 33, who had received a higher command in the SA. The KPD held both Maikowski and Hahn responsible for the

murder and mayhem in Charlottenburg. See Schwurgericht I beim Landgericht, Urteil (500) 1. pol. b K.10.33 (53.33), File 30 (Zauritz), GStALgB, LAB.

63. *Der Angriff*, 31 January 1933.

64. See *Völkischer Beobachter*, 7 February 1933, headlined "Deutschlands Trauermarsch für unsere Toten! Das Staatsbegräbnis für Hans Maikowski und den Polizeiwachtmeister Josef Zauritz" and "Im strömenden Regen zum Invalidenfriedhof; Zehntausende im Zuge." See also *Der Angriff*, 6 February 1933.

65. See photographs of "Das Staatsbegräbnis für die Opfer des 30. Januar," Bilder Sammlung Maikowski, 472, 485, BayHStA. Compare the photograph with the caption "Die Nation trägt die Toten des 30. Januar zu Grabe," in Wilfred Bade, ed., *Deutschland erwacht*, p. 80.

66. Helmut Heiber, ed., *Goebbels Reden: 1932–1939*, vol. I, pp. 64–66. For broad illustrated coverage of the funeral, see *Illustrierter Beobachter*, 11, 18 February 1933, and Maikowski File, Slg. Personen 5682, Sammlung Rehse, BayHStA. Compare "Hans Eberhard Maikowski: Zum bevorstehenden Jahrestag seiner Ermordung," *Berliner Illustrierte*, 28 January 1934. Maikowski, like Wessel, was glorified in many works of poetry. For one example, see Hans-Jürgen Nierentz, "Sturmführer Maikowski," in Herbert Böhme, *Rufe in das Reich*, p. 278.

67. Daluege to Diels, "zu sofortigen Veranlassung," 12 May 1933, 2142, Maikowski File, BDC.

68. Illegible, Berlin, 18 February 1943, "Betrifft: Ermordung Maikowski-Zauritz," "Herrn Generaloberst Daluege vorgelegt." The suggestion that the file be destroyed was initialed "Ja" by Daluege. Hans Maikowski File, BDC.

69. Engelbrechten and Volz, p. 58.

70. See Schwurgericht I beim Landgericht, Urteil (500) 1.pol. b K.10.33 (53.33), File 30 (Zauritz), GStALgB, LAB.

71. Petersen, p. 128. Petersen's remarkable work, written in his Charlottenburg apartment when he was a member of the communist underground movement, was smuggled out of Nazi Germany and was first published in 1936 in Bern and Moscow. For a photograph of the memorial on the Wallstrasse, see Bilder Sammlung Maikowski, 85/52/15, BA. For an insider's story of the anarchy in the Berlin SA in 1933, as well as its reign of terror against the communists, see the account by the first director of the Gestapo, Rudolf Diels, in *Lucifer ante Portas*, pp. 152–58.

72. Petersen, pp. 280–81.

73. Engelbrechten and Volz, p. 177.

74. Ibid., pp. 174–75. Alfred Buske had acted bravely at the side of Hans Maikowski in a fracas outside the Ahlerts Festsäle on the Bismarckstrasse on the night of 9 December 1931 (*Der Weg zum Nationalsozialismus*, pp. 258–61). On this occasion, allegedly a horde of communists were beating "Karl D" to death, when Maikowski and Buske came upon the pack. In the ensuing melee, Maikowski shot three of the communists, one of whom died. The police held Buske and two other SA men responsible for the crime and incarcerated them at the storied "Alex" Prison. From his hiding place—Maikowski had fled Berlin when the wanted posters appeared bearing his name—Hans wrote a full description of the incident to the state prosecutor's office, taking full responsibility for the shooting. As a result, Buske and the others were freed. The "Karl D" mentioned points to Karl Deh, who later testified to the Gestapo that Buske had murdered Maikowski.

75. Engelbrechten and Volz, p. 178. Strangely, Buske's name slipped past the censors when the historical retrospective *Wir wandern durch das nationalsozialistische Berlin* was published by SA Obersturmbannführer J. K. von Engelbrechten and SA Sturmführer Hans Volz in 1937. There Buske was chronicled as having "died on 18 January 1934 as a result of wounds incurred during the 'Kampfzeit.'"

76. Petersen, pp. 238–47. For an excellent photograph of the ceremony, see

Bilder Sammlung Maikowski, 85/52/16, BA; see also the photograph "Gedenkstelle Hans Maikowski," 30 January 1935, Bilder Sammlung Maikowski, 85/52/15, BA.

77. "Über Gräber vorwärts; Nächtliche Weihestunde für Hans Eberhard Maikowski und Joseph Zauritz," *Völkischer Beobachter*, 1 February 1935.

78. "Weihe einer Gedenkstätte für Hans Eberhard Maikowski," *Völkischer Beobachter*, 31 January 1937.

79. Wessel's name was changed to Hans Westmar because Goebbels endeavored to glorify the entire movement. Credits are production, Volksdeutsche Film FmbH; premiere, Capitol Theater, Berlin, 13 December 1933; music and assistance in direction, Ernst Hanfstaengl and Giuseppe Becce; featuring units of the SA Berlin-Brandenburg, Standarte 4, Standarte 5 (Horst Wessel), Standarte 6, Landespolizei-Gruppe Wecke, Kösener SC; featuring Emil Lohkamp, Carla Bartheel, Grete Reinwald, Arthur Schröder, Paul Wegener, Carl Auen, Heinrich Heilinger, Otti Dietze, Gertrud de Lalsky, Irmgard Willers, Wilhelm Diegelmann, Richard Fiedler, Heinz Salfner, Robert Thiem, and Hugo Gau-Hamm.

80. Ewers joined the NSDAP on 1 November 1931 but was seen as an opportunist by the Nazis. Very early on, his bizarre and sometimes perverted behavior embarrassed members of the party, who protested about him to the highest authorities. Walter Buch, head of the USCHLA (the feared intraparty disciplinary commission in Munich), complained bitterly that Ewers's novel *Reiter in deutscher Nacht* was a criminal disservice to the heroic men of the Free Corps. See Buch, undated and unaddressed letter on Reichstag stationery, Hanns Heinz Ewers File, NSDAP/HA, BDC. On another occasion, the Ortsgruppenleiter of Bad Eilsen, Wilhelm Tünnermann, complained about the bizarre activities of Ewers, who was residing in Der Fürstenhof in that spa town. Not only did Ewers feed worms to children at a party he hosted, but his bloviated sputterings also embarrassed all true Germans. See Wilhelm Trümmermann to Reichsleitung der NSDAP, Munich, 6 June 1932, ibid. Walter Buch's acid response (USchlA R.L./I. Kammer, Der Vorsitzende, 13 June 1932, ibid.) warned the official to take no action for the duration and noted: "The time to treat such people and their shoddy and destructive works with the measures they deserve has not yet arrived. We have waited 13 long years and do not want to make our work any more difficult by lunging too soon just as we are nearing victory."

81. See Hanns Heinz Ewers, "Anlage I zu meinem Schreiben vom 20. April 1940," Ewers File, NSDAP/HA, BDC.

82. Ewers, undated letter of 1942, listing his grievances to the Reichsschriftumskammer, ibid. Ewers died in 1943, a broken man.

83. In his lenghty memorandum banning all of Ewers's works, the censor Karl Karsch noted that "der Verfasser eine Neigung und Veranlassung zu Widernatürlichkeiten hat. Dass er seine Grundeinstellung nicht geändert hat, dass er die neue Zeit und ihren Geist nicht begriffen hat, beweist er dadurch, dass er noch heute zu seinem Werke steht." Abs Lektor, S8170/12.6.41–534 1/1, Ewers File, NSDAP/HA, BDC.

84. *Der Angriff*, 27 May 1933. The Schalmeienkapelle of Standarte 5 played at the meeting.

85. Lazar, pp. 177–90.

86. For details on the trial, see *Neue Züricher Zeitung*, 16 June 1934, as well as the Wessel File, BDC, and Lazar, pp. 177–90.

87. See Goebbels's speech, 9 October 1933, "Berlin-Friedrichshain, Hof des Horst Wessel Krankenhauses—Einweihung des Sterbezimmers von Horst Wessel," *Goebbels Reden*, vol. I, pp. 128–30. There are several extant photographs featuring these shrines. The facade of the Wessel boys' birthplace on the Jüdinstrasse in Berlin carried the following message: "In this house Horst and Werner Wessel became

fighters for Germany's honor and freedom." Horst Wessel File, Slg. Personen 3303, Sammlung Rehse, BayHStA. Photographs of the room in which Wessel was shot have the following captions: "The fifth anniversary of the death of the German freedom fighter, Storm Führer Horst Wessel. The room on the Grosse Frankfurter Street in which Horst Wessel was murdered! View of the sofa, decorated with flowers and swastika, on which Horst Wessel collapsed in blood after the deadly shots were fired." See A-B-C-Nr. 16654, 4365A, 4366A, Bilder Sammlung Horst Wessel, BA. See also "The room where Horst Wessel died in Horst Wessel Hospital in Berlin. View of the room in which the National Socialist freedom fighter Horst Wessel died. To the left, the bust of the deceased." A-B-C-Nr. 15082, Bilder Sammlung Horst Wessel, BA. See also "Goebbels spricht am Neugestaltung des Horst Wessel–Platzes in Berlin, März 1934," A-B-C Nr. 1928, Bilder Sammlung Horst Wessel, BA.

88. See "Feierstunden der Berliner SA. am Todestage Horst Wessels," Berlin, 23 February 1936, Horst Wessel File, Slg. Personen 3303, Sammlung Rehse, BayHStA.

89. See "Sturmkamerad Horst Wessel—dein Geist lebt! Appell der Berliner SA vor Gauleiter Dr. Goebbels am 30. Geburtstag des ermordeten Sturmführers," *Völkischer Beobachter*, 11 October 1937. Compare the memorial ceremony in Munich, 24 February 1935, "Kranzniederlegung an der Feldherrnhalle im Gedenken an das Heldentum Horst Wessels," Horst Wessel File, Slg. Personen 3303, Sammlung Rehse, BayHStA. The Nazis even propagandized Wessel abroad. See "Horst Wessel Feier in Stockholm; Schwedischer Dank an den Nationalsozialismus," *Völkischer Beobachter*, 4 March 1934.

90. For an excellent example of the genre, see *Die Jungenschaft. Blätter für Heimabendgestaltung im Deutschen Jungvolk*, Berlin, 25 January 1939, Folge 8.

91. See "Programmfolge; Horst Wessel Gedenkfeier am 22. Febr. 38 im Dietrich Eckart Heim, Kanalstrasse 30; Ausführung: Münchener Jungvolk in Verbindung mit der Volksbildungsstätte München," Horst Wessel File, Slg. Personen 3303, Sammlung Rehse, BayHStA.

92. For a photograph of the Hinckeldey sculpture, see *Hamburger Illustrierte*, 11 October 1937.

93. *Münchener Neusteste Nachrichten*, 18 May 1935.

94. "Unvergessliche Stunde am Horst Wessel Denkmal," Bielefeld, *Völkischer Beobachter*, 25 February 1936. Wessel monuments turned up far and wide throughout the Reich. See "Horst Wessel Denkmal in Hindenburg: Weihe in Gegenwart von ca. 80,000 Personen," *Münchener Neueste Nachrichten*, 21 August 1933, and "Weihe eines Horst Wessel Steins," Bad Elgersburg, *Völkischer Beobachter*, 14 September 1934.

95. Lazar, p. 190.

96. "Das Beispiel: Horst-Wessel-Gedenkfeier der SA. im Rundfunk," *Völkischer Beobachter*, 24 February 1941.

97. Walter Lutze, "Horst Wessel: Das Vermächtnis unseres Sturmführers—zu seinem 10. Todestag," *Völkischer Beobachter*, 23 February 1940, and Lieutenant Hans Zöberlein, "Zum 10. Todestag Horst Wessels," ibid. Also Wessel's old crony in Storm 5, Richard Fiedler, who became SA Brigadeführer in Halle, published a retrospective on his friend and fellow warrior. See *Mitteldeutsche National Zeitung*, 23 February 1939, entitled "Horst Wessel—ewiges Vorbild; Inbegriff des nationalsozialistischen Kämpfers und politischen Soldaten." Compare "Horst-Wessel-Gedenken in München. Feierstunde der Obersten SA. Führung und der Gruppe Hochland," *Völkischer Beobachter*, 24 February 1939.

98. Goebbels to all Reichsleiter, Gauleiter, Kanzlei Rosenberg, 17 October 1939, "Betrifft: Horst Wessel Gedenkfeiern," T-454, Roll 74, 502.

99. See "Kranz des Führers am Grabe Horst Wessel," *Völkischer Beobachter*, 24/

25 February 1940. The tenth anniversary of Wessel's death began with a morning ceremony featuring SA Chief of Staff Viktor Lutze and SA Gruppenführer Prince August Wilhelm. For an example of what Goebbels expected in proper Horst Wessel ceremonials, see SA der NSDAP, Standarte 98, Metz, 7 February 1942, "Betrifft: Horst Wessel Feier," NSDAP, T-81, Roll 92, 106376, NA. Instructions submitted by the party for proper content of a Wessel memorial in 1941 included not only appropriate musical selections played by band or orchestra but also readings from works by Hitler, Wessel, von Schirach, Hanns Flut, Hans Baumann, and Herybert Menzel. Often there were readings from Goebbels's account of his hours spent at the bedside of the dying Horst. See "11. Jahrestag des Todes Horst Wessels," NSDAP, T-81, Roll 92, 106286, NA.

100. See Otto Paust File, NSDAP/HA, BDC, and H. Mersdorf, "Otto Paust, der Dichter der Deutschen Trilogie," *Völkischer Beobachter*, 24 February 1938.

101. See "Heute wie damals: Krieg gegen Moskau! Hans Eberhard Maikowski— Soldat seines Glaubens," *Der Angriff*, 30 January 1943.

V. THE DEATH AND TRANSFIGURATION OF HITLER YOUTH HERBERT NORKUS

1. The smoke of battle is gone . . . the war is over . . .
   with hair grayed by mourning
   we—carried—*Norkus* out to the hill
   still but a child—of sixteen years!
   His dream was the longing, to deliver his homeland,
   from its hellish nightmare . . .
   Then—he—was—bestially—killed
   by wicked murdering hands.

   You German boy! You brave child!
   You died . . . because you spread the word . . .
   The flags, for which you died
   wave in the wind at your grave . . .
   You died like a German hero in raging
   battle,
   aflame with the spirit of freedom!
   And when the German night is long
   forgotten—
   we will never forget you!

Gerhard Mondt, *Herbert Norkus. Das Tagebuch der Kameradschaft Beusselkietz*, pp. 9–10.

2. See Decker, pp. 145–46, 150–51; Weberstedt et al., pp. 134–35; *Herbert Norkus, der Hitlerjunge. Der Weg zum Nationalsozialismus*, pp. 262–64. For an excellent analysis of the violence in Berlin neighborhoods, see Rosenhaft, pp. 128–66.

3. See "Baldur von Schirach" in Joachim C. Fest, *The Face of the Third Reich*, pp. 229–31; Michael H. Kater, "Bürgerliche Jugendbewegung und Hitlerjugend in Deutschland von 1926 bis 1939," pp. 151–52; George L. Mosse, *Nazi Culture*, p. 266.

4. Von Schirach, quoted in Arnold Littmann, *Herbert Norkus und die Hitlerjungen vom Beusselkietz*, p. 6.

5. See Alfred Bauer, *Deutscher Spielfilm Almanach 1929–1950*, p. 191. For a discussion of the film, see Gerd Albrecht, *Arbeitsmaterialien zum nationalsozialistischen Propagandafilm*, pp. 1–40; Manfred Dammeyer, ed., *Der Spielfilm im Dritten Reich*, pp. 34, 51–62, 165–68; Erwin Leiser, *Nazi Cinema*, pp. 34–39; David Stewart Hull, *Film in the Third Reich*, pp. 21, 25, 32–34, 222.

6. Ludwig Norkus offered this testimony to reporters shortly after the murder. *Der Angriff*, 26 January 1932. See also Rudolf Ramlow, *Herbert Norkus?—Hier!* pp. 46–52. Compare Littmann, pp. 9–15.

7. *Zeitprobleme: Wie der Arbeiter wohnt*, produced by the communist controlled Weltfilm Kartell, 1930, Mag. Nr. 394, BA.

8. Ibid.

9. *Mutter Krausens Fahrt ins Glück* (Prometheus, 1929). See Helmut Korte, *Film und Realität in der Weimarer Republik*, pp. 103–68.

10. Baldur von Schirach, May Day address, 1934, NSDAP/HA, Roll 18, Folder 366. See Peter D. Stachura, *Nazi Youth in the Weimar Republic*, pp. 43–70, and, by the same author, "The Ideology of the Hitler Youth in the Kampfzeit," *Journal of Contemporary History*, 7 (July 1973), pp. 155–67.

11. Ramlow, pp. 55–59; Littmann, pp. 77–81.

12. Littmann, pp. 72–73.

13. Littmann, pp. 49–52, 81–82; Ramlow, pp. 52–54.

14. For a reproduction of the flyer, see Mondt, p. 19.

15. Ibid., p. 45.

16. Reichsführer HJ Kurt Gruber, "Verfügung Nr. 2: Die Septemberaktion," *Kommandobrücke*, 20 July 1931, NSDAP/HA, Roll 18, Folder 342.

17. Littmann, p. 112.

18. There is extensive documentation regarding the death of Norkus and the trial of the perpetrators located in the files of the Generalstaatsanwaltschaft bei dem Landgericht Berlin, Rep. 58, Ordner 9 (Herbert Norkus), LAB.

19. According to the Berlin police, Stennes's connections to the KPD were through "Dr. Kempe, Baroness von Bischoffshausen, and a certain Wetzel-Lichtenberg born in Engelwood, New Jersey, in 1906." See "Staatsanwaltschaft bei dem Landgericht Berlin: gegen Simon und Genossen, Anlage zum Protokoll vom 9.7.1932 (Dok. 147)," GStALgB, LAB.

20. Ibid; Kriminalpolizei, Kommissariat, Polizei Revier 22, Abt. I AD II, Berlin, 29 January 1932, GStALgB, LAB.

21. Kriminalpolizei, Kommissariat, Revier 22, Abt. IADII, Berlin, 29 January 1932, GStALgB, LAB. Kuhlmann admitted to the police that he provoked the murder. He countered those who advised against it, saying "you assholes. You blowpipes! Who spared us then, when they cracked our skulls open and stuck a knife in the heart of my comrade! No, I said to the Reds, 'finish him off.' " On the morning of the murder, Kuhlmann had departed on an outing to the country with the "Wanderer and Jujitsu Club," a Stennes cover organization. Kuhlmann told the police that he had been a volunteer with the Free Corps of Captain Pfeffer von Salomon in 1922. According to Kuhlmann, Lichtenberg severely reprimanded him the day after the murder, saying, "Na, siehst du, was du fürn Quatsch gemacht hast!" See Kriminalpolizei, Kommissariat, Polizei Revier 22, Berlin, Dok. 159, Johannes Kuhlmann (b. 1905), 18 February 1932, GStALgB, LAB.

22. See Kriminalpolizei, Kommissariat, Polizei Revier 22, Berlin, I AD II, 29 January 1932, GStALgB, LAB. At his police hearing on 27 January 1932, Georg Stolt offered the alibi that he was asleep at the Marx Gaststätte when the crime occurred. He said that he had played billiards until very late and was too drunk to venture out into the winter night. He allegedly woke up at 8:00 A.M., whereupon he helped Herr Marx clean the tavern. See ibid., 27 January 1932, Georg Walter Stolt, "verhandelt."

23. Report by Berg., Krim. Ass., Kriminal Kommission, Abt. II Ad II, Polizei Revier 22, Berlin, 26 January 1932, GStALgB, LAB.

24. Mondt, pp. 58–59.

25. Ibid., pp. 60–67. See Kriminalpolizei, Polizei am K.J. Ch/Tg, Kommissariat,

4. Bezirk, Polizei Revier 22, Nr. 231, Betrifft: Norkus, Spursicherung, 24.1.32, testimony of Otto Kretschmann, Gerhard Mondt, Willy Moebius, Albert Passin, Georg Bauschuss, Rep. 58, Ordner 9, GStALgB, LAB.

26. Kriminalpolizei, Kommissariat, Polizei Revier 22, Abt. II AD II, Berlin, 27 January 1932, testimony of Johannes Kirsch, 24 January 1932, Rep. 58, Ordner 9, GStALgB, LAB. Kirsch said that he heard screams and scuffling and was able to give the police a description of some of the pursuers.

27. Kriminalpolizei, Kommissariat, Polizei Revier 22, Abt. II AD II, Berlin, 27 January 1932, verhandelt, Plätterin Marie Jobs, Rep. 58, Ordner 9, GStALgB, LAB.

28. On the morning of 24 January the police carried out an inspection at the scene of the crime. They found a trail of blood leading to Zwinglistrasse 4 and considerable blood in the vestibule at that address. See police report of 24 January 1932, ibid. According to the coroner's report, Norkus had been stabbed six times. See report of Laborant Fröminrehen, 26 January 1932, ibid.

29. See Haftbefehl v. Noel, Amtsgerichtsrat, Berlin Mitte, Abt. 128, 6 February 1932, 128.G.32, GStALgB, LAB. For a reproduction of the wanted poster, see Herbert Norkus File, Slg. Personen 1132, Sammlung Rehse, BayHStA. Kriminal-Polizeirat Reinhold Heller of the Berlin police was responsible for the case. See Hsi-Huey Liang, *The Berlin Police Force in the Weimar Republic*, pp. 140–41.

30. See Generalstaatsanwaltschaft bei dem Landgericht, "Urteil gegen Simon und Genossen," 29 July 1932, Rep. 58, Ordner 9, GStALgB, LAB. Stolt, Kuhlmann, and Seeburg received sentences of three years imprisonment; Gundel, one year. Lichtenberg, Scheweit, and Klose received no sentences. Simon, Klingbeil, and Tack succeeded in escaping to the Soviet Union with the help of the Rote Hilfe organization.

31. *Der Angriff*, 26 January 1932. Goebbels visited the murder sight twice immediately after the death of Norkus. He was appalled that the bloodied handprints of the victim were clearly visible on the wall of the vestibule of Zwinglistrasse 4. As if to encourage himself, Goebbels confided to his diary on 24 January 1932: "Just don't lose your nerves! Don't do anything foolish! Wait for the day of revenge! Work, make propaganda, conserve your powers, and don't become discouraged!" See Joseph Goebbels, *Vom Kaiserhof zur Reichskanzlei*, p. 31.

32. *Der Angriff*, 28/30 January 1932. See also *Völkischer Beobachter*, 31 January 1932, headlined "Abschied von Herbert Norkus; Die letzte Fahrt des Hitlerjungen."

33. Goebbels, *Vom Kaiserhof zur Reichskanzlei*, p. 34.

34. Schaumburg-Lippe, pp. 65–66.

35. *Die Welt am Abend*, 25 January 1932.

36. *Der junge Sturmtrupp*, 2, 3 (1. Februar Ausgabe, 1932). Most of the issue was devoted to the Norkus propaganda. Charges that Jewish "subhumans" were behind the murder was a central theme. Hitler Youth members were livid that the communist press had the audacity to blame the death of Norkus on poor parental and school training, thus faulting the victim for the crime, not the murderers. According to the "Jewish-run" *Tempo*, "His educators would have better met their obligations, if this little Party member who was stabbed to death was not a martyr to their so-called principles of education, but instead had remained a living, if perhaps stupid boy." See "Die Juden und der Mord," ibid.

37. Edgar Bissinger in *Der junge Sturmtrupp*, 2, 4 (2. Februar Ausgabe 1932).

38. Domarus, vol. I, pp. 141–42. The enthusiastic group leader Gerdt Mondt wrote of the excitement he felt when meeting Hitler and receiving the medal for "Tapferkeit und Treue" from him: "Das war mein grösster Tag im Leben. . . . Ich habe dem Führer in die Augen geblickt, viel darin gelesen und halte ihm die Treue!" Mondt, pp. 87–88.

39. See von Schirach's message to the Hitler Youth celebrating the group's brav-

ery in *Verordnungsblatt der Reichsjugendführung,* Munich, 22 January 1933, NSDAP/ HA, Roll 18, Folder 337. For the use of the Norkus anniversary in Hitler Youth ceremonials, see Vondung, p. 60.

40. See the photograph with caption "Die Gedenktafel am Mordhause Zwing- listrasse 4 nach der Enthüllung am 26.7.33, davor drei Kameraden mit der Herbert Norkus Fahne," Ramlow, p. 1. On anniversaries, this sacred spot was decorated with flowers and palms, while two Hitler Youth members stood honor guard. See the photograph with caption "Eine Ehrenwache der Hitlerjugend an der Mord- stelle," *Völkischer Beobachter,* 26 January 1935. The Hitler Youth often staged an- niversary marches past this historic place. See "Herbert Norkus zum Gedächtnis," Hitler Youth march, 24 January 1936, Herbert Norkus File, Scherl Bilderdienst, 85/52/22, BA. On 24 January 1935, in the great refectory of the Marienburg, the castle of the Teutonic Knights in East Prussia, Stabsführer Hartmann Lauterbacher blessed the flags of the combined *Jungvolk* with the "Herbert Norkus Fahne." He concluded with the following words: "His eternal spirit bless our flags!" See "Fahn- enweihe auf der Marienburg," *Die Jungenschaft. Blätter für Heimabendgestaltung im Deutschen Jungvolk,* 8 (20 April 1938).

41. See "Die HJ. ehrt Herbert Norkus; Grabsteinenthüllung auf dem Friedhof; Marsch der deutschen Jugend Berlins durch Moabit und den Wedding," *Der Angriff,* 27 February 1933.

42. During the Third Reich, Norkus was the subject of veneration for the Hitler Youth on every anniversary of his death, and there were annual observances in many schools as well. See Rektor Albert Krebs, ed., *Wir Jungen tragen die Fahne. Nationalsozialistische Morgenfeiern der Adolf Hitler Volksschule Stettin,* pp. 31–35. See "Mahnmal für Herbert Norkus: Mit der Hitler-Jugend in Grimma—5000 beim Aufmarsch des Bannes 179," *Leipziger Tageszeitung,* 23 April 1934, and "Essener Jugend ehrt den Hitlerjungen Herbert Norkus; Erhebende Kundgebung auf der Margaretenhöhe," *National Zeitung,* Essen, 25 January 1934. Compare "Norkus- Gedenkfeier am Beusselkietz: Prinz August Wilhelm beim Bahn 201," *Der Angriff,* 25 January 1934, and Günther Röhrdanz, "Opfertod für Deutschland: Herbert Norkus von kommunistischen Mordbuben gemeuchelt am 24. January 1932 in Berlin," *Völkischer Beobachter,* 21 January 1934.

43. Baldur von Schirach, *Revolution der Erziehung,* pp. 18–25. The Norkus grave was often the rendezvous for events of special significance. For example, the Berlin Hitler Youth began their march to the Nuremberg *Parteitag* in 1935 after meeting at the grave of Norkus.

44. Domarus, vol. I, p. 137.

45. Karl Aloys Schenzinger, *Der Hitlerjunge Quex,* was written between May and September 1932 and was published in December of the same year. In 1934 Schen- zinger published another novel in the heroic youth genre entitled *Der Herrgottsbacher Schülermarsch.*

46. This has long been a theme in Teutonic culture. The German historian Gerhard Reinhard Ritter (not to be confused with the Freiburg historian Gerhard Ritter) wrote in 1936 that "the nature of the German is not without reason also a symbol of eternal growth. It is represented most beautifully and significantly in the type of the German youth. Why otherwise would so many great masters of our history have been able to choose as the incarnation of the German people a youth as symbol—Siegfried, Parsifal, Horst Wessel! All of these representations involve the Faustian thought of the eternal seeker in a significant way." See Gerhard Ritter, *Die geschlechtliche Frage in der deutschen Volkserziehung,* p. 207.

47. Schenzinger, *Der Hitlerjunge Quex,* p. 164.

48. Ibid., pp. 60–61.

49. Georg Walther Heyer, *Die Fahne ist mehr als der Tod. "Lieder der Nazizeit,"* pp. 22–23.

50. Schenzinger, *Der Hitlerjunge Quex,* pp. 254–56.

51. For an example of what Goebbels expected from the film industry, see his speeches of 28 March and 19 May 1933 in Gerd Albrecht, *Nationalsozialistische Filmpolitik,* pp. 439–47. David Welch offers an illuminating commentary on *Hitler Youth Quex* in *Propaganda and the German Cinema, 1933–1945,* pp. 59–74.

52. Both von Schirach and the ardent Nazi director Karl Ritter did not want the boys of the Hitler Youth to be confused with actors. As a result, the young man who played Quex, Jürgen Ohlsen, culled from the ranks of the corps, did not receive credits in the billing of the film. See "Wie der Hitlerjunge Quex gefunden wurde," *Die Filmwoche* 37 (13 September 1933).

53. Schirach made no secret of his mystical concept of nationalist aesthetics, which was grounded in racism and the exaltation of the spirit of eternal youth. See Baldur von Schirach, *Die Hitler-Jugend,* pp. 18–19.

54. Thomas Arnold et al., *Hitlerjunge Quex. Einstellungsprotokoll,* pp. 99–101.

55. Ibid., pp. 169–75; Leiser, pp. 36–38.

56. Arnold et al., pp. 208–37. See also the notes of Friedrich P. Kahlenberg, *Ausstellung zur Filmreihe "Jugend im NS Staat,"* pp. 8–12, and Pierre Cadars et al., *Le Cinema Nazi,* pp. 34–41.

57. See "Platzeinteilung der Ehrengäste im Einvernehmen mit der Reichsjugendführung Berlin für Welturaufführung 'Hitlerjunge Quex,' " File *Hitlerjunge Quex,* Deutsches Institut für Filmkunde, Wiesbaden-Biebrich.

58. Oskar Kalbus, *Der Tonfilm,* pp. 121–23.

59. *Kinematograph,* 176, 12 September 1933. The Berlin premiere followed the Munich world premiere on 19 September 1933. Walter Redmann, film critic of the *Berliner Morgenpost,* offered a graphic description of Jürgen Ohlsen in the role of Quex (20 September 1933): "This boy is simply fascinating, especially when one realizes that he is not an actor but simply a boy playing himself with a freshness and spirit that is natural and reflects his idealism. He is the incarnation of the idealism of many thousands of German boys today." See also the very favorable review in *Illustrierte Film-Post,* 9 (20 September 1933).

60. *Kinematograph* 176 (12 September 1933).

61. Goebbels, address to "Fachschaft Film," Kroll Opera, 9 February 1934. *Kinematograph* (13 February 1934), cited in Gert Albrecht, *Film im Dritten Reich: Eine Dokumentation,* pp. 207–08. On the subject of myth and Nazi film, see Robert F. Herzstein, "Goebbels et le Mythe Historique par le Film," in *Revue d'Histoire de la Deuxième Guerre Mondiale* 101 (January 1976), pp. 41–62.

62. Kalbus, p. 123.

63. The Abteilung Film of the Reichspropagandaleitung der NSDAP was very efficient in turning out audiences for its film programs. In 1935 alone, for example, it sponsored 48,615 film assemblies for school children totaling 10,234,815 viewers, as well as 72,730 showings for 11,532,969 adults. Reaching some 21,767,784 people in one year must have set a record in film propaganda annals. Curt Belling, *Der Film in Staat und Partei,* pp. 74–75.

64. Curt Belling et al., *Der Film in der Hitler-Jugend,* p. 69.

65. Dammeyer, p. 52. See also "Educational Film Propaganda and the Nazi Youth" in David Welch, *Nazi Propaganda,* pp. 65–87.

66. Hans Baumann, *Der helle Tag,* pp. 47–48. The attention given the Norkus theme in poetry was notable. Rainer Schlösser, later named by Goebbels as *Reichsdramaturg* to oversee theater in the Third Reich, showed that even seasoned veterans of the Great War could be profoundly moved by the Norkus tragedy. His poem "Mannestränen" (Mondt, p. 17) ended with the following words:

Dir, den erdolcht sie uns zurückgebracht,
Der mehr durchlitt als je wir in der Schlacht.
Dir, kleiner Knabe, dem, als er erbleicht,
Kein Kamerad die Abschiedshand gereicht.
Dir, Herbert Norkus. . . . Weh, das Wort versagt!
So sei beweint und tausendmal beklagt.

Baldur von Schirach's poem "Herbert Norkus" (*Die Fahne der Verfolgten,* p. 8) was essentially a mystical prayer to the soul of the young hero. Its references to the martyr's "death wound" affirm that the blood he shed was redemptive:

O bleib mit mir, Geläuterter, im Bunde
und quäle mich, dass ich nichts andres weiss,
als deine Grösse bis zum tiefsten Grunde
in Not und Kampf und mit der Todeswunde.
Und was ich tue, sei auf Dein Geheiss . . .

67. *Die Jungenschaft* 7 (11 January 1939).
68. See "Dem Gedächtnis: Herbert Norkus (26.7.1916–24.1.1932)," *Die neue Gemeinschaft. Das Parteiarchiv für N.S. Feier und Freizeitgestaltung,* 8 (January 1942).
69. *Völkischer Beobachter,* 9 November 1935.
70. Hitler address, Bürgerbräukeller, Munich, 8 November 1934, Domarus, vol. I, p. 458.
71. Der Reichsminister der Justiz Thierack to Leiter der Partei-Kanzlei, Reichsleiter Bormann, 25 March 1943, "Betrifft: Todesurteil des Sondergerichts Berlin gegen Harry Tack (Mord an den Hitlerjungen Herbert Norkus)," Anlagen: 1 Urteilsabschrift, 1 Gesuch, NSDAP/HA, Roll 41, Folder 810.
72. Gesuch: Harry Tack, Untersuchungs-Gefängnis Moabit, Gef. 1754/39 Abt. C II Zelle 184, to Adolf Hitler, ibid.
73. Martin Bormann to Dr. Thierack, 31 March 1943, "Betrifft: Todesurteil des Sondergerichts Berlin gegen Harry Tack, Ihr Schreiben vom 23. März 1943—IV g.5 1/43," ibid.

VI. GERHARD SCHUMANN: ELITIST POET OF THE VOLK COMMUNITY

1. And bowing in sworn commitment
   We knelt down, with eyes transfixed and hearts aflame.
   And shimmering above us the cathedral, the Reich.

Gerhard Schumann, "Die Lieder vom Reich" (1930), in *Die Lieder vom Reich,* p. 15.
2. This chapter is based on study of most of Gerhard Schumann's extant writings, including his memoirs entitled *Besinnung. Von Kunst und Leben.* The author granted me an interview in his home at Bodman on Lake Constance on 19 May 1985. The Berlin Document Center has extensive material on Schumann, including autobiographical reports on his life and career written for party offices ("Lebenslauf I, 1937" and "Lebenslauf II, 1944"), and an article on literary theory entitled "Der junge Dichter in seiner Zeit," signed in his capacity as an SA Standartenführer and member of the Kulturkreis der SA. The Bayerisches Hauptstaatsarchiv also has extensive files of newspaper clippings (Slg. Personen 4867, Sammlung Rehse) and photographic coverage (Bilder sammlung Schumann) on Schumannn.
3. Schumann, *Besinnung,* pp. 81–92.
4. Ibid., pp. 92–93.
5. Ibid., pp. 98–99.
6. "Deutschland":

Blut strömt aus tausenden Wunden,
Not frisst, das graue Gespenst . . .

Nun dich der Erdball zertreten,
Säumst du nicht frevelnd zugleich?
Türmst nicht in wilden Gebeten
Opfernder Reinheit das Reich?

Hat denn der Gott dein vergessen?
Oder verrietest du dich?

Schumann, *Die Lieder vom Reich*, p. 13.
    7. "Die Lieder vom Reich":

Doch ich erwachte aus dem kalten Traum,
Durch den ich einsam stolz in Hüllen ging.
Doch ich entklirrte brennend diesem Ring,
Der mich umspannte. Siehe: da war Raum. . . .

Und ich war Einer. Und das Ganze floss.
Und siehe: aufwärts schwang die neue Brandung.
Und mit der Strömung war ich gut und gross

Und hingegeben und durchstiess die Wandung
Und brach eratmend vor aus Damm und Deich
Verlor mich selbst und fand das Volk, das Reich.

Und neue Wölbung neuer Himmel flog
In grossen Bogen über der verjüngten,
Der deutschen Erde. . . .

In klarer Wucht, in rein getürmter Schichtung,
Der Stufenbau des Seins, der neue Gral.

Und hingebeugt zu schwörender Verpflichtung
So knieten wir, blickhart und herzenweich.
Und über uns im Licht der Dom, das Reich. . . .

Aus tausend Augen glomm das letzte Hoffen!
Aus tausend Herzen brach der stumme Schrei:
Den Führer! Knecht uns! Herr mach uns frei! . . .

Bis der Befehl ihn in die Kniee zwang.

Doch als er aufstand fuhr der Feuerschein
Des Auserwählten um sein Haupt. Und niedersteigend
Trug er die Fackel in die Nacht hinein.

Die Millionen beugten sich ihm schweigend.
Erlöst. Der Himmel flammte morgenbleich.
Die Sonne wuchs. Und mit ihr wuchs das Reich.

Ibid., pp. 14–20.
    8. Schumann, interview, 19 May 1985. Schumann added: "We conceived of Germany as the core power, to maintain order in a constellation of equal Fatherlands—the French, the English, the Scandinavian peoples—that was our idea of a "Reich Europa" . . . with the center in Germany as a wall against the Asiatic incursions as they had been experienced over the centuries." Compare Friedrich Hielscher, *Das Reich*, pp. 228–29, 290–303, 377–78, and Kurt Sontheimer, *Antidemokratisches Denken in der Weimarer Republik*, pp. 280–306.
    9. Schumann, *Besinnung*, pp. 99–104; see also Schumann File, BDC.
    10. Schumann, *Besinnung*, pp. 112–13.
    11. Schumann, "Lebenslauf II," BDC.

12. "Deutsche Weihnacht":

Rings reckt Verzweiflung die verlorenen Hände
In roter Himmel fahlen Untergang.
Befehlend drängt zu neuer Tat ein Ende
Und fordert, dass die Jugend sich verschwende.
Wir aber ruhen eine Stunde lang.

Wir haben keine Qual und keine Schmach vergessen,
Doch knien wir atmend um den Gottestraum.
So werden wir zu schweigenden Gefässen.
Erfüllt mit Licht . . .

Hand wächst in Hand. Die stumme Bruderschaft
Schliesst ihren Ring, der Herzen gleichen Brand.
Wir fliehen nicht. Wir holen neue Kraft.
Das Wunder bindet wie das Blut uns band.

Schumann, *Die Lieder vom Reich*, p. 30.

13. Schumann, interview, 19 May 1985. For an analysis of the climate of opinion among the theology faculty at Tübingen in this period, see Robert P. Ericksen, *Theologians under Hitler*, pp. 28–78.

14. Schumann, *Besinnung*, p. 133.

15. He was named Hochschulverbindungsführer beim Landesführer V. des Chefs des Ausbildungswesens. After 1935 he assumed the offices of Kulturreferent des Reichspropagandaamtes Württemberg and Gaukulturhauptstellenleiter der NSDAP, as well as being named to the Stab des Kulturreferenten der SA.-Gruppe Südwest. Schumann, "Lebenslauf II, 1944," BDC.

16. Standartenführer Gerhard Schumann, "M.d. Kulturkreises der S.A.," "Der junge Dichter in seiner Zeit," Schumann File, BDC. I have been unable to locate the place and time of this publication, but by every indication it was published in the *Der SA Mann* in 1936.

17. Ibid., and Schumann, interview, 19 May 1985. See also Ralf Schnell, "Was ist nationalsozialistische Dichtung?" *Merkur* 39 (May 1985), pp. 397–405. For a brief analysis of Schumann's conception of National Socialist letters, see Uwe-Karsten Ketelsen, *Von Heroischem Sein und Völkischem Tod. Zur Dramatik des Dritten Reiches*, pp. 11–12.

18. See Schumann, "Politische Kunst?" This article was first published in *Der SA Mann* in 1937. See Gerhard Schumann, *Ruf und Berufung*, pp. 10–14.

19. Schumann, "Lebenslauf II", BDC.

20. Even as Schumann saw himself as a member of the *Volksgemeinschaft*, he stood aside as an observer. His poem "Wer sich dem Reich verschrieb" (1934) graphically illustrates this:

Wer sich dem Reich verschrieb,
Ist ein Gezeichneter.
Auf seiner Stirn entbrennt
Ein jäh durchzuckend Mal.

Den Vielen ist er fremd,
Weil er sich selbst vergass,
Weil ihn ein Sternbild treibt,
Das zwingend vor ihm glüht.

Kaum einer sieht die Sucht.
Nur wenige lieben ihn.
Doch einmal springt sein Wort
Wie Feuer in den Kreis.

Da steht er leuchtend vorn.
Hält flatternd den Befehl.

Schumann, *Die Lieder vom Reich*, p. 5.
  21. Ibid., p. 33.
  22. "Hitler":

In einem Willen alle Wucht getürmt
Von Millionen Lebenden und Toten. . . .

In einer Hand den brüderlichen Gruss
Von Millionen ausgestreckten Händen. . . .

Mit aller Glocken donnernder Gewalt
So läutet seine Stimme in die Welt.

Die Welt wird hören.

Ibid., p. 45.
  23. Gerhard Schumann, *Fahne und Stern*, pp. 58–62.
  24. "Die Reinheit des Reiches":

Und nach den Siegen kommen, die sie feiern.
Dann sind sie gross und der Soldat ist stumm.
Sie teilen reichlich Ruhm aus und sie leiern
Das Blutlied schier zum Gassenhauer um. . . .

Verschleudern Opfer, herb uns abgekargt.
Das Blut der Toten bieten sie zu Markt. . . .
Dafür sind diese Toten nicht gestorben! . . .

Und die im Kampf die scharfe Waffe führten,
Fühlen sich fremd bei Feier und Parade. . . .

Und manchmal hocken sie zu Hauf vergrämt,
In dem Getriebe heimatlos geworden. . . .

Und sehen zornig auf die Hast und scheel
Und schweigen plötzlich. Lauern auf Befehl. . . .
Nun aber steht ein Haufe von Entschlossnen, . . .
Sie träumen Nachts vom Blut, dem hingegossnen, . . .

Dem Führer, der das dunkle Schicksal trägt,
Und von dem Acker, der nach Männern schreit,
Und von dem Strom, der an die Grenze schlägt,
Und von dem Bruder, der die Schuld verzeiht.

Vor ihrem Blick steht das Geheime nicht.
Ihr hartes Wort fällt schwer und wie aus Stahl.
Aus ihren Schritten hallt das Blutgericht.

In ihrer Seele tragen sie den Gral.
Knechte des Führers, Hüter und Rächer zugleich,
In ihnen brennt, mit ihnen wächst das Reich.

Ibid., pp. 58–62.
  25. Schumann, interview, 19 May 1985.
  26. Schumann, *Besinnung*, pp. 154–56.
  27. "Das Gericht":

Und als der Mann die dunklen Worte sprach:
Erschiessen!—war ein schwarzer Raum um ihn.

Und als die Schüsse peitschten durch die Nacht,
Brach jede Kugel in des Führers Herz.

So lange Deutschland lebt, wird in den Nächten
Die Salve Menschen aus den Betten schrecken.

Und blutig wird das Herz des Mannes leuchten,
Der seine Freunde tilgte um das Reich.

Schumann, *Besinnung,* p. 154.

28. Schumann, interview, 19 May 1985.

29. Schumann, *Besinnung,* pp. 154–56.

30. Schumann, interview, 19 May 1985.

31. Philipp Bouhler chaired the "Parteiamtliche Prüfungskommission zum Schutze des nationalsozialistischen Schrifttums."

32. Schumann, *Besinnung,* pp. 155–56.

33. Ibid.

34. Vondung, p. 89.

35. Hermann Dannecker, "Gerhard Schumann," *Völkischer Beobachter,* 19 May 1935.

36. Gerhard Schumann File, BDC.

37. Schumann, *Besinnung,* pp. 140–43.

38. Gerhard Schumann, *Wir aber sind das Korn.*

39. See *Die Tagebücher von Joseph Goebbels. Sämtliche Fragmente,* vol. 3, 28 April 1935 (p. 606) and 27 May 1935 (p. 616); *Völkischer Beobachter,* 27 May 1936; Christian Jenssen, "Ein junger Kampfdichter: Gerhard Schumann," *Münchener Zeitung,* 22 May 1936.

40. Vondung, p. 148.

41. The *Deutsche Allgemeine Zeitung* (2 May 1936) reported that, in addition to Hitler and Goebbels, those attending included Göring, von Blomberg, Himmler, Lutze, Ribbentrop, Hanns Johst, and Richard Strauss.

42. "Heldische Feier":

. . . Denn aus dem Raum, wo Blitz und Donner wachsen,
Und wo die Sterne stürzen aus dem Nichts,
Und wo das Weltall stürmt um seine Achsen,
Fuhr einer zu uns, leuchtenden Gesichts . . .

Wehende Fahne des Lichts!

Uns liebt der Tod, weil wir das Leben lieben . . .
Wir aber sind das Korn . . .

Umdroht von Nächten und von tausend Morden
Verwuchsen wir zu dem verschwornen Orden . . .

Und wenn auch Mütter stehn mit tränennassen
Und wunden Augen, weil sie dies gezollt—
Schon knien sie—und können es kaum fassen,
Wie aus den Gräbern und aus den Gelassen
Der Söhne Geist die Fahne rot entrollt.

Gesegnet sei der Tod, der ihre Schwaden
Mit hartem Schnitt ins Ewige geholt.
Gesegnet sein die stummen Kameraden.
Unsterblichkeit strahlt um die stummen Taten . . .

Ins Ungeheure steigt die Kathedrale, . . .
Der Welt zum ruhelosen Totenmale. . . .

Und plötzlich steht uns über dem Gewimmel
Von Hast, Befehl und werkdurchtobtem Schwalle,
Einsam und gross am aufgebrochnen Himmel,
Das Bild der rot bestrahlten Feldherrnhalle.

Wir baun des Reiches ewige Feldherrnhallen,
Die Stufen in die Ewigkeit hinein,
Bis uns die Hämmer aus den Fäusten fallen.
Dann mauert uns in die Altäre ein.

Schumann, *Wir aber sind das Korn*, pp. 68–77. For a contemporary review of the works of Schumann, see Hans Gstettner, *Völkischer Beobachter*, 5 April 1936.

43. *Deutsche Allgemeine Zeitung*, 2 May 1936, Beiblatt.
44. Ibid. See also Schumann, *Besinnung*, pp. 144–45.
45. *Völkischer Beobachter*, 5 May 1936.
46. Gerhard Schumann, *Herr Aberndörfer*.
47. "Herr Aberndörfer und das Führerprinzip":

Er wurde Blockwart. O wie rann die Ehre
ihm flammend in die welke Brust hinein . . .

der war nun streng, ein kleiner Orts-Satrape,
durchschritt den Block mit kühlem Herrscherblick.
Er kannte den Familienstand, die Habe
und auch den Kochtopf, aller Leid und Glück . . .

Die Stammtischbrüder kannten ihn nicht wieder. . . .
so sah er auf die kleinen Männer nieder,
von denen keiner mehr ihn ganz verstand.

Wenn er einherging unter seiner Herde,
erwartet er von rechts und links den Gruss, . . .

Und neben ihm als rauschende Fregatte,
da geht Frau Blockwart: "Guten Morgen, Leute!"
Und wer zum Staat noch kein Verhältnis hatte,
der wird bestimmt zum neuen Kämpfer heute. . . .

Ibid., pp. 27–29.
48. Schumann, *Besinnung*, pp. 137–38.
49. Gerhard Schumann, *Wir dürfen dienen*.
50. Gerhard Schumann, *Schau und Tat*, pp. 33–38, 81–88. Franz Philipp composed the resounding music for *Volk ohne Grenzen* for full orchestra, organ, und chorus.
51. See Rudolf Erckmann, *Gerhard Schumann*; Hermann Pongs, "Zur Lyrik der Zeit," in *Das Innere Reich* 2, 12 (March 1936), pp. 1574–578; Walter Linden, "Gerhard Schumann," *Die Neue Literatur* 10 (October 1936), pp. 570–79; Hellmuth Langenbucher, *Volkhafte Dichtung der Zeit*, pp. 468–70, and, by the same author, *Die Dichtung der jungen Mannschaft*, pp. 92–102; Heinz Grothe, "Gerhard Schumann," *Westfälische Tageszeitung "Rote Erde,"* Dortmund, 8 March 1936; Josef Magnus Wehner, "Wir aber glaubten . . . ," *Münchner Neueste Nachrichten*, 27 January 1936; Heinz Riecke, "Gerhard Schumann," in "Kritische Gänge," Beilage der *Berliner Börsenzeitung*, 5 May 1935.
52. "Ja (zum 10. April 1938)":

Nach tausendjährigen Wunden
Hat Blut zu Blut gefunden,
Geborsten Wall und Deich!
Vom Nordmeer bis zum Brenner
Nur flammende Bekenner:
Ein Führer, Volk und Reich!

Schumann, *Schau und Tat*, p. 75.

53. Schumann, *Besinnung*, pp. 147–49.
54. Gerhard Schumann, *Entscheidung*. See *Leipziger Bühnenblätter*, Altes Theater, Spielzeit 1938–39, Gerhard Schumann File, BDC. On 24 November 1942 Schumann was present at the fiftieth performance of *Entscheidung*, staged at the Kleines Haus of the Württembergische Staatstheater in Stuttgart. Program in possession of the author.
55. See Dr. Hermann Wanderscheck, "Warum Politisches Drama," in which Schumann described his inspiration for the work: "Ich habe es so gewagt, Menschen unserer Zeit in Worten unserer Zeit die Entscheidung unserer Zeit erlegen, erleiden und bestehen zu lassen und versucht, gleichzeitig das Überzeitliche, das Ewige, das uns alle still in der Hand hält, durch die Handlung und durch die Gestalten scheinen zu lassen. 'Entscheidung' ist kein Schlüsselstück, sondern die apokalyptische Vision einer untergehenden Zeit und eines geahnten neuen Aufbruches." *Leipziger Bühnenblätter*, Herausgegeben vom Intendanten der Städtischen Theater, Altes Theater, Spielzeit 1938–1939, Gerhard Schumann File, BDC. See also Schumann, "Mein Weg zum Drama," ibid.
56. Ibid.
57. Max Geisenheyner, *Frankfurter Zeitung*, 17 January 1939. See also Günther Ströve's commentary in the *Völkischer Beobachter*, 26 January 1939, and the review by Hermann Dannecker in the *NS-Kurier*, 16 January 1939. The play premiered in both Leipzig and Stuttgart. For reviews of the Stuttgart production, see Hermann Missenharter's column in the *Stuttgarter Tagblatt*, 16 January 1939, and the coverage in the *Schwäbischer Merkur*, 16 January 1939.
58. Schumann, *Entscheidung*, pp. 7–48.
59. Ibid., pp. 71–93.
60. Schumann, *Besinnung*, p. 140. Earlier that evening, Goebbels had greeted Schumann very warmly. The Reich minister would later ban the play. But because of its useful anti-Bolshevik content, it enjoyed a revival during the war. To be sure, in Schumann's words, "But from then on, I was no longer a golden boy." See Schumann interview, 19 May 1985.
61. Schumann, *Entscheidung*, pp. 122–34. Very important in Schumann's conception was his determination to play the protagonist off against a worthy foe. As he said, "The greater the opponent is presented, the greater is the victory of the heart for the hero playing opposite him." It was very important to the author that his play force a "decision" upon the audience as well, "therefore a decision for rebellion or for order." See Heinz Grothe, "Der Weg zur 'Entscheidung,' " "Gespräch mit Gerhard Schumann über sein neues Drama," *Völkischer Beobachter*, 11 January 1939.
62. See Gerhard Schumann File, BDC, and Schumann, *Besinnung*, pp. 158–59.
63. See SS Obergruppenführer und General der Waffen SS, Chef des SS Personalhauptamtes to Oberkommando des Heeres, Heerespersonalamt, 10 November 1944, requesting the army's approval for Schumann's appointment in the SS; see also Der Reichsführer SS, SS Hauptamt BI (4c) 21 b Be/Me, Berlin Grünewald, Douglasstrasse 7–11, 10 November 1944, in which Berger called Schumann to his new post. Gerhard Schumann File, BDC.
64. As a leading writer of the era, Schumann fit the mold of the Germanic "warrior-poet," a type often celebrated in Nazi war propaganda. For an example of the genre, see Kurt Ziesel, ed., *Krieg und Dichtung*, pp. 406–10. In works of this nature, Schumann shared the stage with such writers as Werner Beumelburg, Herybert Menzel, Eberhard Wolfgang Möller, Richard Euringer, Paul Alverdes, and Will Vesper.

65. Schumann, "Schwert und Geist. Ein Aufruf," in *Ruf ud Berufung*, pp. 25–27.

66. Schumann, "Krieg—Bericht und Dichtung," *Dichter und Krieger. Weimarer Reden 1942*, ed. Rudolf Erckmann, pp. 59–71. The Weimar writers congress, staged by the propaganda ministry, was held annually in October in connection with Goebbels's birthday.

67. "Führer":

Wir haben dir einmal geschworen.
Nun sind wir auf immer dein.
Wie Bäche, im Strome verloren,
Münden wir in dich ein.

Gerhard Schumann, *Bewährung*, p. 24. See also Schumann's poem "Gelöbnis an den Führer," a hymn of praise to Hitler, which was widely distributed and reprinted in several anthologies. For an example of this mass distribution, see Winterhilfswerk des Deutschen Volkes, *Ewiges Deutschland. Ein deutsches Hausbuch*, p. 93.

68. "Unser Dank ist unsre Treue":

Aus geborstnen Grüften brechen
Heldengeister aller Ahnen.
Unsichtbar mit treuen Kräften
Sind sie vorn beim Sturm der Fahnen.

Schumann, *Bewährung*, pp. 21–22. "Wen der Gott erwählt . . . (zum 8. November 1939)" celebrated Hitler's narrow escape from death at the Bürgerbräukeller in Munich in November 1939. See ibid., p. 25.

69. Gerhard Schumann, "Des Führers Augen," *Die Lieder vom Krieg*, p. 13.

70. "Lied aus der Nacht":

Sie lauschten. Sie hörten: ein Singen . . .
Aus der Hölle ein seliger Psalm.
Da sang es vom Wiesengrunde,
Von der Heimat, vom fernen Lieb,
Dass manchem die süsse Wunde
Tränen ins Auge trieb.

Und wie sich die Stimmen verwoben
Aus Gräbern und Löchern hervor
Stieg leuchtend und tröstend nach oben
Der brüderliche Chor.

Dass ob dem zerfetzten Lande,
Das feurig vom Tod durchweht
Im Graun der Vernichtung brannte
Ihr Lied wie ein stilles Gebet.

Ibid., p. 24–25.

71. "Gebet des Soldaten":

Herrgott, mit Worten sind wir karg.
Hör gnädig unser Beten nun:
Mach uns die Seelen hart und stark.
Das andre wolln wir selber tun.

Behüt daheim die stille Frau,
Wenn sie in dunkler Nacht sich härmt.
Entzünd den Stern im hohen Blau,
Dass ihr sein Trost das Herz erwärmt.

Behüt den Führer und das Land.

Die Kinder lass in Frieden ruhn.
Wir geben sie in deine Hand.
Das Andre wolln wir selber tun.

Schumann, *Bewährung*, p. 27. Eugen Pabst of Cologne composed the music for male choir accompanied by brass instruments. See Schumann, *Die Lieder vom Krieg*, pp. 48–49 and Sigmund Graff, ed., *Eherne Ernte. Gedichte im Krieg 1939–1941*, p. 148.

72. "Meiner Mutter," in Gerhard Schumann, *Gesetz wird zu Gesang*, p. 62. See also "Brief einer Mutter," in Schumann, *Die Lieder vom Krieg*, p. 31.

73. "Einem gefallenen Freund (H.P.H.)":

Kampf stand auf deiner Stirn. Und ohne Beben
Gingst leuchtend du in jede Nacht und Not,
Für deinen Führer dich dahinzugeben.
Wie eine Flamme war dein ganzes Leben.
Und wie du lebtest, bist du stolz verloht.

. . . Doch in den blutig lodernden Standarten
Marschierst du schweigend mit uns in den Sieg.

Schumann, *Die Lieder vom Krieg*, p. 29.

74. "Mein Liebster Bruder!":

Dein Herz war so lauter
Wie ein Kristall.
Deine Treue war
Wie eine feste Burg. . . .
Viele habe ich begraben.
Und mein Herz hat geblutet.
Doch nun sie dich begraben haben,
Mein vollendeter Bruder,
Junger, schweigsamer deutscher Held,
Ist ein Herzstück aus meinem Leben
Herausgebrochen.

Schumann, *Gesetz wird zu Gesang*, pp. 24–25. Uli Schumann was killed in 1942, in a mission originating from his Sicilian Luftwaffe base at Catania. See Schumann, *Besinnung*, p. 91.

75. "Ihr toten Helden," in Schumann, *Bewährung*, p. 30; "Vision an Gräbern," in Schumann, *Die Lieder vom Krieg*, p. 46; "Triumph," in Schumann, *Die Lieder vom Krieg*, p. 45.

76. "Unsterblichkeit":

In Gottes Sterneall kann nichts verwehen.
Der Tod ist nur ein stiller Übergang.
Und alles Leben ein Hinüber-gehen.
Schweigt, lauscht und hört: Gesetz wird zu Gesang.

Schumann, *Gesetz wird zu Gesang*, p. 83.

77. "Sie sind nicht tot" (Eine Rede zum Helden-Gedenktag), March 1942, place unknown, in Schumann, *Ruf und Berufung*, pp. 55–60.

78. Ibid., p. 60.

79. Gerhard Schumann, *Gudruns Tod*. According to Schumann, "My goal was to mold the form of the tragedy to the grand play of destiny found in the *Hildebrandlied* and the *Nibelungenlied*." Schumann, *Besinnung*, p. 220.

80. Ernst Karchow directed the production at the Deutsches Theater in Berlin, which featured the storied Anna Dammann (Gudrun), Albin Skoda (Hartmut), and Gerhard Geissler (Herwig). Richard Biedrzynski, *Völkischer Beobachter*, 11 May 1943.

81. Hanns Johst praised the work in a letter to Schumann: "This is your greatest

creation, poetry, vision, and theater all in one. I like this kind of Trinity!" See Hanns Johst, Oberallmannshausen, Starnberger See, 26 November 1942, letter to Gerhard Schumann, copy in possession of author. *Gudruns Tod* was well received by both the party press and the serious critics of the day. See reviews by Hans Jenkner, *Der Angriff*, 10 May 1943; Werner Fiedler, *Deutsche Allgemeine Zeitung*, May 1943; Ulrich Rothermel, *NS-Kurier*, Stuttgart, 15 February 1943; and Martin Kalliga, *Esslinger Zeitung*, 16 February 1943. See also Hermann Wanderscheck, "Die Tragödie von der Treue," *Kunst im Kriege*, 2/1943, pp. 54–55, and Wolfgang Hultzsch, "Gerhard Schumann auf der Stettiner Bühne," *Das Bollwerk*, 2, 1943, pp. 28–30.

82. Gerhard Schumann, inauguration as president of the Hölderlin Gesellschaft, 7 June 1943. See "Ansprache des Präsidenten Gerhard Schumann," *Iduna. Jahrbuch der Hölderlin Gesellschaft*, 1, 1 (1944), pp. 16–20. For critical judgment on Schumann, especially in relationship to his role as president of the Hölderlin Gesellschaft (1943–45), see Bernhard Zeller, ed., *Klassiker in finsteren Zeiten 1933–1945*, vol. II, pp. 82–83, 99, 122–24.

83. Schumann felt a personal bond with Berger, who was his first SA commander in Tübingen. Gerhard Schumann, letter to the author, 2 April 1986.

84. Ibid. See also Schumann, *Besinnung*, p. 169. In a letter to the author (2 April 1986), Schumann denied having had any knowledge of the Holocaust during the war.

85. Schumann reemerged following the defeat and three years of internment, becoming an active writer for the neo-Nazi cause. He published several volumes of poetry, became a director of the European Book Club, and founded his own publishing firm, the Hohenstaufen Verlag.

VII. HANS BAUMANN: TROUBADOUR OF THE HITLER YOUTH

1. We will keep on marching,
   even if everything is smashed,
   because today Germany belongs to us
   and tomorrow the whole world.

Kulturamt der Reichsjugendführung, *Liederblatt der Hitlerjugend.*

2. Much of the background for this chapter was provided by two personal interviews that Hans Baumann granted me at his home in Murnau an der Staffelsee/Oberbayern, 23 April and 1 May 1985. On the enthusiasm of the Hitler Youth, see Alfons Heck, *A Child of Hitler*, pp. 8–9.

3. Baumann, interview, 23 April 1985. For a biographical précis on Baumann, see the entry by Margarete Dierks, *Lexikon der Kinder und Jugendliteratur*, pp. 116–17.

4. Hans Baumann, *Der Retter Europas. Zum 20. April 1942.*

5. Herbert Böhme, *Rufe in das Reich*, pp. 365–66.

6. Baumann, interview, 1 May 1985.

7. Ironically, the establishment was owned by the Bavarian minister-president, Heinrich Held.

8. Hans Baumann, *Reisepass*, p. 8.

9. Ibid., p. 7.

10. Hans Baumann, *Macht keinen Lärm;* also see Baumann, interviews, 23 April and 1 May 1985. See also the thoughtful article on Baumann by Rudolf Walter Leonhardt, "Der Dichter und Dramatiker Hans Baumann. Versuch eines Beitrages zur sogenannten Bewältigung der Vergangenheit," in *Die Zeit*, 3 February 1962. This essay occasioned a learned response by Franz Schneider of Gonzaga University,

Spokane, Washington, in a letter sent to Leonhardt (23 April 1962) and placed at my disposal by Baumann.

11. For a discussion of the larger dimensions of German youth's call for renewal, see Wohl, pp. 43–84.

12. "Es zittern die morschen Knochen"

Es zittern die morschen Knochen
der Welt vor dem roten Krieg.
Wir haben den Schrecken gebrochen,
für uns wars ein grosser Sieg.

Und mögen die Alten auch schelten,
so lasst sie nur toben und schrein,
und stemmen sich gegen uns Welten,
wir werden doch Sieger sein.

Und liegt vom Kampfe in Trümmern
die ganze Welt zuhauf,
das soll uns den Teufel kümmern,
wir bauen sie wieder auf.

Wir werden weiter marschieren,
wenn alles in Scherben fällt,
denn heute gehört uns Deutschland
und morgen die ganze Welt.

Kulturamt der Reichsjugendführung, *Liederblatt der Hitlerjugend*. There were several changes in the wording of the song over the years. For comparison see the version in Generalkommando des VII. Armeekorps, *Soldatenliederbuch*. Baumann, as well as his original publisher, unsuccessfully attempted to keep the wording "denn heute hört uns Deutschland" (not "gehört"), but it had already become popular in this form.

13. A few of the most successful of Hans Baumann's works include *Feuer, steh auf dieser Erde*. Kantate zur Sonnenwende; *Horch auf Kamerad; Das Jahr überm Pflug*, Ein Bauernchor; *Der Grosse Sturm*. Chor. Spiel.; *Wir zünden das Feuer; Kampf um die Karawanken*. Schauspiel.

14. Undated newspaper clipping, Sammlung Baumann, IfZ. See also "Deutsche Dichter der Zeit. Hans Baumann," *Völkischer Beobachter*, 15 February 1939. Baumann was often abroad on official travel assignments. In a letter to the author, dated 23 August 1986, he wrote, "I was officially the departmental chief for lay theater and very soon became a member of the staff dealing with foreign cultural work—but without office hours, often on trips to Siebenbürgen, Bessarabia, and the Baltic."

15. Sammlung Baumann, IfZ. Baumann was dumb like a fox. He wrote further, "One winter I went to Italy. Michelangelo's *Pieta* and the marble statue of Venus of Cyrene moved me deeply. The theater at Syracuse gave me a premonition of impending disaster." Ibid.

16. This explains the reason why I was unable to find a shred of evidence on Baumann in the massive NSDAP personnel files in the Berlin Document Center. There was only one undated document in the files of the Reichskulturkammer in that depository, a missive from the SS/Reichssicherheitshauptamt, Auskunftstelle, attesting that Baumann had presented an acceptable racial profile (Abstammungs-nachweis). The SS clerk had noted, "Hitler Youth Leader at present has the desk for Foreign Germans Cultural Work in the Reich Youth Central Office. Poet/Writer." A document from Baumann, "Erklärung für die Reichsschriftumskam-mer," dated 23 January 1941, ran but one line: "I am, respectively was in the Army

from 27.8.39." This is indicative of the low opinion Baumann had of the bureau-cracy, whether party or state. See Hans Baumann, Reichskulturkammer Files, BDC.

17. Rainer Maria Rilke, *Die Weise von Liebe und Tod des Cornets Christoph Rilke.*

18. Rudolf Walter Leonhardt attested that "all of us twelve-to-nineteen-year-olds in the Hitler Reich felt something that touched us in Baumann's songs. . . . I know that many sang his songs like they would folk songs." See *Die Zeit,* 3 February 1962. For further evidence of the enthusiasm of youth, see the description of the pageantry surrounding Schlageter Memorial Day in Allen, pp. 210–12.

19. Hans Baumann, *Horch auf, Kamerad,* pp. 28–29.

Jungen, lasst euch nicht irren
. . . Nun sind wir am Marschieren,
keiner die Losung verliert:
Jungen für Deutschland marschieren . . .

20. Baumann, "Ihr rufenden Fanfaren," *Horch auf, Kamerad,* pp. 30–31.
21. Baumann, interview, 23 April 1985.
22. Baumann, "Wieder stehen nun Burgen auf," *Horch auf, Kamerad,* p. 26.
23. Ibid., pp. 86–87.

Nun steht der Dom, nun steht er ganz im Licht . . .
Die Not verging, die unser Volk zerriss . . .
und unser Lied macht sicher und gewiss . . .
So steht der Dom, so steht er ganz im Licht.

Compare the poem "Deutsche Ostern 1933" by the SA poet Heinrich Anacker, *Die Fanfare. Gedichte der deutschen Erhebung,* pp. 112–13. Anacker's poem contained the following remarkable lines: "Germany suffered its Golgatha, too, and was nailed to the cross. . . . For Germany is, like the Blessed Jesus, resurrected in glory."

24. Hans Baumann, "Die neue Stadt," *Wir zünden das Feuer,* pp. 47–55.
25. Ibid., p. 55.

Und haben wir die Treue
und nichts sonst auf der Welt,
das ist genug, und keiner
ist dann vor uns gestellt.
die kann der Tod nicht mähen
mit seinem harten Schnitt.

26. Ibid., p. 54.

Ein neuer Roland wird nun aufgestellt.
Das ist die Treue über diesem Land,
ein stummer Rufer in der lauten Welt.
Und für die Freiheit hebt er seine Hand . . .
So ist ein Roland sicher aufgestellt,
dass vor dem Tor der Welt die Treue steht.

27. Baumann, "Wir sind gekommen mitten her aus Nacht und Sorgen," *Horch auf, Kamerad,* p. 32.
28. Baumann, "Wir treten ohne Gewehre an," *Horch auf, Kamerad,* p. 40. In his introduction to the copiously illustrated indoctrination pamphlet dedicated to the twenty-one martyred Hitler Youths (*Unsterbliche Gefolgschaft,* ed. Heinz Görz und Franz-Otto Wrede), von Schirach claimed that "*die unsterbliche Gefolgschaft* marschiert an der Spitze der jungen deutschen Generation."
29. Baumann, *Horch auf, Kamerad,* pp. 36–37. Compare the assertion of Hans-Jürgen Nierenz, a youthful writer of the era: "Flag, whom you touch is in union with the times. Flag, whom you touch is consecrated! Flag, you flag leading us to eternity." Paul Gerhardt Dippel, *Dichtung der jungen Nation,* p. 150.

30. *Call of the East* was published in a collection of cantatas entitled *Wir zünden das Feuer* (pp. 5–14), which also included *Das Jahr überm Pflug, Unter Sternen wachsen Taten, Den Müttern,* and *Ans Werk.*

31. "Ruf aus dem Osten":

> In den Ostwind hebt die Fahnen,
> denn im Ostwind stehn sie gut,
> dann befehlen sie zum Aufbruch,
> und den Ruf hört unser Blut. . . .

> Macht euch stark! Wer baut im Osten,
> dem wird keine Not erspart. . . .

"Ruf und Antwort":

> Deutschland, du Strom der Gewalten . . .
> Strom aus dem Herzen Gottes . . .
> Hier bist du einmal gegangen,
> hier ist dein alter Lauf . . .
> Deutschland, hier ist dein Strombett
> in die Unsterblichkeit.

> Im Osten steht unser Morgen,
> steht Deutschlands kommendes Jahr,
> dort liegt eines Volkes Sorgen,
> dort wartet Sieg und Gefahr.

Baumann, *Call of the East.*

32. The *Völkischer Beobachter,* 3 July 1939, carried the heading "*Rüdiger von Bechelaren;* Uraufführung von Hans Baumanns Weihespiel in Anwesenheit des Reichsjugendführers/Arbeitstagung des Reichsbundes der Deutschen Freilicht und Volksschauspiele in Passau/Appell an die Dichter." Baumann himself noted, "Passau is going all out for the 'Rüdiger' production, and friends are coming from throughout the Reich. The city presents me with a small plot of land at the castle." Undated newspaper clippings, Sammlung Baumann, IfZ. The *Weihespiele* were generally not popular among the youths and were usually command performances.

33. "Kameraden, hebt die Fahnen":

> Kameraden, hebt die Fahnen,
> lasst die Trommeln brausend gehn!
> Was die anderen nur erahnen,
> wird in unsern Herzen stehn.
> Führer, gib die Marschbefehle,
> die uns kein Zweifel bricht.
> Leuchtend steht vor unsrer Seele
> Deutschland gross im Morgenlicht.

Hans Baumann, *Der helle Tag,* pp. 55–60.

34. "Eid des Fähnrichs":

> Über tapferer Männer Beben,
> über meines Herzens Not
> werde ich, vom Leid umloht,
> händelos die Fahne heben.
> Wenn die Lüfte jäh zerspringen,
> wenn der Strom erschrocken steht,
> werde ich, vom Krieg umweht,
> mit verstummten Munde singen.

> Tausend fallen, tausend türmen

zum Gebirg der Leiber Feld.
Ich werd, tausendmal gefällt,
auf den Knien stehn und stürmen.

Hans Baumann, *Atem einer Flöte*, p. 54.
35. The text was reproduced in a memorial book honoring the war dead, *Den Gefallenen. Ein Buch des Gedenkens und des Trostes*, p. 17.
36. Hans Baumann, *Gelöbnis der Jugend*. The occasion for the speech on Heroes Memorial Day was the keynote address at the opening of the "3. Berliner Erzählerwoche." German troops were quickly cured of this perverted idealism in the killing fields of Russia.
37. Ibid.
38. Hans Baumann, interview, 1 May 1985.
39. See "Die Bewährung des Dichters. Rede beim Deutschen Dichtertreffen in Weimar 1941," *Das Innere Reich*, 8, 9 (December 1941), pp. 461–71.
40. Hans Baumann, *Der Wandler Krieg. Briefgedichte 1941*.
41. "Inschrift":

Wenige fallen
freudigen Angesichts.
Doch die Erkorenen
bluten die Zukunft,
veratmen die Jugend
in ihre Freunde.

Baumann, *Atem einer Flöte*, p. 56.
42. "Tod und Krieg":

Schwankend im Regen des Stahls, vom Glanz
der Waffen geblendet, naht
der Tod und klagt:

Wer hat den Sommer gewendet, wer
die Wälder gefällt und die Äcker
sengend verwüstet?

Wo blieb der Lerchen Gesang, wo
der Birken Gellüster, der Bäche
heimliches Lied? . . .

Ibid., p. 57. Baumann commented on this new tone of realism: "During our discussion you asked me more than once why *death* was so often the subject of my early songs. I have thought about this. I think that there is a simple answer that explains it. These early songs were composed in a period of unbridled exuberance and immaturity, when strong language was the order of the day. But with the experience of the war, when one saw death every day, one got over this very soon." Baumann, letter to author, 2 May 1985.
43. Karl H. Ruppel, *Berliner Schauspiel*, pp. 339–46. See Hans Baumann, *Alexander*.
44. See Baumann, interviews, 23 April, 1 May 1985, and letter to author, 13 April 1988. Compare Boguslaw Drewniak, *Das Theater im NS-Staat*, pp. 242–43.
45. Baumann, interview, 1 May 1985.
46. Baumann, *Alexander*, p. 150.
47. Ibid., p. 153.
48. See Hans Baumann, *Morgen marschieren wir. Liederbuch der deutschen Soldaten*.
49. Hans Baumann, *Der Retter Europas*, and Hans Baumann, *Soldatenbrevier*.
50. Baumann, interview, 23 April 1985. See also *Die Zeit*, 3 February 1962.

51. Baumann, interview, 1 May 1985. See also letter to the author, 23 August 1986.

VIII. KARL RITTER AND THE HEROIC NAZI CINEMA

1. "Selbst die Heldentaten eines Nibelungenliedes verblassen gegenüber dieser Sinfonie von Heroismus, Leidenschaft, Mut und Todesverachtung. In furchtbaren Stahlgewittern stieg das Geschwader siegreich zur Sonne, Tod und Verderben bringend, wo es auf den Feind stiess." Hermann Göring, Kommandeur des Jagdgeschwaders Richthofen, *Filmwelt*, No. 52, 23 December 1938.

2. Karl Ritter File, Slg. Personen 3303, Sammlung Rehse, BayHStA; Karl Ritter File, Deutsches Institut für Filmkunde, Wiesbaden; Kurt Höllger, *Karl Ritter*.

3. Karl Ritter File, BDC. Ritter's NSDAP membership was number 23040. Curiously, both he and Erika let their party memberships lapse in 1928. The reason for this might well have been the stringent financial condition of the Ritters at that time. An appeal from Erika Ritter to Reichsleiter Alfred Rosenberg, dated 24 June 1938, asked his support in approaching Reichsschatzmeister F. Xaver Schwarz. Making the case that she and her husband were eligible for the Golden Party Badge of the NSDAP, Erika pointed out that only financial reverses had necessitated their leaving the party. Further, she noted that in 1930 they both applied for readmission to the party in Berlin, but that conditions in the Ortsgruppe Zehlendorf had delayed their request until March 1932. Rosenberg supported the Ritter appeal, pointing out to the party treasurer that the Ritters "are old Party comrades, and the Führer has known them from the earliest days." But Schwarz was firm in his refusal, noting that on the orders of the Führer the Golden Party Badge was to be awarded only to individuals who had an uninterrupted membership from 1 October 1928. See Erika Ritter to Alfred Rosenberg, 24 May 1938; Rosenberg to F. Xaver Schwarz, 24 June 1938; Schwarz to Rosenberg, 5 July 1938, Karl Ritter File, BDC.

4. "Mehr Weltanschauung im Film: Karl Ritter sprach über 'Zeitfilm-Zeitgeschichte,'" *Berliner Börsenzeitung*, 13 December 1936. Compare Ritter, "Reportage-und-Spielfilm," in *Der Deutsche Film*, Sonderausgabe 1940/41, quoted in Ulrich Kurowski, ed., *Deutsche Spielfilme 1933–1945*, pp. 152–53. See also "Spielleiter" Karl Ritter, "Zum Film-Volkstag am 28. Februar 1938. Filmkunst, nicht Filmindustrie," *Stuttgarter Neues Tageblatt*, 26 February 1938.

5. Ufa, *Verräter* (1936); script: Leonard Fürst; music: Harold M. Kirchstein; Herstellungsgruppe/Spielleitung: Karl Ritter. Ufa, *Patrioten;* premiered 14 May 1937; script: Philipp Lothar Mayring, Felix Lützkendorff, and Karl Ritter; music: Theo Mackeben; "Staatspolitisch und künstlerisch besonders wertvoll."

6. Ufa Tonfilm, *Unternehmen Michael*, premiered 7 September 1937 (Nuremberg) and 19 November 1937 (Berlin); music: Herbert Windt; camera: Günther Anders; sets: Walter Röhrig. Karl Ritter's son, Karl Gottfried (born 1916), directed the cutting desk. See *CineGraph*, F 4, and *Ufa-Werbedienst* booklet for theater owners, GFD/MPS/LOC. The film received the designation "Staatspolitisch und künstlerisch wertvoll," Bauer, p. 391.

7. Drehbuch, *Unternehmen Michael*. For advertising material on the film, see *Ufa-Werbedienst*, GFD, MPS, LOC.

8. Drehbuch, *Unternehmen Michael*, p. 15.

9. Ibid., p. 15.

10. Ibid., p. 17. The original play by Hans Fritz von Zwehl had the General affirm, "If we are victorious here, then the world will be ours. But, if we are defeated, we won't even have Germany anymore." See commentary by von Zwehl in Reichspropagandaleitung der NSDAP, Amtsleitung Film (Dr. Walther Günther), *Staatspolitische Filme*, vol. 7, *Unternehmen Michael*, p. 5.

11. Drehbuch, *Unternehmen Michael*, pp. 26–27.

12. Ibid., p. 37.

13. The model for this decision might well have been Field Marshal Ludendorff, who set a precedent in 1914. Ludendorff took command of the Fourteenth Brigade in Belgium after the death of General Wussof, thus guaranteeing the success of the assault on Liege. See Walther Günther, "Verhältnis des Films zur Wirklichkeit," in *Staatspolitische Filme, Unternehmen Michael,* p. 19.

14. See Drehbuch, *Unternehmen Michael.*

15. *Völkischer Beobachter,* 9 September 1937.

16. "*Unternehmen Michael; Ufa* Palast. "Stürmischer Beifall für einen grossen Film," *Berliner Lokal Anzeiger,* 19 November 1937.

17. Ibid. Compare the favorable review by Edith Hamann in *Filmwoche,* 1 December 1937.

18. Ludwig Eberlein, in a review headlined " 'Urlaub auf Ehrenwort.' Ein deutscher Filmsieg im Ufa-Palast am Zoo," in *Berliner Morgenpost,* 21 January 1938. See also von Arndt's review in the *Völkischer Beobachter,* 20 January 1938, headlined "Grosse Leistungen der Schauspieler. 'Urlaub auf Ehrenwort' ein überwältigendes Erlebnis." See also Kurowski, *Deutsche Spielfilme 1933–1945* and Albert Schneider, "Eine Grosstat deutschen Filmschaffens," in *LichtBildBühne,* 20 January 1938.

19. Kilian Koll, *Urlaub auf Ehrenwort: Geschichten um den Krieg,* p. 12. On Kilian Koll, see the autobiographical sketch in Kurt Ziesel, *Krieg und Dichtung,* p. 282.

20. Koll, *Urlaub auf Ehrenwort,* pp. 13–14.

21. Bauer, p. 392.

22. See *Ufa-Werbedienst,* GFD/MPS/LOC.

23. Ibid.

24. Drehbuch, *Urlaub auf Ehrenwort,* Ufafilm No. 932, Ufaproduktion 37–38 Plan No. U 12, Spielleitung: Karl Ritter; Herstellungsgruppe: Karl Ritter, p. 7.

25. Drehbuch, *Urlaub auf Ehrenwort,* p. 55.

26. Ibid., p. 39.

27. Ibid., pp. 216–21. Sex and the demimonde were ever the danger zones for Ritter. Across town at the Artistenhotel Aurora, the Hungarian singer Ilonka seduces the seventeen-year-old schoolboy-recruit Kurt Hellwig.

28. On this theme, see the brilliantly eccentric work by Klaus Theweleit, *Männerphantasien.*

29. Those attending the premiere of *Urlaub auf Ehrenwort* included Reich Press Chief Dietrich, State Secretary Hanke, Police President Graf Helldorf, and the highly esteemed actor Emil Jannings.

30. *Das 12 Uhr Blatt,* 20 January 1938, headlined "Das Hohelied vom verdammten Pflichtgefühl." See also the following reviews: Günter Schwark, *Filmkurier,* 20 January 1938; Wilhelm Staar, *8 Uhr-Abendblatt,* 20 January 1938; Paul Otte, *Berliner Volks-Zeitung,* 20 January 1938; Erik Krünes, *Berliner Illustrierte Nachtausgabe,* 20 January 1938; Karl Macht, *Der Angriff,* 20 January 1938; Ernst von der Decken, *BZ am Mittag,* 20 January 1938; Felix Dargel, *Berliner Lokal-Anzeiger,* 21 January 1938.

31. "To the director Karl Ritter in thankful recognition of his exemplary pioneering contribution to German film on the occasion of the great success of his film 'Urlaub auf Ehrenwort.' " Thereafter, Ritter proudly posed in his home for the press with Goebbel's photograph as a stage prop for added prestige. See *Licht-Bild-Bühne,* 21 January 1938, V.B. Film-Archiv, Deutsches Institut für Filmkunde, Wiesbaden.

32. *Ufa, Pour le Mérite,* 1938; director: Karl Ritter; script: Fred Hildenbrand, Karl Ritter; music: Herbert Windt; assistant to director: Gottfried Ritter.

33. *Völkischer Beobachter,* 11 June 1938.

34. Karl Ritter File, BDC.

35. See Gerhard Schoenberner's chapter "Das Preussenbild im deutschen Film," in Axel Marquardt and Heinz Rathsack, eds., *Preussen im Film*, Eine Retrospektive der Stiftung Deutsche Kinemathek, p. 33.

36. See the article entitled "Im Geiste Richthofens, *Pour le Mérite*, ein Film vom deutschen Opfergang," *Filmwelt*, 23 December 1938. The Richthofen legend had indeed caught the public's imagination. For a fascinating account of the reinterment of von Richthofen's body in the *Invaliden Friedhof* in Berlin, 18 November 1925, see Whalen, pp. 32–35.

37. Herbert Holba et al., *Reclams deutsches Filmlexikon*, p. 321.

38. Bauer, p. 428 and *Ufa*, program for *Pour le Mérite*, GDF, MPS, LOC.

39. Drehbuch, *Pour le Mérite*.

40. Ibid., p. 5.

41. Ibid., p. 11.

42. Ibid., pp. 12–13.

43. Ibid., p. 27.

44. Ibid., p. 29.

45. Ibid., p. 35.

46. Ibid., p. 37.

47. *Lichtbildbühne*, 10 December 1938, cited in Julian Petley, "Karl Ritter," *CineGraph*, E1.

48. *Filmwelt*, 6 January 1939. See also the review in *Völkischer Beobachter*, 12 December 1938.

49. See *Das Schwarze Korps*, 20 December 1938.

50. *Ufa*, *Kadetten*, premiered 2 December 1941 (Danzig) and 18 December 1941 (Berlin). For reviews of *Kadetten*, see *Deutsche Allgemeine Zeitung*, 5 December 1941 and *Steglitzer Anzeiger* (Berlin), 19 December 1941.

51. See Bauer, p. 539, and *Ufa-Werbedienst*, GFD, MPS, LOC.

52. Commenting on this episode, Ritter revealed, "I'm a little frightened by my own courage. I am filming my new production *Kadetten* with nine boys who have never before stood in front of a camera. But I need the naturalness of these youths. The action of my film calls for a militarily disciplined corps of boys. And so I went out to Potsdam with my colleague Mathias Wieman, and there in the Napola we chose two dozen cadets to appear for screen tests. . . . It was really a joy to work with these spirited and unspoiled boys." See "Knabenmut und Mannestreue," an interview with Karl Ritter, in Karl Ritter File, Deutsches Institut für Filmkunde, Wiesbaden. See also "Unterhaltung mit Felix Lützkendorff," ibid.

53. *Ufa* film program, *Kadetten*, GFD, MPS, LOC. The *Kadettenlied* was so effective that, according to A. U. Sander, *Jugend und Film*, German children who saw the film during the war often whistled and sang the lyrics as they left the theater.

54. Wilhelm Utermann, " 'Kadetten.' Karl Ritters Preussenfilm in Berlin erstaufgeführt," *Völkischer Beobachter*, 20 December 1941.

55. Friedrich P. Kahlenberg, "Preussen als Filmsujet in der Propagandasprache der NS-Zeit," in Marquardt and Rathsack, pp. 153–55. See also Friedrich P. Kahlenberg, ed., *Ausstellung zur Filmreihe "Jugend im NS-Staat,"* pp. 19–20; "Kadetten stehen ihren Mann. Ein Jungenschicksal des Jahres 1760—im Film gestaltet," Deutsches Institut für Filmkunde, Wiesbaden; David Welch, "Educational Film Propaganda and the Nazi Youth," in Welch, *Nazi Propaganda*, pp. 65–87.

56. *Ufa*, *Stukas*, written by Karl Ritter and Felix Lützkendorf, with music by Herbert Windt, premiered 27 June 1941. Ritter's son, Heinz, worked on the camera crew for the film. It was judged "Staatspolitisch wertvoll, künstlerisch wertvoll, Volkstümlich wertvoll, and Jugendwert."

57. *Illustriertes Filmprogram 1941*, quoted in Dammeyer, pp. 175–77.

58. Friedrich Hölderlin, "Der Tod fürs Vaterland," Hsgn. vom Volksbund Deutsche Kriegsgräberfürsorge e.V., *Den Gefallenen. Ein Buch des Gedenkens und des Trostes*, p. 17.

59. "Stukalied":

> Wir sind die schwarzen Husaren der Luft,
> Die Stukas, die Stukas, die Stukas.
> Immer bereit, wenn der Einsatz uns ruft,
> Die Stukas, die Stukas, die Stukas.
> Wir stürzen vom Himmel und schlagen zu
> Wir fürchten die Hölle nicht und geben nicht Ruh'.
> Bis endlich der Feind am Boden liegt,
> Bis England, bis England, bis England besiegt,
> Die Stukas, die Stukas, die Stukas.

Compare David Welch, *Propaganda and the German Cinema, 1933–1945*, pp. 214–15, and Leiser, *Nazi Cinema*, pp. 66–67.

60. Curt Belling, "*Stukas*. Karl Ritters neuer Fliegerfilm im Ufa-Palast am Zoo," *Völkischer Beobachter*, 29 June 1941.

61. For an extended treatment of Nazi propaganda against the Soviet Union, see Baird, pp. 147–98, and Robert Edwin Herzstein, *The War That Hitler Won*, pp. 351–69.

62. For a devastating treatment of this subject, see Reichsführer SS, SS Hauptamt, *Der Untermensch*.

63. Bauer, p. 569. See also *Das Programm von Heute*, Nummer 1837. *G.P.U.* premiered on 14 August 1942.

64. See Dorothea Hollstein, *Antisemitische Filmpropaganda. Die Darstellung des Juden im nationalsozialistischen Spielfilm*, pp. 156–60.

65. *Ufa, Besatzung Dora*; script: Fred Hildenbrand and Karl Ritter; music: Herbert Windt, Zensur November 1943 (Verbot).

66. "Zum Film 'Besatzung Dora'; Ein Geleitwort von Professor Karl Ritter," *Ufa, Bild-und Text-Informationen, Besatzung Dora*, Deutsches Institut für Filmkunde, Wiesbaden.

67. In a letter to the late author Peter A. Hagemann of the Stiftung Deutsche Kinemathek, Berlin, Karl Ritter wrote: "One reason that *Besatzung Dora* was not released was the letter from State Secretary Gutterer to Karl Ritter of 14 April 1943, conveying Goebbels's criticism that the film was not in the spirit of National Socialism. Considering the great amount of work that went into it—and how dangerous it was to make—this criticism was especially depressing." See Kraft Wetzel and Peter A. Hagemann, *Zensur-Verbotene deutsche Filme 1933–1945*, pp. 61–63.

68. On the concluding phase of Ritter's life, see Julian Petley's article in *CineGraph*, B2.

IX. HITLER, HEROES, AND *HELDENTOD*:
THE MYTH OF DEATH IN WORLD WAR II

1. "The giving of one's own life for the existence of the community is the ultimate meaning of sacrifice" (Adolf Hitler). Reichspropagandaleitung/Hauptamt Kultur, *Die Heldenehrungsfeier der NSDAP* (Berlin 1942), Sonderdruck, *Die neue Gemeinschaft*, p. 2.

2. See George L. Mosse, "Two World Wars and the Myth of the War Experience," *Journal of Contemporary History*, 21, 4 (October 1986), pp. 491–513.

3. Heinz Boberach, ed., *Meldungen aus dem Reich. Auswahl aus den geheimen Lageberichten des Sicherheitsdienstes der SS 1939–1944*, pp. 8–9, and Baird, pp. 52–53.

4. Goebbels, *Das Reich,* June 9, 1940, p. 1.

5. For an analysis of the Hitler myth during this period, see Ian Kershaw, *Der Hitler-Mythos,* pp. 131–34. On German wartime film, see Welch, pp. 186–237.

6. *Sieg im Westen* (Noldan 1940), directed by the army press group of the OKW/WPr in cooperation with the film section of the propaganda ministry. For official coverage of the film, see OKW/WPr., ed., *Sieg im Westen. Der Kriegsfilmbericht des Heeres.*

7. Heinrich Anacker File, BDC. See also Hellmuth Langenbucher, *Volkhafte Dichtung der Zeit,* pp. 454–56.

8. "Seemanns Lied":

> Der Tag war grau, der Tag war schwer,
> Und stürmisch ging die See.
> Nun klart es auf von Westen her . . .
> Der mich in goldne Träume wiegt—
> Antje, mein blondes Kind!
> Hörst du nicht von ferne unser Schifferklavier?
> Antje, das Lied soll dich grüssen von mir!
> Geht alles so, wie's Gott gefällt,
> Und Seeleut' gibt's noch mehr . . .
> Ein andrer kommt, der um dich fragt,
> Antje, mein blondes Kind!

Heinrich Anacker, *Bereitschaft und Aufbruch. Gedichte aus dem Kriegswinter 1940,* p. 29.

9. "Ostmärkisches Alpenjägerlied":

> Von Stavanger bis nach Trondheim weht
> Deutschlands stolze Fahne, sturmgebläht.
> Selbst auf Narviks schroffem Felsenthron
> Wacht der Ostmark treuer Alpensohn!
>
> Starb ein Kamerad den Heldentod,
> Blüht's im Schnee wie Alpenrosen rot . . .
> Und für ihn, der fern der Heimat schied,
> Singen wir als letzten Gruss das Lied:
> "Aus dem Steirerland und vom Tirol,
> Aus den Kärntner Bergen sind wir wohl.
> Hoch im Norden kämpft in Schnee und Eis
> Hitlers Alpenkorps vom Edelweiss!"

Ibid., pp. 80–81.

10. Es steht aus *einem* Guss
> Die Batterie!
> Wir senden Schuss für Schuss,
> Dem Feind den Eisengruss—
> Ja, die Kanone kracht
> Und macht bum, bum!

Heinrich Anacker, *Über die Maas, über Schelde und Rhein. Gedichte vom Feldzug im Westen,* p. 36.

11. "Stille vor dem Sturm":

> Volldampf voraus! Die Flaggen sind gehisst!
> Und eher kommt das Schwert nicht in die Scheide,
> Als bis Britanniens Macht zerbrochen ist!

Heinrich Anacker, *Heimat und Front. Gedichte aus dem Herbst 1939,* p. 8.

12. "England ist Schuld":

Die Toten, die Frau'n mit verweintem Gesicht
Erheben die Klage und werden Gericht,
Das vor der Geschichte sein Urteil spricht:
England ist schuld!

Ibid., p. 54.
13. Anacker, "Royal Oak," in *Heimat und Front*, p. 56.
14. See "Der Tod geht um Engeland!" Anacker, *Bereitschaft und Aufbruch*, p. 16.
15. *Frankreichlied:*

Kamerad, wir marschieren im Westen,
Mit den Bombengeschwadern vereint—
Und fallen auch viele der Besten,
Wir schlagen zu Boden den Feind!
Vorwärts! Voran! Voran!
Über die Maas, über Schelde und Rhein
Marschieren wir siegreich nach Frankreich hinein—
Marschieren wir, marschieren wir
Nach Frankreich hinein!

Anacker, *Über die Maas, über Schelde und Rhein*, p. 5. See Willi A. Boelcke, ed., *Kriegspropaganda 1939–1941*. Geheime Ministerkonferenzen im Reichspropagandaministerium, p. 359.
16. "Flandern":

Auf Flanderns weiten Fluren,
Da blüht der Mohn so rot . . .
Es wissen Flanderns Fluren,
Wohl vom Soldatentod!"

Nun ist auf neu in Flandern
Ein rotes Blühn erwacht;
Nun tobt aufs neu in Flandern
Die blutig-heisse Schlacht.
Den Sieg erkämpft im Frühlingsschein
Grossdeutschland, jung und stark,
Und bringt der Toten Ernte ein
Bei Ypern und Langemarck!

Anacker, *Über die Maas, über Schelde und Rhein*, p. 12.
17. Anacker, "Der graue Rock," in *Heimat und Front*, p. 12.
18. Anacker, "Der Führer bei seinen Soldaten," in *Heimat und Front*, p. 38.
19. "Compiegne":

Nun führt er als Feldherr Grossdeutschlands Heer
Zum Sieg vom Argonner Wald bis zum Meer.
Motoren donnern und dröhnen dumpf—
Sie künden des deutschen Schwertes Triumph
Im Walde von Compiegne!

Anacker, *Über die Maas, über Schelde und Rhein*, p. 54.
20. "Der Führer in Compiegne":

Unsichtbar ewigen Ruhmes Adler kreiste . . .
All', was geschah, geschah aus Hitlers Geiste,
Der zukunftsträchtig in den Morgen führt!

Ibid., p. 55.
21. "Der Führer am Heldengedenktag 1940," Zeughaus, Berlin, RPL/HKA, *Die*

Heldenehrungsfeier der NSDAP, Die Neue Gemeinschaft, 1942, pp. 42–44, and Domarus, pp. 1477–479.

22. *Der ewige Jude* (Defi 1940) was produced by the Reichspropagandaleitung; *Jud Süss* (Terra Film 1940), directed by Veit Harlan, featured a stellar cast including Ferdinand Marian, Werner Krauss, Heinrich George, and Kristina Söderbaum.

23. Alfred Ingemar Berndt and Hasso von Wedel, eds., *Deutschland im Kampf,* 43, 4 (June 1941), pp. 73–79.

24. DW 564–755, LOC.

25. Newsreel of 16 July 1941, DW 567, LOC.

26. See DW 567–69 (July 1941) and DW 663 (May 1943), LOC. On these and other topics related to the Nazi media blitz against the Soviet Union, see Baird, pp. 147–259, and Herzstein, pp. 351–69.

27. For a devastating treatment of this subject, see Reichsführer SS, SS Hauptamt, *Der Untermensch.*

28. See DW 569, July 1941, LOC. *Das Sowjetparadies* (1942), *Europa bekämpft dem Bolschewismus* (1942), and *Im Walde von Katyn* (1943) were all produced by the propaganda ministry's film section.

29. Joseph Goebbels, *Der steile Aufstieg. Reden und Aufsätze aus den Jahren 1942/ 43,* pp. 95–102.

30. Ibid., p. 97.

31. Ibid., pp. 101–02. Goebbels attested that his remarks had nothing whatsoever to do with romanticism. The German people had formed a community, united in their destiny (*Schicksalsgemeinschaft*), in which all considerations of class had given way to social unity. Theirs was a front experience of equals, to be distinguished from the *Fronterlebnis* of the Great War, which was based on class hierarchy. Members of the former aristocracy now died side by side with farmers and workers.

32. George H. Stein, *The Waffen SS: Hitler's Elite Guard at War, 1939–1945,* pp. 122–23. For an admirable analysis of the Waffen SS troops, see Charles W. Sydnor, *Soldiers of Destruction: The SS Death's Head Division, 1933–1945,* pp. 313–42. See also SS-Hauptamt/IV, Berlin W 35, *Lehrplan für Sechsmonatige Schulung* (n.d.), IfZ, 5692177, Dc 29.36.

33. Stein, pp. 122–23.

34. *Treuelied der SS:*

Wenn alle untreu werden, so bleiben
wir doch treu,
dass immer noch auf Erden für euch
ein Fähnlein sei.
Gefährten unsrer Jugend, ihr Bilder
bessrer Zeit,—die uns zu Männertugend
und Liebestod geweiht.

Josef Ackermann, *Heinrich Himmler als Ideologe,* p. 150.

35. Der Reichsführer SS, SS Hauptamt, *Vorschläge für die Abhaltung einer Totenfeier* (Manuskript: Nur für den Dienstgebrauch), NSD41/238, BA. On the SS "new man," see Robert A. Pois, *National Socialism and the Religion of Nature,* pp. 84–86.

36. Gottlob Berger distributed the Himmler order in RFSS/SS Hauptamt, Berlin, 31 August 1942, "Feierliche SS-mässige Gestaltung der Beerdigung von gefallenen und gestorbenen SS Angehörigen," SS, T-175, Roll 190, 2727842, NA. Himmler ordered the SS Hauptamt to name an officer to assume responsibility for each burial, and all higher-ranking SS officers and police officials were to serve at his disposal. For elaboration on the basic order for SS funerals, as well as those for SS wives, see Berger, RFSS/SS Hauptamt, Berlin, 19.7. 1943, AI (1d)-Az.:4 b Do/

Si., "Toten-und Gedenkfeiern zu Ehren gefallener und verstorbener SS-Angehö-riger und SS Frauen," Bezug: RFSS-Befehl vom 26.8.1942, BA. For ideological and liturgical directives on SS funerals, see Der Reichsführer SS, SS Hauptamt, *Vor-schläge für die Abhaltung einer Totenfeier*, NSD41/238/BA.

37. Hitler had awarded the first "Oberste Stufe des Deutschen Ordens" to Reich Minister for Armaments Fritz Todt, who was killed in 1942. For a record of the state funeral, see *Reinhard Heydrich*, ed. Reichssicherheitshauptamt, *Völkischer Beo-bachter*, 5 June 1942, pp. 1–2; 9 June, p. 1; and 10 June, pp. 1–2. For photographs of the ceremony, see 69/52/69 and 69/58/27, Reinhard Heydrich File, Bilder Samm-lung, BA. From time to time when he was in Berlin, Himmler visited Heydrich's grave. In a letter to Frau Heydrich dated 23 May 1944, the Reichsführer wrote, "Some difficult days lie ahead for you. My thoughts will be with you and the children, especially out there at the cemetery. When I was in Berlin for a few days recently, I visited Reinhard again." See SS, T-175, Roll 82, 2602260, NA.

38. "Des Führers Wölfe!":

Der Leitwolf fiel—
Und bildet—noch vom Kampf erhitzt—
Einen Ring der Treue um den Herrn,
der diese Meute sich zu seinem Schutz erkor.

Der stärkste Wolf springt wieder vor!
Mit wachen Lichtern überprüft er kühn das Feld—
Und schlägt voll Ingrimm seine Fänge in der Feinde Masse,
Indes das Rudel sichernd um den Hügel streift.

Was ihr auch noch ersinnen mögt
An Niedertracht aus eurem feigen Hinterhalt—
Ihr Kreaturen haltet die Lawine doch nicht auf.
Wer eurem niedren Hass auch noch zum Opfer fallen möge,
Uns ist es gleich!
Wir trau'n auf unsern Stern und harren des Befehls!
Und unser Schlachtruf bleibt: "Das Reich!"

Richard Wolff, SS Sturmbannführer im SD des RFSS, "Nach dem Staatsakt im Mosaiksaal der Neuen Reichskanzlei anlässlich des Todes des SS-Obergruppen-führer Reinhard Heydrich," *SS Leitheft*, 8:2, 1942, p. 6.

39. Freiherr von Wangenheim, *Der Letzte Appell: Des SS-Oberjunkers Radewitz Taten, Traum und Tapferer Tod.*

40. See Lieutenant Hasser, "Die Front hat das Wort!" NSDAP/RPL/HKA, *Kul-turpolitisches Mitteilungsblatt*, 15 June 1942, p. 21.

41. See *SS Leitheft*, October 1944, pp. 6–8.

42. "Brief eines gefallenen SS-Mannes an seine Eltern," *SS Leitheft*, December 1943, pp. 41–42.

43. "Das Testament eines SS-Mannes," *SS Leitheft*, June 1942, pp. 12–13. "SS-Mann Heinz H." died on 28 March 1942 in Russia. His last letter to his brother reflected human warmth when he drew fond recollections of his years as a cadet at the Napola Köslin, one of the preeminent National Socialist leadership schools for boys. He took pride in the ethos of the school: "Believe, Obey, Fight!" Köslin and its teachings had truly inspired his life. His farewell concluded, "Whoever searches for the meaning of German heroic death must be on the right path if he always returns to these words: 'Fallen for Führer and Volk, with Belief in the Eternity of the Reich.'"

44. Herbert Lange, *Der Brückenschlag über den Tod: Aus dem Tagebuch eines Ge-fallenen*, "Geschrieben als Soldat im Sommer und Herbst 1942."

45. Ibid., pp. 22–23.

46. *SS Leitheft,* February 1943, pp. 24–25.

47. "Meinem gefallenen Mann," *SS Leitheft,* Ausgabe S, vol. 3. The poem featured a mother surrounded by three children munching bread and marmalade, with the following caption: "He who calls such riches his own knows what he is fighting for." Compare Reichsführer SS/SS Hauptamt/Schulungsamt, *Sieg der Waffen—Sieg des Kindes* (n.p., n.d.), with the following foreward from Himmler: "Every people fighting for its existence has two weapons at its disposal: its military forces and its natural fertility. Never forget that military strength alone cannot guarantee the future of a people, but that alongside it there must be the continuous source of fertility. Read this publication and act accordingly, so that the victory of the German weapons is accompanied also by the victory of the German child."

48. RPL/HKA, *Die Heldenehrungsfeier der NSDAP,* p. 8; see also Vondung, p. 90.

49. RPL/HKA, *Die Heldenehrungsfeier der NSDAP,* p. 8.

50. Reichspropagandaleitung/Hauptamt Reichsring, *Reichsring Mitteilungen* 2/1944, NSDAP/HA, Roll 16, Folder 291.

51. "Die letzte Nachricht," in Volksbund Deutsche Kriegsgräberfürsorge, ed., *Den Gefallenen. Ein Buch des Gedenkens und des Trostes,* pp. 66–67. Compare "Nachricht vom Tod des Sohnes," Hermann Gerstner, *Den Müttern der toten Kämpfer,* p. 10, Reihe, *Fahrt und Feier,* vol. 11.

52. Walther Tiessler, Reichsring für Volksaufklärung und Propaganda, Hauptamt Propaganda, to Goebbels, "Betrifft: Brief eines Divisionspfaffers an die Eltern eines Gefallenen," 3 February 1942. The original complaint was made by the Gauhauptstellenleiter of the Nationalsozialistische Kriegsopfer Versorgung, Gaudienststelle Niederdonau, to Pg. Goger of the Gaupropagandaamt of Gauleitung Niederdonau, Vienna, 13 January 1942. The official grumbled that, although the "theologians" generally were sent to the medical corps, they "should be sent to the front lines, so that if things go wrong they can be ordered forward in God's name." See NSDAP, T-81, Roll 675, 5483633, NA.

53. Himmler Befehl is included in correspondence of Chef des SS Hauptamtes to Verteiler V, Berlin, 23 April 1940, RFSS, T-175, Roll 199, 2739977, NA.

54. See, for example, Chef des Sicherheitspolizei und des SD, Berlin, "Heldenehrungsfeiern: Zunehmende Aktivität der Kirche," 12 October 1942, "Meldungen aus dem Reich," RFSS, T-175, Roll 264, 2757772, NA.

55. Ibid.

56. Ibid.

57. Ibid.

58. Ibid.

59. Gerhard Seeger-Ahlert, "To Our Dead":

So hat sich das Volk gefunden,
Und für wenige Sekunden
Wird das Herz der Stärksten weich.
—Doch nun höher die Standarten!
Deutschland soll nicht länger warten,
Stehe fest, du heil'ges Reich!

RPL/HKA, *Die Helden-Ehrungsfeier der NSDAP, Die Neue Gemeinschaft,* 1942. In smaller towns, the name of every fallen soldier was read by the SA Standortführer, accompanied by muffled drum rolls. See the report on the heroes memorial ceremony in Reutlingen, n.d., in ibid. Compare Vondung, pp. 76–776, and Gamm, pp. 151–55.

60. See NSDAP/Reichsleitung, RPL, "Auszug aus der Anweisung des Reichs-

propagandaleiters," 20 February 1943, in *Die Neue Gemeinschaft,* February 1943, p. 11.

61. Domarus, pp. 1999–2003.

62. See Reinecke, OKW, Nr. 760/43 AWA/W Allg. (III), 5 February 1943, "Betrifft: Heldengedenktag 1943," in *Die Neue Gemeinschaft,* February 1943, pp. 16–17.

63. See RPL/Chef des Propagandastabes to all Gauleiter and Gaupropagandaleiter, 13 February 1943, and "Anlage 5, Ausführungsbestimmungen des Hauptamtes Propaganda," ibid., pp. 12–14. Compare "Heldengedenkfeier 1944," in NSDAP/RPL/HKA, *Unsere Feier. Richtlinien zur Fest-und Feiergestaltung,* Nr. 3/1944, in NSDAP, T-81, Roll 133, 166474, NA.

64. See "Gefallenenehrungsfeiern der NSDAP. Aus den Berichten," RPL/HKA, *Kulturpolitisches Mitteilungsblatt,* 1 May 1943, p. 3.

65. See RPL/HKA, *Die Neue Gemeinschaft,* 1943, p. 12.

66. Friedrich Wilhelm Hymmen, *Briefe an eine Trauernde. Vom Sinn des Soldatentodes.* Another favored work given as consolation was Alwin Rüffer, *Frei vor dem Tod.* It also embodied the National Socialist cult of death, at many points reaching the outer limits of primitive mysticism.

67. Hymmen, pp. 21–22.

68. Ibid., pp. 35–38.

69. See "Die Mutter unseres Fliegerhelden Werner Mölders zum Tode ihres Sohnes," in RPA/HKA, *Gebt euren Toten Heimrecht!,* n.p., NSD 12/107, BA.

70. Ibid. For a glorification of the hero, see Major Fritz von Forell, *Mölders und seine Männer.*

71. Ibid. Compare RPL/HPA, *Den Müttern und Frauen zum Muttertag 1944. Deutschland . . . Kein Opfer . . . ist dafür zu gross!* NSD 12/110, BA.

72. See Claudia Koonz, *Mothers in the Fatherland,* pp. 248–49, and Dorothee Klinksiek, *Die Frau im NS-Staat,* pp. 66–67, 84–86, 108–11.

73. "Meiner Mutter":

Wenn etwas Gutes in mir ist,
dann weil Du meine Mutter bist.
Bin ich Dir auch so furchtbar fern,
ich seh Dich doch, du stiller Stern
Bist Du auch hoch und ich nur hier
mein Leben sei der Weg zu Dir.

Baldur von Schirach, *Die Fahne der Verfolgten,* p. 55.

74. Hans Baumann, *Die helle Flöte,* p. 63.

75. Meine liebe Mutter, diesen letzten Brief
wirst du haben, wenn ich in der Erde,
die mich unaufhörlich zu sich rief,
mit den andern Kameraden liegen werde.

Meine liebe Mutter, diesen armen Sand
musst du lieben, der mein Leben schlürfte.
Doch was gäb ich, wenn ich deine Hand
einmal noch, nur einmal streicheln dürfte.

Eberhard Wolfgang Möller, *Berufung der Zeit. Kantaten und Chöre,* pp. 65, 70. Compare V. A. Frey, *Mütter und Männer. Ein Buch vom tapferen Herzen,* a collection of stories and poems exalting the eternal bond between mothers and sons.

76. Hermann Gerstner, *Requiem für einen Gefallenen,* Reihe, *Fahrt und Feier,* vol. 9, and *Den Müttern der toten Kämpfer,* in Reihe, *Fahrt und Feier,* vol. 11.

77. Für alle hebst du deine Hand empor
und segnet die Kolonne in der Gruft,
die sich dereinst zum Todessturm verschwor.

Du atmest tief im Licht die sanfte Luft
des Frühjahrs, und du lauscht, ob nicht im Tor
des Himmels einer steht und nach dir ruft.

Gerstner, *Den Müttern der toten Kämpfer,* p. 15.

78. Nun ruhst du unterm Tag und bist vereint
den Freunden, die das gleich Schicksal traf.
Du weisst nicht mehr, dass um den dunklen Schlaf
der Gruft die Liebe einer Mutter weint.

Gerstner, *Requiem für einen Gefallenen,* p. 11.

79. Gerstner, "Gespräch mit meinem Töchterchen," in Kurt Ziesel ed., *Krieg und Dichtung,* pp. 161–65.

80. Bodo Schütt, *Gestirn des Krieges. Gedichte,* pp. 64–68.

81. "Den Müttern":

O Mutter, in Demut bewahre
und mehre das edle Blut!
Unmässig verschwenden die Jahre
des Schwertes das teuerste Gut,
und Väter und Söhne erkühnen
des Todes sich, Helden gleich.

Ibid., p. 62.

82. Agnes Miegel, "Die Mütter an die Jugend im Krieg":

Aber dann zuckt das Herz und weiss wieder das grosse, bittere Wort
und weiss, er zog so wie damals sein Vater fort!
Und wir sind tapfer, so wie wir es damals waren,
und wieder bereit, geduldig auf Botschaft zu harren!
Aber dieses ist schwer: dass ihr uns schützt, nicht mehr wir
euch schützen, geliebte Jungen, ihr!

Und wir schliessen die Augen, müde von Arbeit und Sorgen,
fühlen mit euch uns vereint und mit allen Müttern geborgen,
denken dankbar, dass wir so stolz auf euch sind,
sagen—o sanft kommt der Schlaf—:
Draussen steht auch mein Kind!

Sigmund Graff, ed., *Eherne Ernte. Gedichte im Krieg 1939–1941,* pp. 139–40. Compare Herybert Menzel, "Frauen Sind Heimat," *Die Neue Gemeinschaft,* 8 (April 1942), p. 167.

83. Wenn einst der Schlussakkord gesungen,
wird man von der deutschen Jugend sagen:

Dass sie gleich den Helden unserer Sagen
sich um ihres Führers Fahne scharte,
dass sich Deutschland in uns offenbarte,
Deutschland, das wir tief im Herzen tragen.

Wenn ich falle, Mutter, musst du's tragen,
und dein Stolz wird deinen Schmerz bezwingen,
denn du durftest ihm ein Opfer bringen,
das wir meinen, wenn wir Deutschland sagen.

Die Neue Gemeinschaft, 8 (April 1942), p. 174.

84. Koonz, pp. 185–86. For an analysis of the origins of Mother's Day, see

Karin Hausen, "Mother's Day in the Weimar Republic," in Renate Bridenthal et al., *When Biology Became Destiny: Women in Weimar and Nazi Germany*, pp. 131–52.

85. For an example of the kind of propaganda employed, see Tiessler, Reichspropagandaleitung, Rundschreiben Nr. 77 an alle Gaupropagandaleiter und Gauringleiter, 14 July 1942, under the rubric "Sieg der Waffen—Sieg der Wiegen," HA, Reel 16, Folder 291.

86. See Goebbels an alle Gauleiter, Betrifft: Muttertag 1944, 31 March 1944, in RPL/HKA, *Unsere Feier. Richtlinien zur Fest-und Feiergestaltung*, Nr. 5/44, 31 March 1944, "Muttertag 1944," Anlage Nr. 1., NSDAP, T-81, Roll 167, 306406, NA.

87. Ibid. For an excellent photograph of these ceremonies as well as a remarkable photograph of several happy women wearing their official "Ehrenkreuz der Deutschen Mutter" with the caption "Five Generations under One Roof," see Norbert Westenrieder, *Deutsche Frauen und Mädchen: Vom Alltagsleben 1933–1945*, p. 38.

88. RPL/HKA, *Unsere Feier. Richtlinien zur Fest- und Feiergestaltung*, Nr. 5/44, 31 March 1944, "Muttertag 1944," NSDAP, T-81, Roll 167, 305406, NA. See also Tiessler, RPL/Hauptamt Reichsring, Hotel Kaiserhof, Berlin, 25 April 1942, Rundschreiben Nr. 41, to all Mitglieder und Verbindungsmänner des Reichsrings/Gauleiter zur Kenntnis, "Betrifft: Muttertag 17 May 1942," NSDAP/HA, Roll 16, Folder 291. The Reichsbund der Kleingärtner was pressed into service as well. It was expected to provide free of charge garlands of flowers for the mothers of the fallen.

89. RPL/HKA, *Unsere Feier. Richtlinien zur Fest- und Feiergestaltung*, Nr. 5/44, 31 March 1944, "Muttertag 1944," NSDAP, T-81, Roll 167, 306406, NA.

90. "Feierstunde der NSDAP, Muttertag, 17 May 1942, "Für Dich, Mutter!" *Die neue Gemeinschaft*, 8 (April 1942), pp. 190–93.

91. There was often a fine line between propaganda and truth. The last letter of one "P. B.," who was killed in February 1944, to his sister contained the thought that "when we speak of homeland and Fatherland, of culture and tradition, which is why we are out here, these are values and concepts, which are only in part a link to the irrational. But through our children we are bound to the most elemental connections of blood. We are defending our blood here in the East. This realization provides the strength for all our undertakings. Isn't it really worthwhile to put our lives on the line for our children? Nor is danger foreign to you mothers. . . . " *Den Gefallenen. Ein Buch des Gedenkens und des Trostes*, p. 77.

92. Because the Mother's Day ceremony was to be characterized by a tone of joy, the booklets distributed to each mother who had lost a son or husband during the war were not presented at this time. Instead, during the week of Mother's Day, a party functionary visited each home and tactfully gave the official book of inspiration for that particular year.

93. RPL/HKA, *Unsere Feier*, Nr. 5/44, 31 March 1944, NSDAP, T-81, Roll 167, 306406, NA. For exercises in celebration of the coming of Mother's Day in the Hitler Youth, see Rektor Albert Krebs, ed., *Wir Jungen tragen die Fahne*, pp. 127–30.

94. See Gerald Kirwin, "Allied Bombing and Nazi Domestic Propaganda," *European History Quarterly*, 15, 3 (July 1985), pp. 341–62.

95. For example, on 7 February 1941, Goebbels called for honest reporting on the number of deaths in the air war at his daily press conference. Boelcke, *Kriegspropaganda 1939–1941*, p. 65. As early as 19 February 1941, the OKW/WPr objected to a proposed commemorative notice of the deaths of eighty-nine people in a raid on Hanover, which Gauleiter Hartmann Lauterbacher intended to publish in a local newspaper. See OKW/WPr, T-77, Roll 985, 4476928, NA.

96. Boelcke, p. 344. According to Goebbels, "Die Berichterstattung soll hierdurch beitragen, dass das Ertragen von Luftangriffen als Kampf gewertet und

empfunden wird." See Vertrauliche Informationen Nr. 183/41, 17 July 1941, Sammlung Oberheitmann, ZSg 109/23, BA.

97. See Goebbels's press conference of 11 August 1942, in Willi A. Boelcke, ed., *"Wollt Ihr den totalen Krieg?" Die geheimen Goebbels-Conferenzen 1939–1943*, pp. 269–70.

98. Hitler, speech delivered 8 November 1943, Löwenbräukeller, Munich, Domarus, p. 2056. On public opinion, see response to Goebbels's air war propaganda and his *Das Reich* editorial of 16 August 1942 entitled "Konzentration der Kräfte," SD, Reichssicherheitshauptamt report of 20 August 1942, R58/174, BA.

99. NSDAP, T-81, Roll 152, 0155783, NA.

100. See the text of Goebbels's speeches on the subject of the air war in Helmut Heiber, ed., *Goebbels Reden, 1939–1945*, Berlin, 5 June 1943, p. 218–39; Kassel, 5 November 1943, pp. 259–85; Hanover, 5 November 1943, pp. 305–13; Nuremberg, 4 June 1944, pp. 323–41.

101. *Das Reich*, 2 January 1944. See also Goebbels's editorial "Das Leben geht weiter," *Das Reich*, 16 April 1944.

102. Wächter/Berndt, Reichsministerium für Volksaufklärung und Propaganda, Propagandaparole Nr. 59, 7 August 1943, NSDAP, T-81, Roll 672, NA.

103. SD, R58/144, BA.

104. Vertrauliche Informationen der Parteikanzlei, Betrag 996, 27 November 1942.

105. *Reichsverfügungsblatt*, Rundschreiben 166/43, 2 December 1943, NSDAP, T-81, Roll 659, 5466343, NA.

106. Georg Grabenhorst, "Die Opfer in der Heimat," *Den Gefallenen*, pp. 78–81.

107.

Zwischen Ruinen eilen wir hin aller Stunden,
Wissen Leichen im Schutt und denken vorbei,
Schwatzen ein Weilchen und lachen und hehlen die Wunden,
Sagen, was harmlos, und verschweigen den Schrei.

Alltag und Tote . . . in hellem und schwarzem Mäander
Tod und Leben. Leben wir selber nur halb?

Wilhelm Pleyer, "Zwischen Ruinen," *Den Gefallenen*, p. 85. See also Gertrud von le Fort, "Die Kathedrale nach der Schlacht," ibid., p. 84.

108.   Er spaltete es auf in tausend Schreie
        und trug sie steigend in das weite Freie
        und in den Stürmen wurden sie ein Meer
        verzweifelten Gebetes. Aber hier
        ist eine Stille weniger. Die Steine
        verwandelt dieser Untergang in reine
        Erwartung. Aber was warten wir . . . ?

Oskar Gitzinger, *Nacht und Brand*, p. 15. For an analysis of German morale during the bombing campaign, see Earl R. Beck, *Under the Bombs*, pp. 107–71.

109. "Gedenkfeier der NSDAP für die Opfer des Luftkrieges in D.," *Die neue Gemeinschaft*, 11 (January 1945), pp. 35–37. As the air war dragged on, the cries for revenge became louder and louder. As one propaganda pamphlet threatened, "Der Deutsche ist nicht rachsüchtig. Er hat in seiner langen und leidenvollen Geschichte viel erduldet und viel verziehen. Wenn er aber diese Tausende qualvoller Nächte, diese Hunderttausende gemeltzelter Kinder und Frauen, diese Millionen Ruinen je vergässe und verziehe,—dann wäre er das Schicksal wert, zu dem ihn britische Blasphemie im voraus verdammt hat. Dieser Terror kennt nur eine Ant-

wort: VERGELTUNG! Und der Tag der Vergeltung wird kommen. Signed: 'Ein Deutscher.' "

110. See Welch, pp. 221–37, and Richard Taylor, *Film Propaganda: Soviet Russia and Nazi Germany*, pp. 216–33.

111. Goebbels, quoted in *Ein Mann. Des Seefahrers und aufrechten Bürgers Joachim Nettelbeck wundersame Lebensgeschichte von ihm selbst erzählt*, p. 427.

Bibliography

ARCHIVAL SOURCES

BAYERISCHES HAUPTSTAATSARCHIZ, MUNICH

Sammlung Rehse (Sammlung Personen)
    4590 Hans Baumann
    2778 Langemarck
    5682 Hans Maikowski
    7008 Eberhard Wolfgang Möller
    1132 Herbert Norkus
    5802 Karl Ritter
    3796 Albert Leo Schlageter
    4867 Gerhard Schumann
    2784 Verdun
    4747 Josef Magnus Wehner
    3303 Horst Wessel
    3229 Hans Zöberlein
Bildersammlung (Sammlung Personen)
    Hans Maikowski
    Herbert Norkus
    NS-Gedenkfeier 1934, 1936, 1937
    Albert Leo Schlageter
    Horst Wessel

BERLIN DOCUMENT CENTER

NSDAP Personnel Files. Reichsschriftumskammer.
    Heinrich Anacker
    Hans Baumann
    Hanns Heinz Eweis
    Alfred Götze
    Hanns Johst
    Hans Maikowski
    Otto Paust
    Theodor von der Pfordten
    Karl Ritter
    Albert Leo Schlageter
    Otto Schneider
    Dr. Max Erwin von Scheubner-Richter
    Gerhard Schumann
    Horst Wessel
    Hans Zöberlein

BUNDESARCHIV, KOBLENZ

NL 118/62 Nachlass Goebbels
NSD 41/238 Reichsführer SS. SS Hauptamt. *Vorschläge für die Abhaltung einer Toten-feier.* Manuskript. Nur für den Dienstgebrauch.
R 43 I/710–12; II/1287–89. Reichskanzlei. "Friedhöfe, Denkmäler und Gedenk-feiern für die im Kriege Gefallenen 1919–1944."

R43 11/1306 Reichskanzlei. "Planung für Ehrenmalen und Ehrenfriedhöfen. Generalbaurat für die Gestaltung der deutschen Kriegerfriedhöfe 1940–1943."
ZSg 109/23 Sammlung Oberheitmann. Reichsministerium für Volksaufklärung und Propaganda. "Vertrauliche Informationen."
R58/174 SD. Reichssicherheitshauptamt. "Meldungen aus dem Reich."

Photographs Section
Joseph Goebbels 85/52/19
Reinhard Heydrich 69/52/69, 69/58/27.
Langemarck 85/52/23
Horst Wessel A-B-C No. 9302, 9303, 16654, 4365A, 4366A, 15082, 1924, 1928.
Hans Maikowski 85/52/15, 85/52/16.
Herbert Norkus 85/52/22
9 November 1935 85/52/13
Albert Leo Schlageter 85/52/17, 85/52/18

DEUTSCHES INSTITUT FÜR FILMKUNDE, WIESBADEN

File Karl Ritter
Besatzung Dora
G.P.U.
Kadetten
Pour le Mérite
Patrioten
Stukas
Urlaub auf Ehrenwort
Unternehmen Michael
Verräter
File Hans Steinhoff
Hitlerjunge Quex

DEUTSCHES LITERATUR ARCHIV, SCHILLER NATIONALMUSEUM (MARBACH AN DER NECKAR)

Sammlung Hans Grimm
Bestand Willi Rehkopf
Albert Leo Schlageter: Dokumentation

HOOVER INSTITUTION

NSDAP Hauptarchiv
Early Hitler speeches, Roll 2, Folder 59
Polizeidirektion München, 2 November 1925, Roll 2, Folder 23
Die Blutfahne und ihre Träger, Roll 4, Folder 93.
Die Toten der Bewegung/Gedenkfeiern, Roll 4, Folder 103
NSDAP/München (1923), Roll 5, Folder 116.
Hauptamt Reichsring-Reichspropagandaleitung 1939, 1941–1944, Roll 16, Folder 291.
S. A. Oberkommando/Verfügungen, Roll 16, Folder 296, 301.
Von Schirach papers, Roll 18, Folder 336.
K.P.D. Verschiedenes, Roll 41, Folder 810.
9 November 1923 (Blutfahne Trambauer), Roll 53, Folder 1278.
Horst Wessel, Roll 53, Folder 1280.
Gedenkfeiern, Roll 54, Folder 1291.

INSTITUT FÜR ZEITGESCHICHTE, MUNICH

MS 8/1(a), MS 8/2(a) Dr. Armand Dehlinger. *Architektur der Superlative. Eine Kritische Betrachtung der N. S. Bauprogramme von München und Nürnberg.*
Reichsjugendführung. *Die Jungenschaft. Blätter für Heimabendgestaltung im Deutschen Jungvolk.* Berlin. Bundesarchiv.
Reichspropagandaleitung. Hauptkulturamt. *Die neue Gemeinschaft. Das Parteiarchiv für N. S. Feier und Freizeitsgestaltung* 1939–1945.
Reichspropagandaleitung. Hauptkulturamt. *Kulturpolitisches Mitteilungsblatt.*
SS, *SS Leithefte.*

INTERVIEWS

Hans Baumann. Murnau an der Staffelsee. 23 April, 1 May 1985.
Dr. Fritz Hippler. *Reichsfilmintendant.* Berchtesgaden. 18 January 1988.
Gerhard Schumann. Bodman/Bodensee. 19 May 1985.
Dr. Werner Naumann. Staatssekretär im Reichsministerium für Volksaufklärung und Propaganda. Bad Homburg, 17 November 1969; Klingenberg/Main, 11–12 July 1970; Lüdenscheid, 6 August 1970.

LANDESARCHIV BERLIN

Generalstaatsanwaltschaft beim Schwurgericht, Landgericht Berlin
Rep. 58/2046 (Alfred Götze). "Meineid Schlageter."
Rep. 58, Lfd. No. 11, 1 J 126/30, "Rubrum: Höhler und Andere. Sachverhalt: Ermordung des Studenten Horst Wessel, Urteil."
Rep. 58/30 (Zauritz/Maikowski). Urteil (500), 1.pol.b K.10.33 (53.33).
Rep. 58/9 (Herbert Norkus)

LIBRARY OF CONGRESS

Motion Pictures Section
Ufa-Werbedienst: Karl Ritter Files
Prints and Photographs
LC-USZ 62–42896 Horst Wessel
Lot 11384 Klaus Weill, Leibstandarte "Adolf Hitler," field burial, snapshot album presented to Hitler.
Lot 11382 W. Schmitt, photograph album presented to Hitler, Schlageter memorial ceremonies, Düsseldorf, 27–28 May 1933

NATIONAL ARCHIVES

Chef des Sicherheitspolizei und des SD. "Heldenehrungsfeiern. Zunehmende Aktivität der Kirche, 12 October 1942. "Meldungen aus dem Reich." SS, T-175, Roll 264, 2757772.
Goebbels, Rundschreiben an alle Reichspropagandaämter, 1 October 1942, Reichspropagandaleitung/Hauptamt Reichsring, NSDAP, T-81, Roll 675, 5483729.
Goebbels, Horst Wessel Gedenkfeiern, 17 October 1939, T-454, Roll 74, 502.
Horst Wessel Feier, 7 February 1942, NSDAP, T-81, Roll 92, 106376.
"11. Jahrestag des Todes Horst Wessels," NSDAP, T-81, Roll 92, 106286.
NSDAP. Parteikanzlei, Rundschreiben No. 156/42 Nov. 1942, NSDAP-Reichsring f.V.und P.-Hauptamt Pro., T-81, Roll 675, 5483725.
NSDAP. Reichspropagandaleitung. Hauptkulturamt. *Unsere Feier. Richtlinien zur Fest-und Feiergestaltung.* No. 3/1944. NSDAP, T-81, Roll 133, 166474.
Oberkommando der Wehrmacht. Abteilung für Wehrmachtspropaganda. T-77, Roll 985.
Dr. Walter Luetgebrune Akten, T-253, Roll 1, 1453005.

Reichsführer SS. SS Hauptamt. "Feierliche SS-mässige Gestaltung der Beerdigung von gefallenen und gestorbenen SS Angehörigen." SS, T-175, Roll 190, 2727842.
Reichsministerium für Volksaufklärung und Propaganda. "Propagandaparolen." NSDAP, T-81, Roll 672.
Walther Tiessler. Reichsring für Volksaufklärung und Propaganda. Hauptamt Propaganda. NSDAP, T-81, Roll 675.

STADTARCHIV MÜNCHEN

Stadtrat der Landeshauptstadt München
    Bürgermeister und Rat 458/2, 458/3. "Betreuung der Feldherrnhalle 1933–1945."
    Bürgermeister und Rat 512. "Der in den Städt. Friedhöfen Münchens befindlichen Grabstätten der Gefallenen vom 9. November 1923."
Photographs
    Miscellaneous
        1938 9 November 1933 Führer entourage
        4087 9 November 1934 Kranzniederlegung am Ehrenmal
        1980 9 November 1935 Feldherrnhalle
    Sammlung Nortz
        3669 9 November 1935 Überführung d. Opfer des 9 Nov. 1923

STIFTUNG DEUTSCHE KINEMATHEK, WEST BERLIN

Filmscripts: Films of Karl Ritter

DOCUMENTARY FILMS

Bundesarchiv
    Der 9. November in München. Agfa 1933. Mag. Nr. 192.
    Deutsche Wochenschauen: 1940–1945
    Ewige Wache. NSDAP/RPL. 1936. Mag. Nr. 68.
    Für Uns. NSDAP/RPL. 1937. Mag. Nr. 77.
    Im Geist der Alten Garde. Bavaria Wochenschau. 1936. Mag. Nr. 252.
    N.S.-Feiern und 9. November 1933–1938. Ufa Wochenschauaufnahmen. Mag. Nr. 273.
    NS-Ton-Bild Bericht Nr. 2. 1933.
    8. und 9. November 1935. Wochenschauaufnahmen. Mag. Nr. 781.
    Ufa-Tonwoche: 1936–1940
    Zeitprobleme. Wie der Arbeiter wohnt. Weltfilm Kartell, 1930. Mag. Nr. 394.
Library of Congress
    Begräbnis Horst Wessel. NSDAP/RPA. 1933.
    Das Sowjetparadies. NSDAP/RPL. 1943.
    Der ewige Jude (Fritz Hippler 1940)
    Europa bekämpft dem Bolschewismus. NSDAP/RPL. 1942.
    Im Walde von Katyn. NSDAP/RPL. 1943.
    Jahre der Entscheidung. NSDAP/RPL. 1939. FAA 1084.
    Sieg im Westen (Noldan 1940)

FEATURE FILMS: BUNDESARCHIV. STAATLICHE FILMARCHIV DER DDR.

Library of Congress
Besatzung Dora (1943 Karl Ritter)
GPU (1942 Karl Ritter)
Hans Westmar (1933 Franz Wenzler)

Jud Süss (1940 Veit Harlan)
Kadetten (1941 Karl Ritter)
Kreuzer Emden (1932 Louis Ralph)
Morgenrot (1933 Gustav Ucicky)
Mutter Krausens Fahrt ins Glück (1929 Prometheus)
Patrioten (1937 Karl Ritter)
Pour le Mérite (1938 Karl Ritter)
Stukas (1941 Karl Ritter)
Unternehmen Michael (1937 Karl Ritter)
Urlaub auf Ehrenwort (1937 Karl Ritter)
Verräter (1936 Karl Ritter)

OTHER DOCUMENTARY SOURCES

Newspapers, journals, and NSDAP publications
    Die Welt am Abend
    Bergisch-Märkische Zeitung/Elberfelder Zeitung
    Berliner Lokal-Anzeiger
    Berliner Illustrierte
    Berliner Morgenpost
    Berliner Volkszeitung
    Breisgauer Zeitung
    CineGraph
    Das Innere Reich. Zeitschrift für Dichtung, Kunst und deutsches Leben.
    Das Reich
    Das Schwarze Korps
    Der Angriff
    Der junge Sturmtrupp. Kampfblatt der werktätigen Jugend Grossdeutschlands
    Der Montag
    Der SA Mann
    Deutsche Allgemeine Zeitung
    Die Bewegung (Nationalsozialistische Deutsche Studentenbund)
    Die Filmwoche
    Essener Volkszeitung
    Esslinger Zeitung
    Filmkurier
    Filmwelt
    Filmwoche
    Fränkische Kurier
    Germania
    Hamburger Illustrierte
    Illustrierte Film-Post
    Illustrierter Beobachter
    Kinematograph
    Kölnische Zeitung
    Kunst im Kriege
    Kyffhäuser Wehrkorrespondent
    Leipziger Tageszeitung
    LichtBildBühne
    Morgenpost (Munich)
    Mitteldeutsche National Zeitung
    Münchener Abendblatt
    Münchener Illustrierte
    Münchener Neueste Nachrichten

Münchener-Augsburger Abendzeitung
Münchener Zeitung
National Zeitung (Essen)
N. S. Kurier
Neue Badische Zeitung
Rote Erde. Generalanzeiger für die werktätige Bevölkerung des Industriegebietes (Peckenloh)
Rote Fahne
Schwäbische Merkur
Stuttgarter Tagblatt
Tempo (Berlin)
Völkischer Beobachter (Berlin/Munich)
Volksparole (Düsseldorf)
Vorwärts
Vossische Zeitung

NEWSPAPER ARTICLES

Belling, Curt. " 'Stukas.' Karl Ritters neuer Fliegerfilm im Ufa-Palast am Zoo." *Völkischer Beobachter*, 29 June 1941.

Berchtold, J. "14 Jahre Rotmord." *Der SA Mann*, 10 August 1932.

Brüchle, Franz. 1. Vorsitzender der Angehörigen ehem. K.B. 6. Res.-Feld.-Art.-Regts. "Allerheiligen 1914, Langemarck-Wytschaete." *Völkischer Beobachter*, 1 November 1935.

D'Alquen, Günter. "Auf dem Kemmel." *Völkischer Beobachter*, 5 June 1940.

Dannecker, Hermann. "Gerhard Schumann." *Völkischer Beobachter*, 19 May 1935.

"Deutsche Dichter der Zeit. Hans Baumann." *Völkischer Beobachter*, 15 February 1939.

Eberlein, Ludwig. "Urlaub auf Ehrenwort": Ein deutscher Filmsieg im Ufa-Palast am Zoo." *Berliner Morgenpost*, 21 January 1938.

Ehmer, W. "Kriegsfreiwillige Berliner Jugend: Das Sterben von Dixmude." *Völkischer Beobachter*, 28 October 1934.

"Essener Jugend ehrt den Hitlerjungen Herbert Norkus." *National Zeitung*, 25 January 1934.

Fiedler, Richard. "Horst Wessel—ewiges Vorbild. Inbegriff des nationalsozialistischen Kämpfers und politischen Soldaten." *Mitteldeutsche National Zeitung*, 23 February 1939.

Grothe, Heinz. "Gerhard Schumann." *Westfälische Tageszeitung "Rote Erde"*, 8 March 1936.

———. "Der Weg zur 'Entscheidung'; Gespräch mit Gerhard Schumann über sein neues Drama." *Völkischer Beobachter*, 11 January 1939.

Gstettner, Hans. "Gerhard Schumann." *Völkischer Beobachter*, 5 April 1936.

"Hans Eberhard Maikowski: Zum bevorstehenden Jahrestag seiner Ermordung." *Berliner Illustrierte*, 28 January 1934.

Haur, Walter. "Die von Langemarck: Von einem alten Langemarckkämpfer." *Völkischer Beobachter*, 8 December 1934.

Hersdorf, H. "Otto Paust, der Dichter der Deutschen Trilogie," *Völkischer Beobachter*, 24 February 1938.

"Heute wie damals: Krieg gegen Moskau! Hans Eberhard Maikowski—Soldat seines Glaubens." *Der Angriff*, 30 January 1943.

Hultzsch, Wolfgang. "Gerhard Schumann auf der Stettiner Bühne." *Das Bollwerk 2*, 1943.

Jenssen, Christian. "Ein junger Kampfdichter: Gerhard Schumann." *Münchener Zeitung*, 22 May 1936.

Johst, Hanns. "Langemarck. Bekenntnis zu Josef Magnus Wehners Rede." *Münchener Neueste Nachrichten*, 4 August 1932.

"Langemarck," *Der SA Mann*, 12 November 1932.

Leonhardt, Rudolf Walter. "Der Dichter und Dramatiker Hans Baumann. Versuch eines Beitrages zur sogennanten Bewältigung der Vergangenheit." *Die Zeit*, 3 February 1962.

Lutze, Walter. "Horst Wessel. Das Vermächtnis unseres Sturmführers—zu seinem 10. Todestag." *Völkischer Beobachter*, 23 February 1940.

"Mahnmal für Herbert Norkus." *Leipziger Tageszeitung*, 23 April 1934.

Riecke, Heinz. "Gerhard Schumann." "Kritische Gänge." Beilage der *Berliner Börsenzeitung*, 5 May 1935.

Ritter, Karl. "Reportage- und Spielfilm." *Der Deutsche Film*. Sonderausgabe 1940/41.

"Spielleiter" Karl Ritter. Zum Film-Volkstag am 28. February 1938. Filmkunst, nicht Filmindustrie." *Stuttgarter Neues Tageblatt*, 26 February 1938.

Uterman, Wilhelm. " 'Kadetten.' Karl Ritters Preussenfilm in Berlin erstaufgeführt." *Völkischer Beobachter*, 20 December 1941.

Wehner, Josef Magnus. "Stirb und werde." *Illustrierte Beobachter*, 30 September 1933.

Weiskopf, Hermann. "Sinn und Opfer der Mütterlichkeit. Den Müttern unserer S.A.-Männer in Verehrung zum Muttertag 1930." *Der SA Mann*, 19 November 1932.

———. "Wir aber glaubten." *Münchener Neueste Nachrichten*, 27 January 1936.

Zöberlein, Leutnant Hans. "Zum 10. Todestag Horst Wessels." *Völkischer Beobachter*, 23 February 1940.

PRIMARY SOURCES

Albert Leo Schlageter. Dem deutschen Helden zum Gedächtnis. Zusammengestellt von der Sturmabteilung Schlageter (N.S.D.A.P.) Munich: Verlag der nationalen Propaganda, Briennerstrasse 29, n.d

Albert Leo Schlageter. Ein deutscher Freiheitsheld. Deutsches Wollen. Schriften für die deutsche Jugend. Bochum: Verlag Ferdinand Kamp, 1939.

Albert Leo Schlageter. Seine Verurteilung und Erschiessung durch die Franzosen in Düsseldorf am 26.5.1923. Dargestellt von den einzigen beteiligten Augenzeugen Rechtsanwalt Dr. Sengstock, Gefängnispfarrer Fassbender und Gefängniskaplan Roggendorff. Düsseldorf: 1927.

Albrecht, Gert. *Film im Dritten Reich. Eine Dokumentation.* Karlsruhe: Doku Verlag, 1979.

Anacker, Heinrich. *Die Fanfare.* Gedichte der deutschen Erhebung. Munich: Eher Verlag, 1934.

———. *Wir wachsen in das Reich hinein.* Munich: Eher Verlag, 1938.

———. *Bereitschaft und Aufbruch. Gedichte aus dem Kriegswinter 1940.* Munich: Franz Eher, 1940.

———. *Heimat und Front. Gedichte aus dem Herbst 1939.* Munich: Franz Eher, 1940.

———. *Über die Maas, über Schelde und Rhein. Gedichte vom Feldzug im Westen.* Munich: Franz Eher, 1940.

Arnold, Thomas, et al. *Hitlerjunge Quex. Einstellungsprotokoll.* Institut für historischsozialwissenschaftliche Analysen, no. 4. Munich: Filmland Presse, 1980.

Bade, Wilfred, ed. *Deutschland erwacht. Werden, Kampf und Sieg der NSDAP.* Hamburg: Cigarettenbilderdienst Hamburg-Bahrenfeld, 1933.

———. *Die SA erobert Berlin. Ein Tatsachenbericht.* Munich: Knorr & Hirth, 1943.

Baeumler, Alfred. *Männerbund und Wissenschaft*. Berlin: Junker & Dünnhaupt, 1940.

Baumann, Hans. *Alexander*. Jena: Diederichs, 1941.

―――. *Atem einer Flöte*. Jena: Diederichs, 1940.

―――. *Das Jahr überm Pflug*. Ein Bauernchor. Junges Volk, Reihe Fahrt und Feier, no. 3. Munich: Eher Verlag, 1935.

―――. *Der grosse Sturm*. Chor. Spiel. Potsdam: Voggenreiter 1935.

―――. *Der helle Tag*. Potsdam: Voggenreiter, 1940.

―――. *Der Retter Europas. Zum 20. April 1942*. Schriftenreihe zur Truppenbetreuung, no. 3. Die "Grauen Hefte" der Armee Busch. Die Propaganda Kompanie: "Feldzeitung von der Maas bis an die Memel," 1942.

―――. *Der Wandler Krieg*. Briefgedichte 1941. Jena: Diederichs, 1943.

―――. "Die Bewährung des Dichters. Rede beim Deutschen Dichtertreffen in Weimar 1941." *Das Innere Reich* 8 (December 1941): 461–71.

―――. *Die helle Flöte*. Lieder. Wolfenbüttel/Zürich: Möseler, 1980.

―――. *Feuer, steh auf dieser Erde*. Kantate zur Sonnenwende. Junges Volk. Reihe Fahrt und Feier, no. 8. Munich: Eher, 1935.

―――. *Gelöbnis der Jugend*. Berlin: Graphischer Grossbetrieb Oscar Brandstetter, 1940.

―――. *Horch auf Kamerad*. Lieder. Potsdam: Voggenreiter, 1936.

―――. *Kampf um die Karawanken*. Schauspiel. Deutsche Reihe, no. 73. Jena: Diederichs, 1938.

―――. *Macht keinen Lärm*. Munich: Kösel & Pustet, 1933.

―――, ed. *Morgen marschieren wir. Liederbuch der deutschen Soldaten*. Im Auftrag des Oberkommandos der Wehrmacht. Potsdam: Voggenreiter, 1941.

―――. *Reisepass*. Stuttgart: K. Thienemanns Verlag, 1978.

―――. *Wir zünden das Feuer*. Jena: Diederichs, 1936.

Behrendt, Erich F. *Soldaten der Freiheit*. Berlin: E. C. Etthofen, 1935.

Belling, Curt. *Der Film in Staat und Partei*. Berlin: 1936.

Belling, Curt, and Schütze, Alfred. *Der Film in der Hitler-Jugend*. Berlin: 1937.

Berndt, Alfred Ingemar (RMfVP), and Wedel, Hasso von (OKW/WPr), eds. *Deutschland im Kampf*. Berlin: Otto Stollberg, 1939–1944.

Beumelburg, Werner. *Von 1914 bis 1939. Sinn und Erfüllung des Weltkrieges*. Leipzig: Philipp Reclam jun., 1939.

Binding, Rudolph G. *Deutsche Jugend vor den Toten des Krieges*. Dessau: Karl Rausch, 1924.

―――. *Stolz und Trauer*. Frankfurt am Main: Literarische Anstalt Rütten & Loening, 1923.

Boberach, Heinz, ed. *Meldungen aus dem Reich. Auswahl aus den geheimen Lageberichten des Sicherheitsdienstes der SS 1939–1945*. Neuwied/Berlin: Luchterhand, 1965.

Boelcke, Willi A., ed. *Kriegspropaganda 1939–1941. Geheime Ministerkonferenzen im Reichspropagandaministerium*. Stuttgart: Deutsche Verlags-Anstalt, 1966.

―――, ed. *Wollt Ihr den totalen Krieg? Die geheimen Goebbels-Konferenzen 1939–1943*. Stuttgart: Deutsche Verlagsanstalt, 1967.

Böhme, Herbert. *Rufe in das Reich. Die heldische Dichtung von Langemarck bis zur Gegenwart*. Berlin: Junge Generation Verlag, 1934.

Brandt, Rolf. *Albert Leo Schlageter. Leben und Sterben eines deutschen Helden*. Hamburg: Hanseatische Verlagsanstalt, 1926.

Braun, Otto. *Von Weimar zu Hitler*. Hamburg: Norddeutsche Verlagsanstalt, 1949.

Decker, Will. *Kreuze am Wege zur Freiheit*. Leipzig: K. F. Koehler, 1935.

Der Gute Kamerad. Schriftenreihe zur Truppenbetreuung, no. 21. "Die 'Grauen Hefte' der Armee Busch." Die Propaganda-Kompanie: Feldzeitung von der Maas bis an die Memel," n.d.

Der Unbekannte SA Mann. Ein guter Kamerad. Munich: Eher Verlag, 1930.

Der Weg zum Nationalsozialismus. Die Ruhmeshalle der SA, SS and HJ, des früheren Stahl-helms und der für das Dritte Reich gefallenen Parteigenossen. Fürstenwalde/Spree: Militär Verlag, n.d.

Diels, Rudolf. *Lucifer ante Portas.* Zürich: Interverlag, n.d.

Dippel, Paul Gerhardt. *Dichtung der jungen Nation.* Berlin: Büchergilde Gutenberg, 1938.

Domarus, Max. *Hitler. Reden und Proklamationen 1932–1945.* 4 vols. Munich: Süd-deutscher Verlag, 1965.

Dreysse, Wilhelm. *Langemarck 1914. Der heldische Opfergang der Deutschen Jugend.* Minden i.W.: Wilhelm Köhler Verlag, 1934.

Dwinger, Edwin Erich. *Wir Rufen Deutschland.* Jena: Diederichs, 1932.

Elser, Johann Georg. *Autobiographie eines Attentäters. Aussage zum Sprengstoffanschlag im Bürgerbräukeller, München am 8. November 1939.* Edited by Lothar Gruch-mann. Stuttgart: Deutsche Verlags-Anstalt, 1970.

Engelbrechten, J. K. von. *Eine braune Armee entsteht. Die Geschichte der Berlin-Bran-denburger SA.* Munich/Berlin: Franz Eher, 1937.

Engelbrechten, J. K. von, and Volz, Hans. *Wir wandern durch das nationalsozialistische Berlin. Ein Führer durch die Gedenkstätten des Kampfes um die Reichshauptstadt.* Mun-ich: Eher Verlag, 1937.

Erckmann, Rudolf. *Gerhard Schumann.* Reihe "Künder und Kämpfer." Edited by Paul Gerhardt Dippel. Munich: Deutscher Volksverlag, 1938.

Euringer, Richard. *Deutsche Passion 1933.* Oldenburg i. O.: Gerhard Stalling, 1933.

Ewers, Hanns Heinz. *Horst Wessel. Ein deutsches Schicksal.* Stuttgart/Berlin: Cotta, 1934.

Ewiges Deutschland. Ein deutsches Hausbuch. Winterhilfswerk des Deutschen Volkes. Berlin/Hamburg: Georg Westermann, 1942.

Flex, Walter. *Der Wanderer zwischen beiden Welten: Ein Kriegserlebnis.* Munich: C. H. Beck'sche Verlagsbuchhandlung, 1937.

Forell, Fritz von. *Mölders und seine Männer.* Berlin: Verlag Scherl, 1941.

Frank, Hans. *Im Angesicht des Galgens.* Munich-Gräfelfing: Beck Verlag, 1953.

———. *Theodor von der Pfordten.* Munich: Franz Eher, n.d.

Frey, V. A. *Mütter und Männer. Ein Buch vom tapferen Herzen.* Stuttgart/Berlin: Georg Truckenmüller, n.d.

Ganzer, Karl Richard. *9. November 1923. Tag der ersten Entscheidung.* Munich: Lan-gen-Müller, 1936.

Generalkommando des VII. Armeekorps. *Soldatenliederbuch.* Munich: Franz Eher, 1940.

Gerstner, Hermann. *Den Müttern der toten Kämpfer.* Reihe Fahrt und Feier, no. 11. Munich: Zentralverlag der NSDAP, n.d.

———. *Requiem für einen Gefallenen.* "Reihe Fahrt und Feier," no. 9. Munich: Franz Eher, n.d.

Giessler, Hermann. *Ein Anderer Hitler. Bericht seines Architekten Hermann Giessler* (Leoni am Starnberger See: Druffel Verlag, 1978.)

Gitzinger, Oskar. *Nacht und Brand.* Karlsruhe: C. F. Müller, 1947.

Glombowski, Friedrich. *Organisation Heinz (O. H.). Das Schicksal der Kameraden Schla-geters.* Berlin: Reimar Hobbing Verlag, 1934.

Goebbels, Joseph. *Das Tagebuch von Joseph Goebbels 1925/26.* Edited by Helmuth Heiber. Schriftenreihe der *Vierteljahrshefte für Zeitgeschichte.* Stuttgart: Deutsche Verlagsanstalt, 1960.

———. *Der Angriff. Aufsätze aus der Kampfzeit.* Munich: Franz Eher, 1935.

———. *Der steile Aufstieg. Reden und Aufsätze aus den Jahren 1942/43.* Munich: Franz Eher, 1943.

———. *Die Tagebücher von Joseph Goebbels. Sämtliche Fragmente.* 4 vols. Edited by Elke Fröhlich. Munich: K. G. Saur, 1987.

———. *Goebbels Reden: 1932–1939.* 2 vols. Edited by Helmut Heiber. Düsseldorf: Droste, 1971.

———. *Michael. Ein Deutsches Schicksal in Tagebuchblättern.* Munich: Eher Verlag, 1934.

———. *Vom Kaiserhof zur Reichskanzlei.* Munich: Eher Verlag, 1937.

———. *Wetterleuchten. Aufsätze aus der Kampfzeit.* Munich: Eher Verlag, 1939.

Goote, Thor. *Kam'raden, die Rotfront und Reaktion erschossen. Ein Buch vom Opfertode unserer braunen Kameraden.* Berlin: Verlag E. S. Mittler & Sohn, 1934.

Görgen, Hans-Peter. *Düsseldorf und der Nationalsozialismus.* Düsseldorf: L. Schwann, 1969.

Görz, Heinz, and Wrede, Franz-Otto, eds. *Unsterbliche Gefolgschaft.* Unter Verwendung des Archivs der Reichsjugendführung der Hitler Jugend. Berlin: 1936.

Graff, Sigmund, ed. *Eherne Ernte. Gedichte im Krieg 1939–1941.* Munich/Berlin/Leipzig: Karl H. Bischoff Verlag, 1943.

———. *Unvergesslicher Krieg.* Leipzig: Breitkopf & Härtel, 1936.

Günther, Hans F. K. *Ritter, Tod und Teufel. Der heldische Gedanke.* Munich: J. F. Lehmanns Verlag, 1928.

Gutachten des Instituts für Zeitgeschichte. Munich: Selbstverlag des Instituts für Zeitgeschichte, 1958.

Hanfstaengl, Ernst. *Zwischen Weissem und Braunem Haus. Memoiren eines politischen Aussenseiters.* Munich: Piper, 1970.

Harbeck, Karl-Heinz, ed. With Karl Dietrich Erdmann (Historische Kommission bei der Bayerischen Akademie der Wissenschaften) and Wolfgang Mommsen (Bundesarchiv). *Akten der Reichskanzlei. Weimarer Republik. Das Kabinett Cuno: 22. November 1922–12. August 1923.* Boppard am Rhein: Harald Boldt Verlag, 1968.

Hay, Gerhard. "Rundfunk und Hörspiel als 'Führungsmittel' des Nationalsozialismus." Horst Denkler and Karl Prümm. *Die deutsche Literatur im Dritten Reich.* Stuttgart: Reclam, 1976.

Heck, Alfons. *A Child of Hitler: Germany in the Days when God Wore a Swastika.* Frederick, Colorado: Renaissance House, 1985.

Herbert Norkus, der Hitlerjunge. "Die Fahne hoch! Die braune Reihe," no. 20. Berlin: Neues Verlagshaus für Volksliteratur, 1934.

Heyer, Georg Walther, ed. *Die Fahne ist mehr als der Tod. "Lieder der Nazizeit".* Munich: Wilhelm Heyne Verlag, 1980.

Hielscher, Friedrich. *Das Reich.* Berlin: Verlag Das Reich, 1931.

Hitler, Adolf. *Mein Kampf.* Munich: Eher Verlag, 1943.

Hoffmann, Heinrich. *Mit Hitler im Westen.* Munich: Eher Verlag, 1940.

Hölderlin. Gedenkschrift zu seinem 100. Todestag. 7. Juni 1943. Iduna. Jahrbuch der Hölderlin Gesellschaft 1 (1944): 16–20.

Höllger, Kurt. *Karl Ritter.* Berlin: Curtius, 1940.

Hügenell, Wilhelm. *Schlageter.* Munich: Verlag der Deutschvölkischen Buchhandlung, Franz Eher Nachf., 1923.

Hymmen, Friedrich Wilhelm. *Briefe an eine Trauernde. Vom Sinn des Soldatentodes.* Sonderdruck für das Hauptkulturamt in der Reichspropagandaleitung der NSDAP. Stuttgart: J. Engelhorns Nachf. Adolf Spemann, 1942.

Johst, Hanns. *Schlageter.* Munich: Langen-Müller, 1933.

Jünger, Ernst. *The Storm of Steel.* New York: Howard Fertig, 1975.

———. *Der Kampf als inneres Erlebnis.* Berlin: E. G. Mittler & Sohn, 1926.

Kahlenberg, Friedrich P. *Ausstellung zur Filmreihe "Jugend im NS Staat." Katalog.* Bundesarchiv. Koblenz: 1978.

Kalbus, Oskar. *Vom Werden deutscher Filmkunst.* vol. I: *Der Tonfilm.* Altona-Bahren-feld: Cigaretten-bilderdienst, 1935.

Kaufmann, Günter, ed. *Langemarck. Das Opfer der Jugend an allen Fronten.* Berlin: n.d.

———. "Einführung der Jugend in den Frontkämpfergeist."

Kern, Erwin Friedrich. *Albert Leo Schlageter und seine Heimat.* Schönau-Wiesenthal: Verlag Jungdeutscher Orden, n.d.

Koll, Kilian. *Urlaub auf Ehrenwort. Geschichten um den Krieg.* Munich: Langen-Müller, 1937.

Krebs, Alfred, ed. *Wir Jungen tragen die Fahne. Nationalsozialistische Morgenfeiern der Adolf Hitler Volksschule Stettin.* Frankfurt am Main: Verlag Moritz Diesterweg, 1942.

Kuratorium für das Reichsehrenmal Tannenberg. *Tannenberg. Deutsches Schicksal-Deutsche Aufgabe.* Oldenburg i. O./Berlin: Gerhard Stalling, 1939.

Kurfess, Franz. *Albert Leo Schlageter. Bauernsohn und Freiheitsheld.* Hirts Deutsche Sammlung, Gruppe VI: Persönlichkeiten. Breslau: Ferdinand Hirt, 1935.

Lange, Herbert. *Der Brückenschlag über den Tod. Aus den Tagebuch eines Gefallenen.* Sonderausgabe für die Truppenbetreuung der Waffen SS und Polizei. Berlin: Elsnerdruck, n.d.

Langenbucher, Hellmuth. *Die Dichtung der jungen Mannschaft.* Hamburg: Hanseatische Verlagsanstalt, 1936.

———. *Volkhafte Dichtung der Zeit.* Berlin: Junker und Dünnhaupt, 1937.

Linden, Walter. "Gerhard Schumann." *Die Neue Literatur* 10 (October 1936): 570–79.

Littmann, Arnold. *Herbert Norkus und die Hitlerjungen vom Beusselkietz. Nach dem Tagebuch des Kameradschaftsführers Gerd Mondt und nach Mitteilungen der Familie.* Berlin: Steuben Verlag, 1934.

Mann, Erika. *School for Barbarians.* New York: Modern Age Books, 1938.

Möller, Eberhard Wolfgang. *Berufung der Zeit.* Berlin: Theaterverlag Albert Langen/Georg Müller, 1935.

Mondt, Gerhard. *Herbert Norkus. Das Tagebuch der Kameradschaft Beusselkietz.* Berlin: Traditions-Verlag Kolk, 1941.

Müller, Franz. *Drei Sturmtrupplieder zur Deutschen Freiheitsbewegung. Dem Helden Schlageter gewidmet.* Kirchheim-Teck: Fr. Späth's Nachf. J. Weixler, 1923.

Mulot, Arno. *Der Soldat in der deutschen Dichtung unserer Zeit.* Stuttgart: J. B. Metzlersche Verlagsbuchhandlung, 1938.

NSDAP. *9. November 1923- 1933.* Munich: 1933.

NSDAP. Traditionsgau München-Oberbayern. *Zum 9. November 1936.* Munich: 1936.

Oberkommando der Wehrmacht/Abteilung für Wehrmachtspropaganda. *Sieg im Westen. Der Kriegsfilmbericht des Heeres.* Berlin: 1940.

Pantel, Gerhard. *Fähnlein Langemarck.* Munich: Jugendverlag Hochland, 1934.

Petersen, Jan. *Unsere Strasse. Eine Chronik Geschrieben im Herzen des faschistischen Deutschlands 1933/34.* Berlin/Weimar: Aufbau Verlag, n.d.

Pongs, Hermann. *Krieg als Volksschicksal im deutschen Schrifttum.* Stuttgart: J. B. Metzlersche Verlagsbuchhandlung, 1934.

Ramlow, Rudolf. *Herbert Norkus?—Hier! Opfer und Sieg der Hitler-Jugend.* Stuttgart/Berlin/Leipzig: Union Deutsche Verlagsgesellschaft, 1933.

Reichsführer SS. SS Hauptamt. Schulungsamt. *Sieg der Waffen—Sieg des Kindes,* n.p., n.d.

Reichspropagandaamt. Hauptkulturamt. *Gebt euren Toten Heimrecht!* Berlin: Erasmusdruck, 1941.

Reichspropagandaleitung. Hauptamt Kultur. *Die Heldenehrungsfeier der NSDAP*. Sonderdruck, *Die Neue Gemeinschaft*. Berlin: 1942.

Reichsjugendführung. Kulturamt. *Liederblatt der Hitlerjugend*. Wolfenbüttel/Berlin: Georg Kallmeyer Verlag, 1936.

Reichspropagandaleitung. Hauptpropagandaamt. *Den Müttern und Frauen zum Muttertag 1944. Deutschland . . . Kein Opfer . . . ist dafür zu gross!* Berlin: Erasmusdruck, 1944.

Reichspropagandaleitung der NSDAP, Amtsleitung Film. *Unternehmen Michael.* "Staatspolitische Filme," no. 7. Berlin: Frickert, n.d.

Reichssicherheitshauptamt, ed. *Reinhard Heydrich.* Berlin: Verlag Ahnenerbe Stiftung, 1942.

Reitmann, Erwin. *Horst Wessel. Leben und Sterben.* Berlin: Steuben Verlag, 1932.

Rilke, Rainer Maria. *Die Weise von Liebe und Tod des Cornets Christoph Rilke.* Leipzig: Inselverlag, 1899.

Ritter, Gerhard. *Die geschlechtliche Frage in der deutschen Volkserziehung.* Berlin/Cologne: Marcus & Weber, 1936.

Ritter, Gustav, and von Oetinger, Edler. *In Ketten von Ruhrgebiet nach Saint-Martin de Re. Erlebnisse politischer Gefangener im Ruhrgebiet, im Rheinland und in Frankreich 1923/1924.* Essen: Verlag Julius Hergt, 1925.

Rittich, Werner. "Heroische Plastik," *Die Kunst im Dritten Reich* 10 (December 1937): 28–34. Schriftenreihe zur Truppenbetreuung, no. 21.

Roden, Hans, ed. *Deutsche Soldaten.* Unter Mitarbeit der Deutschen Gesellschaft für Wehrpolitik und Wehrwissenschaften und des Schlageter Gedächtnis Museums. Leipzig: Breitkopf & Härtel, 1935.

Rossbach, Gerhard. *Mein Weg durch die Zeit.* Weilburg/Lahn: Vereinigte Weilburger Buchdruckereien, 1950.

Roth, Bert, ed. *Kampf. Lebensdokumente deutscher Jugend von 1914–1934.* Leipzig: Reclam, 1934.

Ruppel, Karl H. *Berliner Schauspiel.* Berlin/Vienna: Paul Neff Verlag, 1943.

Saar, Wilhelm F. von der. *Der deutsche Martyr 'Schlageter' und der Französische Sadismus an Ruhr und Rhein.* Stuttgart: Wilhelm Baltrusch Verlag, 1923.

Salomon, Ernst von. *Die Geächteten.* Gütersloh: C. Bertelsmann, 1930.

———, ed. *Das Buch vom deutschen Freikorpskämpfer.* Hrsg. im Auftr. der Freikorpszeitschrift 'Der Reiter gen Osten.' Berlin: Wilhelm Limpert Verlag, 1938.

———. *Fragebogen.* New York: Doubleday, 1955.

Sander, A. U. *Jugend und Film.* Berlin: Eher Verlag, 1944.

Schaumburg-Lippe, Friedrich Christian Prinz zu. *Als die Goldne Abendsonne. Tagebücher 1933–1937.* Wiesbaden: Limes Verlag, 1971.

Schauwecker, Franz. *Aufbruch der Nation.* Berlin: Frundsberg, 1929.

Schenzinger, Karl Aloys. *Der Herrgottsbacher Schülermarsch.* Berlin: Zeitgeschichte Verlag, 1934.

———. *Der Hitlerjunge Quex.* Berlin: Zeitgeschichte Verlag, 1932.

Schirach, Baldur von. *Die Fahne der Verfolgten.* Berlin: Zeitgeschichte Verlag, n.d.

———. *Die Hitler-Jugend. Idee und Gestalt.* Berlin: Zeitgeschichte Verlag, 1934.

———. *Revolution der Erziehung. Reden aus den Jahren des Aufbaus.* Munich: Franz Eher, 1938.

———. *Vom Glauben der Gemeinschaft.* Berlin: Graphischen Kunstanstalt Albert Frisch, 1935.

Schlageter, Albert Leo. *Deutschland muss leben. Gesammelte Briefe von Albert Leo Schlageter.* Edited by Friedrich Bubendey. Berlin: Paul Steegemann Verlag, 1934.

Schlageter. Eine Auseinandersetzung. Karl Radek/P. Fröhlich/Graf Ernst Reventlow/Möller van den Bruck. Kommunismus und nationale Bewegung. Berlin: Vereinigung Internationaler Verlagsanstalten, 1923.

Scholtz, Gerhard. *Tag von Langemarck.* Leipzig: Schmidt & Spring.
Schrade, Hubert. *Das Deutsche Nationaldenkmal.* Munich: Langen-Müller, 1934.
Schütt, Bodo. *Gestirn des Krieges. Gedichte.* Jena: Diederichs, 1941.
Schumann, Gerhard. *Besinnung. Von Kunst und Leben.* Bodman/Bodensee: Hohenstaufen Verlag, 1974.
————. *Bewährung.* Munich: Langen-Müller, 1940.
————. *Die Lieder vom Krieg.* Feldpostausgabe. Munich: Langen-Müller, 1941.
————. *Die Lieder vom Reich.* Munich: Langen-Müller, 1935.
————. *Entscheidung.* Munich: Langen-Müller, 1943; reprint ed., Munich: Hohenstaufen Verlag, 1980.
————. *Fahne und Stern.* Munich: Langen-Müller, 1934.
————. *Gesetz wird zu Gesang.* Vienna/Berlin/Leipzig: K. H. Bischoff Verlag, 1943.
————. *Gudruns Tod.* Vienna: K. H. Bischoff Verlag, 1943; reprint ed., Esslingen/Neckar: Hohenstaufen Verlag, 1963.
————. *Herbstliche Ernte.* Bodman/Bodensee: Hohenstaufen Verlag, 1986.
————. *Herr Aberndörfer.* Leipzig: Arweg Strauch, 1937.
————. "Krieg—Bericht und Dichtung." *Dichter und Krieger. Weimarer Reden 1942.* Edited by Rudolf Erckmann. Hamburg: Hanseatische Verlagsanstalt, 1943.
————. "Mein Weg zum Drama." *Leipziger Bühnenblätter.* Herausgegeben vom Intendanten der Städtischen Theater, Altes Theater, Spielzeit 1938–1939.
————. *Ruf und Berufung.* Munich: Langen-Müller, 1943.
————. *Schau und Tat. Gedichte.* Munich: Langen-Müller, 1938.
————. *Wir aber sind das Korn.* Munich: Langen-Müller, 1936.
————. *Wir dürfen dienen.* Munich: Langen-Müller, 1937.
Sellg, Wolfram, ed. *Chronik der Stadt München 1945–1948.* Munich: Stadtarchiv München, 1980.
Severing, Carl. *Mein Lebensweg.* Cologne: Greven Verlag, 1950.
Steguweit, Heinz. *Der Jüngling im Feuerofen.* Munich: Langen-Müller, 1932.
Sturm 33: Hans Maikowski. Geschrieben von Kameraden des Toten. Berlin: Verlag Deutsche Kultur-Wacht, 1934.
Troost, Gerdy, ed. *Das Bauen im Dritten Reich,* 2 vols. Bayreuth: Bauverlag Bayreuth, 1943.
Überhorst, Horst. *Elite für die Diktatur. Die nationalpolitischen Erziehungsanstalten 1933–1945. Ein Dokumentarbericht.* Düsseldorf: Droste, 1969.
Uetrecht, Fred-Erich. *Jugend im Sturm: Ein Bericht aus den schicksalsschweren Jahren 1917–1933.* Berlin: Verlag Ullstein, 1936.
Volksbund Deutsche Kriegsgräberfürsorge e.V. *Den Gefallenen. Ein Buch des Gedenkens und des Trostes.* München/Salzburg: Akademischer Gemeinschaftsverlag, 1952.
Wangenheim, Freiherr von. *Der Letzte Appell. Des SS-Oberjunkers Radewitz Taten, Traum und Tapferer Tod.* Berlin: Nordland, 1943.
Weberstedt, Hans, and Langner, Kurt. *Gedenkhalle für die Gefallenen des Dritten Reiches.* Munich: Franz Eher, 1935.
Wehner, Josef Magnus. *Langemarck. Ein Vermächtnis.* Munich: Langen-Müller, 1932.
————. *Sieben vor Verdun.* Munich: Langen-Müller, 1930.
Wer war Schlageter? Hrsg. vom Verlag Das Andere Deutschland. Berlin: 1931.
Wessel, Ingeborg. *Mein Bruder Horst. Ein Vermächtnis.* Munich: Franz Eher, 1934.
————. *Horst Wessel. Sein Lebensweg, nach Bildern zusammengestellt.* Munich: Eher Verlag, 1933.
Wetzel, Kraft, and Hagemann, Peter A. *Zensur—Verbotene deutsche Filme 1933–1945.* Stiftung Deutsche Kinemathek. Berlin: Verlag Volker Spiess, 1978.
Wulf, Joseph, ed. *Theater ud Film im Dritten Reich.* Hamburg: Rowohlt, 1966.
Zeller, Bernhard, ed. *Klassiker in finsteren Zeiten 1933–1945.* Eine Austellung des

Deutschen Literaturarchiv im Schiller-Nationalmuseum. Marbach am Neckar. 2 vols. Marbach: Deutsche Schillergesellschaft e.V., 1983.

Ziesel, Kurt, ed. *Krieg und Dichtung. Soldaten werden Dichter—Dichter werden Soldaten. Ein Volksbuch.* Vienna: Wiener Verlag 1943.

Zöberlein, Hans. *Der Glaube an Deutschland.* Munich: Franz Eher, 1931.

SECONDARY SOURCES

Ackermann, Josef. *Heinrich Himmler als Ideologe.* Göttingen: Musterschmidt, 1970.

Allen, William Sheridan. *The Nazi Seizure of Power: The Experience of a Single German Town, 1922–1945.* Rev. ed. New York: Franklin Watts, 1984.

Albrecht, Gerd. *Arbeitsmaterialien zum nationalsozialistischen Propagandafilm. Hitlerjunge Quex. Ein Film vom Opfergeist der deutschen Jugend. Die Information* 2 (1983): 1–40.

———. *Nationalsozialistische Filmpolitik. Eine soziologische Untersuchung über die Spielfilme des Dritten Reichs.* Stuttgart: Enke, 1969.

Baird, Jay W. *The Mythical World of Nazi War Propaganda, 1939–1945.* Minneapolis: University of Minnesota Press, 1974.

Beck, Earl R. *Under the Bombs.* Lexington: University of Kentucky Press, 1986.

Bessel, Richard. *Political Violence and the Rise of Nazism: The Storm Troopers in Eastern Germany, 1925–1934* New Haven/London: Yale University Press, 1984.

Bracher, Karl D.; Sauer, Wolfgang; and Schulz, Gerhard. *Die nationalsozialistische Machtergreifung.* Cologne: Westdeutscher Verlag, 1962.

Bramsted, Ernst K. *Goebbels and National Socialist Propaganda, 1925–1945.* East Lansing: Michigan State University Press, 1965.

Bridenthal, Renate; Grossmann, Atina; and Kaplan, Marion, eds. *When Biology Became Destiny: Women in Weimar and Nazi Germany.* New York: Monthly Review, 1984.

Brinkmann, Jürgen. *Orden und Ehrenzeichen des "Dritten Reiches."* Minden/Westphalen: Auktionator Jürgen Brinkmann, 1976.

Broszat, Martin. *Hitler and the Collapse of Weimar Germany.* Leamington Spa/Hamburg/New York: Berg, 1987.

Cadars, Pierre, and Courtade, Francis. *Le Cinema Nazi.* Paris: Losfeld, 1972.

Cornebise, Alfred E. *The Weimar in Crisis: Cuno's Germany and the Ruhr Occupation.* Washington: University Press of America, 1977.

Dallin, Alexander. *German Rule in Russia, 1941–1945.* London: Macmillan, 1957.

Dammeyer, Manfred, ed. *Der Spielfilm im Dritten Reich.* XII. Westdeutsche Kurzfilmtage. Oberhausen, 13–19 February 1966.

Diehl, James M. *Paramilitary Politics in Weimar Germany.* Bloomington/London: Indiana University Press, 1977.

Drewniak, Boguslaw. *Das Theater im N. S.-Staat. Szenarium deutscher Zeitgeschichte 1933–1945.* Düsseldorf: Droste Verlag, 1983.

Eksteins, Modris. "War, Memory, and Politics: The Fate of the Film *All Quiet on the Western Front.*" *Central European History* 13 (March 1980): 60–82.

Ericksen, Robert P. *Theologians under Hitler.* New Haven/London: Yale University Press, 1985.

Fest, Joachim C. *The Face of the Third Reich.* New York: Pantheon, 1970.

Fischer, Conan. *Stormtroopers: A Social, Economic, and Ideological Analysis, 1929–1935.* London: Allen & Unwin, 1983.

Fosten, D. S. V., and Marrion, R. J. *Waffen-SS.* London: Altmark, 1971.

Fowkes, Ben. *Communism in Germany under the Weimar Republic.* New York: St. Martin's Press, 1984.

Franke, Manfred. *Schlageter. Der erste Soldat des 3. Reiches.* Cologne: Prometh Verlag, 1980.

Gamm, Hans-Jochen. *Der braune Kult. Das Dritte Reich und sein Ersatzreligion.* Hamburg: Rütten & Loening, 1962.

———. *Führung und Verführung. Pädagogik des Nationalsozialismus.* Munich: List, 1964.

Gordon, Jr., Harold J. *Hitler and the Beer Hall Putsch.* Princeton: Princeton University Press, 1972.

Giles, Geoffrey J. *Students and National Socialism in Germany.* Princeton: Princeton University Press, 1985.

Heer, Friedrich. *Der Glaube des Adolf Hitler.* Munich: Bechtle Verlag, 1968.

Herzstein, Robert E. "Goebbels et le Mythe Historique par le Film." *Revue d'Histoire de la Deuxième Guerre Mondiale* 101 (January 1976): 41–62.

———. *The War That Hitler Won: The Most Infamous Propaganda Campaign in History.* New York: Putnam, 1978.

Hoch, Anton. "Das Attentat auf Hitler im Bürgerbräukeller." *Vierteljahrshefte für Zeitgeschichte* 17 (October 1969): 383–413.

Hollstein, Dorothea. *Antisemitische Filmpropaganda. Die Darstellung der Juden im nationalsozialistischen Spielfilm.* München-Pullach/Berlin: Verlag Dokumentation, 1971.

Hull, David Stewart. *Film in the Third Reich.* Berkeley: University of California Press, 1969.

Jarausch, Konrad H. "German Students in the First World War." *Central European History* 17 (December 1984): 310–29.

———. *Students, Society, and Politics in Imperial Germany.* Princeton: Princeton University Press, 1982.

Kamenetsky, Christa. *Children's Literature in Hitler's Germany.* Athens/London: Ohio University Press, 1984.

Kater, Michael H. "Ansätze zu einer Soziologie der SA bis zur Röhm Krise." Ulrich Engelherdt et al. *Soziale Bewegung und politische Verfassung.* Stuttgart: 1976.

———, "Bürgerliche Jugendbewegung und Hitlerjugend in Deutschland von 1926 bis 1939." *Archiv für Sozialgeschichte* 17: 151–52.

———. "Generationskonflikt als Entwicklungsfaktor in der NS-Bewegung vor 1933." *Geschichte und Gesellschaft* 11 (1985): 217–43.

———. *Studentenschaft und Rechtsradikalismus in Deutschland 1918–1933.* Hamburg. Hoffmann und Campe, 1975.

Kershaw, Ian. *Der Hitler-Mythos. Volksmeinung und Propaganda im Dritten Reich.* Schriftenreihe der Vierteljahrshefte für Zeitgeschichte. Stuttgart: Deutsche Verlagsanstalt, 1980.

Ketelsen, Uwe-Karsten. *Heroisches Theater. Untersuchungen zur Dramatheorie des Dritten Reiches.* Bonn: Bouvier, 1968.

———. *Von Heroischem Sein und Völkischen Tod. Zur Dramatik des Dritten Reiches.* Bonn: Bouvier Verlag, 1970.

Kirwin, Gerald. "Allied Bombing and Nazi Domestic Propaganda." *European History Quarterly* 15 (July 1985): 341–62.

Klinksiek, Dorothee. *Die Frau im NS-Staat.* Schriftenreihe der Vierteljahrshefte für Zeitgeschichte. Stuttgart: Deutsche Verlagsanstalt, 1982.

Koonz, Claudia. *Mothers in the Fatherland: Women, the Family, and Nazi Politics.* New York: St. Martin's Press, 1987.

Korte, Helmut. *Film und Realität in der Weimarer Republik.* Frankfurt: Fischer Taschenbuch Verlag, 1980.

Kurowski, Ulrich, ed. *Deutsche Spielfilme 1933–1945.* Materialien III. 2d rev. ed. Munich: Stadtmuseum München, 1981.

Laqueur, Walter. *Russia and Germany*. Boston: Little-Brown, 1965.

Lazar, Imre. *Der Fall Horst Wessel*. Stuttgart/Zürich: Belser Verlag, 1980.

Leiser, Erwin. *Nazi Cinema*. New York: Collier, 1974.

Lerner, Warren. *Karl Radek: The Last Internationalist*. Stanford: Stanford University Press, 1970.

Liang, Hsi-Huey. *The Berlin Police Force in the Weimar Republic*. Berkeley: University of California Press, 1970.

Lidtke, Vernon L. "Songs and Nazis: Political Music and Social Change in Twentieth-Century Germany." *Essays on Culture and Society in Modern Germany*. Edited by Gary D. Stark and Bede Karl Lackner. College Station: Texas A&M University Press, 1982.

Loewenberg, Peter. "The Psychohistorical Origins of the Nazi Youth Cohort." *American Historical Review* 76 (December 1971): 1457–502.

Marks, Sally. "Black Watch on the Rhine: A Study in Propaganda, Prejudice, and Prurience." *European Studies Review* 13 (July 1983): 297–334.

Marquardt, Axel, and Rathsack, Heinz. *Preussen im Film*. Eine Retrospektive der Stiftung Deutsche Kinemathek. Berlin: Rowohlt, 1981.

Merkl, Peter H. *The Making of a Stormtrooper*. Princeton: Princeton University Press, 1980.

Mitchell, Otis C. *Hitler over Germany: The Establishment of the Nazi Dictatorship, 1918–1934*. Philadelphia: Institute for the Study of Human Issues, 1983.

———. *Nazism and the Common Man*, 2d ed. Washington, D.C.: University Press of America, 1981.

Moltmann, Günter, and Reimers, Karl F. *Zeitgeschichte in Film und Tondokument*. Göttingen: Musterschmidt, 1970.

Mosse, George L. *The Nationalization of the Masses*. New York: Howard Fertig, 1975.

———. "National Cemeteries and National Revival: The Cult of the Fallen Soldiers in Germany." *Journal of Contemporary History* 14 (January 1979): 1–20.

———. *Nazi Culture* (New York: Grosset & Dunlap, 1966.

———. "Two World Wars and the Myth of the War Experience." *Journal of Contemporary History* 21 (October 1986): 491–513.

Noakes, Jeremy. *The Nazi Party in Lower Saxony, 1921–1933*. London: Oxford University Press, 1971.

Pfeiler, William K. *War and the German Mind: The Testimony of Men of Fiction Who Fought at the Front*. New York: Columbia University Press, 1941.

Prinz, Friedrich. *Trümmerzeit in München*. Munich: Beck Verlag, 1984.

Rosenhaft, Eve. *Beating the Fascists? The German Communists and Political Violence*. Cambridge: Cambridge University Press, 1983.

Schmeer, Karlheinz. *Die Regie des öffentlichen Lebens im Dritten Reich*. Munich: Verlag Pohl, 1956.

Schneeberger, Guido. *Nachlese zu Heidegger*. Bern: Suhr, 1962.

Sontheimer, Kurt. *Antidemokratisches Denken in der Weimarer Republik. Die politischen Ideen des deutschen Nationalismus zwischen 1918 und 1933*. Munich: Nymphenburger, 1962.

Stachura, Peter D. "The Ideology of the Hitler Youth in the Kampfzeit." *Journal of Contemporary History* 7 (July 1973): 155–67.

———. *Nazi Youth in the Weimar Republic*. Santa Barbara: Clio Books, 1975.

Stein, George H. *The Waffen SS: Hitler's Elite Guard at War, 1939–1945*. Ithaca/London: Cornell University Press, 1966.

Stokes, Lawrence D. "Der Fall Radke. Zum Tode eines nationalsozialistischen 'Märtyrers' und die Folgen in Eutin, 1931–1933." Erich Hoffmann and Peter Wulf, eds. *"Wir bauen das Reich". Aufstieg und erste Herrschaftsjahre des Nationalsozialismus*

in Schleswig-Holstein. Quellen und Forschungen zur Geschichte Schleswig-Hol-
   steins, vol. 81. Neumünster: Karl Wachholtz Verlag, 1984.
Sydnor, Charles W. *Soldiers of Destruction: The SS Death's Head Division, 1933–1945.*
   Princeton: Princeton University Press, 1977.
Taylor, Richard. *Filmpropaganda: Soviet Russia and Nazi Germany.* London: Croom
   Helm, 1979.
Taylor, Robert R. *The Word in Stone.* Berkeley: University of California Press, 1974.
Theweleit, Klaus. *Männerphantasien.* Frankfurt: Roterstern, 1978.
Vondung, Klaus. *Magie und Manipulation. Ideologischer Kult und politische Religion des
   Nationalsozialismus.* Göttingen: Vandenhoeck & Ruprecht, 1971.
Waite, Robert G. L. *Vanguard of Nazism: The Free Corps Movement in Postwar Germany,
   1918–1923.* New York: Norton, 1969.
Welch, David. *Propaganda and the German Cinema, 1933–1945.* Oxford: Clarendon
   Press, 1983.
———. *Nazi Propaganda: The Power and the Limitations.* London: Croom Helm, 1983.
Wessels, Wolfram. " 'Der 9. November,' Weihvollster Tag im Dritten Reich." *Stu-
   dienkreis Rundfunk und Geschichte: Mitteilungen* 10 (1984): 88–89.
Westenrieder, Norbert. *Deutsche Frauen und Mädchen. Vom Alltagsleben 1933–1945.*
   Düsseldorf: Droste, 1984.
Whalen, Robert Weldon. *Bitter Wounds: German Victims of the Great War, 1914–1939.*
   Ithaca/London: Cornell University Press, 1984.
Wohl, Robert. *The Generation of 1914.* Cambridge: Harvard University Press, 1979.
Zeman, Z. A. B. *Nazi Propaganda.* London: Oxford University Press, 1964.

Index